The Cyber Risk Handbook

Founded in 1807, John Wiley & Sons is the oldest independent publishing company in the United States. With offices in North America, Europe, Australia, and Asia, Wiley is globally committed to developing and marketing print and electronic products and services for our customers' professional and personal knowledge and understanding.

The Wiley Finance series contains books written specifically for finance and investment professionals as well as sophisticated individual investors and their financial advisors. Book topics range from portfolio management to e-commerce, risk management, financial engineering, valuation and financial instrument analysis, as well as much more.

For a list of available titles, visit our web site at www.WileyFinance.com.

The Cyber Risk Handbook

Creating and Measuring Effective Cybersecurity Capabilities

DOMENIC ANTONUCCI

WILEY

Library of Congress Cataloging-in-Publication Data:

ISBN 9781119308805 (Hardcover)
ISBN 9781119309727 (ePDF)
ISBN 9781119308959 (ePub)

Printed in the United States of America

10 9 8 7 6 5 4 3 2 1

This book is dedicated to my wife Jenni, my son Nathan, my daughter Megan, and to the rest of my family.

Contents

CHAPTER 4

Cybersecurity Policies and Procedures 35
The Institute for Risk Management (IRM)
Elliot Bryan, IRM and Willis Towers Watson, UK
Alexander Larsen, IRM, and President of Baldwin
    Global Risk Services Ltd., UK

CHAPTER 5

Cyber Strategic Performance Management 67
McKinsey & Company
James M. Kaplan, Partner, McKinsey & Company, New York, USA
Jim Boehm, Consultant, McKinsey & Company, Washington, USA

CHAPTER 6

Standards and Frameworks for Cybersecurity   **81**

*Stefan A. Deutscher, Principal, Boston Consulting Group (BCG),
   Berlin Germany*
*William Yin, Senior Partner and Managing Director, Boston Consulting
   Group (BCG), Hong Kong*

CHAPTER 9
Treating Cyber Risks Using Process Capabilities   123
ISACA
Todd Fitzgerald, CISO and ISACA, USA

CHAPTER 10
Treating Cyber Risks—Using Insurance and Finance   143
Aon Global Cyber Solutions
Kevin Kalinich, Esq., Aon Risk Solutions Global Cyber Insurance
Practice Leader, USA

CHAPTER 11

Monitoring and Review Using Key Risk Indicators (KRIs) **159**
Ann Rodriguez, Managing Partner, Wability, Inc., USA

CHAPTER 12

Cybersecurity Incident and Crisis Management **171**
CLUSIF Club de la Sécurité de l'Information Français
Gérôme Billois, CLUSIF Administrator and Board Member
Cybersecurity at Wavestone Consultancy, France

CHAPTER 13

Business Continuity Management and Cybersecurity   185
Marsh
Sek Seong Lim, Marsh Risk Consulting Business Continuity Leader for Asia, Singapore

CHAPTER 14

External Context and Supply Chain   193
Supply Chain Risk Leadership Council (SCRLC)
Nick Wildgoose, Board Member and ex-Chairperson of SCRLC, and Zurich Insurance Group, UK

CHAPTER 15
Internal Organization Context 207

Domenic Antonucci, Editor and Chief Risk Officer, Australia
Bassam Alwarith, Head of the National Digitization Program, Ministry of
    Economy and Planning, Saudi Arabia

Foreword
The State of Cybersecurity

Ron Hale, ISACA, USA

If cybercrime were compared to other global criminal enterprises, it would rank fourth out of five high-impact crimes in terms of the cost as a percentage of the global gross domestic product (GDP). Only transnational crime (1.2 percent), narcotics (0.9 percent), and counterfeiting/piracy (0.89 percent) rank higher in terms of financial impact. Cybercrime, however, is pushing toward the top, representing 0.8 percent of the global GDP, according to a 2014 study conducted by the Center for Strategic and International Studies. While many may not be aware of the worldwide cost of cybercrime, enterprises everywhere are certainly feeling the consequences of intrusions and compromise. It is hitting the bottom line in corporate financial statements.

Cybercrime is also gaining the attention of legislators, regulators, and boards as reports of intrusions and their consequences are released on a daily basis. Everyone is becoming alarmingly aware of cybercrime, as it is constantly in the news. Cybercrime is also very personal because each of us have probably had the experience of receiving notifications that our financial and other personal information may have been compromised in an attack. The incidence of cybercrime is eroding public trust as well.

THE GLOBAL CYBER CRISIS

We are in what can best be described as a global cyber crisis, and the future does not look promising. The June 2014 Center for Strategic and International Studies report estimated that the global impact of cybercrime was between $375 and $575 billion. As cyber incidents are frequently undetected and infrequently reported, it is difficult to arrive at a more accurate understanding of the extent of cybercrime. The Center's best estimate is $445 billion, given that the four largest economies, the United States, China, Japan, and Germany collectively account for at least $200 billion of this amount.

Despite the lack of details on the extent of cybercrime, we know that it is having a significant negative impact on business and that instead of slowing, cyber attacks are escalating at what could be considered an alarming rate. Even without verified and complete numbers, we calculate that the Internet economy generates between $3 and $5 trillion dollars globally and that cybercrime extracts between 15 percent and 20 percent of this value. The Center for Strategic and International Studies commented that cybercrime is a rapidly growing industry because of the high potential rate of return on investment and the low risk of detection and prosecution. Many legitimate enterprises would love to have the same economic opportunity that cybercriminals currently enjoy.

The April 2016 Internet Security Threat Report produced by Symantec highlights the extent of the cyber crisis. According to their analysis, 430 million new and unique pieces of malware were discovered in 2015. This represents an increase of 36 percent from the prior year. While this is a huge number, we know that malware does not go out of style in the underground cybercrime community. Attack tools and malicious code that were produced over the past several years are still commonly used and remain very effective. It is impossible to know the full extent of the library of malicious code that is either currently in use or available to hackers. The result, however, is that one-half billion personal records were either lost or stolen in 2015. This comes as the result of the known 1 million attacks that were launched against individuals each and every day in 2015. The state of cybersecurity can best be described as "hackers gone wild." There seems to be no system that cannot be compromised and no information that is safe.

While the daily impact of cybercrime is alarming, the most significant impact cybercriminals can have is on emerging technologies and business activities. The history of cybercrime demonstrates that as technology advances, so, too, do attacks against systems and the resulting damage that attacks bring. We are in an early stage of global transformation where the combined impact of cloud computing, mobile technologies, big data, analytics, robotics, and the interconnected world of smart devices has the potential to change everything. We have seen demonstrations where self-driving cars can be compromised and hackers can access avionics systems in flight. We know that devices such as insulin pumps and pacemakers are vulnerable.

How can we expect that advanced technology applications are safe when technologies that we have relied on and are business critical are not secure? The Symantec 2016 Internet Security Threat Report found that 78 percent of scanned web sites were vulnerable and that 15 percent had critical security flaws. The report also identified that zero day vulnerabilities increased by 125 percent between 2014 and 2015. If a technology with which we have long-term experience, such as web site deployments, is so ill protected from even traditional attack mechanisms, how prepared can we expect to be from zero day attacks and the even more insidious advanced persistent threats?

ISACA research recognizes that enterprises are more aware of the risk of advanced persistent threats (APTs) and are taking action to better manage this risk. Sixty-seven percent of respondents to the 2015 Advanced Persistent Threat Awareness survey were familiar or very familiar with APTs. Unfortunately, many organizations are relying on traditional defense and detection mechanisms, which may only be minimally effective against persistent threats. While Web intrusions resulting from configuration or other security lapses are possible and APTs are likely, there is a growing trend to attack mobile devices. The Symantec Threat Report indicated a 214 percent increase in mobile vulnerabilities in 2015.

While we see greater recognition of the cyber problem and its impact on business, this does not equate to implementing cyber defense better. What is needed is a rethinking of how information and cybersecurity are governed, managed, and implemented. What is needed is a more holistic, business-focused approach to cybersecurity, and recognition that cybersecurity is a business issue and not just a technical problem.

THE TIME FOR CHANGE

The need to innovate, the accelerated integration of business and technology, the drive for better performance, and the exploitation of new technologies for business benefit can realistically happen only if cybersecurity is how business is done, instead of being addressed as an afterthought. While many organizations continue to see cybersecurity as a technical problem, we are beginning to see changes that will only enhance the effectiveness of cyber risk management.

The State of Cybersecurity: Implications for 2016

A joint research activity by the RSA Conference and ISACA, shows that cybersecurity is increasingly being seen as a business enabler. As organizations strive to become fully digital, and as they exploit benefits derived from emerging technology solutions, security must become a core organization capability involving all departments and not just information technology (IT). We see from the ISACA research that most boards of directors (82 percent) are concerned or very concerned about cybersecurity. Board concern should translate into action. A possible consequence of board attention is that most organizations have developed and are enforcing their cyber policies (66 percent) and are providing what security leaders believe is appropriate funding (63 percent). More importantly, perhaps, 75 percent of those responding to the survey indicated that their cyber strategy is now aligned with enterprise objectives.

Connecting cyber activities to business goals and aspirations is perhaps the most important element in becoming a cyber risk–managed organization. While many security leaders felt that they were adequately funded, board and executive leader attention is resulting in budget increases for 61 percent of the organizations participating in the study. Investments are necessary to do more than keep up with cyber threats. As cyber becomes integral to how new products, services, and capabilities are developed, additional funding is required. Participants in the ISACA/RSA survey reported that this additional funding will provide increased compensation for skilled cyber specialists, enhanced training, broader awareness activities, and more effective response and recovery planning.

INCREASING CYBER RISK MANAGEMENT MATURITY

Best-performing organizations, with more mature cyber risk management capabilities, share several common characteristics. They commonly:

- Recognize the importance of cybersecurity and address it as a board issue and value enhancer.
- Ensure that executive management is engaged in leading cyber efforts and support cybersecurity as a business issue.
- Manage cyber risks within an enterprise risk management approach providing the necessary human and capital support for programs and initiatives.
- Follow established cybersecurity standards or frameworks in building, managing, and monitoring the enterprise cyber program.
- Continuously evaluate cybersecurity performance against business goals and objectives.
- Track and report cybersecurity performance against the international standards and frameworks used to design and implement their program.
- Fine-tune cybersecurity priorities and activities as enterprise needs and threats change.

What sets best-performing organizations apart from the crowd is that they address cybersecurity as an essential part of how products and services are designed and delivered. These organizations look at cybersecurity as an integral part of business that involves everyone from the board to computer users throughout the organization.

For those who recognize that cybersecurity is a business issue and that cyber risks need to be considered within the context of an enterprise risk management program, the consequences are significant. Best-performing organizations typically experience fewer incidents, the impact of incidents is less severe, and recovery times are quicker. More mature organizations, in summary, better manage cyber risk and are more resilient. Reaching this level of cyber preparedness and defense has been a challenge, however, since business leaders, who need to understand their role, did not have business-oriented guidance available to them. Information and cybersecurity have appeared as a technical issue and not a core part of how things are done and how the business operates. Value has been seen as coming from new products or the adoption of new technologies without connecting the need for protection with value enhancing business strategies.

The Cyber Risk Handbook changes this. It is written from the perspective of, and in a language that will resonate with, both technology and business unit leaders. It captures the elements of organization theory and design that have been shown to be essential in creating mature organizations that experience exceptional performance.

A major advancement in thinking that business executives will appreciate is found in the concept of the business model information security as presented in Figure 1.1 in our Introduction. This drawing demonstrates the essential elements found in every organization and the interconnectedness of these elements. Every organization can be described in terms of the organization structure, the people, the technology they leverage, and the processes that bind organization, people, and technology together to achieve business goals. What is less often considered is the importance of the culture connecting people within the organization, the human factors that need to be considered in making technology useful for both customers and staff, and the effectiveness of the technology design or architecture in supporting the business. Often missed in reference guides for cybersecurity practitioners and business leaders is the enabling power of governance connecting organization design to processes, and how technology needs to foster more effective processes and how processes support business enablement through technology. The mature organization understands how these elements come together and how intrinsic they are to creating superior risk management capabilities.

Understanding cybersecurity as part of a system will lead boards and management to a better understanding of cyber defense within the organization and the components of the business that need to be energized to create the culture, structures, and programs required for an effective risk management system. While this understanding is essential, concepts need to be connected with concrete guidance. This is achieved in *The Cyber Risk Handbook* by leveraging COBIT 5: A Business Framework for the Governance and Management of Enterprise IT and COBIT 5 for Information Security. Of particular importance is the presentation of the seven COBIT 5 enablers, shown in Figure 1.2, and the use of these enablers as the guiding structure for *The Cyber Risk Handbook*. While cybersecurity leverages security technology, what separates mature organizations from others is the ability to effectively exploit the interconnectedness of security principles, processes, and frameworks with enterprise-wide processes, structures, culture and behavior, and services and infrastructures and to effectively integrate information as part of the enterprise risk management program.

In planning and executing attacks against organizations, hackers and adversaries often take a holistic approach. Hackers and adversaries are attackers that consider how best to overcome the significant defenses that organizations have constructed to protect their sensitive business and personal information as well as their critical resources. Attackers consider where there are avenues of weakness understanding that the organization's culture and behavior as well as services and applications can become easy access paths for compromise instead of competent defenses. Creating convincing e-mail messages to entice users to open an attachment or visit an infected web site, or to disclose security credentials in response to a contrived message from the support desk, are frequent attack mechanisms that prove very successful. A mature risk-managed organization creates awareness that seemingly legitimate messages should not be trusted when they run counter to established processes and where the organization culture supports the idea that it is acceptable to question the legitimacy of a request.

The Cyber Risk Handbook provides a perspective of cybersecurity that breaks the barriers between those whose job is technology provisioning and administration and those who are responsible for business innovation, program development, and front-line customer support. It provides cybersecurity guidance that is understandable since it builds on common experience demonstrating how cybersecurity can build on this experience to create a different outcome. *The Cyber Risk Handbook* will be an invaluable tool in helping organizations reach a level of cyber protection required to support your organizations goals and objectives.

ABOUT ISACA

As an independent, nonprofit, global association, ISACA engages in the development, adoption, and use of globally accepted, industry-leading knowledge and practices for information systems. Previously known as the

Information Systems Audit and Control Association, ISACA now goes by its acronym only, to reflect the broad range of IT governance professionals it serves. Incorporated in 1969, ISACA today serves 140,000 professionals in 180 countries. ISACA provides practical guidance, benchmarks, and other effective tools for all enterprises that use information systems. Through its comprehensive guidance and services, ISACA defines the roles of information systems governance, security, audit, and assurance professionals worldwide. The COBIT framework and the CISA, CISM, CGEIT, and CRISC certifications are ISACA brands respected and used by these professionals for the benefit of their enterprises.

ABOUT RON HALE

Ron Hale, PhD, CISM is the cief knowledge officer at ISACA. He brings wide professional experience gained from serving as a forensic investigator, information security manager, security consultant, and researcher. In his current position he represents the professional and career needs of ISACA's constituents across the professional areas of specialization ISACA represents. Ron was admitted to the Directorship 100 by the National Association of Corporate Directors (NACD) for his contributions to corporate governance. He has a master's degree in criminal justice from the University of Illinois (United States) and a doctorate in Public Policy from Walden University (United States).

About the Editor

Domenic Antonucci is a practicing international chief risk officer overseeing cybersecurity and a former counterterrorist intelligence officer. An Australian expatriate based in Dubai UAE, Domenic specializes in bringing capabilities within organization risk management systems "up the maturity curve" for enterprise and program and for specialized risks such as cybersecurity. Formerly with Marsh, Shell and Red Cross, he enjoys over 35 years' experience in risk, strategic planning, and business management consulting across many sectors in Europe, Africa, Middle East, Asia, and Australia-Pacific. A Specialist with IRM (SIRM), he is a certified ISO 31000 ERM lead trainer and BCMS business continuity lead implementer as well as a former RMP-PMI risk management professional and PMP project management professional. A regular international conference presenter and author, he is the content author for risk maturity model software called Benchmarker™ and the author of the book *Risk Maturity Models: Assessing Risk Management Effectiveness.*

List of Contributors

Mete Bireciki
June Chambers
Andrew Cox
Nicola Crawford
Paul Dwyer
Baris Ekdi
Jennifer Friedberg
Mary E. Galligan
Ron Hale
Nicole Hockin
Waqas M. Hussain
Scott Krugman

Ian Livesy
Malcolm Marshall
Asha Nair
Pam Randall
Victoria Robinson
George M. Shaw
Nagesh Suryanarayana
Bob Sydow
Clive Thompson
Marcus Turner
Carolyn Williams
Caroline Woolley

Acknowledgments

A big thanks to Stig Sunde, a senior audit professional who never tired of my endless questions. My bigger thanks go to my wife Jenni for her forbearance and support, as well as to my editors, Tula, Christina, and Vincent, for their trust and enthusiasm.

All my contributor-authors deserve applause for "volunteering" to contribute to this handbook, especially as they were all so pressed for time and came from all parts of the globe. We did not want to just throw together a loose collection of white papers but to strive toward a cogent enterprise-wide handbook with a story and solutions. I know that for some authors, their initial cynicism grew into trust and support, while for a few, the task turned into hard and disciplined work as I pushed back for revision after revision.

Some of those contributor-authors deserve my special mention for going "above and beyond" in assisting me as editor. These include Ron Hale in the United States, Didier Verstichel in Belgium, and Bassam Alwarith in Saudi Arabia. To all, I tip my hat.

CHAPTER 1

Introduction

Domenic Antonucci, Editor and Chief Risk Officer, Australia

THE CEO UNDER PRESSURE

Tom is sitting at his chief executive officer's desk staring into his early-morning coffee cup. His chairperson, Tara, has just reminded him that he has only one day before he must personally present to the board regarding his organization's cyber risk management capabilities. "Also, include an assessment of how effective our cyber risk management is across all our enterprise-wide operations—not just IT," she added.

Tom has never presented on cyber before. He had delegated such matters in the past to his chief information officer (CIO). Tom struggled to remember his last internal briefing on the matter. He was aware that they had recently hired a chief information security officer (CISO) with a focus on cybersecurity, who reported to him directly. Tom started to protest, "Tara, my CISO or CIO can present ..." but was interrupted: "No, *you* own cybersecurity, *we* oversee it alongside the board. By 'system,' I don't mean our IT approach, I mean our whole-of-organization capabilities to manage cyber threats."

Noting the dazed look on Tom's face, Tara gave Tom a tip. "Tom, cyber risk is not just an IT risk, it is an enterprise, strategic, commercial, and organization-wide risk. We at the top are accountable. You've introduced our first enterprise-wide risk management (ERM) system together with a risk maturity strategy and risk maturity model to assess and measure how we are improving the ERM system over time. Fine. But cyber risk is now an urgent priority and the specific capabilities required are a subset of the enterprise risk management system. You need to integrate the two. I suggest you dedicate your whole day today to having your team define the *right set of capabilities* in cyber risk management that our organization needs and how we can measure them. The board expects to see your road map first thing tomorrow."

The Need for a Cyber Risk Handbook

"But what is the board worrying about, Tara?" Tom quizzed. Tara paused, "Cyber threats, social media, mobile devices, massive data storage, artificially intelligent products, the Internet of Things (IoT), privacy requirements, and continuity of our business-as-usual—and more. These require heavy information security measures and organization capabilities. Tom, I'm going to leave you with a couple of recent survey results and you'll understand what our board is worrying about. Read the highlights."

Tom picked up the two reports and read the highlights.

Eighty-eight percent of companies don't believe their information security fully meets their organization's needs ... Sixty-nine percent of businesses recognize that they should be spending more on cybersecurity than they currently do, and learning about making the most of that essential investment is critical.

—*EY's Global Information Security Survey 2015:* "Creating Trust in the Digital World," www.ey.com/giss

In November and December 2015, the ISACA and RSA Conference conducted a global survey of 461 cybersecurity managers and practitioners. Survey participants confirmed that the number of breaches targeting organizational and individual data continues to go unchecked and the sophistication of attack methodologies is evolving. The current state of global cybersecurity remains chaotic, the attacks are not expected to slow down, and almost 75 percent of respondents expect to fall prey to a cyber attack in 2016. Cybercriminals are the most prevalent attackers and continue to employ social engineering as their primary initial attack vector. ... Eighty-two percent of security executives and practitioners participating reported that boards are concerned or very concerned about cybersecurity.

—Text from *ISACA Report, March 2016. Source:* State of Cybersecurity: Implications for 2016 ©2016 ISACA. All rights reserved. Used by permission.

"So, how do you suggest I start?" queried a concerned Tom. As she left the room, Tara looked back and said simply, "Get the perspectives of all your organization functions as they are all stakeholders for cyber risk, and not just your information security guys. Pull together an enterprise play-book to cover what they need to create and measure effective cybersecurity capabilities. Call it your cyber risk handbook."

TOWARD AN EFFECTIVELY CYBER RISK–MANAGED ORGANIZATION

Cyber risk is not new. It has been around since the start of the digital age, but cyber threats to organizations are now growing in scale and sophistication at an unprecedented rate due to advancing technologies, criminal and state-level avarice, and changing work practices (such as big data, remote access, cloud computing, social media, and mobile technology). There is increasing media and insurance industry attention. This is spotlighting high-profile and highly disruptive and damaging security breaches. These threaten financial, physical, and reputation damage across critical organization (and state) infrastructures.

Cyber risk is now widely regarded as a top risk for organizations and *the* top risk for many. Organization vulnerability across all sectors is increasing. The *do-nothing* option is increasing becoming unrealistic. This is due to legislative, corporate, national security, and regulatory requirements to dem-onstrate that organizations are protecting sensitive information and digital assets (i.e., any equipment which contains a microprocessor) as well as man-aging their internal cyber risk management system effectively.

There is no internal or external consensus among cybersecurity agents (the "Goodies") on which set of clear and specific organization capabili-ties represent an "effectively cyber risk–managed organization"—one that is sustainability resilient against cybersecurity threat agents (the "Baddies"). This calls for clarity regarding specific internal enterprise-wide capabilities in cybersecurity.

Effectiveness Is All About *Doing the Right Things*

Tom is our handbook's fictional protagonist, but he is representative of an organizational leader. Tom returns at the start of each chapter and else-where to help pull together our developing journey and to emphasize the need for an enterprise-wide and integrated approach to cyber risk manage-ment maturity and effectiveness for the modern organization. Today, noth-ing should be stopping an organization moving up the cyber risk maturity curve—a curve that is dynamically changing all the time as cyber threats increase and transform themselves. Our epilogue explains our maturity approach in greater detail.

While efficiency is about "doing things right," effectiveness is all about "doing the right things." That means the modern challenge for any organization is keeping up with the right capabilities to protect the digital enterprise against faster-paced threat agents.

This handbook sets about normalizing cyber risk as enterprise risk and its risk management system as a subset of the ERM system. It represents a call to arms from the functional perspectives of the CEO and all organization managers—not just the IT department—to understand how they must work together as a team. How they must together play their part in building and measuring a constantly improving right set of *capabilities* needed to deliver ongoing and fast cyber risk management effectiveness.

This handbook arms the CEOs, functional managers, and front and support lines of a modern organization with a reference guide devoted to the specific subject of integrating a cyber risk management system and cyber risk maturity at the digital enterprise level.

HANDBOOK STRUCTURED FOR THE ENTERPRISE

Conceptualizing Cybersecurity for Organization-Wide Solutions

Tom is realizing that information security and organizations are inextricably interwoven today. Cyber attacks and data breaches are not just IT risks. They are enterprise-wide risks requiring joint solutions across nearly all organizational functions. To help unify his approach with his team members, Tom penciled a diagram. This conceptualized how cybersecurity did not just sit in one corner under technology but was part of an interrelated triangle with the organization at the top. See Figure 1.1.

Theming the Right Set of Capabilities

Tom was well aware of his existing organization chart and how his team worked by function under him. He regarded his functional heads as the strategic drivers working as a team to build the combined right set of capabilities needed to protect the digital enterprise.

Drivers in turn need enablers. Tom did not want to reinvent any wheels. So on the advice of his CISO and CIO, Tom adapted the COBIT 5 enablers to the information security process as a way to theme and modularize the right set of cyber risk management capabilities he wanted to define and measure. COBIT 5 is an information security management system (ISMS) backed by ISACA, an international professional association serving a broad range of IT governance professionals and a framework accepted by many assurance and governance professionals.

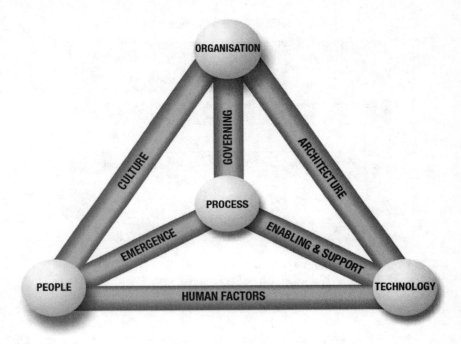

FIGURE 1.1   Conceptualizing information security within the organization
Source: The Business Model for Information Security ©2010 ISACA. All rights reserved. Used with permission.

Tom now had seven parts for his handbook, representing the seven sets of capabilities he wanted to build and measure. As adapted from COBIT 5 Framework (ISACA®, *Cobit 5® An ISACA® Framework: A Business Framework for the Governance and Management of Enterprise IT*, USA, 2012), Figure 1.2 visualizes how the seven capability sets work together in a sequential way that Tom could take to his managers (rather than the holistic way of Figure 1.1).

Figure 1.1 begins with *principles, policies, and frameworks* as mechanisms acting as hand-rails guiding desired behavior for day-to-day management (see handbook chapters 1 to 6 and our epilogue). *Processes* describe an organized set of practices and activities to achieve certain objectives and produce a set of outputs in support of achieving cybersecurity objectives aligned to enterprise objectives (see chapters 7 to 13). *Organizational structures* are the key decision-making entities in an enterprise (see chapters 14 to 15). *Culture, ethics, and behavior* of individuals and of the enterprise are a key success factor in governance and management

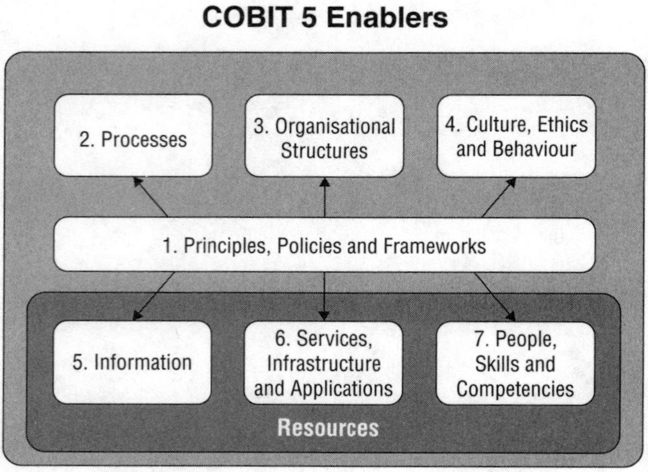

COBIT 5 Enablers

FIGURE 1.2 How seven sets of capabilities work together
Source: COBIT 5 ©2012 ISACA. All rights reserved. Used by permission.

activities (see chapters 16 to 18). *Information* is organization pervasive and includes all information produced and used by the enterprise. Information is not only required to keep the organization running and well governed, but is often the key product of the operational enterprise (see chapter 19). *Services, infrastructure, and applications* include the infrastructure, technology, and applications that provide the enterprise with information technology processing and services (see chapters 20 to 23). *People, skills, and competencies* are linked to people and are required for successful completion of all activities and for making correct decisions and taking corrective actions (see chapters 24 to 26).

Enterprise Functions Together Drive the Right Set of Capabilities   Over that long day collating contributions from all his team, Tom's handbook was able to make sense and unify his team's contributions into chapters under these seven parts. It enabled him to matrix out not only who in the future should be responsible for which capability, but who should be accountable, supported, consulted, and informed as well. Tom's RASCI Matrix can be found in Chapter 15, "Internal Organization Context."

Cyber Risk Maturity Model Measures Improvements in Capabilities

Tom's handbook ended up with 26 chapters and an epilogue. Each chapter concluded with a capability statement succinctly describing the set of capabilities required. In this way, the organization could understand what cybersecurity meant—not just the IT or cyber technical specialists.

By collating each capability title into a cyber risk maturity model, Tom was able to assess an overall index score (see epilogue). This then could be integrated into the chief risk officer's ERM-level risk maturity model, which held one entry for an overall cyber risk management capability. Tom was now ready to present to his board how he was going to build and measure effective cybersecurity capabilities.

HANDBOOK STRUCTURE, RATIONALE, AND BENEFITS

I am a practicing chief risk officer with cyber and enterprise risk management experience stewarding the needs of organizations sitting anywhere along the risk maturity curve. My emphasis in this handbook is less on which idealistic capabilities are required at the top of the cyber risk maturity curve and more on *what it takes to move up* this ever-moving curve for nontechnical managers. These are addressed by interrelated chapters each written by a different subject matter expert. These capabilities are then collated in an epilogue to form a new cyber risk maturity model for adaptation and ongoing measurement by any organization.

The overall handbook structure is designed to offer several advantages and unifying approaches for enterprise leaders and managers.

Balance and Objectivity

First, it is an edited book based on robust chapter contributions by many types of subject matter experts from around the world. This imparts more overall balance and objectivity from an enterprise perspective to the cybersecurity domain than a single or technical author work may provide.

It is focused on threats to *organizations*. While the target audience for this handbook is not state-sponsored or military-sponsored cyber agencies, this is not to say that organizations should not factor these agencies as their own sources of risk (and perhaps opportunity?). It is focused on the *nontechnical* approach to cyber threats directed against *organizations of any type*, be they for-profits, not-for-profits, or nongovernmental organizations (NGOs)—not just large corporations. It is focused on the *globalization* of cyber risk, bringing together varying perspectives from an array of subject-matter chapter contributors originating from not just the United States but many countries, including (in alphabetical order): Australia, Belgium, Canada, France, Germany, Hong Kong, India, Italy, Norway, Saudi Arabia, Singapore, South Africa, the Netherlands, United Arab Emirates, and United Kingdom. Chapter contributors also represent not just IT/cybersecurity backgrounds but a wide *variety of functional* backgrounds in risk management, insurance, finance/accounting, supply chain, and internal audit. Moreover, they represent the *varying perspectives* of the major consulting firms, professional institutes, and associations. The "About" sections at the end of each chapter attest to the diverse experience the chapter contributors bring to bear.

Enterprise-wide Comprehensiveness

Second, the seven parts guiding the chapters take an *enterprise-wide* approach to cyber risk content. This helps non-IT managers to understand cybersecurity but also helps IT managers understand how all enterprise managers need to work together. It treats the cyber risk management system as a subset to the modern enterprise risk management system (ERM) in nontechnical language more familiar to non-IT managers. ISO 31000:2009, *Risk management—Principles and guidelines* is the leading risk management global standard and the standard that is becoming central to, or the "umbrella" for, all ISO standards. This includes those relevant to cyber and information security. Those familiar with ISO 31000 can easily "crosswalk" from our chapter structure to the standard (see Chapter 3, "Principles behind Cyber Risk Management").

Moving Up the Risk Maturity Curve

Third, enterprise risk managers are familiar with risk maturity strategy (ISO 31000 annex A) and risk maturity models, just as IT professionals are with the capability maturity models that have been around since the late 1980s. So collating the handbook's contents into one cyber risk maturity model in our epilogue is a proven methodology to road-map and measure gap-capability improvement over time.

WHICH CHAPTERS ARE WRITTEN FOR ME?

Fourth, the handbook structure aggregates a growing accumulation of organization cybersecurity capabilities, chapter by chapter. This is handy for a reader with a particular functional or other perspective who may scan the handbook content more easily for the pertinent part they want to find at the time. It also lends itself to broader management uptake and on-boarding from a handbook than purely a process focus or an IT focus or technical focus, or a loose collection of best practices or case studies.

Managers in modern organizations complain they are time poor. To help readers from different organization functions zero in on key chapters and content that are likely to be of immediate interest to them, we offer Table 1.1, an alternative to the table of contents. Readers who self-identify by a function—whether as a CEO or in operations—may use the key in Table 1.1 to go directly to the chapters of likely interest to them, if not written for them.

TABLE 1.1   Chapters Listed by Interest to Functional Type in Alphabetical Order

	Go to chapters …	Also see …
Audit Committee	01 Introduction 02 Board cyber risk oversight 18 Assurance	Epilogue & Ch 15 RASCI Tables 15.3 to 15.7
Board	01 Introduction 02 Board cyber risk oversight 17 Legal and compliance 18 Assurance All chapter introductions	Epilogue & Ch 15 RASCI Tables 15.3 to 15.7
Business Continuity	13 Business continuity management	Epilogue & Ch 15 RASCI Tables 15.3 & 15.15
CEO	01 Introduction 05 Cyber strategic performance 02 Board cyber risk oversight 11 Monitoring & review - KRIs 17 Legal and compliance 18 Assurance All chapter introductions	Epilogue & Ch 15 RASCI Tables All tables
Compliance	17 Legal and compliance 18 Assurance	Epilogue & Ch 15 RASCI Tables 15.3 & 15.17
Corp. Comms.	12 Cybersecurity incident and crisis management	Epilogue & Ch 15 RASCI Tables 15.3 & 15.22
Finance	10 Treating cyber risks using insurance and finance	Epilogue & Ch 15 RASCI Tables 15.3, 15.13 & 15.16
Human Resources	15 Internal context 16 Culture and human factors Chapters 22, 24, 25 & 26	Epilogue & Ch 15 RASCI Tables All tables
Info. Security	All	Epilogue & Ch 15 RASCI Tables All tables
Info. Technology	15 Internal organization context Chapters 19 to 23	Epilogue & Ch 15 RASCI Tables 15.3 & 15.8
Insurance	10 Treating cyber risks using insurance and finance	Epilogue & Ch 15 RASCI Tables 15.3 & 15.13
Internal Audit	02 Board cyber risk oversight 15 Internal context 18 Assurance	Epilogue & Ch 15 RASCI Tables 15.3 to 15.6
Legal	17 Legal and compliance	Epilogue & Ch 15 RASCI Tables 15.3 & 15.17
Operations	14 External context and supply chain	Epilogue & Ch 15 RASCI Tables 15.3, 15.15, 15.19 & 15.20

(Continued)

TABLE 1.1 *(Continued)*

	Go to chapters ...	Also see ...
Risk	All	Epilogue & Ch 15 RASCI Tables All tables
Security	20 Physical security	Epilogue & Ch 15 RASCI Tables 15.3 & 15.14
Strategy	5 Strategic performance 11 Monitoring and review—KRIs	Epilogue & Ch 15 RASCI Tables 15.3 & 15.18
Supply Chain	14 External context and supply chain	Epilogue & Ch 15 RASCI Tables 15.3, 15.15, 15.19, & 15.20

CHAPTER 2

Board Cyber Risk Oversight

What Needs to Change?

Tim J. Leech, Risk Oversight Solutions Inc., Canada
Lauren C. Hanlon, Risk Oversight Solutions Inc., Canada

The introduction to this book opens with a succinct statement from Tara to Tom, the CEO who has attempted to delegate accountability for responding to the board's request for a cybersecurity road map to his chief information security officer. Tara told Tom: "No, you own cybersecurity; we oversee it alongside the board . . . I don't mean our IT approach, I mean our whole-of-organization capability to manage cyber threats." This type of clarity and direction to CEOs is relatively new, but one that is gaining traction globally.

From a pragmatic perspective, the key question well-intending boards need to be asking is "what specifically do we and the organization's CEO need to do differently to meet these new cybersecurity expectations?" The problem they will immediately confront is a veritable ocean of advice on how to do this. This chapter focuses on the following three questions: (1) what are boards expected to do now?; (2) what barriers to action will well-intending boards face?; and (3) what practical steps should boards and organizations take now to respond? Be warned, however; the steps proposed in this paper are a radical departure from status quo thinking.

WHAT ARE BOARDS EXPECTED TO DO NOW?

The *first* short answer is the frustrating and quite common *"It depends."* It depends on what country your organization is in, the focus and approach of regulators in that country, the business sector the organization is in, the evolution of legal duty of care, the frequency of major governance crises linked to cybersecurity breaches, the culture of the organization, and more.

For busy directors, new expectations and calls for change are often best received and embraced when the communication comes from other board members. In 2014 the National Association of Corporate Directors (NACD) in the United States recognized the emerging need for director guidance following a flurry of major scandals involving breaches of information technology (IT) security. The NACD produced a well-researched, readable, and succinct "Cyber Risk Oversight" guide. This report is available without charge by registering at https://www.nacdonline.org/cyber.

The NACD guidance distilled what the authors believe directors should do to five core principles:

1. Directors need to understand and approach cybersecurity as an enterprise risk management (ERM) issue, not just an IT issue. (Authors' note: This is the key principle.)
2. Directors should understand the legal implications of cyber risks as they relate to their organization's specific circumstances.
3. Boards should have adequate access to cybersecurity expertise, and discussions about cyber risk management should be given regular and adequate time on the board meeting agenda.
4. Directors should set the expectation that management will establish an enterprise-wide cyber risk management framework with adequate staffing and budget.
5. Board-management discussion of cyber risk should include identification of which risks to avoid, accept, mitigate, or transfer through insurance, as well as specific plans associated with each approach.[1]

The board should define the risk appetite for the organization and approve the likelihood and impact scale at the enterprise level. The board may be involved in the insurance aspect, depending on the contract value and possibly the choice of the insurer. Then it is up to management to address the risks that are above the threshold.

For those directors willing to invest more time skilling up on cybersecurity, the U.S. government has produced the widely acclaimed "Framework for Improving Critical Infrastructure Cybersecurity" version 1.0.[2] It is important to note that the U.S. National Institute of Standards and Technology (NIST) IT security framework does not emphasize the key role of the board of directors. Unlike some other more silo-leaning IT security guides, the NIST framework does promote the need to see cybersecurity as a subset of ERM. It proposes a cybersecurity maturity framework linked to risk management and what NIST calls an "integrated risk management program." Unfortunately, the NIST guidance doesn't give much practical advice on how to transition IT security assessments from what is often a silo-based approach to one that is fully integrated with an effective enterprise risk management framework.

The Short Answer

A quick scan of global developments confirms that, although the specific answer to the question will evolve over time on a country-by-country and sector basis, the answer can be summarized simply as "a lot more." However, the central message in this chapter is that it should not be "a lot more *of the same*," referring to the siloed, specialist-driven approach in use in a large percentage of organizations today. Cyber risk management and assurance needs to be reengineered globally.

WHAT BARRIERS TO ACTION WILL WELL-INTENDING BOARDS FACE?

Most boards will face difficulty as they attempt to address cyber risk management. The five main categories of barriers to action can be identified as follows:

1. Lack of senior management ownership of IT security.
2. Failure to link cybersecurity assessments to key organization objectives.
3. Omission of cybersecurity from entity-level objectives and strategic plans.
4. Too much focus on internal controls.
5. Lack of reliable information on residual risk status.

These barriers are discussed in further detail in the following sections.

Barrier 1: Lack of Senior Management Ownership

In many organizations the perception is that IT security is the IT department's and internal audit's problem, not something the CEO and C-suite own. Senior management is ultimately responsible for all major threats to an organization, so it is critical that the C-suite takes ownership of this and assesses IT security in the context of key business objectives. IT security is often treated as a separate silo, with the majority of the work being done by IT, internal audit, and outside IT consultants that often lack "big picture" perspectives and experience.

This is compounded by a lack of clear line management ownership for assessing and reporting upwards on the state of residual risk linked to key value creation and value preservation objectives. All too often, ERM programs are relegated to an annual/semiannual update of the organization's risk register and a collection of spot-in-time internal audits, not an ongoing process owned by management to continuously identify, assess, and treat key risks, including cyber risks, to important business objectives.

A key point that is often lost is that *IT security should only be seen as important to the extent it significantly impacts the achievement of important business objectives that add significant value and/or preserve value for the organization*. Because management in these organizations often do not have to formally assess, treat, and report upwards on risks that impact on the achievement of key organization objectives and related residual risk status, they do not actively participate in identifying cybersecurity-linked risks as part of a holistic enterprise-wide process. More importantly, boards are often not told which top value creation and potentially value eroding objectives are significantly threatened by low levels of cybersecurity risk treatments.

Barrier 2: Failure to Link Cybersecurity Assessments to Key Organization Objectives

A large percentage of boards are populated with pragmatic and very experienced executives who have learned to focus their scarce time and attention on objectives key to the success of the business. They are often quite attuned to the organization's key objectives. Unfortunately, for a variety of reasons, a large percentage of the cybersecurity work done in many organizations is not directly tied to specific organization objectives. Boards are often not told which of the organization's most important value creation and value preservation objectives are likely to be impacted by weak or nonexistent cybersecurity treatments and to what degree. In its most extreme form, the message communicated implicitly, and sometimes explicitly, by the IT security assessors is that having high levels of computer security should be seen as an objective in its own right. This premise can sometimes be promoted by well-intending regulators charged with raising IT security levels without specific cost-benefit analysis linked to the organization objectives impacted.

Senior management and boards have a difficult time deciding how much of the organization's scarce resources should be dedicated to this area without high-quality information to assess which organization objectives are most likely to be impacted, and to what degree by low/nonexistent cybersecurity risk treatments. At the current time, based on Institute of Internal Audit (IIA) surveys globally, only a small percentage of internal audit, IT security, and ERM specialists link their risk and controls assessment work directly to the organization's top, most important value creation and value preservation objectives.

Barrier 3: Omission of Cybersecurity from Entity-Level Objectives and Strategic Plans

In companies that have ERM functions, cybersecurity threats are often included in risk registers, which may or may not be directly linked to the organization's top strategic plan and value-creation objectives. In order for cybersecurity to be robust and overarching, it *must* be included in objectives and strategic plans at the highest level of the organization. Many IT information security functions focus exclusively on IT security, often without directly linking how IT security impacts key organization objectives. *Risk universes* and *audit universes* that are developed by management, risk functions, or internal audit are often carved out as separate risk and audit topics and separated from the organization objectives the risks link to and potentially impact.

Barrier 4: Too Much Focus on Internal Controls

Too large a percentage of the ERM and internal audit work done today still focuses on identifying *internal controls*. Auditors make the primary decision in their audits and risk assessments if these cybersecurity internal controls are deficient or in need of improvement. The most extreme form of this is the binary approach imposed by Sarbanes-Oxley section 404. The groups doing this work often do not use processes aligned with ISO 31000:2009 Risk Management. This means that they do not assess risks in the context of specific, related organization objectives or deploy the full range of risk treatment options available, which are:

- Avoiding the activity that gives rise to the risk.
- Taking or increasing the risk in order to pursue an opportunity.
- Removing the risk source.
- Changing the likelihood.
- Changing the consequences.
- Sharing the risk with other parties (e.g., risk financing, contracts).
- Retaining the risk by informed decision.

Perhaps most importantly, when accepting some level of residual risk linked to key objectives, which is always the case, evaluate whether acceptance of the risk is appropriate in light of the organization's and board's risk appetite and tolerance.

Barrier 5: Lack of Reliable Information on Residual Risk Status

Higher-quality information is needed for senior management and boards to properly assess whether current levels of cybersecurity are appropriate and cost justified. The information should clearly answer the following questions:

- Which critical organization objective or objectives are impacted by cyber risks?
- How well are those objectives currently being achieved with the current risk treatment strategy?
- What are the potential impacts to reputation, cost, remuneration, and so on if an important business objective is not achieved in whole or part because of a cybersecurity risk realization?
- What viable risk treatments are available and could be used to reduce relevant cybersecurity risks, and at what cost, that are not being used?
- What information is available on current performance and risk indicators and any impediments management and the organization face?

WHAT PRACTICAL STEPS SHOULD BOARDS TAKE NOW TO RESPOND?

There are four steps, outlined in this section, that boards can take to respond to risk. They are as follows:

1. Use a "five lines of assurance" approach.
2. Include top objectives and specific owners.
3. Establish a risk management framework.
4. Require regular reporting by the CEO.

Practical Step 1: Use a "Five Lines of Assurance" Approach

The "five lines of assurance" approach to risk oversight and governance (Figure 2.1) models how an organization can operate effectively in the realm of cybersecurity. The five lines are, on one side, internal audit and specialist units; and on the other side, the C-suite and work units that report to them. All four of these lines provide information to the board of directors, the fifth line, and also directly execute and oversee risk-management programs.

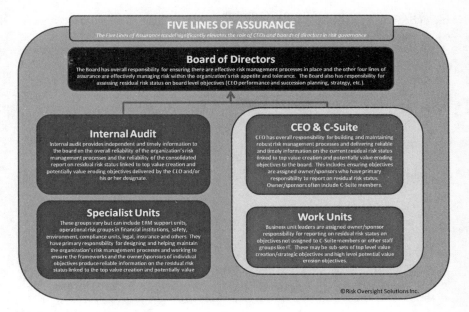

FIGURE 2.1 Five lines of assurance

Cybersecurity deficiencies linked to the organization's top value creation and value preservation objectives are often obfuscated and managed suboptimally. This will continue as long as:

- Senior management and work units are not expected to complete formal risk assessments on top value creation and preservation objectives and report upwards to the board on residual risk status.
- ERM groups build their work plans around "risk registers" with little direct linkage to organization's value creation strategy.
- Internal audit departments continue to use "audit universes" as their primary work foundation and perform point-in-time direct report audits and form subjective opinions on "control effectiveness."

It should be the CEO and C-Suite that decide which organization objectives warrant the cost of combined assurance overseen by the organization's board of directors. The board and CEO should be seen as key players in a "five lines of assurance" approach—not mere recipients of reports. The CEO or his/her designate should be responsible for providing reliable consolidated reports on residual risk status linked to all top value creation and preservation objectives, including those that are being, or could be, impacted by cybersecurity threats. Boards need to oversee the overall effectiveness of the organization's enterprise approach to risk management—including defining which objectives they want residual risk status information on and the level of risk assessment rigor.

Practical Step 2: Include Top Objectives and Specific Owners

For risk management to be effective, objectives registers must include the top value creation/preservation objectives and specify owners and sponsors at the highest organizational levels. These registers must clearly define risk assessment rigor and combined assurance levels. An organization's ERM and combined assurance resources are costly. The C-suite should take the lead deciding which objectives warrant the cost of formal risk treatment, combined assurance work, and inclusion in the organization's objectives register. The board should oversee that process. The objectives register should provide the foundation for the majority of formal risk treatment work done by management, risk specialists, and internal audit. Objectives included should be the objectives with the highest potential to increase entity value, as well as those with the highest potential to erode entity value. Cybersecurity risks are often relevant to both types of objectives. Each objective should have an owner/sponsor who has primary responsibility for assessing and reporting upward on residual risk status on a real-time basis.

Practical Step 3: Establish a Risk Management Framework

For risk assessment and treatment to be effective, it must be done using a framework focused on providing reliable information. Decision makers need to fully understand the composite residual risk status linked to top value creation and value preservation objectives. The framework should be designed to serve this purpose, and using it should be a requirement.

All risk assessment and treatment work should be done using an approach consistent with the ISO 31000:2009, *Risk management—Principles and guidelines* global standard, but more importantly, it should also put high importance on direct linkage of the risks assessed and treated to the relevant organization objective(s) and, most importantly, developing a reliable picture of residual risk status linked to top objectives for decision makers. Figure 2.2 describes key elements of the risk status approach.

Owners/sponsors of each objective are required to complete risk assessments and treatments on those objectives with specified levels of risk assessment and treatments rigor defined by the C-suite and board and report a "Composite Residual Risk Rating" (CRRR) for each objective. In cases where the owner/sponsor believes no additional or stronger risk treatments

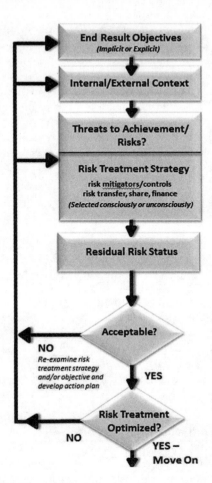

FIGURE 2.2 Risk status approach to assessment and treatment

are warranted but significant levels of residual risk are still being accepted by the organization, this needs to be communicated to the board, including cases where high levels of cybersecurity residual risk is being accepted.

Practical Step 4: Require Regular Reporting by the CEO

If, ultimately, the CEO is to be held accountable for cybersecurity, he or she must be fully aware of how the program is working. This can be accomplished by having the CEO deliver consolidated reports to the board on a regular basis. These reports should cover the residual risk status linked to the organization's formal objectives. Internal audit should also report on the reliability of the CEO's consolidated report.

Boards should be provided with reliable reports on the residual risk status linked to the organization's top objectives on a regular basis, ideally quarterly. This should include a concise report on the objectives that currently have residual risk status outside of the organization's risk appetite and tolerance, and what is being done about them, as well as areas where high levels of residual risk are being accepted by senior management. This report should put cybersecurity risks in the context of the end result organization objectives they relate.

CYBERSECURITY—THE WAY FORWARD

The way forward, if real progress is to be achieved, requires major changes in the way that a large percentage of organizations have historically approached risk governance generally, and cybersecurity in particular. Radical change rarely comes easily. Regulators, professional associations, boards of directors, senior management, internal auditors, and risk specialists must embrace the need for radical change in the area of enterprise risk governance and map out formal change management strategies. Cyber risks should not continue to be treated as yet another silo. Like many big undertakings, change needs to start with some small steps. Are you willing to advocate risk oversight and governance change at your organization?

BOARD CYBER RISK OVERSIGHT

Boards and senior management around the world have relied on traditional ERM and internal audit paradigms to help them oversee cyber risk. These paradigms need to change if boards and senior management are going to meet the new expectations. More of the same cybersecurity approaches will not do the job. Boards need to insist that all ERM and internal audit work is directly linked to their organization's top value creation and value preservation objectives and require regular reports on the state of residual risk linked to those objectives. Cybersecurity needs to be focused on its potential impact on key business objectives, not as a priority on its own regardless of its impact on the organization's sustained success. To accomplish this shift boards and senior management must call for fundamental change in the way ERM and internal audit services are delivered.

NOTES

1. Cyber-Risk Oversight Director's Handbook Series 2014. National Association of Corporate Directors.
2. Framework for Improving Critical Infrastructure Cybersecurity, Version 1.0. National Institute of Standards and Technology, February 12, 2014.

ABOUT RISK OVERSIGHT SOLUTIONS INC.

Risk Oversight Solutions is a boutique consulting and training firm based in Toronto, Ontario, Canada, and Sarasota, Florida, that helps clients who want more integrated and effective risk and assurance frameworks that cost less and deliver more. Figure 2.2 is trademarked as RiskStatusline™ approach to assessment and treatment. More information on what needs to happen for Board risk oversight can be found in the July 2015 article "Reinventing Internal Audit," published in *Internal Audit* magazine, and the summer 2016 article Paradigm Paralysis in ERM and Internal Audit in Ethical Boardroom.

ABOUT TIM J. LEECH, FCPA, CIA, CRMA, CFE

Tim has over 35 years of global experience in the areas of board risk oversight, ERM, internal audit, and forensic accounting fields, with a focus on helping public- and private-sector organizations with ERM and internal audit transformation initiatives. His April 2015 article "Reinventing Internal Audit" was awarded the 2016 Outstanding Contributor award by the Institute of Internal Auditors.

ABOUT LAUREN C. HANLON, CPA, CIA, CRMA, CFE

Lauren Hanlon has spent over 20 years providing insight on risk management, internal audit, and internal controls for public and private companies in various industries. She has provided innovative solutions and a fresh approach to ERM methodology and technology training for numerous organizations and risk specialists, including the Big 4 audit partners, in countries around the world.

CHAPTER 3

Principles Behind Cyber Risk Management

RIMS, *the* risk management society™
Carol Fox, Vice President, Strategic Initiatives at RIMS, USA

Tom was wondering why his head of human resources, Grace, was sitting alongside his chief strategy officer George. Tom asked, "So what do our people have to do with principles guiding our cyber strategy, risks, and actions?" Grace replied, "Lots. Our people enact the principles—principles that provide the foundation for desirable and positive behavior."

CYBER RISK MANAGEMENT PRINCIPLES GUIDE ACTIONS

Principles provide the foundation for people's desirable and positive behavior in carrying out their respective responsibilities within an organization. Principles aid in determining whether decisions and the resulting actions are helpful or harmful.

Principles from the ISO 31000:2009 international risk management standard can support an organization that chooses to implement COBIT 5 GEIT[2] and its five principles:

1. Meeting stakeholder needs.
2. Covering the enterprise end-to-end.
3. Applying a single, integrated framework.
4. Enabling a holistic approach.
5. Separating governance from management.

In this chapter, principles from the ISO 31000:2009, *Risk management—Principles and guidelines*[3] are described to guide desirable and positive actions that are in line with the organization's enterprise-wide approach to governance and management of enterprise information technology (IT). The two sets of principles are organized in Table 3.1. At times, the word *cyber* is inserted in the text to emphasize an IT-specific risk management perspective. However, the noted risk management principles are meant to apply across the entire organization, whether or not decisions and activities are related to IT.

TABLE 3.1   COBIT 5 GEIT Principles

	COBIT 5 GEIT PRINCIPLES				
	Meet stakeholder needs:	*Covering the enterprise end-to-end:*	*Applying a single, integrated framework:*	*Enabling a holistic approach:*	*Separating governance front management:*
ISO 31000 RISK MANAGEMENT PRINCIPLES	Risk management is transparent and inclusive.	Risk management creates and protects value.	Risk management is systematic, structured, and timely.	Risk management is an integral part of all organizational processes.	Risk management facilitates continual improvement of the organization.
	Risk management is dynamic, iterative, and responsive to change.	Risk management is tailored.		Risk management takes human and cultural factors into account.	
		Risk management explicitly addresses uncertainty.		Risk management is part of decision making.	
				Risk management is based on the best available information.	

MEETING STAKEHOLDER NEEDS

The first COBIT 5 principle "addresses the need to align individual and departmental objectives and priorities with enterprise and stakeholders needs."[4] The principle recognizes that stakeholder needs and enterprise goals change over time.

Being Transparent and Inclusive

One of the principles noted in the ISO 31000 standard holds that "risk management is transparent and inclusive." The principle states that "appropriate and timely involvement of stakeholders and, in particular, decision makers at all levels of the organization, ensures that [cyber] risk management remains relevant and up-to-date."

Examples of stakeholders in cyber risk assessment processes might include:

- Customers, clients, stockholders, employees, contractors, and supply chain partners (e.g., outsourced partners and critical infrastructure suppliers);
- Government and regulatory authorities;
- Nongovernmental organizations;
- Civil society groups; and
- Members of the public (including the media).[5]

This principle is demonstrated when the organization can answer questions such as "What is each stakeholder expecting from the organization when it comes to managing cyber risk?"; "What are the regulations that apply to the digital information and sensitive data that is accessed, used, stored, and transmitted by the organization?"; and "What are the voluntary or contractual obligations that the organization has taken on with respect to its network, systems and data availability, reliability, security, and privacy?" The answers may differ depending on the stakeholder.

Being Responsive to Change

Once these questions are asked and answered, the risk management principle that "risk management is dynamic, iterative, and responsive to change" applies in meeting changing stakeholder needs. This principle explicitly states that [cyber] "risk management continually senses and responds to change. As external and internal events occur, context and knowledge change, monitoring and review of risks take place, new risks emerge, some change, and others disappear."[6] Given the disruptive nature of technology and speed of change, this principle addresses the intersection between stakeholders (and their respective and, at times, differing needs) and changes in internal and external circumstances. Technology refreshes, operational process changes, new applications/software solutions—and changes in how each of the stakeholders access and use the organization's network, systems, and data—all create opportunities as well as threats.

This principle is demonstrated when uncertainties and changes that modify IT assets, the organization's objectives or stakeholder needs are integrated into the organization's formal and informal change management processes, wherever these processes occur.

COVERING THE ENTERPRISE END TO END

This COBIT 5 principle recognizes that managing IT as an asset is an essential element of business value creation, covering "all functions and processes within the enterprise" to "enable the enterprise to achieve the goal of satisfying stakeholder needs."[7] Accountability for managing IT assets in this regard rests with business managers rather than IT functional roles.

Creating and Protecting Value

Three ISO 31000 principles relate to this foundational element. The first, "risk management creates and protects value," focuses on the idea that [cyber] risk management "contributes to the demonstrable achievement of objectives and improvement of performance. ..." This principle is demonstrated when the process for considering uncertainties and decisions related to IT assets by business managers includes recognition of the organizational value to be gained or the value protected.

Tailoring

The second, "risk management is tailored," emphasizes that [cyber] "risk management is aligned with the organization's external and internal context and risk profile." The principle acknowledges the potential differences in the entity's operations, stakeholders, and business environment, with the expectation that these differences are taken into account. This principle is demonstrated when assessment methodologies, decisions, and resulting actions are customized based on the circumstances, proprietary knowledge, and the set of risks under consideration.

Addressing Uncertainty

The third, "risk management explicitly addresses uncertainty," relates to behaviors in which people acknowledge that the future can be different from the past. This principle encourages "risk management [that] explicitly takes account of uncertainty, the nature of that uncertainty, and how it can be addressed." The principle recognizes that not everything can be known, that circumstances change, and that ambiguity requires planning so that the enterprise can adapt in an unpredictable environment. This principle may be demonstrated through the use of assessment methodologies that examine potential factors and emerging issues that could affect desired outcomes, scan for changes in the organization's environment, consider various scenarios, and make plans for management action.

APPLYING A SINGLE, INTEGRATED FRAMEWORK

In this third COBIT 5 principle, the use of an overarching framework that incorporates relevant standards and frameworks—including the ISO 31000 risk management series—is provided as a "consistent and integrated source of guidance … addressing specific GEIT aspects … in an effective way."[8] ISO 31000 is noted to apply within two areas in COBIT 5: (1) Evaluate, Direct, and Monitor; and (2) Align, Plan, and Organize, while being interconnected with a number of complementary standards at the same time.

Being Structured

One of the ISO 31000 principles, "risk management is systematic, structured, and timely" states that "a systematic, timely and structured approach to [cyber] risk management contributes to efficiency and to consistent, comparable and reliable results." This principle infers that people apply management-directed criteria, metrics, and processes that can be replicated and used whenever and wherever decisions concerning IT assets and related environments are made. In order to achieve consistency and effectiveness throughout the enterprise, the criteria, metrics, and processes for considering risk should be aligned with that used for non-IT related issues. This principle is demonstrated when the enterprise establishes and communicates a clear and naturally integrated way of dealing with risk that is appropriate for business management to meet stakeholder needs, and is applicable to governing and managing enterprise IT.

ENABLING A HOLISTIC APPROACH

The fourth COBIT 5 principle "emphasizes that efficient and effective implementation of GEIT requires a holistic approach that takes into account several interacting components or mechanisms ..."—"enablers" in COBIT terms.[9] Four of these enablers (processes; culture; information; and people, skills, and competencies) relate directly to four ISO 31000 principles.

Integrating into the Organization

The first, "risk management is an integral part of all organizational processes" explains that [cyber] "risk management is not a stand-alone activity that is separate from the main activities and processes of the organization. Risk management is part of the responsibilities of management and an integral part of all organizational processes, including strategic planning and all project and change management processes." Since all activities of an organization involve risk, risk management is a natural intersection for incorporating legal, human resources, operations, IT management and protection, information security, physical security, privacy, and compliance functions and processes needed for a holistic cyber risk approach. Figure 3.1 illustrates how risk management unifies the organizational processes across the cyber enterprise.

This principle is demonstrated by people working collaboratively across the various organizational systems in managing cyber risks to influence

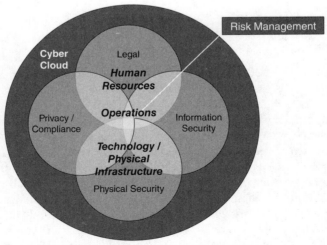

FIGURE 3.1   Risk management unifies processes

people, processes, and technology. It is further demonstrated when risk management is embedded into processes, such as strategic planning and change management, which influence the direction and modifications necessary to achieve the enterprise mission.

Considering Human and Cultural Factors

A different principle, "risk management takes human and cultural factors into account," is closely aligned with COBIT's enabler of culture, ethics, and behavior. In this ISO 31000 principle, "risk management recognizes the capabilities, perceptions, and intentions of external and internal people that can facilitate or hinder achievement of the organization's objectives." The principle suggests that evaluation of these capabilities, perceptions, and intentions can provide insights into external uncertainties, such as disruptive consumer preferences, behavior of industry or supply chain participants, and competing inventions. Internal uncertainties, such as innovation, ethical behavior, and motivations can be evaluated for consistency with the expectations set by management and rewarded through performance. This principle is demonstrated internally through management's clear expectations and rewards for behaviors consistent with the enterprise's core values, and is carried out through the decisions and resulting actions that individuals take. This principle is further demonstrated when the organization can answer questions such as:

- Is this project, initiative, or activity consistent with cultural expectations for managing cyber risk?
- Will the people involved, both internally and externally, behave in the way we anticipate?
- If not, are there other alternatives or actions that can be taken to reduce the potential negative effects of the related uncertainty and increase the potential positive effects of the related uncertainty?

The answers may differ depending on the project, initiative, or activity as well as the individuals or groups of individuals involved.

Being Part of Decision Making

A related ISO 31000 principle, "risk management is part of decision making," connects two COBIT 5 enablers: culture (as discussed earlier) and people, skills, and competencies. This principle emphasizes that [cyber] "risk management helps decision makers make informed choices, prioritize actions and distinguish among alternative courses of action." Decisions are made by all individuals within an enterprise as they carry out their activities. Most are automatic and made in the moment, requiring no formal risk assessments, but are highly dependent on the competencies and skills of the individual for managing risk. People who are making decisions that are of significant importance or are complex, such as those involved in a project or initiative, benefit from using risk management techniques to assess and evaluate the uncertainties related to each of the available options and identify potential unintended consequences. Those who are making decisions that have a strategic importance and are complex benefit from using more formal decision-making and risk management processes, applying multiple risk management techniques.[10]

All decisions, however, are influenced by the biases of those making decisions, as well as by the individuals' respective skills and competencies. As noted in the ANSI/ASIS/RIMS Risk Assessment Standard RA.1-2015, "Biases may sometimes lead to perceptual distortion, inaccurate judgment, and illogical analysis of information. There is a common tendency to acquire and process information by filtering it through one's own likes, dislikes, and experiences. Inherent bias is the effect of underlying factors and assumptions that impact information collection and analysis. Cognitive biases are tendencies to think in certain ways or a failure to imagine plausible alternatives." Bias considerations can be flagged and addressed using a vigorous [cyber] risk management lens.

This principle is demonstrated when people responsible for complex decisions (such as those related to strategy, projects, and initiatives, particularly those that are of significant or strategic importance) apply formal risk decision quality and management processes and techniques, and when risk management techniques and process are used in less complex projects and initiatives. It is further demonstrated by coaching and training people who are expected to take risk into account in their daily decision-making activities.

Using the Best Available Information

Another ISO 31000 principle, "risk management is based on the best available information"—which is directly related to the COBIT 5 enabler "information"—notes that "inputs to the process of managing risk are based on information sources, such as historical data, experience, stakeholder feedback, observation, forecasts and expert judgement." This principle encourages a fact-based approach, while recognizing limitations of data, modeling, and divergence of opinion among experts. The importance of agreeing to the validity of the underlying information to be used is key. This principle is demonstrated by clear agreement as to what constitutes verifiable evidence and, when unavailable, what constitutes reliable information or estimates.[11]

SEPARATING GOVERNANCE FROM MANAGEMENT

The fifth COBIT 5 principle "makes a distinction between governance and management."[12] The principle separates governance activities of evaluating, directing, and monitoring (based on business needs) from the management activities of planning, building, running, and monitoring. Both sets of activities are supported by GEIT processes. This principle contemplates a repeatable, closed-loop system in which management feedback is given "to ensure alignment with the direction that was set by the governance body and, thus, achieve the enterprise objectives."[13] While not specifically stated, such a feedback system naturally and continually improves the IT capabilities of the enterprise as it achieves its objectives.

Maturity Strategy and Continual Improvement

This principle is closely aligned with the ISO 31000 principle "risk management facilitates continual improvement of the organization." This principle holds that "organizations should develop and implement strategies to improve their [cyber] risk management maturity alongside all other aspects of their organization." This principle views continual improvement as being driven through a risk maturity strategy that aligns naturally with activities and processes found in *separating governance from management*. As people use risk management processes and techniques, they gain insights into the uncertainties that affect objectives, weigh alternatives, and make decisions that result in beneficial actions. As their risk management capabilities improve and mature over time, they naturally and consistently apply the above principles in determining whether decisions and the resulting actions are helpful or harmful. This principle is demonstrated when cyber risk management is embedded not only in IT-related governance and management activities and decisions, but in all the governance and management activities of the enterprise.

CONCLUSION

The cyber risk management statement in the "Principles Guide Actions" box represents those organizational capabilities the CEO and board expect to be demonstrated in terms of *cyber risk management principles to guide actions*.

PRINCIPLES GUIDE ACTIONS

Actions are taken by people in order to achieve the goals and objectives of an enterprise. Principles form the foundation of desirable and positive behavior for people in carrying out their respective responsibilities. Risk management principles in a COBIT 5 approach *meet stakeholder needs* by being transparent, inclusive, dynamic, iterative and responsive. Principles *covering the enterprise* guide people to create and protect value, tailor to their own environment, and explicitly address uncertainty. In *applying* a *single, integrated framework*, being systematic, structured, and timely is key. *Enabling a holistic approach* is supported by making risk considerations integral in all processes and decision making, while considering human factors, and using the best available data. Finally, the principle of facilitating continual improvement through a risk maturity strategy aligns naturally with activities and processes found in *separating governance from management*.

NOTES

1. ISO 31000:2009(E) International Standard: Risk Management—Principles and Guidelines, ISO 1st ed. 2009-11-15.
2. COBIT® 5 Implementation: A Business Framework for the Governance and Management of Enterprise IT, ISACA, 2012. *GEIT* stands for Governance of Enterprise Information Technology.
3. ISO 31000:2009(E) International Standard: Risk Management—Principles and Guidelines.
4. COBIT 5 Principles: Where Did They Come From? An ISACA COBIT series white paper, 2014, p. 5.
5. ANSI/ASIS/RIMS Risk Assessment Standard RA.1-2015, p. 8.
6. ISO 31000:2009(E) International Standard: Risk Management—Principles and Guidelines.
7. COBIT 5 Principles: Where Did They Come From?, p. 6.
8. Ibid., p. 8.
9. Ibid., p. 10.
10. ANSI/ASIS/RIMS Risk Assessment Standard RA.1-2015, p. 30.
11. Ibid., p. 11.
12. COBIT 5 Principles: Where Did They Come From?, p. 11.
13. Ibid.

ABOUT RIMS

As the preeminent organization dedicated to advancing the practice of risk management, RIMS, *the* risk management society™, is a global not-for-profit organization representing more than 3,500 industrial, service, non-profit, charitable and government entities throughout the world. Founded in 1950, RIMS is dedicated to advancing risk management for organizational success, bringing networking, professional development, and education opportunities to its membership of more than 11,000 risk management professionals who are located in more than 60 countries. For more information on RIMS, visit www.RIMS.org.

ABOUT CAROL FOX

Carol Fox, ARM, is the Vice President, Strategic Initiatives at RIMS, *the* risk management society™. While at RIMS, she's led the development of numerous RIMS publications, including *An Overview of Widely Used Risk Management Standards and Guidelines, ERM Best Practices in the Cyber World, and RIMS Strategic Risk Management Implementation Guide.*

A Miami University graduate, she's held progressively responsible risk management positions in the customer care, telecommunications, manufacturing, defense, and insurance industries. Prior to joining RIMS, she was senior director of risk management at Convergys Corporation with responsibility for business continuity, crisis management, safety, and claims. At the direction of the chief technology officer, she launched and managed a cross-functional IT security project that protected $100 million in recurring revenue.

Carol is the chair of the U.S. Technical Advisory Group for the ISO 31000 family of risk management standards, is a participant on the COSO ERM Advisory Council, and serves on Miami University's William Isaac & Michael Oxley Center of Business Leadership Advisory Board. Known for her risk management experience and writings, she received RIMS's prestigious 2009 Harry & Dorothy Goodell Award. In 2011, Treasury & Risk named her as one of the 100 Most Influential People in Finance.

CHAPTER 4

Cybersecurity Policies and Procedures

The Institute for Risk Management (IRM)
Elliot Bryan, IRM and Willis Towers Watson, UK
Alexander Larsen, IRM, and President of Baldwin Global Risk Services Ltd., UK

Tom, the CEO, was surprised. He challenged his chief risk officer, Nathan, and chief information security officer, Maria: "Are you telling me there is not one but six types of policies I need to sign off for cyber risk?" The two answered in tandem: "Yes! Social media, ransomware, cloud computing/third-party vendors, Big Data analytics, the Internet of Things, and bring-your-own-device (BYOD)/mobile devices."

SOCIAL MEDIA RISK POLICY

Social media is an Internet-based communication tool and platform that increases and enhances the sharing of information and media. It is often overlooked as an area of risk by organizations that underestimate its potential negative impact—particularly on reputation.

A McDonald's social-media effort is one example of a known social media risk being realized. The fast-food leader set up the hashtag #McDstories on Twitter to encourage users to share and promote positive stories about the restaurant. It didn't take long for people to use the hashtag to post mostly negative stories of their experiences, derailing the campaign and embarrassing McDonald's.

Understand Your Social Media Risks

Currently, there are literally thousands of social media platforms with over 2 billion active users. These include forums, blogs, networking sites, and image/video-sharing sites.

From a risk perspective, there are two key areas that companies on social media are exposed to that need to be considered. These are:

1. *Employee use* of social media by mobile phone or computer exposing the organization to risk (e.g., intellectual property and data leakage, viruses, password loss).
2. *Corporate use* of social media such as having a Twitter account or Facebook profile exposing the organization to risk (e.g., negative posts about your organization, campaigns backfiring, inefficient use of social media).

Prepare for Your Social Media Policy

The best form of prevention is for your organization to be well prepared before it enters into the social media sphere. Six preparations are recommended:

1. Engage a *multidisciplinary team*. Since social media affects a wide range of functions, an effective strategy should bring together senior representatives from human resources (HR), legal, information technology (IT), risk, and any other affected functions.
2. Clarify the *objective* of using social media. For example, to improve reputation, attract talent, increase sales, or improve customer engagement.
3. Undertake a *risk assessment*.
4. Obtain *senior management mandate* and commitment.
5. Understand *legal implications* of the do's and don'ts, monitoring of staff, and disciplinary action. This is where having the legal department on your team can be useful.
6. *Train all staff* in the basics of the social media because media policy is essentially useless without the right training.

Choose between Social Media Policy Options

There are a number of options and considerations when creating a social media policy. These include how many policies to have and how extensive they should be. Should it even be called a *policy?* Employees are hardly likely to feel enthusiastic about a policy, so perhaps *social media guidelines* or something along those lines may be more appropriate.

Choose between One versus Many Policies   Decide if your organization needs to write *one complete* social media policy that addresses all currently available social media, or write *many policies as you need them*. It may seem excessive to have a policy for each network, and indeed, a company may choose to include these into one policy; however, it is important to understand the different impacts each network may have on the company.

Something to keep in mind is that when a company has multiple social media policies, it can become difficult to keep updated. Social Media networks update their content, features, and terms and conditions on a regular basis, and having specific policies would require them to keep up to date with all these changes.

For many companies, having separate policies may be critical. Military, police, IT companies, health care, and political parties, for example, may want to be very specific with regard to what employees can't do or share online. Loss of sensitive data, such as patient records, staff addresses, political views, and so on, could lead to major reputation loss, danger to staff, or breach of legal requirements.

For other companies, however, it could be more beneficial for a company to have a social media guidance policy that focuses more on behavior and refers to all social media.

Choose between Format Options   Social media policies range from being *extensive* documents to being *short* and to the point. There is no right or wrong approach to this, and it will all depend on an organization's industry, organizational culture, their risks, and motivations for participating in social media. Words and phrases that are familiar from other policies or visions within the organization may be a great way for staff to remember and understand the policy, too.

Examples of Social Media Policies

Rather than going through one or two examples of policies, it is recommended that you look online. There are over 100 policies from various organizations available online from Social Media Governance, a web site created by technology advisor Chris Boudreaux (www.socialmediagovernance.com/policies/). Some examples include:

- Employee Code of Conduct for Online Communications
- Employee Code of Conduct for Organization Representation in Online Communications
- Employee Blogging Disclosure Policy
- Employee Personal Blog Policy
- Employee Personal Social Network Policy

- Employee LinkedIn Policy
- Corporate Blogging Policy (including guidelines for comments)
- Corporate Facebook Brand Page Usage Policy (including guidelines for public comments and messages)
- Corporate Twitter Account Policy
- Corporate YouTube Policy (including guidelines for public comments)
- Organization Password Policy

Finding the right combination from these examples can help organizations cover all three major social media risk categories (i.e., personal, employee, and corporate use of social media).

It is considered a leading international practice to have at least two social media policies: one for employees using social media *for their job* and the other for employees using social media in their *personal lives*. Recommendations on content for both types of accounts are covered in the boxes "Personal Social Media Policy for Employees" and "Social Media Policy for Corporate Accounts." This first is for employees' individual use of social media. It focuses on employees' personal use of social media and should give employees information about what they can and cannot say about your organization on their personal site.

PERSONAL SOCIAL MEDIA POLICY FOR EMPLOYEES

INTRODUCTION
Outline research and work done in preparation and organization objectives for the social media program.

DEFINITIONS
Be clear from the outset as to what the organization considers its intellectual property, critical data, confidential information, competitors, and other *no-go* areas to be.

BOUNDARIES AND GUIDELINES
Outline appropriate rules for internal approval processes and information to disclose about the organization and the range of opinions expressed if an employee tweets or blogs views or comments that are work related. Outline appropriate rules for the range of opinions they may express if an employee tweets or blogs personal views or comments (e.g., many organizations restrict political or other sensitive

issues being discussed). Remind employees of organization's policy on bullying and harassment.

OFF-LIMITS CONTENT

Address the content that should obviously be totally off limits on social media (e.g., confidential information, negative comments about competitors, anything illegal).

SAFE USE

Remind employees to regularly update social networking passwords and check privacy settings in order to minimize hacking or virus incidents that could lead to identity theft or a virus on organization networks.

PERSONAL USE

Clarify whether employees can use the organization's Internet and company e-mail system for personal use. Provide staff with clear wording to be added to e-mails and Internet posts that state that the views in the e-mail or post are the views of the employee and not the organization.

REPORTING

Provide employees with an e-mail address to report cases of organization-related content posted online that they feel should be responded to. This could be negative comments, fake pages, or inappropriate competitor posts.

PROFESSIONALISM AND RESPECT

Remind everyone about the importance of professionalism and respect for others. While there are no clear boundaries when discussing professionalism and respect for others, it can often remind people to think twice when posting something.

DATA PROTECTION AND MONITORING

An employer needs to be up front with its employees if they plan on monitoring employees' use of social media. Ideally, it can be communicated as a positive—as a way to protect both employer and employee. An alternative is to have an opt-in program that allows staff to access social media freely as long as they add the organization as a follower

(continued)

(Continued)

or friend in order to allow the employer to monitor in a less controlled manner.

LINKS TO OTHER POLICIES
Cross-reference your social media policy with other policies already in place such as IT, bullying and harassment, code of organization ethics, and other relevant policies.

CONSEQUENCES
Refer to current disciplinary procedures and be clear that these also apply to behavior online. Provide examples of serious infringements and what disciplinary actions could result.

FREQUENTLY ASKED QUESTIONS
Having an FAQ will allow staff to quickly find answers to questions they may be looking for rather than rereading, or in most cases not bothering to reread, the full policy.

A second policy focuses on official professional and corporate social media activities. This should cover everything from defining the team to articulating roles and responsibilities, establishing branding guidelines, and becoming clear about what internal and external policies must be complied with.

SOCIAL MEDIA POLICY FOR CORPORATE ACCOUNTS

RESPONSIBILITIES
Identify employees responsible for setting up and managing accounts, posting comments, and responding to comments. Also identify who is responsible for monitoring the use of brand and fake user names or pages.

DEALING WITH CUSTOMER COMMENTS
Outline key do's and don'ts for responding to positive or negative comments such as avoiding deleting comments or negative posts and

avoiding aggressive comments. Link this to a communication plan that provides preapproved messages depending on the stakeholders and social media platform.

DEALING WITH FAKE USER NAMES, PAGES, AND PROMOTIONS/COMPETITIONS
Provide key steps to take should a social networking site refuse to take down a user name or page using the organization's name. Highlight key information to gather, whom to contact within the legal department, and other such details.

DEALING WITH PROMOTIONS/COMPETITIONS
Outline key do's and don'ts for promotions and competitions including who should review social networking's site terms and conditions to ensure compliance. State how to deal with users who cheat by, for example, setting up multiple accounts.

RANSOMWARE RISK POLICIES AND PROCEDURES

The year 2016 has often been described as *the year of the ransomware attack*. In just the first three months of 2016, attacks increased tenfold over the entire previous year, with *reported* victim costs at more than $200 million.[1] Ransomware is a type of malware that is used by an attacker to effectively kidnap an organization's data and prevent it from using it by encrypting it. This renders your data and files useless until you gain access to the decryption key, for which the attacker will demand a ransom. Attackers know that organizations are becoming more dependent on data for their organization to function and the motivation for hackers to launch an attack increases as the financial value of data is increasing on the black market (also commonly referred to as the "dark web").

Here are a few examples of known recent ransomware attacks:

- Attacks on U.S. police departments—various U.S. police departments have been hit, losing data on open cases.[2]
- Attack on the University of Calgary, Canada, and Brunel University in London—the University of Calgary was forced to pay approximately C$20,000. The attack encrypted all of the university's e-mails and files.[3]

- Hollywood Hospital in Los Angeles paid a ransom of $17,000 after having lost access to all of its data and faced an extortion demand of $3.4 million.[4]

Understand Your Ransomware Risks

Ransomware is often spread through opening infected e-mail attachments, programs, and compromised web sites. An attacker will often try and persuade an unsuspecting employee to inadvertently download ransomware, usually by displaying messages on a web site and directing them to take an action to resolve a fictitious virus. It is this very action that *downloads* the ransomware onto the computer and permeates your organization's network.

An attacker will often send a spam e-mail out to tens of thousands of unsuspecting victims with no real intended target, until an employee accidentally downloads the ransomware. These e-mails can quite often bypass anti-spam filters. The user then receives a message that pops up on their PC stating that their files have been encrypted, or "this operating system has been locked for security reasons." These e-mails will then usually place a demand (usually in online currency bitcoin) to settle the ransom over a short time period (usually with a ticking clock) in exchange for the decryption key.

It is at this point that your organization faces a choice to either pay the ransom or attempt to negotiate with the attacker. Both options are undesirable. If, for example, the attacker exploits a vulnerability in your organization's computer network and your organization pays the ransom at the first time of asking—then there would be nothing to stop the attacker exploiting that vulnerability again and sustaining repeated attacks. There is also no guarantee that the attacker will pass on the decryption key, after having received a ransom payment. If the affected organization chooses to negotiate, they also lose access to critical data for that period of time, which could result in a paralysis of organization operations and loss of revenues.

How Cybercriminals Spread Ransomware   New methods to spread ransomware are *constantly being innovated*. Only prevention via a robust cyber risk management system—including employee education—can help your organization manage ransomware risk effectively. The methods commonly used by criminals include:

- Spam e-mail campaigns.
- Bypassing vulnerable software and password protection.

- Internet traffic redirecting targets to malicious web sites, very commonly from legitimate web sites.
- SMS messages (targeting mobile devices).
- Legitimate web sites that have malicious code injected into their web pages.
- Drive-by downloads, a user inadvertently visiting a web site that is running malicious code.[5]

Prepare for Your Ransomware Policy

Your policies and overriding message should make it clear from the outset that protection across ransomware threats is the responsibility of *all* employees and not just the IT security function.

Be Proactive   As ransomware attacks are becoming so frequent, these policies are framed on the presumption that it is more a case of *when*, and not *if*, your organization is targeted.[6] The purpose of this key policy content is to enable the organization to *be proactive* in preventing avoidable threats to your organization from ransomware attacks. Ransomware attacks are often sophisticated enough to bypass defensive IT anti-virus software, so it is vital that capabilities are deployed across the entire network to identify and contain the malicious activity.

Education, Education, Education   Run regular—at a minimum every three to six months—phishing e-mail *tests* with all employees, and mandatory training for all new employees. A *training* module for a large organization could also include a set of e-mails with unsolicited web links, and the employee has to decide which ones to avoid. Help employees become part of the security process, perhaps by getting them developing *posters* to increase employee awareness of ransomware attacks.[7]

Have a Clear Internal Escalation Procedure   Ensure that employees know where to send a suspicious e-mail, including on how to mark the e-mail header to avoid them inadvertently passing the virus to someone else.

Choose between Ransomware Policy Options   While an organization might want to focus on having a *single* policy (including IT and employee best practices), it may be worth having *separate* ones to avoid diluting the importance of having buy-in your employees. While leading practice IT hygiene can underpin the success of the employee policy, it is important to realize that the IT and employee practices must work together, as a weakness in either policy will undo all of the good work that you have done in the other.

Employees are often cited as the weakest link in IT security management.

RANSOMWARE POLICY KEY CONTENT

BACK UP DATA REGULARLY
Perform and test regular data backups that are perhaps daily, weekly, or monthly to an online backup service to limit the impact of data or system loss and to speed up the recovery process in the event of an attack.

SEGREGATE YOUR DATA
Store your data in different locations, so that an attack on a single point does not hold all of your data to ransom.

KEEP ANTIVIRUS SOFTWARE UP TO DATE
These updates can often be automated, but if not, ensure that the update is always chosen and implemented instantly.

EMBRACE BEST-IN-CLASS "ANTI-SPAM" SOFTWARE
A lot of ransomware attacks come from phishing e-mails, so make your first layer of protection as robust as possible by preventing as many unwanted and inappropriate e-mails as possible.

USE STRONG PASSWORDS
Have minimum length of passwords, including upper- and lowercase letters and rules on the use of names and birthdays.[8] Change passwords regularly.

USE BLACKLISTING SOFTWARE[9]
Limit the potential for visits to harmful and malicious web sites by restricting access through blacklisting software. Enable specified programs to run on computers to block categories of web sites that may include (but are not limited to) content from the following categories:

- Adult, sexually explicit
- Criminal activity
- Gambling
- Intolerance and hate
- Violence and weapons
- Phishing, fraud, spam[10]

There may also be others, but by having a policy it avoids you documenting a list of categories that employees are unable to visit. This has the added benefit of enhancing employee productivity.

LIMIT APPLICATION USE
Use a standardized and restrictive set of applications that are essential only for work use, and limit these to a manageable number. Use a mainstream browser that supports safe browsing.[11]

APPLY THE PRINCIPLE OF "LEAST PRIVILEGE"
Restrict employee access to only the critical folders and data that are required for their job role. Use an application procedure for access to a folder and process that requires permission for access.

CLOUD COMPUTING AND THIRD-PARTY VENDORS

Cloud computing can offer many operational efficiencies and can greatly enhance your organizations access to resources. Typically, a cloud provider hosts a network of remote servers that store, manage and process huge volumes of data on the Internet. This offers an alternative to an organization using the limited space and flexibility of a hard drive. Examples of cloud services include Google Drive, Apple iCloud, Dropbox, and Amazon Cloud Drive. Key benefits include:

- *Flexibility.* Employees can access data from servers remotely that aren't hard-wired in-house servers, thus creating a more flexible and mobile work lifestyle for your organization. Cloud resources are scalable for large corporations and affordable for small ones.[12]
- *Cost savings.* Hard-wired IT infrastructure is costly to implement and may not offer the return on investment that had been anticipated. Cloud providers often operate on pay-per-use models that ensure that you are allocating your resources efficiently.[13]
- *Reliability.* Cloud computing allows your organization to benefit from the cloud provider's economies of scale. The cloud provider is possibly more likely to be able to provide 24/7 support in the event of an outage, and have the expertise in their staff to support the infrastructure.[14]

■ *Enhanced security.* While there are risks that come with trusting the cloud provider's network security, their security and encryption capabilities often supersede most organizations' internal security capabilities.[15]

Understand Your Cloud Computing Risks

The three primary risks that emerge related to cloud computing emerge from Internet dependency, concentration of data, and poorly executed contracts. Internet dependency is a risk that seems unavoidable in today's digital business world. An Internet outage can prevent and delay important business functions, including transactions. While outages from Internet service providers can cause outages, cloud-computing sites can also go down. Even a temporary interruption of service can cause major problems for clients.

An organization that relies on cloud providers also relies on a third party to safeguard their centralized data. If the cloud provider's network is compromised, this could result in the client's loss of access to data, resulting in a damaged reputation. Using a cloud provider that does not adequately protect data can have tremendous negative consequences for organizations, employees, and customers.

Additional risk can emerge from weak service contracts with a cloud provider. Once an agreement is signed, it is very difficult to resolve any problems it causes or fails to address. Should anything go wrong, organizations will, at best, suffer from being stuck in a fractured service relationship. In a worst-case scenario, a client organization can face unexpected liabilities.

Prepare for Your Cloud Computing Policy

Clarify the purpose of your cloud computing policy as to how your organization may reap the benefits of using a cloud service while limiting the threats such as reputation loss and liabilities (should the service not perform as expected). It is vital that organizations both procure cloud provider services effectively and understand the contract language and negotiate key terms.

It is *vital* that you procure your cloud services and achieve a customer agreement and service level agreement that enables your organization to achieve its desired outcomes, prevent disputes and ensure that your organization does not assume *all* of the risk should the cloud fail. Getting the front-end processes right during the procurement stage is key in preventing problems further down the line and helps migrate your applications to the cloud successfully. More detail is provided below.[16]

Procure Cloud Provider Services Effectively

Some key processes that can help you procure cloud providers effectively are discussed in detail in this section.

Identify Your Desired Outcomes from a Cloud Provider Issue an invitation to tender (ITT) that communicates your key desired outcomes to your chosen short list of providers. This could be for a migration of your application software to a state-of-the-art data center, enhanced cost savings, and access to better IT security and reliability of organization continuity, or a combination of all three. This will help your organization narrow your short list.[17]

Review Request and review your shortlisted providers' standard contracts. Rank these contracts with the assistance of a legal advisor in terms of favorability.[18] Do thorough due diligence, and ensure that they retain security certification, and have positive audit results. Review your cloud providers' security, privacy, and data storage policies.

Be Selective Consider only providers that have agreed to meet your outcomes and make this a condition of your contract.[19]

Scope Have a precontractual scope with your chosen provider. Agree on a transition plan for moving applications to the new virtual environment. Discuss scenarios precontract and understand who would be liable in the event of something going wrong. Identify key owners for the various tasks and operate on deadlines. Ensure that the project is only finished when applications are successfully transferred to the cloud and organization as usual is achieved. Obtain evidence that your provider can meet these objectives.[20]

Draft Start drafting the contract by using incentivized payment provisions that are linked to the predetermined outcomes. Use acceptance provisions to hold your cloud provider accountable. Remove "Agreements to Agree" from standard contracts, as these are not operative, potentially discharging the cloud provider's liability.[21] Check the architecture works. Only sign the contract as soon as organization as usual has been achieved and the migration is complete and works effectively.[22]

Clarify Understand the contract language and negotiate key terms. As is common with an industry in its infancy, there are frequently errors in cloud contracts. These contracts (especially with larger providers) tend to be heavily weighted in their favor. There are also the added complications of finite case law and the fact that the choice of law governing these contracts is often overseas meaning that the settlement of a dispute could potentially be very costly.[23] This applies in particular, if your organization is the controller for personal data such as:

- Account numbers and balances of clients.
- Personal information of your customers.
- Personal information of employees.
- Medical history of patients if you're a health care provider.

It is vital that you contract with providers with best-in-class security and the contract does not totally exonerate them from liability in the event of a data breach. It is also better to have a bespoke contract rather than a standard contract, as quite often cloud providers can change their standard terms and post them on their web site without necessarily warning their customers.[24]

Generally, the customer service agreements are usually split into four sections:

- Customer agreement
- Acceptable use policy (AUP)
- Service-level agreement
- Privacy policy[25]

The box "Customer Agreement Key Content" highlights key content that you should pay close attention to when negotiating a contract with a cloud provider.

CUSTOMER AGREEMENT KEY CONTENT

LIMITATIONS OF LIABILITY

This section stipulates the maximum amount the provider would be liable for in the event of deletion or damage to data or any monetary loss created by the inability of the customer to access the service. Ensure that the provider's aggregate limit liability isn't capped too low. Disclaimers often exclude cases where the provider is grossly negligent, so ensure that the clause works both ways and that the clause protects you as well as the provider. Negotiate broad time periods for indemnity claims.[26]

DISASTER RECOVERY

Ensure that your provider is aware of your recovery time objectives and can meet these. Store data in different locations to mitigate the impact of a cyber attack.

TERMS AND TERMINATION

Advance notice should be in excess of 30 days. Ensure that the provider retains the data for a minimum period during transition to a new provider.[27]

SUSPENSION OF SERVICE

Ensure that there is a minimum period of notice given should the cloud provider decide to suspend the service, and aim for a minimum of 60 days.[28]

EXCLUSIONS

Fully understand these exclusions and ask identify which scenarios would not fall on the provider should they occur. Ensure cloud providers retain liability for data safety, and for outages. Many provider standard contracts contain "agreements to agree,"[29] that are not operative contractually, meaning that they can't be relied upon if the cloud provider fails to deliver on its services.[30] You must also ensure that there are no caveats and assumptions.

ACCEPTABLE USE POLICY (AUP)

These can often change without warning, so it is vital you keep up to date with changes. Be sure that your organization and employees do not violate the AUP as there are often significant consequences of doing so. It may be prudent to update your IT policy guide accordingly for employees, if your organization decides to adopt the use of cloud. Request clarification on vague terms and clarify what actions the provider deems unacceptable.[31]

SERVICE-LEVEL AGREEMENT

Review your provider's service availability guarantees and credits and negotiate to get the most favorable terms. Automate a process for detecting and logging outages.[32] Be mindful of your provider's commitment exclusions.

(continued)

(*Continued*)

SECURITY AND PRIVACY POLICY

Negotiate with your provider *where* your data should be located, after understanding how sensitive the data is to the location, and select an appropriate cloud provider that ensures compliance and understanding of local data regulations.[33] Ensure provider commitment to physical security procedures. Since provider-led contracts tend to place the onus of obligations on the customer you should understand the provider's data security posture and how your data would be replicated, backed up, encrypted, and deleted when it becomes redundant.[34] Enforce tight notification provisions. Make sure that provider notifies you in the event of any security breaches or suspicious activity.[35] Review whether your provider outsources administration and whether these administrators have strong levels of security.[36]

BIG DATA ANALYTICS

The benefits of Big Data analytics are being felt across many organizations. While these are numerous, the key benefit is the enhanced capability of being able to collect large volumes of data and apply analytical tools, to help assist organizations in identifying where to focus their marketing efforts and allocate resources efficiently.

Understand Your Big Data Risks

While the use of Big Data analytics unlocks huge possibilities for organizations (i.e., opportunities), it can also open organizations to new threats. Hackers are aware of this shift and are growing both more persistent and more savvy in how they unlawfully access networks. There are two main types of threats:

1. *Increased risk of privacy breaches.* Big data analytics relies on the aggregation of huge amounts of *personal* data. A personal data event could result in reputational damage, regulatory fines, and potential liabilities to those data subjects.
2. *Regulatory compliance.* Globally, there are trends toward more onerous requirements in safeguarding personal data. The new EU General Data Protection Regulations, due to be enforced in May 2018, will impose

requirements on companies to have a compliance-first approach to the use of data. Failure or negligence in providing the relevant safeguards can lead to regulatory fines of up to 4 percent of global turnover. Compliance projects can also drain productivity in achieving organization tasks.

Prepare for Your Big Data Policy

Clarify that the purpose of your big data policy is to not only be regulatory compliant and avoid unwanted headlines but to maintain factual and secure data that will help drive organization growth.[37]

Again, as this the case with ransomware attacks, organizations can opt to have individual IT and employee policies.

A significant number of data breaches occur through negligent employee practices, so it is vital that employees are full engaged and educated in good IT hygiene in securing confidential organization data and customer data.

While, there are numerous policies available, it is best practice to follow the "privacy by design" principle. Privacy by design requires an organization to minimize harm to a data customer by designing a set of rules and processes for acquiring and creating data, migrating that data into systems, and best practice storage and uses of that data.[38] This is a key requirement for organizations' subject to the EU's new General Data Protection Regulation requirements that are due to be enforced in May 2018 and enforced by heavy penalties.

BIG DATA "PRIVACY BY DESIGN" KEY CONTENT

REDUNDANT DATA
Delete redundant data, that is, data that is no longer relevant for analytical purposes.[39]

ANTIVIRUS PROTECTION
Adopt best in class antivirus protection and make sure updates and patches are updated regularly or if possible, automated.[40]

ENCRYPT DATA
Encrypt data both in rest and in transit. Data at rest is typically data that is not moving, and is usually copied data that is stored on backup

(continued)

(*Continued*)

drives or on hard drives. Data at transit, conversely, is data that is moving between networks and would apply heavily in use of big data analytics. This practice is often termed "end-to-end encryption." Enable careful management of decryption keys.[41]

SPREAD DATA STORAGE
Storing data in multiple locations minimizes the impact of a data breach of one of those locations.

LAWFUL COLLATION AND PROCESSING
Ensure compliance with your governing regular to ensure that collection is necessary, explicit consent has been achieved and through the movement of networks between countries, if applicable.[42]

PCI COMPLIANCE
PCI-DSS is an industry standard for organizations that collect payment data. The goal of this is to ensure that card data issued by the major card provider is stored and processed appropriately. A data breach may result in costly assessments from representatives of the major credit card organizations, in conjunction with fines.[43]

THIRD-PARTY VENDORS
If the organization uses third-party administrators or cloud providers to process or store data, thorough due diligence should be undertaken of their security and privacy protection procedures. Contracts should also be tightly worded, to minimize liability on behalf of your organization should a breach occur.[44]

Big Data may mean certain amendments need to be made to existing or other organization policies.

EMPLOYEE POLICY KEY CONTENT AMENDMENTS FOR BIG DATA

EDUCATION
All employees and new joiners should undergo regular tests on the data protection laws that they are subject to, and completion of scenarios

that ensure they fully understand the principle of good data house-keeping. Passwords and decryption keys should never be stored in an easily accessible place.[45]

USB AND EXTERNAL STORAGE
Prevent employees from using their own personal USBs at work and ensure that authorized USB's are encrypted.

BRING YOUR OWN DEVICE (BYOD POLICY)
Guidelines around password protection and two factor authentication of employees' personal devices (phones and laptops) should be taken, and necessary disciplinary action should these guidelines not be adhered to. As discussed later in this chapter, ensure employees are compliant with your organization's BYOD policy and appropriate security measures are taken if your organization decides to implement it.

THE INTERNET OF THINGS

The Internet of Things (IoT) has the potential to deliver untold benefits for organizations. McKinsey Global estimates that it can deliver between $2.7 billion and $6.2 trillion of value to the global economy by 2025, with the number of connected devices to exceed 50 billion by 2020.[46] Essentially, IoT enables the linking together of physical "connected" devices via the Internet that help organizations collect data, complete tasks more efficiently, and thus develop and sell tailored customer solutions. The major advantage to an organization is the ability to use the vast amounts of data to collate big data analytics.

Understand Your IoT Risks

The Internet of Things means more connected devices, and a potential "wild west" type scenario in which a hack into one device can make it easier to hack into others.[47] This is particularly poignant, as an organization may be fairly far removed from the chain in a device that gets hacked and yet suffer significant reputational damage even if your organization was not the initial target. Some examples:

- In 2015 Fiat Chrysler had to recall of 1.4 million vehicles to fix a vulnerability that allowed an attacker to wirelessly hack into the vehicle.[48]

- In 2014 a German Steel Mill blast furnace suffered massive damage, after hackers gained access to controls through hacking employee e-mails and gaining access to the plant's office network.[49]

Categories of IoT threats include:

- Data protection—huge sources of personal data are gathered from all aspect of an individual's life, making them more easily identifiable. This creates potential liabilities, fines, and reputational damage.
- More connected devices—increasing likelihood of a hack.
- Speed of change—the speed at which devices become connected and the growth of IoT technology may outstrip the rate at which appropriate security controls of the connected devices are implemented. The organization may lose control of how many devices are connected to their data, leading to liabilities that have not been accounted for in risk registers. An example are smart meters, where mobile phones can be used to regulate temperature control within a home.[50]
- Increased likelihood of outages—sheer volumes of servers communicating huge volumes of data traffic can overwhelm the server and lead to downtime.[51]
- Security lags—unencrypted links are often used to communicate between devices.[52]

Prepare for Your "Internet of Things" Policy

Clarify that the purpose of this policy is to assist your organization to reap the opportunities from the Internet of Things by gaining a handle on the new risks that your organization will now face. The policy content should factor in security of the data that you collect on your own devices but also should include provisions for other organizations that operate the other connected devices.

"INTERNET OF THINGS" KEY CONTENT

- Identify all stakeholders (regulators, individuals, those using the devices, members of the public, data owners).
- Identify worst case scenarios.
- Encrypt data from the data center to the end point.
- Segregate IoT network from critical corporate data.[53]

- Identify and map (as best you can) all devices that are connected to the device or devices that you sell to your customers, in particular how they collect data and how they communicate with each other and how these links are protected.[54]
- Focused policies on appropriate collection, use, and protection of consumer data.[55]
- Document permissible uses. Make sure that other organizations that have networks that connect with your device have a clear set of guidelines for what your device can be used for.[56]
- Restrict use on applications and limit liability within your contracts.
- Install best in class antivirus and firewall software, and thoroughly audit any resellers security policies and practices.

MOBILE OR BRING YOUR OWN DEVICES (BYOD)

The working environment is changing fast, and companies are responding to calls from employees for increased flexibility in their working practices. This is part of a tidal shift toward agile working, with employees choosing to centralize all aspects of their lives into a single device. In turn, companies are looking to reap the benefits of lower costs and increased employee productivity. These mutual benefits have led to staggering adoption rate of BYOD schemes by companies; it is estimated that around 85 percent of companies now allow employees to bring their own devices to work.[57] There is, however, a darker side to BYOD[58]; it is inevitable that emerging work practices will lead to emerging risks, in particular around data protection.

Understand Your BYOD Risks

The principles of BYOD are largely around giving employees more freedom in how and where they work. The fact remains that the company, as a data controller, has overall responsibility for the data, yet it will retain significantly less control over an employee's devices, than it would its own device.[59] Employees are often seen as a weak link in the data security chain, and the risks of reputational damage are amplified. All of the positives benefits around increased productivity, or reduced hardware costs could soon be eliminated through a single oversight or irresponsible act.

The key risks associated with BYOD are as follows:

- Accidental or intentional data breach leading to harm to customers, reputational damage, and fines.
- Employees connecting to unsecured networks, opening up vulnerabilities.
- Theft of sensitive corporate data and intellectual property, leading to missed opportunities and revenue loss.
- Merging of end user data and corporate data.[60]
- Interception of data between the personal device and corporate system leading to reputational damage and fines.[61]
- Loss of device and hack.
- Privacy regulations, use abroad could open up additional risks in relation to privacy regulations.[62]
- Malware infection leading to data leakage and data corruption.[63]

Prepare for Your BYOD Policy

An enterprise-wide BYOD policy will assist your company in locking in the benefits of employee satisfaction, productivity, and reduced costs while avoiding potentially large-scale embarrassments. Following are some key steps that will help your company prepare toward developing a successful mobile device strategy.

Determine How the Mobile Devices Will Be Used   Be clear on how you expect the mobile devices to benefit your business.[64] Companies should ask themselves if they want the devices to connect with the existing network infrastructure, process sensitive information or act as a tool to help your sales and marketing employees. This will assist you in determining the tightness of the control environment and levels of password protection required.[65]

Get All Company Functions to Contribute   It is vital that the BYOD policy has input across the company from Human Resources, Legal, IT, accounting and the employees.[66] This is crucial in helping the company get a broader understanding of its emerging risks, underpinning the policy. It will also ensure wider accountability across the company, rather than being an "IT" issue. Consider using interactive games or tests to help employees truly understand the risks rather than getting them to search through pages of documents. They will, however, have to eventually read and fully understand the policy.

Understand the Emerging Risks   The implementation of BYOD should not introduce vulnerabilities into already secure networks.[67] Be clear on agreements that you have with other companies and ensure that the BYOD does not contravene these agreements.[68] The emerging risks can be documented, and can seamlessly link in with your other policies such as your overall IT security and social media policies to form the foundation of your policy.

Consider Mobile Device Management   Mobile device management solutions underpin secure BYOD policies and can assist in mitigating many of the merging risks. Examples of these solutions include SOTI MobiControl, Vmware AirWatch, Citrix Xen Mobile, and IBM MaaS360.[69] It is crucial that these are procured carefully and matched with the objectives of the BYOD. Mobile device management can provide all-encompassing solutions such as enforcing a pass code, encrypting stored data, and wiping a device if it gets lost.[70]

Audit Your Data   Understand the data that you hold as an organization, consider how many sensitive data records that you hold, and be clear on which personal data are permitted to be processed on a personal device.

Separate End-User Data and Corporate Data   Cloud adoption is also increasing, and many end users may use their devices to store personal documents, contacts, and e-mails in iCloud.[71] End users must be clear on the acceptable use of the cloud when adopting BYOD, to avoid leaking personal data into the cloud and accidental data breaches.[72]

Protect and Encrypt   All devices should retain a strong password, and two-factor authentication. Encryption should be used to store data on the device effectively, and locks should be in place should an incorrect password be entered in too many times. Support and guidance for the end user is crucial in this regard. Encryption at rest is a useful risk prevention procedure should a device be lost or stolen.

Employee Responsibility   An *end-user agreement* is essential in clarifying that personal data must not be shared. The end-user agreement illustrates the need for employees to be held accountable, and the signing of this agreement is a demonstration of their understanding of their responsibilities and the risks involved when adopting BYOD. They must also have clearly defined parameters as to how the devices can and should not be used.[73] It is crucial that restrictive practices are communicated to the end user, with a support network available.[74] The end-user agreement can be used in conjunction with the company's security policy to cover the life cycle of the device, including loss scenarios, disposal, and when an employee leaves the company.[75]

Choose between BYOD Policy Options

It is vital that companies find a balance between achieving the objectives of the organization without compromising security. Your organization could choose one of the following options.

Disallow BYOD   This is the ultimate risk-avoidance measure. BYOD is fast becoming a work "norm" and preventing BYOD will limit the benefits that a company achieves and may result in employee frustrations and flouting the prohibitions on use.[76]

The "Do Nothing" Approach   Some companies may choose to offer this approach in order to enable extensive take up by employees or avoid stifling creativity and innovation. This is potentially dangerous in that it can lead to serious personal data leakage and a lack of control over their intellectual property, resulting in reputational damage and harm to customers.[77]

Corporate Devices Only   This option helps the company retain more control over their IT assets, policies, baseline security measures, and configurations. While this option ensures consistent security baselines and retained account-ability within the organization, it can lead to increased costs per person and a higher number of connected devices.[78]

Have a Managed BYOD Policy   A managed BYOD policy documents the responsibilities and ensures accountability of the employee through the use of an end-user agreement. It allows employees flexibility but limits the introduction of new risks. The security controls, limitations of use, and types of devices used are largely dependent on the volume and sensitivity of the company data and how the device is intended to be used.[79] Clear communication with employees is vital in helping them understanding the risks associated with using company data on mobile devices. The policy does need to be continuously monitored and improved where necessary with clear internal escalation points for queries by end users.

Examples of BYOD Policies

There are numerous BYOD policies available, many of which contain the following sections:

- Acceptable use (end-user agreement)
- Devices and support

- Reimbursement
- Security
- Risks/Liabilities/Disclaimers[80]

BYOD POLICY KEY CONTENT

Acceptable use

- Agreement to use the mobile device in compliance with company policies, such as the data protection, IT usage and risk policy.
- Blocking of web sites during work hours.[81]
- Compliance with acceptable usage of device on company time.
- Limiting what devices may or may not be used for, such as storing illicit material or transferring proprietary information.[82]
- Zero tolerance policy for texting, calling, or e-mailing while driving.[83]

Devices and Support

- Choose-your-own-device (CYOD) policy. Essentially this limits employee choice of devices to a preapproved list, set by the company, giving IT more control and mitigating unforeseen security and management issues.[84]
- The list is at the company's discretion and may include iPhone and Android, as well as the necessary models.[85]
- IT verifying the device before granting permission for BYOD.[86]

Reimbursement

- This section details where the company will reimburse employees for use of the device during work hours.[87]

Security
Agreement of minimum security provisions as detailed by the Mobile Device Management (MDM).[88]

- Minimum password lengths, containing capital letters and symbols.[89]
- Acknowledgement of password policy, and lockout should an incorrect one be entered in more than a defined number of times.[90]

(continued)

(Continued)

- Locked by password or pin if the device is idle.[91]
- Details on where company data is prohibited from being saved and edited.

Risks/Liabilities/Disclaimers

- Reporting time constraints should a device be lost or stolen.[92]
- Full liability for the employee should there be complete loss of company data and introduction of bugs or malware.[93]
- The company reserves the right to disconnect the device or disable services.[94]
- Employee to take additional precautions such as backing up e-mail and contacts.[95]
- Expectations of adherence to acceptable use policy.[96]

CONCLUSION

The following cyber risk management statement represents those organization capabilities CEO and board expect to be demonstrated in terms of *cyber risk policies.*

CYBER RISK POLICIES

An appropriate mix of tailored cyber risk management–specific policies and procedures guide processes, practices and organization risk management activities. These put cyber risk principles into effect and are systematically applied through the cyber risk management process. The organization can *demonstrate* to all stakeholders how it manages cyber risk. At a minimum, policies and procedures are fully in effect to cover: mobile devices, ransomware, social media, third-party vendors/cloud computing, "Big Data Analytics" and Internet of Things. Various approaches are deployed to make such risks the responsibility of *all* employees, not just the IT function. A cycle of continuous improvement throughout the organization allows development along the risk maturity curve. The policies provide a platform for companies to maximize digital opportunities while managing the threats associated with advances in technology, data-driven insight, and evolving work practices.

NOTES

1. Chris Francescani, "Ransomware Hackers Blackmail U.S. Police Departments," April 26, 2016, http://www.cnbc.com/2016/04/26/ransomware-hackers-blackmail-us-police-departments.html
2. Ibid.
3. Barry Salmon, "Freedom of Information Requests Reveal 6 out of 10 Universities Have Been Ransomware Victims," August 24, 2016, http://www.vigilance-securitymagazine.com/industry-news/case-studies/8241–freedom-of-information-requests-reveal-6-out-of-10-universities-have-been-ransomware-victims
4. Alex Dobuzinskis and Jim Finkle, "California Hospital Makes Rare Admission of Hack, Ransom Payment," February 19, 2016, http://www.reuters.com/article/us-california-hospital-cyberattack-idUSKCN0VS05M
5. Andra Zaharia, Heimdal Security, "What Is Ransomware and 15 Easy Steps to Keep Your System Protected (Updated)," July 7, 2016, https://heimdalsecurity.com/blog/what-is-ransomware-protection/
6. Cisco Local Government and Security teams, "Tackling the Ransomware Threat—Guidance and Recommendations from the Cisco Security Team," 2016, https://www.cisco.com/.../cisco...government/.../local_government_security_steps.pdf
7. Peter Mackenzie, "Security vs Convenience: The Story of Ransomware Spread by Spam Email," naked security by Sophos, https://nakedsecurity.sophos.com/2016/03/14/security-vs-convenience-the-story-of-ransomware-spread-by-spam-email/
8. Sophos, "Checklist of Technology, Tools and Tactics for Effective Web Protection." Available online at: https://www.sophos.com/en-us/medialibrary/Gated-Assets/white-papers/checklist-of-technology-tools-and-tactics-for-effective-web-protection.pdf?la=en
9. Zaharia, July 7, 2016.
10. Sophos
11. Ibid.
12. Level Cloud, "Advantages and Disadvantages of Cloud Computing," http://www.levelcloud.net/why-levelcloud/cloud-education-center/advantages-and-disadvantages-of-cloud-computing/
13. Ibid.
14. Ibid.
15. Michael Haws, "Innovation without Boundaries: Why the Cloud Matters," September 30, 2015, http://www.digitalistmag.com/technologies/cloud-computing/2015/09/30/innovation-without-boundaries-cloud-matters-03517496

16. Best Practice Group, "Cloud Computing: How to Successfully Contract for Cloud Services," 2017, free whitepaper available online: http://www.bestpracticegroup .com/guides/cloud-computing-contracts/

17. Ibid.

18. Ibid.

19. Ibid.

20. Ibid.

21. Ibid.

22. Allan Watton, "Outsourcing Contracts: The Top 10 Clauses that Service Providers Try to Manipulate," August 20, 2012, http://www.bestpracticegroup.com/ outsourcing-contracts-clauses/

23. Best Practice Group.

24. Ibid.

25. Megan Berry, *IT Manager Daily*, "Cloud Computing Policy Template," http:// www.itmanagerdaily.com/cloud-computing-policy-template/

26. Cloud Standards Consumer Council, "Public Cloud Service Agreements: What to Expect and What to Negotiate Version 2.0.1," August 1, 2016.

27. Ibid.

28. Ibid.

29. Best Practice Group.

30. Ibid.

31. Cloud Standards Consumer Council, August 1, 2016.

32. Ibid.

33. Best Practice Group.

34. Dina Gerdeman, "Negotiating Cloud Contracts": A New Era for CIOs," October 2015, http://searchcio.techtarget.com/feature/Negotiating-cloud-contracts-A-new-era-for-CIOs

35. Cloud Standards Consumer Council, August 1, 2016.

36. Ibid.

37. Rebecca Herold, "10 Big Data Analytics Privacy Problems," 2016, https:// www.secureworldexpo.com/10-big-data-analytics-privacy-problems

38. ICO, "The Guide to Data Protection," May 11, 2016, https://ico.org.uk/for-organisations/guide-to-data-protection/privacy-by-design/. Information Commissioners Office.

39. ICO, "Big data and data protection," July 28, 2014, Information Commissioners Office.

40. Andra Zaharia, Heimdal Security, "The 13 Step Guide to Secure Your PC After a Fresh Windows Installation (Updated)," April 21, 2016.

41. Computer Weekly, "Encryption Key Management Is Vital to Securing Enterprise Data Storage," February 2010, http://www.computerweekly.com/feature/ Encryption-key-management-is-vital-to-securing-enterprise-data-storage

42. ICO, May 11, 2016.

43. Ryan Goldman, Cloudera, "Credit Cards and Big Data: The Challenge of PCI Compliance," September 22, 2014, https://vision.cloudera.com/credit-cards-and-big-data-the-challenge-of-pci-compliance/

44. Cloud Standards Consumer Council, "Public Cloud Service Agreements: What to Expect and What to Negotiate Version 2.0.1," August 1, 2016.

45. Computer Weekly, February 2010.
46. Intel, "Policy Framework for the Internet of Things (IOT)," 2014, p. 1.
47. Dell, "Dell Shares Best Practices for Organizations Creating Secure Policies for the Internet of Things," January 9, 2015, http://www.dell.com/learn/us/en/id/press-releases/2015-09-01-dell-shares-best-practices-for-internet
48. Bernie Woodall and Joseph Menn, "Fiat Chrysler Recall Highlights Cyber Risk of Connected Cars, Telematics," *Insurance Journal,* July 27, 2015, http://www.insurancejournal.com/news/national/2015/07/27/376356.htm
49. BBC News, "Hack Attack Causes 'Massive Damage' at Steel Works," December 22, 2014, http://www.bbc.co.uk/news/technology-30575104
50. Kiran Chand, Bond Dickinson, "Internet of Things: The Legal Implications," May 10, 2016, http://www.bonddickinson.com/insights/publications-and-briefings/internet-things-legal-implications
51. Ernst & Young, "Cybersecurity and the Internet of Things," Insights on Governance, Risk and Compliance, March 2015.
52. Ernst & Young, March 2015.
53. Dell, January 9, 2015.
54. Karen Rose, Scott Eldridge, and Lyman Chapin, "The Internet of Things: An Overview: Understanding the Issues and Challenges of a More Connected World," The Internet Society, October 2015.
55. ICO, May 11, 2016.
56. Mike Turner, "How to Secure the Internet of Things," Computer Weekly, June 2015, http://www.computerweekly.com/opinion/How-to-secure-the-internet-of-things
57. Ashley Wainwright, "10 Stats That Show It's Time to Prepare for BYOD Network Design," Securedge Networks, 2017, http://www.securedgenetworks.com/blog/10-Stats-that-Show-it-s-Time-to-Prepare-for-BYOD-Network-Design
58. Dean Evans, "What Is BYOD and Why Is It Important? The Opportunities and Risks of People Using Their Own Devices at Work," October 7, 2015, http://www.techradar.com/news/computing/what-is-byod-and-why-is-it-important-1175088
59. Ibid.
60. William Long, "BYOD: Data Protection and Information Security Issues," October 2013, http://www.computerweekly.com/opinion/BYOD-data-protection-and-information-security-issues
61. Alastair Allison, "Mobile Devices"; Chapter 9 "Cyber Risk Resources for Practitioners," Institute of Risk Management; Hoboken, NJ: Wiley, 2014, pp 121-140.
62. Lisa Phifer, "BYOD Security Strategies: Balancing BYOD Security Risks and Rewards," TechTarget, SearchSecurity, 2013, http://searchsecurity.techtarget.com/feature/BYOD-security-strategies-Balancing-BYOD-risks-and-rewards
63. Allison, 2014.
64. Ibid.
65. Ibid.
66. Ibid.
67. Ibid.
68. Long, October 2013.

69. Paul Ferrill, "The Best Mobile Device Management (MDM) Solutions of 2016," *PC Mag UK,* June 13, 2016, http://uk.pcmag.com/cloud-services/76018/guide/the-best-mobile-device-management-mdm-solutions-of-2016
70. Allison, 2014.
71. Ibid.
72. Ibid.
73. Sarah K. White, "How to Implement an Effective BYOD Policy," *CIO,* September 26, 2016, http://www.cio.com/article/3124127/byod/how-to-implement-an-effective-byod-policy.html
74. Allison, 2014.
75. Ibid.
76. Ibid.
77. Ibid.
78. Ibid.
79. Ibid.
80. Megan Berry, "BYOD Policy Template," IT Manager Daily, http://www.itmanagerdaily.com/byod-policy-template/
81. Ibid.
82. Ibid.
83. Ibid.
84. Michael Kienzie, "BYOD vs CYOD: What Is the Difference?" digium blogs, The Asterisk Company, http://blogs.digium.com/2015/05/19/byod-vs-cyod-difference/
85. Berry,
86. Ibid.
87. Ibid.
88. Allison, 2014.
89. Ibid.
90. Ibid.
91. Ibid.
92. Allison, 2014.
93. Berry,
94. Ibid.
95. Ibid.
96. Allison, 2014.

ABOUT IRM

Founded in 1983 with a head office in London and international membership chapters, the Institute for Risk Management is a specialist institute that continues to develop professional risk qualifications, courses, events, and publications. In 2014, IRM hosted a major Cyber Risk summit and published *Cyber Risk* as member-led thought leadership research to give risk professionals the practical knowledge they need.

ABOUT ELLIOT BRYAN, BA (HONS), ACII

Elliot is an associate and an account executive for Finex Cyber and TMT practice at Willis Towers Watson, London, United Kingdom. In this role, he specializes in advising on, negotiating, and placing cyber, professional indemnity for technology companies, and intellectual property insurance for clients, across a wide range of industry sectors. Elliot advises clients on program design, placement, and risk profiling with a particular focus on policy wording and coverage analysis.

He is a graduate of the University of Sheffield and an associate of the Chartered Insurance Institute.

ABOUT ALEXANDER LARSEN, FIRM, PRESIDENT OF BALDWIN GLOBAL RISK SERVICES

Alexander is a strategic/enterprise and project risk manager who holds a degree in risk management from Glasgow Caledonian University and is a fellow of the Institute of Risk Management (IRM). He is also currently President of Baldwin Global Risk Services based in the United Kingdom.

He has 15 years of experience working in the United Kingdom, Middle East, and Asia, within risk management across a wide range of sectors, including oil and gas, construction, utilities, finance, and the public sector. He has considerable expertise in training and working with organizations to develop, enhance, and embed their enterprise risk management (ERM), project risk management (PRM), business continuity management (BCM), and partnership management processes.

He has attended conferences globally as an expert speaker and to run master classes and contributes articles to various risk publications. In 2015, he contributed a chapter titled "Implementing Risk Management within Middle Eastern Oil and Gas Companies," based on his experiences from around the Middle East including Iraq, for the John Wiley & Sons publication *Implementing Enterprise Risk Management: Case Studies and Best Practices.*

CHAPTER 5

Cyber Strategic Performance Management

McKinsey & Company
James M. Kaplan, Partner, McKinsey & Company, New York, USA
Jim Boehm, Consultant, McKinsey & Company, Washington, USA

"If you don't measure it, you can't manage it," said George, the chief strategy officer, to a nodding CEO Tom.

Cybersecurity performance can be managed, but only if measured.

The ability to measure performance has always been at the heart of effective management, underlying decisions about how to allocate resources, which practices to employ and whom to reward. Much more so than in the past, this is an age of granular and systematic performance management. Senior executives are exploiting massive amounts of data to understand which products generate profits, which salespeople sell effectively, and which operational teams execute with the highest degree of efficiency.

Sadly, in many respects, cybersecurity is an outlier to this trend. Measuring cybersecurity performance is hard. Traditional business performance metrics like revenue or cost are not really relevant. Analogues to market risk and credit risk metrics like value at risk do not exist for cybersecurity. And measuring cybersecurity incidents might lead you to believe you are doing a good job protecting the organization—when in fact you are doing such a bad job monitoring the environment you cannot even detect ongoing attacks.

The difficulty in measuring cybersecurity performance does not make it any less important. The dynamic nature of the cybersecurity environment—with threats escalating rapidly, new technologies introduced constantly, and operational practices evolving quickly—makes it dangerous for cybersecurity executives to rely on experience and instinct in making decisions.

Fortunately, there is a better way. With enough creativity and true understanding of sources of value, cybersecurity elements worth managing can be measured (even if only by proxy). Measuring performance—and organizational health—is critical to catalyzing progress, instilling accountability, and ultimately achieving an organization's strategic aspirations.

PITFALLS IN MEASURING CYBERSECURITY PERFORMANCE

There are a number of pitfalls organizations should avoid in measuring cybersecurity, including:

- *Irrelevant metrics.* Many reports to the senior management team we see include some reference to the millions of attacks the organization faces per week or per day. While eye-catching, this number is entirely irrelevant. The overwhelming number of those attacks come from "script kiddies" that a minimally competent security capability can deflect with ease. For most organizations, the tiny percentage of attacks from sophisticated attackers represents the true risk.
- *Focusing on lagging indicators to the exclusion of leading indicators.* The frequency and severity of security incidents is important information but is inherently a lagging indicator—representing an output— rather than a lever or an input that a management team could choose to affect directly.
- *Assuming more is better.* Even those organizations that look at leading indicators (e.g., extent of encryption) can make the mistake of assuming more controls and tighter controls are always the right answer. Ten years ago, when environments were more likely to be wide open, this might have been the case. Today, organizations can very easily incur too much cost and create too much complexity by creating metrics that encourage the encryption of every piece of data and the application of two-factor authentication to every system when in many cases neither may be necessary.
- *Relying on subjectivity.* In a world where quantitative metrics are challenging, cybersecurity executives may be inclined to report that their data loss prevention (DLP) program or identity and action management (IAM) program is "red," "yellow," or "green." Even if the team performing the color coding has the best intentions in terms of objectivity, subjective assessments like this one will always be less than credible with senior management in terms of driving decisions unless those colors are tied to specific measurable or milestone-driven targets.
- *Measuring the cybersecurity organization rather than enterprise resilience.* We are fond of saying 80 percent of what you have to do to be

secure happens outside the chief information security officer's (CISO) organization. The cybersecurity team cannot write secure code for developers or apply patches quickly for data center managers, even though both actions are critical to an organization's overall security posture. As a result, it is easy to focus cybersecurity metrics on what the security team does directly, rather than what it is supposed to achieve by driving resiliency across the entire organization.

CYBERSECURITY STRATEGY REQUIRED TO MEASURE CYBERSECURITY PERFORMANCE

Organizations can measure cybersecurity performance only in the context of a cybersecurity strategy that tightly connects with an organization's overall business strategy. Otherwise, they will stumble into one or more of the pitfalls described above.

At its core an effective cybersecurity strategy has four components: a business risk assessment, an enabling set of capabilities, a target state to get to, and a portfolio of initiatives.

Organization Risk Assessment

The underpinning of all cybersecurity strategy comes to us from Frederick the Great, who told his commanders, "Little minds try to defend everything at once, but sensible people look at the main point only; they parry the worst blows and stand a little hurt if thereby they avoid a greater one. If you try to hold everything, you hold nothing." Perhaps if he had lived in the twenty-first century, he would have said that only ineffective CISOs try to protect all data to the same level.

Cybersecurity strategy starts with business and cybersecurity executives having a frank discussion about which data is most critical to the business, most attractive to attackers and therefore the most important to protect. Is customer data more sensitive than intellectual property or vice versa? What types of intellectual property (IP) are most important—pricing data or production plans? How does that vary by region or line of business?

Cybersecurity Capabilities

Once an organization understands its risks, it can start to determine what types of capabilities its needs to build to protect itself. Naturally, there are many frameworks organizations can select from. We like organizations to think how far they can progress in putting in place the seven hallmarks of digital resilience that we developed in conjunction with the World Economic Forum:

- *Prioritize information assets based on business risks.* Most organizations lack insight into what information assets need protecting and which are the highest priority. Cybersecurity teams must work with businesses leaders to understand business risks across the entire value chain and then prioritize the underlying information assets accordingly.
- *Differentiate protection based on the importance of assets.* Few organizations have any systematic way of aligning the level of protection they give information assets with the importance of those assets to the business. Putting in place differentiated controls (e.g., encryption or multifactor authentication) ensures that organizations are directing the most appropriate resources to protecting the information assets that matter most.
- *Integrate cybersecurity into enterprise-wide risk management and governance processes.* Cybersecurity is an enterprise risk and must be managed as such. The possibilities of a cyber attack must be integrated with other risk analyses and presented in relevant management and board discussions. Moreover, the implications of digital resilience should be integrated into the broad set of governance functions such as human resources, vendor management, and compliance.
- *Enlist front-line personnel to protect the information assets they use.* Users are often the biggest vulnerability an organization has—they click on links they should not, choose insecure passwords, and e-mail sensitive files to broad distribution lists. Organizations need to segment users based on the assets they need to access, and help each segment understand the business risks associated with their everyday actions.
- *Integrate cybersecurity into the technology environment.* Almost every part of the broader technology environment affects an organization's ability to protect itself—from application development practices to policies for replacing outdated hardware. Organizations must lose a crude *bolt-on security* mentality and instead train their entire staff to incorporate it into technology projects from day one.
- *Deploy active defenses to uncover attacks proactively.* There is a massive amount of information available about potential attacks—both from external intelligence sources and from an organization's own technology environment. Organizations will need to develop the capabilities to aggregate and analyze the most relevant information, and tune their defense systems accordingly.
- *Test continuously to improve incident response across business functions.* An inadequate response to a breach—not only by the technology

team but also from marketing, public affairs, or customer service functions—can be as damaging as the breach itself. Organizations should run cross-functional "cyber-war games" to improve their ability to respond effectively in real time.[1]

It is easy to want the highest level of capability, but there are real constraints to consider. Achieving the hallmarks of digital resilience requires real organizational change across many business functions, so organizations have to ask what level of appetite exists for change. It also requires a level of skill in sophistication in the cybersecurity team that many organizations do not have and would have a hard time obtaining.

On the other hand, organizations also have to balance challenges like these against imperatives for change: How important is sensitive information to the future of the business? How sophisticated are attackers? What is the level of regulatory scrutiny? How important are cybersecurity capabilities and protections to customers?

Target State Protections

Once an organization has assessed its business risks and determined what types of capabilities it is going to develop, it can determine how it will protect its sensitive data. What information assets will be encrypted? How tightly should access to data be controlled? Do systems containing some times of information have to be hosted on a segregated, more secure network segment? Where will the organization push most rigorously for secure coding practices and patch management? How to do all this in a way that does not create confusion and complexity?

Organizations have to create tiers of protection that span many types of controls and protection and develop clear, criteria-based standards for what types of data get what tier of protection (e.g., all pricing strategies for high-margin businesses require tier-3 protection, which implies encryption at rest and two-factor authentication).

Given the wide variety of data assets that many organizations have, they will have to determine the target state of protections on a business line-by-business line basis.

Portfolio of Initiatives

Almost any effective cybersecurity strategy will imply significant business, technology and organizational change. As with any other strategy, these changes will, require a portfolio of initiatives. Each initiative should imply substantial change in a given area (e.g., secure coding, network security, identity and access management)—and should include a description of the future state aspiration, required funding, required management support, required skills, key milestones, and timing.

Some of the initiatives may be enabling in nature—they will reshape or enhance the organization. Many cybersecurity functions we know of are seeking to expand their use of managed services—not so much to reduce cost as to free up capacity to focus on higher order and more value added activities. Therefore, these organizations have initiatives to go-to-market for services like L1 security monitoring, vulnerability scanning or penetration testing. Many organizations also have initiatives to enhance the talent level of the cybersecurity team through a combination of external hiring and training. We believe training members of the cybersecurity team in relevant business issues, general problem solving, financial management, and executive communications can be especially powerful. Some of the initiatives will likely address governance by creating the structures and mechanisms to involve required business leaders in cybersecurity decision making and ensure alignment between the cybersecurity program and business strategy over time.

CREATING AN EFFECTIVE CYBERSECURITY PERFORMANCE MANAGEMENT SYSTEM

To effectively manage the success of its cybersecurity strategy, organizations should put in place a cybersecurity performance management system. This system should have at least three components: measuring progress against initiatives, measuring capability, and measuring protection.

Measuring Progress against Initiatives

Necessarily, to get anything done, organizations need to decompose their cybersecurity strategy into a series of initiatives. Each of those initiatives should have a simple range of metrics decked against it: percentage of applications remediated, reduction in click-through rates on phishing tests, and so on; the exact metric will depend on the initiative in question.

Each initiative should have a least one metric that is indicative of medium-term (i.e., within a two- to three-year window) success, including the following:

- Data loss prevention (DLP) system(s) have decreased incidents related to inadvertent information release to fewer than 100 per annum.
- We will achieve 90 percent patch currency rates on all external-facing operating and network system components within two calendar years.

- One hundred percent of all software projects include security-enhancing components like continuous build and security component-related sprints within the first 10 percent of the project's anticipated development life cycle.
- We will stop more than 99 percent of all attacks detectable by our information security systems by the end of the next calendar year.
- For every high-priority attack, we will identify the attacker (or attacking entity) within one quarter.
- At least 80 percent of managers attend one advanced-level cyber awareness training session per annum.
- Workforce click-through rates on annual phishing attack tests is less than 30 percent.

These metrics can be supplemented with additional, interim markers that indicate whether the organization is making sufficient progress against its strategic cybersecurity initiatives. Simply, "markers" act as "milestones" for the organization.

For example, for the metric, "DLP system(s) have decreased incidents related to inadvertent information release to fewer than 100 per annum," some example may be:

- There is a DLP system installed, and it is managed by a member/team within the organization.
- The DLP system has been "tuned" with rules to prevent inadvertent release of information.
- Accurate reporting is in place to measure the number of inadvertent releases of information due to DLP "misses."
- Inadvertent information release is seen to be decreasing since the DLP system was tuned.

Done well, markers lay out the roadmap for each initiative sequentially, such that when the organization is at one marker it can clearly see the path to the next. The steps along the path from the marker it is presently at to the one it is moving towards further breaks down into the *activities* and *actions* that are ultimately compiled into the initiative team's implementation work plan.

The path between each marker is made up of sequential activities, with each activity broken into a series of actions assigned to specific people or teams. Laying out actions in a Gantt-style work plan, grouped by activity and divided according to the boundaries of each marker, helps tracking, transparency, and identifying organizational, financial, technical, or other dependencies.

This is a relatively basic level of transparency, and it enables senior management to ensure the organization is making progress against the

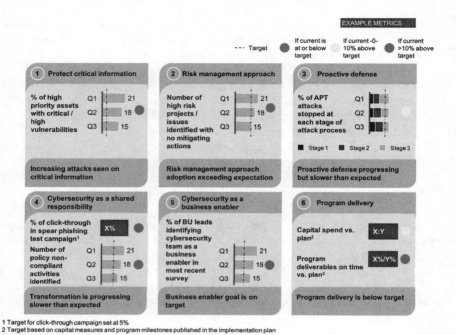

FIGURE 5.1   Measuring progress against initiatives

agreed-on cybersecurity strategy. It creates accountability for individual initiative leaders and can spur required discussions with various stakeholders about their level of engagement with and participation in critical initiatives. Figure 5.1 are example metrics for a six-step approach to measuring progress against initiatives.

Measuring Capability

In addition to measuring progress against initiatives, it is equally important to holistically measure an organization's level of cybersecurity capability. There are a number of ways to do this, but we like to measure enterprise capability in terms of the seven hallmarks of digital resilience with our digital resilience assessment (DRA).

For each of the seven hallmarks described above, DRA measures performance against between 10 and 20 specific, tangible practices in how organizations capture risks or simulate the response to a potential breach. Any assessment of practices runs the risk of subjectivity, but DRA accounts for this in multiple ways:

- *Structure of questions.* DRA never asks "how good are you" at a certain practice; it asks "which of the following things do you do" and provides a scorecard for the respondent to compare current practices.
- *Nature of respondents.* In many cases, many people from a single organization will participate in DRA. This provides three benefits. First, it provides increased granularity—for example, incentives for developers to write secure code might be vastly different in two different business units. Second, it tends to average away respondents' individual biases. Third, variations in responses tend to lead to very productive discussion about differences in assumptions and practices.
- *Validation.* Simply going through responses with each participant and asking why they responded as they did, tends to rebaseline or remove overly optimistic answers.

In the end, the DRA process provides an integrated, holistic, granular and actionable view of whether an organization has the capabilities to protect itself without creating undue cost and complexity for the organizations to manage. Figure 5.2 is an illustrative example of how DRA provides insight into cybersecurity capabilities.

■ ≥3.0 (High)　2.0-2.9　■ <2.0 (Low)

		BU 1	BU 2	BU 3	BU 4	BU 5	BU 6
1 Prioritize information assets and business risks in a way that helps engage business leaders	Asset and risk prioritization	2.2	3.4	2.4	1.6	1.3	2.3
	Risk appetite and thresholds	1.0	4.0	2.0	3.0	2.0	2.0
	Strategy and roadmap	2.0	3.7	3.0	3.3	1.7	3.3
2 Enlist front-line personnel – helping them understand value of information assets	Awareness, training and risk culture	2.1	2.7	2.1	1.6	1.9	1.7
	Employee and contractor security	1.5	2.0	1.5	1.5	1.5	1.0
	Talent development and recruiting	2.0	3.0	2.0	2.0	2.0	2.0
3 Integrate cyber-resilience into enterprise-wide management and governance processes	Product security	2.2	3.0	1.3	2.0	1.8	2.7
	Vendor and other third-party mgmt.	1.0	3.0	1.5	2.5	1.5	2.0
	Risk reporting and metrics	2.0	2.6	2.0	1.8	1.8	2.0
	Organization structure and roles	1.5	2.5	1.5	1.5	2.0	2.0
4 Integrated incident response across business functions, enhanced by realistic testing	Security incident response and simulations	2.3	2.3	2.3	1.2	1.6	2.0
5 Develop deep integration of security into the technology environment to drive scalability	Asset, config. and patch mgmt.	1.0	1.5	0.0	1.0	1.5	0.5
	Cloud security	2.0	2.5	n/a	2.0	2.0	2.0
	Secure app. and systems dev.	2.0	1.5	0.0	0.0	0.0	1.5
	Secure architecture	2.0	3.0	2.5	2.5	1.5	2.0
	Logical security	1.2	2.5	1.0	1.2	0.8	1.8
	Physical security	4.0	2.0	2.0	3.0	2.0	2.0
6 Provide differentiated protection for most important assets	Policies and standards	1.5	3.3	1.5	2.0	2.0	1.3
	Assessment and diagnostics	2.7	4.0	3.0	3.7	3.0	2.0
	Compliance and audit	2.0	3.0	3.0	3.0	3.0	3.0
	Program and project management	1.0	2.0	2.0	0.0	1.0	1.0
7 Deploy active defenses to respond to emerging attacks in real time	Cyber intelligence and vulnerability awareness	3.0	3.0	3.0	3.0	3.0	3.0
	Monitoring and analytics	3.0	3.0	3.0	3.0	3.0	3.0

FIGURE 5.2 DRA provides insight into cybersecurity capabilities

Measuring Protection

While measuring progress against strategic initiatives and measuring overall
level of capability are incredibly valuable and relatively straightforward, neither directly answers the question, "are we protecting our most critical data?"

Doing that requires digging a level deeper and measuring the degrees
of protection against an organization's most important information assets:

- If an organization knows what its most important data is.
- And the organization knows what systems that data sits on.
- And the organization knows how those systems are currently protected.
- And the organization is aligned on how each type of data should be
  protected (e.g., level of encryption, two-factor authentication, etc.).

Figure 5.3 is an example output dashboard for the "crown jewels,"
or how to measure the protection of the most critical information to the
organization.

Then the organization can start to measure and report on whether it
is protecting critical data sufficiently. The cybersecurity team can initiate
discussions with senior management along the lines of:

- We have agreed, as a matter of policy, that customer information for
  our high net worth segment should be encrypted at rest, should require
  two-factor authentication and should require validation of access rights
  every 90 days.

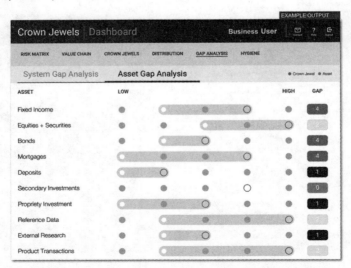

FIGURE 5.3 Measuring protection of most critical information
Courtesy of John Greenwood of McKinsey & Co.

- However, less than half of the systems hosting this type of information meet all of these commitments: Operations does the best with 70 percent of data protected to specification; Trading is in the middle with about 55 percent of data protected to spec. The real problem is in distribution, which protects only 25 percent of the spec.
- Within distribution the biggest problem is encryption—that drives 80 percent of the gap the specified commitments.

With this type of information the cybersecurity team and senior management can, if required, revisit whether the level of protection agreed on was realistic or needs to be adjusted. They can align on clear problem areas that need to be addressed, what the root cause of the issues might be, who is responsible and what actions to take to remediate the situation.

CONCLUSION

Like any other business function, effective management of cybersecurity strategy requires effective measurement. Certainly, for a number of structural reasons designing and implementing a good performance management system for cybersecurity is hard—but does not make it any less essential.

Fortunately, with appropriate management focus and attention, organizations can get effective mechanisms for managing cybersecurity in place. The key is to start with a practical strategy that addresses business risks, underlying capabilities, and target levels of protections with specific initiatives.

Once organizations do this, they can measure progress against those initiatives, assess the overall level of enterprise-level cybersecurity capability and understand the degree to which they are appropriately protecting their most critical data.

The following cyber risk management statement represents those organization capabilities CEO and board expect to be demonstrated in terms of a *cyber risk strategic performance system.*

STRATEGIC PERFORMANCE MANAGEMENT SYSTEM

The organization has a strategic performance management system to measure implementation of a tailored cyber strategy delivering digital resilience. The cyber strategy shares the organization's business risks, target state capabilities, target state level of protection and required

(continued)

(*Continued*)

initiatives. The organization goes beyond cyber risk-mitigating controls and considers cyber as a capability-building enabler. A digital resilience assessment frames a baseline maturity to a set of metrics (key performance indicators [KPIs]/key risk indicators [KRIs]) of three types—measuring progress against initiatives, measuring overall level of capability and measuring protection to specification for the most critical information. The metrics align with an appropriate set of principles and are automated, simple, repeatable and on demand. There is a forum to cascade for each of the three dimensions the aligned initiatives, markers, activities, actions, and resources (people and funding) necessary to drive each action to successful completion. Tracking the "status" and "progress" of each initiative surfaces the blockers and bottlenecks to the cyber strategy.

NOTE

1. See James M. Kaplan, Tucker Bailey, and Derek O'Halloran, *Beyond Cybersecurity: Protecting Your Digital Business* (Hoboken, NJ: John Wiley & Sons, Inc., 2015), 149–154.

ABOUT MCKINSEY COMPANY

McKinsey Company is a global management consulting firm that serves leading businesses, governments, nongovernmental organizations, and not-for-profits. McKinsey assists organizations in developing cybersecurity strategies that maximize business value and accelerate cybersecurity programs.

ABOUT JAMES KAPLAN

James is a partner with McKinsey & Co. in New York, New York, USA. James leads McKinsey's capabilities in cybersecurity, which helps large organizations in implementing cyber-security strategies, conducting cyber-war games, optimizing enterprise infrastructure environments, and exploiting cloud technologies. He has published on a variety of technology topics in the *McKinsey Quarterly,* the *Financial Times,* the *Wall Street Journal,* and the *Harvard Business Review* Blog Network. James is co-author of the book *Beyond Cybersecurity: Protecting Your Digital Business* (Wiley, 2015).

ABOUT JIM BOEHM

Jim is a consultant with McKinsey & Co. in Washington, D.C., USA. Jim is a manager in McKinsey's Cyber Solution and helps organizations design and deliver integrated cybersecurity strategies, implement bespoke cyber operations capabilities, assess digital resilience, and determine appropriate levels of enterprise protection. Prior to McKinsey, Jim was a U.S. Navy officer and national security program manager focusing on Agile development of cyber-analysis software and computer network operations.

CHAPTER 6

Standards and Frameworks for Cybersecurity

Stefan A. Deutscher, Principal, Boston Consulting Group (BCG), Berlin Germany
William Yin, Senior Partner and Managing Director, Boston Consulting Group
(BCG), Hong Kong

As Tom scrambled to put together his board presentation, he had three very practical concerns: First, how to get up to speed quickly, and avoid reinventing the wheel—or just parts of a wheel? Secondly, how to make sure nothing essential was overlooked, so that the wheel (reused or new) kept on turning in the right direction and at the right speed? And third, how to communicate such an elusive topic at the right level of detail, or aggregation, to his target audience—in this case, his supervisory board?

PUTTING CYBERSECURITY STANDARDS AND FRAMEWORKS IN CONTEXT

There are a multitude of cybersecurity standards in existence today that have been developed by various bodies addressing specific needs, and the list continues to grows, but it is important for an enterprise to identify those that bring the most value to the agenda of organization. More importantly, aligning to the "right" standards help facilitate the sharing and transparency on the most recent cyber attacks within the industry and beyond the internal enterprise.

Diversity as a Blessing and Curse

According to Merriam-Webster's Dictionary, a *framework* is "the basic structure of something." That underlying something can be fairly diverse—for instance, ideas, concepts, guidelines, rules, check lists, requirements, facts, or physical parts. And, in this context, diversity may be a blessing and a curse.

There are a large number of cybersecurity and information technology (IT) risk management *frameworks* out there. These are issued by technology vendors, professional services firms, public institutions, nonprofit organizations, and public private partnerships—and all provide a different focus. The types of standards and frameworks include:

- Local, regional, and global frameworks.
- Generic and industry-specific frameworks.
- Value-focused and threat-focused frameworks.
- Very technical frameworks, which are of most use to those concerned with the technical aspects of cybersecurity.
- Governance and organizational frameworks.
- Product assurance, process assurance, and environment assurance frameworks.
- Compliance-focused frameworks useful for interactions with regulators.
- High-level maturity frameworks, which tell you where you stand but not necessarily what to do about it.
- Collections of best practices aimed to cover the basics or more.
- Controls focused frameworks, which can be of tremendous use to auditors as they tend to be built around inputs or ingredients which good security would typically need.
- Capability-focused frameworks, aiming more at outcomes of what good security would typically accomplish, which makes them very powerful but also harder to use for assessments.
- Information-sharing frameworks focused on exchange and collaboration of cybersecurity-related information (e.g., threats, breaches, mitigation measures, best practices).
- Specialized cybersecurity frameworks and holistic frameworks aiming to cover also other security domains like information security, IT security (in general or, for instance, network or end-point security in particular), physical security, people security (be that of key executives, their assistants, systems administrators with elevated access privileges, or contractors), or even security of cyber-physical systems touching on safety, health, and environmental protection.

Obviously, all of these types of frameworks have their merits. Frameworks are a tool chest to structure thinking about, and acting on, security in a given context, and a given set of objectives.

No "Best" Cybersecurity Standard

Standards, as "a level of quality, achievement, etc., that is considered acceptable or desirable [...] established by authority, custom, or general consent as a model or example" (*Merriam-Webster's*), can augment frameworks. Again turning to the *Merriam-Webster's* for a definition, we see that standards are "a level of quality, achievement, etc., that is considered acceptable or desirable [...] established by authority, custom, or general consent as a model or example." Standards play a related role whereby they formalize and serve as guiderail for cybersecurity. There is a similar breadth of standards as there is for frameworks.

This variety exists for a reason. As new technologies and delivery mechanisms develop it will continue to accommodate change and expand in order to address fields such as digital, Internet of Things, Big Data, or simply the cloud. So there is no "best" cybersecurity standard or framework. But there are already many good tools for the job at hand—and less appropriate ones.

First Steps

So where was CEO Tom to start?

Before selecting a cybersecurity framework to use, or a standard to follow, a first but important step is to clarify the organization's objectives or purpose regarding risks and issues that it is attempting to address or mitigate against.

The objectives may range from very operational tasks at hand (e.g., configuration of employee computers) to daily governance issues (e.g., design of an information security policy) and board-level responsibilities (e.g., ensuring that the executive team provides risk oversight for cybersecurity). Other purposes may include:

- To establish a common language and taxonomy allowing technical people, organization people, and risk managers to start communicating around cybersecurity.
- To provide transparency by assessing the current state of cybersecurity against a yard stick accepted by and understandable to the intended target audience (which, in turn, may be any group of people, from technical experts to board members, from customers to regulators).
- To provide a guideline to for action against known gaps, threats, or identified areas for development.

- To ensure and demonstrate compliance with relevant regulation or laws, enable an organization to compete on security, or to establish security beyond compliance.
- To normalize cyber related risk, allowing it to be treated and included in enterprise risk management like any other risk to an organization.

The organization context can be regulated (as, for example, financial services, health care, food and beverage industries, and critical national infrastructure) or nonregulated with respect to cybersecurity requirements. Or it can be at global scale or confined to particular geographies. Or the organization may be running in a "business-as-usual" state or face an exceptional situation (e.g., about to launch a new—possibly digital—product, to execute a corporate transaction like a merger or a carve-out, to bid for an especially large deal). Or the organization may even be facing an emergency (such as having learned that its own security or that of an essential partner in its supply chain has been breached and compromised).

Tailoring a Choice of Frameworks

Since there are many frameworks and standards available, and they typically are largely compatible at the core but differentiated at the fringes, organizations often benefit from an informed combination of several frameworks to best match their particular need and tailored to their objectives, context, and risk profile. The exception to this rule, of course, is if one or the other is required by regulation or particular key customers. For multinationals operating in several jurisdictions, using more than one framework, or complying with more than one standard, may not even be a choice but a must.

So out of the plethora of cybersecurity frameworks and standards, which ones should Tom consider at a minimum? Here, we list a selection of some of the most commonly used frameworks.

COMMONLY USED FRAMEWORKS AND STANDARDS (A SELECTION)

The following frameworks and standards are considered to outline globally accepted best practices.

ISO/IEC 27000 Family

This framework series, sometimes also referred to as ISO 27k, covers a very broad series of topics, such as providing general vocabulary (ISO 27000), outlining requirements for an information security management program (ISO 27001), giving a code of practice for information security management (ISO 27002) or a description of information security risk management (ISO 27005), providing guidance on fairly technical topics like network security (ISO 27033) or application security (ISO 27034), and implementation guidance for particular industries, like, for instance, the information security management in health using ISO/IEC 27002 (ISO 27799). This is just a small selection, and the framework is in active development, several more standards are in preparation, for instance, to address security in supplier relationships or to provide guidance on analysis and investigation around digital evidence.

The framework is often considered the information security equivalent of ISO 9000, and also provides a certification. Parts of it (like ISO 27005) are also informed by, and can be seen as a specialized addition to, ISO 31000, which provides a family of standards relating to risk management.

Obviously, such broad and deep coverage demands a premium of shelf real estate—it is by far the largest set of standards in this overview. Among all of these standards comprising the ISO 27k family, ISO 27001 would be the best point to start for Tom—even more since at some point he could decide to get certified against this standard.

The organization describes itself as follows:

The ISMS family of standards (see Clause 4) is intended to assist organizations of all types and sizes to implement and operate an ISMS ... and specifically, ISO/IEC 27001:2013 specifies the requirements for establishing, implementing, maintaining and continually improving an information security management system within the context of the organization. It also includes requirements for the assessment and treatment of information security risks tailored to the needs of the organization. The requirements set out in ISO/IEC 27001:2013 are generic and are intended to be applicable to all organizations, regardless of type, size or nature.[1,2]

Author/Issuer: International Organization for Standardization (ISO) and the International Electrotechnical Commission (IEC), Geneva, Switzerland.

Extent: The whole standard family has over 1,500 pages and parts of it were last updated in 2016; the particular ISO 27001 standard comes on 23 pages and was last updated in 2013.

Region/Type: Global, international standard.

Industry: All types of organizations and industries.

Primary audience: Information security, risk, and IT functions.

COBIT 5 for Information Security

COBIT is a comprehensive IT governance risk management framework especially suited for organizations accustomed to external auditing. It comprises, among other things, process descriptions, implementation guidelines, and extensive descriptions of goals, controls, related metrics, and even Responsible-Accountable-Consulted-Informed-Matrix (RACI) suggestions for IT governance. Several of the processes it documents deal with or touch on information security topics, such as "Evaluate, Direct, and Monitor (EDM) #03: Ensure Risk Optimization," "Align, Plan, and Organize (APO) #013: Manage Security," or "Deliver, Service, and Support (DSS) #05: Manage Security Services," and a version placing an information security "lens" over the framework was published separately as "COBIT 5 for Information Security." Since it provides a comprehensive set of controls it lends itself well to auditing, and is very often used by firms to achieve compliance with the Sarbanes-Oxley rules. The organization describes itself as follows:

> COBIT 5 is the overarching organization and management framework for governance and management of enterprise IT. COBIT 5 for Information Security provides guidance to help IT and security professionals understand, utilize, implement and direct important information security-related activities, and make more informed decisions while maintaining awareness about emerging technologies and the accompanying threats.[3]

Author/Issuer: ISACA (previously known as Information Systems Audit and Control Association but now going by its acronym only to reflect the broad range of professionals it serves), United States.

Extent: The most current version, COBIT 5, as well as the lens for information security was published in 2012, each comprising about some 220 pages.

Region/Type: Global quasi-standard.

Industry: All, especially common in financial services and industries where regulatory compliance is highly important.

Primary audience: All stakeholders, especially information security, risk, and IT functions.

NIST Computer/Cybersecurity Frameworks

NIST use three Special Publications (SP) subseries to publish guidelines, recommendations and reference materials related to cybersecurity, computer security, and information security: Series SP800: "Computer Security,"

Series SP500: "Computer Systems Technology," and Series SP1800: "NIST Cyber Security Practice Guide." SP800 appears to be currently the center of gravity of NIST's security work and can be seen as a repository covering a large body of topics, such as protection of controlled unclassified information (SP800-171), fairly technical things like Secure Virtual Network Configuration for Virtual Machine (VM) Protection (SP800-125B) or a Guide to Industrial Control Systems (ICS) security (SP800-82r2), and also an Information Security Handbook/Guide for managers (SP800-100), or a description of Security and Privacy Controls for Federal Information Systems and Organizations (SP800-53r4). The latter comprises an extensive catalog of controls for security and for implementation of an information security program and is being used, for instance, by U.S. government agencies to comply with the requirements of the Federal Information Processing Standard (FIPS) 200.

SP500 tends to be more technical even and these days focused less on security as such, a Cloud Computing Security Reference Architecture guide (SP500-299) started in 2013 is still in draft. SP1800, finally, has since its inception in 2015 already produced several draft documents for instance on Securing Electronic Health Records on Mobile Devices (SP1800-1) or IT Asset Management in Financial Services (SP1800-5).

In addition to these, NIST also created and continues to develop a Cyber Security Framework aimed at Improving Critical Infrastructure Cybersecurity with guidelines to assess current capabilities and prioritize improvements. So, depending on the industry Tom's organization is active in, he would find a rich repository of materials to structure his cybersecurity program and focus on security beyond compliance, but to create a plan that can be audited, SP800-53r4 would be a good starting point.

The organization describes itself as follows:

SP800 is NIST's primary mode of publishing computer/cyber/ information security guidelines, recommendations and reference materials, while SP1800, created to "complement the SP800s; targets specific cybersecurity challenges in the public and private sectors, practical, user-friendly guides to facilitate adoption of standards-based approaches to cybersecurity," and SP500 was used "prior to the SP800 subseries for computer security publications." The special "Framework for Improving Critical Infrastructure Cybersecurity" was "created through collaboration between industry and government, the NIST Framework consists of standards, guidelines, and practices to promote the protection of critical infrastructure. The prioritized, flexible, repeatable, and cost-effective approach of the Framework helps owners and operators of critical infrastructure to manage cybersecurity-related risk."[4,5]

Author/Issuer: U.S. National Institute of Standards and Technology (NIST), United States.

Extent: Several thousands of pages across the repository. For instance, the Guide for Managers (SP800-100) was last updated in 2007 and spans about 180 pages; the "Security and Privacy Controls for Federal Information Systems and Organizations" in its most recent 2015 update (SP800-53r4) takes about 460 pages, and the cybersecurity framework was last updated in 2014 (with a scheduled update in 2016) and comprises about 40 pages.

Region/Type: U.S. national standard but used globally by practitioners.

Industry: Often applied or even mandated in a U.S. government context, but applicable to, and used in, all industries.

Primary audience: Information security, risk, and IT functions, also managers and auditors.

ISF Standard of Good Practice for Information Security

Authored by an international member organization, this framework covers security governance, security requirements, controls, monitoring/improvement and addresses risk from people, processes, and technology. It is broader and more prescriptive than ISO, and aims to also enable compliance with ISO27001/2, COBIT 5 for Information Security, and the SANS Top 20 Critical Controls, and to help comply with the UK Cyber Essentials Scheme and the U.S. NIST Cyber Security Framework. The framework is accompanied by a set of tools and benchmark offerings for ISF members.

The organization describes itself as follows:

The ISF Standard of Good Practice for Information Security (the Standard) is the most comprehensive information security standard in the world, providing more coverage of topics than ISO. It covers the complete spectrum of information security arrangements that need to be made to keep the organization risks associated with information systems within acceptable limits, and presents good practice in practical, clear statements.[6]

Author/Issuer: Information Security Forum (ISF), United Kingdom.

Extent: About 300 pages (2011 version) and was last updated in 2014.

Region/Type: Global quasi-standard with member chapters in several regions of the world.

Industry: Large organizations from the public and private sector.

Primary audience: Information security, risk, and IT audit functions, organization and IT managers.

SANS Top 20

The SANS Top 20 CIS Critical Security Controls form deliberately not a complete framework, but rather are a widely adopted list of the top 20, specific and actionable cyber defense controls, based on the NIST framework and on regularly updated industry intelligence of attack patterns and vulnerabilities. In its most recent version, this top 20 list addresses topics such as inventory of devices and software, malware defense, secure configuration, wireless access control, incident response and management, and penetration testing.

While these top 20 controls don't provide metrics for measuring success, they are broadly accepted as a good starting point for organizations aiming to establish foundational cyber hygiene or embarking on the quest of building a cybersecurity capability, and as an additional check list for security professionals. Looking at the tight deadline, for our CEO Tom, they would be an excellent first step towards his supervisory board meeting, allowing him to structure and communicate his intent.

The organization describes itself as follows:

The CIS Critical Security Controls are a recommended set of actions for cyber defense that provide specific and actionable ways to stop today's most pervasive and dangerous attacks. A principle benefit of the Controls is that they prioritize and focus a smaller number of actions with high pay-off results. The Controls are effective because they are derived from the most common attack patterns highlighted in the leading threat reports and vetted across a very broad community of government and industry practitioners. They were created by the people who know how attacks work—NSA Red and Blue teams, the US Department of Energy nuclear energy labs, law enforcement organizations and some of the nation's top forensics and incident response organizations—to answer the question, "what do we need to do to stop known attacks."[7]

Author/Issuer: The SANS Institute (registered as The Escal Institute of Advanced Technologies, Inc.)/Center For Internet Security, United States.

Extent: 94 pages, last updated in 2016.

Region/Type: Global quasi standard.

Industry: All.

Primary audience: Information security, risk, and IT functions.

IT Capability Maturity Framework—Information Security Management (IT-CMF:ISM)

This framework is developed and maintained by practitioners and academics from a large consortium of member companies across all industries, and it aims to become the gold standard for the management of IT value and IT-enabled innovation. The framework is designed around 35 IT capabilities and associated capability building blocks rather than on processes or specific controls. In addition to the capability building blocks, it also provides a maturity assessment methodology, benchmarks, practices, outcomes, and metrics (POMs). Information security management is treated as one such IT capability and the framework is informed by many of the existing information security frameworks and standards. Its purpose is not to replace them but rather to unlock organizations investment in them by moving beyond controls to an organization value focused approach to measuring and optimizing information security maturity.

The organization describes itself as follows:

> *The IT-CMF provides a concise management roadmap to optimize organization value derived from IT investments. The Information Security Management module includes a comprehensive maturity profile, assessment method, and improvement roadmap, each expressed in business language that can be used to guide discussions on setting goals and evaluating performance. The module helps organizations build a competent and effective organization capability to manage IT security, protect business value and business success and demonstrate effective security for stakeholders and regulators.*[8]

Author/Issuer: Innovation Value Institute (IVI), Ireland.

Extent: Ten pages plus extensive accompanying materials, last updated in 2014.

Region/Type: Global, capability framework.

Industry: Any.

Primary audience: Information Security and IT management functions.

Payment Card Industry (PCI) Data Security Standard (PCI-DSS)

De facto standard for the protection of credit card account data, widely adopted in financial services and retail. This standard addresses six objectives (from "Build and Maintain a Secure Network and Systems" to "Maintain an Information Security Policy") by means of 12 actionable key requirements, and combines them with testing procedures, guidelines, and best practices. It is positioned by its authors as a minimum set of requirements for protection of cardholder data, which may be enhanced by additional controls and its specific focus on protection of cardholder data only makes it very actionable. Compliance with PCI-DSS is mandated by law in some countries for payments processing industries and systems, and in any case, most, if not all, credit and payment card issuers require their merchants and service providers to comply with the PCI DSS. So if Tom's company was to process any card data, chances are he would already have someone in his organization familiar with the standard.

The organization describes itself as follows:

> *The Payment Card Industry Data Security Standard (PCI DSS) was developed to encourage and enhance cardholder data security and facilitate the broad adoption of consistent data security measures globally. PCI DSS provides a baseline of technical and operational requirements designed to protect account data. PCI DSS applies to all entities involved in payment card processing—including merchants, processors, acquirers, issuers, and service providers. PCI DSS also applies to all other entities that store, process or transmit cardholder data (CHD) and/or sensitive authentication data (SAD).*[9]

Author/Issuer: Payment Card Industry (PCI) Security Standards Council, United States.

Extent: In its current version 3.2, it comprises about 140 pages and was last updated in 2016.

Region/Type: Global industry standard.

Industry: Financial services, retail, and other card data processing industries of any size.

Primary audience: Information security and IT functions.

World Economic Forum Cyber Risk Framework (WEF-CRF)

This framework provides a holistic high-level approach to addressing and calculating the risk posed by cyber attacks. Looking at value at risk,

potential attacker profiles, and organizational maturity, it allows understanding of cyber risks and response readiness and provides recommendation and a roadmap for collaborative action against cyber threats. In a
pending framework aimed specifically at boards, the forum is also looking
at cyber risk from a supervisory board perspective with the aim to normalize cyber risk.

The organization describes itself as follows:

> *The Forum approaches the issue from a leadership and governance
> perspective and outlines a "cyber value-at-risk" framework that
> seeks to unify all dimensions of cyber threats and encourages or-
> ganizations to create robust cyber risk models. This should help
> increase confidence regarding decisions to invest, distribute, offload
> and/or retain cyber risks.*[10]

Author/Issuer: The World Economic Forum, Geneva, Switzerland.

Extent: Twenty pages plus supporting reports, last updated in 2015.

Region/Type: Global framework.

Industry: Any.

Primary audience: Information security, risk, and IT functions.

European Union Agency for Network and Information Security (ENISA)

The European Union Agency for Network and Information Security (ENISA),
appears to be currently focusing on topics related to critical infrastructure
protection and national cybersecurity strategies of its member states, while
also paying attention to the cybersecurity needs of small and medium-sized
enterprises (SMEs), which form the backbone of many economies.

To that end, ENISA has issued, and keeps issuing, a number of publications such as the "Evaluation Framework on National Cyber Security Strategies" (12/2014) or a study on "Information Security and Privacy Standards
for SMEs" (12/2015). ENISA is apparently not set on contributing to the
proliferation of security framework with another one of their own making,
but instead is advocating the use of existing frameworks like the ones mentioned above.

The organization describes itself as follows:

> *"Securing Europe's Information Society": The mission of ENISA
> is to contribute to securing Europe's information society by raising
> "awareness of network and information security and to develop*

and promote a culture, of network and information security in society for the benefit of citizens, consumers, enterprises and public sector organizations in the Union.

ENISA's strategic objectives are derived from the ENISA regulation, inputs from the Member States and relevant communities, including private sector.[11]

Author/Issuer: European Union Agency for Network and Information Security, Greece.

Extent: Several specific publications available from the ENISA web site.

Region/Type: European Union.

Industry: Government agencies, national critical infrastructure, SMEs.

Primary audience: Information security, risk, and IT functions.

CONSTRAINTS ON STANDARDS AND FRAMEWORKS

These are but a selection of the most important frameworks and standards. Although there are more and different ones—created for different purposes, industries, audiences, or specific regions—it is key to remember that they all of these can have their merit if employed as a tool for the right purpose.

Likewise, it is important to keep in mind that risk methods and frameworks may be affected by some constraints and fundamental limitations. For example, there are limits in a "reductionist approach," a lack of variety, limits of a "fixed-state" approach, a lack of feedback and control, and the danger of losing risk signals in the "security noise," and assumed determinability. These are nicely summarized in an article by the UK Communications Electronics Security Group (CESG), the information security arm of the GCHQ.[12]

Good Practice Consistently Applied

But in the end, real security comes from first deciding together within the organization on the appropriate security strategy and its overall objectives (compliance versus security beyond compliance, partnering versus competing on security, etc.), and then adopting an appropriate framework. Usually, any framework needs to be adapted somewhat to the situation at hand and enriched with practices as needed, or augmented with relevant elements from other frameworks. Indeed, many companies follow such an approach. A next step would be to run a risk assessment, then to build a road map for implementation of a cybersecurity/cyber risk management system and to establish the required capabilities to keep all of this functioning, monitored, and up to date. Obviously, it is prudent to prioritize and close obvious or already previously identified gaps quickly, rather than waiting for the end of a more comprehensive cybersecurity transformation project.

Good practice, consistently applied still beats sporadic pockets of best practice. But even then, regardless of the particular framework selected, the consistent pursuit of cybersecurity comes at a cost and will need skilled internal resources, assigned roles and not only documented but also accepted responsibilities support from outside assessors and so on. These requirements should be taken into account when selecting a framework to ensure that its application will be economically feasible and sustainable for the organization.

Given the time at hand, Tom, our hypothetical CEO, would probably be well advised to first run an IT-CMF:ISM assessment or any other enterprise-wide focused cybersecurity health check, explore the SANS Top 20 and then take a step back for a more informed pick among the other, more comprehensive frameworks. With a bit more time, Tom would also be well advised to familiarize himself with the upcoming Cyber Resilience Guidelines for Boards the World Economic Forum is currently developing—because this may well be what the board members who requested his presentation will use to gauge his preparedness.

CONCLUSION

The following cyber risk management statement represents those organization capabilities CEO and board expect to be demonstrated in terms of *cyber risk standards and frameworks*.

STANDARDS AND FRAMEWORKS

The appropriate mix of global key standards and frameworks for cybersecurity are in evidence, monitored, reviewed and tailored to the organization context. These include voluntary codes such as the ISO/IEC 27000 series, COBIT 5, NIST, ISF, SANS Top 20 controls, IT-CMF, WEF, and ENISA. These can be tailored singly, or in combination and with local regulatory codes that may apply to the organization. They provide the organization with effective cyber risk management guidance and benchmarking. Management understands that consistently applied good practice beats sporadic pockets of "best" practice. There is a road map for implementation of the cyber risk management system and to establish the required capabilities to keep it functioning, monitored, and up to date. Cyber-related risks are treated and included in enterprise risk management (ERM) like any other risk to an organization and are aligned with the umbrella ISO 31000:2009, *Risk management—Principles and guidelines* standard.

NOTES

1. https://www.iso.org/obp/ui/#iso:std:iso-iec:27000:ed-3:v1:en
2. http://www.iso.org/iso/catalogue_detail?csnumber=54534
3. http://www.isaca.org/cobit/pages/info-sec.aspx
4. http://csrc.nist.gov/publications/PubsSPs.html
5. https://www.nist.gov/cyberframework/background-framework-improving-critical-infrastructure-cybersecurity
6. https://www.securityforum.org/tool/the-standard-of-good-practice-for-information-security
7. https://www.sans.org/critical-security-controls
8. http://www.webopedia.com/TERM/I/IT_Capability_Maturity_Framework.html; https://ivi.ie/critical-capabilities/; https://content.ivi.ie/sites/default//files/media/Final%20deck%20Information%20Security%20Management_Jan2014_b.pdf
9. https://www.pcisecuritystandards.org/documents/PCI_DSS_v3-2.pdf
10. https://www.weforum.org/reports/partnering-cyber-resilience-towards-quantification-cyber-threats/
11. https://www.enisa.europa.eu/about-enisa/mission-and-objectives
12. https://www.cesg.gov.uk/guidance/critical-appraisal-risk-methods-and-frameworks

ABOUT BOSTON CONSULTING GROUP (BCG)

The Boston Consulting Group (BCG) is a global management consulting firm and the world's leading advisor on business strategy and transformation. We partner with clients from the private, public, and not-for-profit sectors in all regions to identify their highest-value opportunities, address their most critical challenges, and transform their enterprises. Our customized approach combines deep insight into the dynamics of companies and markets with close collaboration at all levels of the client organization. This ensures that our clients achieve sustainable competitive advantage, build more capable organizations, and secure lasting results. Founded in 1963, BCG is a private company with 85 offices in 48 countries. For more information, please visit bcg.com.

ABOUT WILLIAM YIN

William is a senior partner and managing director of the Boston Consulting Group. He is the leader of BCG's Technology Advantage practice for Greater China and leader of BCG's Cyber Security and IT Risk Management practice in Asia-Pacific. He is based in BCG's Hong Kong office.

ABOUT DR. STEFAN A. DEUTSCHER

Stefan is a principal at the Boston Consulting Group and BCG's global topic leader for Cyber Security and IT Risk Management. He is based in BCG's Berlin office.

CHAPTER 7

Identifying, Analyzing, and Evaluating Cyber Risks

Information Security Forum (ISF)
Steve Durbin, Managing Director, Information Security Forum Ltd.

The chief risk officer, Nathan, put it plainly to CEO Tom: "To say that cybersecurity presents complex challenges is an understatement. The scope of risk to sensitive information has grown exponentially during the twenty-first century. Those risks not only involve technical factors, but human, cultural, and legal factors, as well as economics. Of course, the profession of cybersecurity has struggled to grow in tandem with these challenges. But nobody has the resources to ensure complete data security. Figuring out where security investments are justified requires a sophisticated understanding of the risk landscape."

THE LANDSCAPE OF RISK

Hardly a day goes by when the evening news does not include a report about a major institution reluctantly announcing that its files have been hacked. The stories tend to follow a familiar pattern: expressions of official regret, attempts at reassurance, and pledges to do whatever is required to prevent its future recurrence.

Attacks on institutional and corporate databases have become the new normal. A generation of workers comfortable with information sharing has also grown accustomed to its negative consequences. The capabilities of cybercriminals continue advancing at an alarming pace. And the losses associated with major data attacks, which run into the millions, are increasingly seen as just another cost of doing business.

At the same time, however, there is a growing understanding of those consequences. A movement in the leadership ranks of both business and government agencies to manage cyber risks more effectively and to improve the resilience of security tools already in place, has followed. This is a welcome development because, until fairly recently, most senior managers and board members regarded cybersecurity as essentially a technical problem for their IT departments—not as an existential issue requiring greater investment as well as the engagement of personnel throughout the organization. That said, however, some of the issues really do involve the organization's network technology.

Technology flaws—whether in design, encryption, event logging or software malfunction—create opportunities for attackers to infiltrate an organization's technical infrastructure. Understanding and realistically assessing the vulnerabilities of an organization's system components is essential. But it is people, far more than technology, that present the greatest risks.

THE PEOPLE FACTOR

Most high-profile attacks on corporate servers and institutional networks originate outside of the victimized organizations—in many cases from halfway around the world. But the network openings that allow cyber attackers to burrow in, infect databases, and potentially take down an organization's file servers, overwhelmingly originate with trusted insiders. There are three categories of insider threats, as illustrated in Figure 7.1.

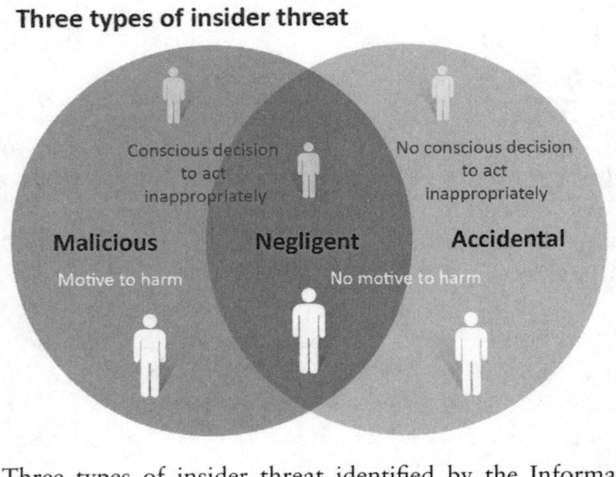

Three types of insider threat

Conscious decision to act inappropriately

No conscious decision to act inappropriately

Malicious

Negligent

Accidental

Motive to harm

No motive to harm

FIGURE 7.1 Three types of insider threat identified by the Information Security Forum (ISF)
Source: Copyright ISF. Used with permission.

In some cases, those insiders are driven by malicious intent—the desire to enrich themselves through the sale of sensitive data or to retaliate for perceived slights or mistreatment in other instances. Deceptive behavior—sometimes referred to as social engineering—is used to trick employees into divulging proprietary codes, passwords, or other private company information. There are also cases where an organization's third-party contractors, vendors, or temporary workers, essentially privileged users, have been responsible for their client's network breaches, either through malice or by accident.

However, according to a survey of Information Security Forum (ISF)[1] members, the vast majority of those network openings were created innocently through accidental or inadvertent behavior by insiders without any intention of harming their employer. In a number of cases, that vulnerability was the ironic result of a trusted employee doing something seemingly ordinary like taking files home to work on in their spare time.

That risk is exacerbated by personal mobile devices. Welcome or not, they have become inexorably tied into corporate information systems. And their use frequently reflects their owners' relaxed consumer habits.

Therein lies the rub: the cost associated with data leaked, hacked, stolen, or compromised for most private individuals is comparatively low—perhaps limited to personal embarrassment. But for a multinational corporation, it can be huge. Marketing plans, product road maps, pricing strategies, personnel records, customer account data, confidential correspondence, and other types of sensitive information, if stolen, corrupted, or held hostage for ransom can have a disastrous impact on an organization's operations and its reputation. It can also enrage loyal customers who expect—and the courts require—that their private information remains private.

Indeed, for anyone, irrespective of where they may be located, if they operate using personal information relating to European citizens, the stakes have just been significantly raised. The EU's General Data Protection Regulation (GDPR)[2] has penalties of up to 4 percent of global turnover just waiting to be applied to organizations unfortunate enough to be hacked and suffer the loss of EU citizen personal information. The EU GDPR comes into force in 2018 and adds another layer of complexity, not to mention potential cost and associated resources, to the issue of critical information asset management that so many organizations are struggling to come to terms with.

As a result, there is now a much clearer recognition of both the immediate and longer-term costs associated with cyber attacks. Identifying an organization's vulnerabilities is key to developing effective responses. Organizations must deploy a multiphase process, to assess cyber threats—whether these threats are deliberate, unintentional, or the results of environmental incidents such as floods or power failures. Here is how it works.

A STRUCTURED APPROACH TO ASSESSING AND MANAGING RISK

There are different tools and software available in the market to help risk managers assess their information vulnerabilities. Symantec, Trend Micro, NetIQ, ISF, and others are reputable firms with applications and techniques focused on different aspects of risk management. They all have satisfied users. A robust information risk assessment methodology should not simply be a piece of software but a comprehensive procedure to identify, analyze, evaluate, and manage a variety of information risks throughout their organizations in a structured manner, and then to generate risk profiles in terms that are meaningful to the organization's business. See Figure 7.2, which illustrates the six phases of the ISF IRAM2,[3] which identifies the distinct stages of risk management.

In fact, the need for a structured approach to the identification and management of risk has never been greater than in today's always-on, constantly communicating, cyber-enabled business environment. A realistic and disciplined assessment of the worst-case scenarios for business in advance of this need, is to prioritize the organization's investments in defending against cyber attacks.

Such an approach typically involves six phases:

- The first provides guidance for generating an integrated view of information risk, ranging from an organization's business processes through to its technology.
- The second offers guidance for realistically assessing worst-case scenarios—the potential business impact if information assets become compromised.
- The third involves mapping different types of threats, both malicious and accidental, that could potentially affect the business.
- The fourth involves assessing your vulnerabilities to different threat events and the strength of any controls already in place.

The six phases of IRAM2

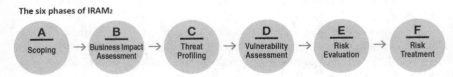

FIGURE 7.2   The six phases of the ISF IRAM2
Source: Copyright ISF. Used with permission.

- The fifth stage evaluates the organization's risk appetite and likelihood of a successful threat in light of the previous findings.
- The sixth and final phase involves developing practical approaches to addressing the information risks which have been identified.

In essence, it provides companies with a highly structured and practical method for assessing risks to guide critical business decisions. By taking a comprehensive view of risk exposure and focusing attention on the most significant ones, organizations may predict and prevent attacks instead of simply reacting to them after they occur.

SECURITY CULTURE

Accurately assessing the attributes of cyber threat and an organization's resilience to them involves examining factors including organization capability, commitment, people competence, and user privilege patterns. Common threat attributes could include simple deception used in phishing attacks, stealthy taps into unsecured wireless networks, or using "accidentally misplaced" removable media to inject malware into the targets network.

But one of the most significant factors is the organization's culture, which often mirrors the society where it is located. For the multinational organization, that means taking into account the ways in which different cultures view protecting data and the way in which those cultures respond to directives about safeguarding digital devices and commingling corporate and personal business on those same devices.

A study commissioned by Cisco[4] almost a decade ago found that risky behavior and rampant disregard for their organization's security policies occurred at alarming rates among employees in all parts of the world, although some were worse than others. Those personal patterns do not appear to have changed that much. But a 2016 international survey by PricewaterhouseCooper[5] offered some encouraging news about an important turnaround at the institutional level. It found that 65 percent of those organizations surveyed now collaborate to improve their cybersecurity, 69 percent use cloud-based cybersecurity services, and many more follow a risk-based cybersecurity framework, most frequently ISO 27001 guidelines.

There is also a generational difference. Generation Y employees, as a whole, do not feel as though requirements for securing sensitive information apply to them as much as they do to their more senior colleagues. Instead, among recent entrants into the job market, the prevailing view is that it is the organization's job to make sure information is secure—not the individual's.

But while there has been a welcome growth in security awareness among senior management, the view that security is the responsibility of higher-level employees is frequently misplaced. A recent Nasdaq survey[6] highlights alarming gaps between awareness and accountability at the highest levels of global enterprises: too many board members and executives are unable to understand security briefings and unwilling to accept responsibility for data breaches. Indeed, for many organizations, the more senior someone is, the less aware they tend to be of the way data needs to be secured. Some senior executives seem to think they're immune from security threats altogether.

Another reason that deferring to senior colleagues on security matters may be misguided is that those senior colleagues are of the same generation that formerly nourished their newer employees' relaxed attitudes. Most of today's employees have gone through educational institutions where they are encouraged by their mentors to share information. Go to any university in the United States, and you will be given ready access to a host of information sources all across the country.

But while we encourage people to share information, we do not teach that there are also security considerations around the ways they use that information. So when those students eventually become employees, they are thrust into a completely different, and far less forgiving, information security environment.

REGULATORY COMPLIANCE

In highly regulated environments, like financial services, there are a number of statutory requirements an organization needs to comply with. And that has tended to drive institutional behavior; they're compliant because they have to be. But if you are going to avoid innovative attacks, compliance will not necessarily help. A compliance-driven strategy might satisfy the authorities, but it will do little to discourage a creative hacker.

At the same time, there are banks and other organizations that see compliance only as a starting point. That is because by the time a regulation goes into effect, it is usually out of date. Compliance regulations come about because of something that happened in the past. They have been put in place to prevent a past act from repeating itself. It is like preparing today to win a previous war.

However, cyber is different than other types of risk. Cyber is exceptionally fast moving. It is not like slip-and-fall injuries or vandalism, embezzlement, or any of the other conventional risks an organization faces. A lot of the cyber attacks that take place are unprecedented. They have never been seen before. As a result, if you follow only a compliance approach, you are looking backwards and leaving yourself open to attacks that seem to come out of nowhere.

It is a balancing act. First, you really do have to be compliant. And second, you have to do everything reasonable to protect your organization's mission-critical information. That realization has prompted some leading organizations to take a slightly different approach. In the past, they have tried to protect things like devices; they have tried to protect networks; they have tried to protect the perimeter on the assumption that if you can stop somebody from coming in, you can be secure.

Unfortunately, there are plenty of holes in those perimeters. There are lots of ways a hacker or attacker can come in. Maybe it is through a third party; perhaps through a faulty device, possibly through human error, maybe through an outside contractor, or even through an insider who either willfully hands over information or innocently makes a mistake that allows a hacker to gain access. A number of intrusion-penetration test methodologies are commercially available to help identify holes at different points in the network.

MATURING SECURITY

As recently as 10 years ago, cybersecurity was primarily a function of IT departments. Organizations tended to treat their data protection as a technology matter—one best left to its techies. The organization's established risk managers tended to focus instead on the organization's traditional insurance coverages. And its product line managers rarely felt any connection to the cybersecurity function. That is all starting to change.

There are different levels of maturity in cybersecurity across enterprises. The most mature ones have moved into a broader risk function. Those coming up the maturity curve still tend to view their work as part of IT, where security concerns were initially focused. But as the economy assumes a more resilience-oriented approach to preventing and recovering from attacks, we need to view security as a holistic business issue—not just an IT issue.

In an ideal world, there should not be any barriers separating data security from the organization's core business functions. In reality, however, most security departments are still not consulted—nor are they viewed as business enabling. Instead, they are viewed as being the "No" guys—the ones who prevent things from happening and keep employees from downloading their favorite software, logging onto sports and entertainment web sites, going onto social media, or checking their Gmail.

However, once an organization has been attacked, it is likely to get the religion of security rather quickly because a hack is typically more than a transient business disruption—it impacts your brand, your reputation, your operations, and creates costs for cleanup, forensics, investigations, and so on. In organizations that have been attacked, as well as their competitors, there typically follows a sharp uptick in their focus on data security.

PRIORITIZING PROTECTION

Years ago, securing an organization's information was synonymous with safeguarding its computers. But the recent explosion of devices and users and interconnection channels has made it essential to shift from a focus on devices—which actually form the perimeter of a network—to their core: the information it contains.

Today, with so many devices and so many users touching the data, protecting them all is impossible. Instead, organizations need to focus on what is important from a business standpoint: protecting mission-critical information, regardless of who might want to access it, irrespective of the devices they might be using, and no matter where they might be coming from.

That represents a sea change from the earlier device-centric safeguards. Today, the approach to security begins and ends with the organization's data. How do I protect my data? Which data is truly mission critical? And who really needs to access it?

Going through that exercise leads you to think about data in a somewhat different way: What are my organization's crown jewels? How do I need to protect them? What behaviors am I trying to protect against? Who actually needs to access this information, and when?

Safeguarding an organization's mission-critical information is a process involving a number of moving parts—technology, leadership, culture, policy, environment, and more. They are all subject to change over time, and adversaries who want to attack those assets are constantly on the lookout for any opportunities those changes create. Regularly and systematically assessing your organization's technological defenses, its potential business impact scenarios, its matrix of threats, and the resilience of its current configuration to potential attacks are all essential to developing a pragmatic plan to resist and, if worse comes to worst, to recover from an assault on your most critical data.

CONCLUSION

The following cyber risk management statement represents those organization capabilities CEO and board expect to be demonstrated in terms of *identifying, analyzing, and evaluating (i.e., assessing) cyber risks.*

IDENTIFYING, ANALYZING, AND EVALUATING CYBER RISKS

The organization realistically assesses the vulnerabilities of its digital system components not just for technology flaws (such as in design, encryption, event logging or software malfunction) but for human factors. Trusted insiders present the highest risk (motivated either by malice or more commonly by accident) as well as third-party contractors, vendors, or temporary workers (essentially privileged users). The organization commits to a robust and structured approach to assessing and managing risk and an information risk assessment methodology. This involves a six-part approach to (1) generating an integrated view of information risk; (2) realistically assessing worst case; (3) mapping different types of threats, both malicious and accidental; (4) assessing vulnerabilities to different threat events and the strength of any controls already in place; (5) evaluating risk appetite and likelihood of a successful threat; and (6) developing practical approaches to addressing the information risks that have been identified. Other factors examined include organization capability, security culture, commitment, people competence, user privilege patterns, technology, leadership, policy, and environment. There is a balance between regulatory compliance and doing everything reasonable to protect mission-critical information. Cybersecurity maturity avoids barriers separating data security from the organization's core business functions and does not rely on device-centric safeguards. The focus begins and ends with the organization's data: how it is protected, which data is truly mission critical, what behaviors need to be protected against, and who really needs to access it and when.

NOTES

1. Information Security Forum, "Managing the Insider Threat: Improving Trustworthiness," Based on analysis of findings in Verizon 2015 Data Breach Investigation Report, http://www.verizonenterprise.com/verizon-insights-lab/dbir/
2. European Commission, "Reform of EU Data Protection Rules," 2015, http://ec.europa.eu/justice/data-protection/reform/index_en.htm
3. Information Security Forum, "Information Risk Assessment Methodology 2," 2016, https://www.securityforum.org/tool/information-risk-assessment-methodology-iram2/

4. Cisco Systems, Inc., "Data Leakage Worldwide: Common Risks and Mistakes Employees Make," 2008, http://www.cisco.com/c/en/us/solutions/collateral/enterprise-networks/data-loss-prevention/white_paper_c11-499060.html
5. PricewaterhouseCooper LLP, "The Global State of Information Security® Survey 2016—Turnaround and Transformation in Cybersecurity," http://www.pwc.com/gx/en/issues/cyber-security/information-security-survey.html
6. Tanium Inc. and Nasdaq, Inc., "The Accountability Gap: Cybersecurity & Building a Culture of Responsibility," 2016, http://www.infosecisland.com/blogview/24788-A-View-from-the-Top-The-C-Suite-Steps-Up-as-Cyber-Security-Threats-Surge.html

ABOUT THE INFORMATION SECURITY FORUM (ISF)

Founded in 1989, the Information Security Forum (ISF) is an independent, not-for-profit organization whose members include many of the world's Fortune 500 and Forbes 2000 organizations. It is dedicated to investigating, clarifying and resolving key issues in information security and risk management by developing best-practice methodologies, processes, and solutions to meet the business needs of its members.

The ISF offers a trusted and confidential environment in which members' in-depth knowledge and practical experience can be shared. This collaborative approach enables the ISF to harness the collective insights and knowledge of its members to deliver comprehensive leading-edge solutions that are both pragmatic and effective.

The ISF has developed a proprietary, second-generation Information Risk Assessment Methodology known as IRAM2. It is not simply a piece of software. Rather, it is a comprehensive procedure—largely the product of members' input—that helps companies identify, analyze, evaluate and manage a variety of information risks throughout their organizations in a structured manner, and then to generate risk profiles in terms that are meaningful to the organization's business.

ABOUT STEVE DURBIN

Steve Durbin is managing director of the Information Security Forum. His main areas of focus include strategy, information technology, cybersecurity and the emerging security threat landscape across both the corporate and personal environments. He is a frequent speaker and commentator on technology and security issues including cloud, Big Data, the Internet of Things and the impact of cybersecurity on business growth and profitability.

Formerly at Ernst & Young, Steve was responsible for the entrepreneurial markets business in Europe, Middle East, India, and Africa. He has been involved with initial public offerings and mergers and acquisitions of fast-growth companies across Europe and the United States, and has also advised a number of Nasdaq and New York Stock Exchange–listed global technology companies.

Previously, as global head of Gartner's consultancy business, Steve developed a range of strategic marketing, business, and IT solutions for international investment and entrepreneurial markets. He also served as a Digital 50 advisory committee member in the United States, a body established to improve the talent pool for Fortune 500 boards around cybersecurity and information governance. In 2014, he was ranked as one of the top 10 individuals shaping the way that organizations and leaders approach information security careers.

CHAPTER 8

Treating Cyber Risks

**John Hermans, Cyber Lead Partner Europe, Middle East, and Africa
at KPMG, The Netherlands
Ton Diemont, Senior Manager at KPMG, The Netherlands**

CEO Tom challenged his chief risk officer, Nathan. "So give me the right guidelines for how to treat cyber risk and bring cybersecurity back to basics."

Cybersecurity has been in the spotlight for the past few years. Due to the number and seriousness of cyber incidents, the media's focus on such incidents, and the importance of tackling cyber issues in the extensive digitization of most organizations, this area requires the attention of directors and managers everywhere. But it needs to be tackled in the appropriate way and with the required subtlety, as a component of integral risk management.

INTRODUCTION

The fact that cybersecurity is important to every organization needs no further explanation. On an almost daily basis, various incidents demonstrate how great the risks are and that individual hackers and professionally organized cybercriminals are extremely active. The heads of organizations need to ensure that their organizations have set the proper priorities. To many, however, this is not a simple task because the world of cybersecurity seems elusive due to its specialist character and the technical jargon used. Generalists have difficulty grasping the complexities. In addition, it is difficult to distinguish between primary and secondary issues, while media coverage contributes to a culture of fear leading to the idea that almost every organization is helpless prey to malevolent forces. Almost no distinction is made between imposters on eBay, hackers who crash web sites, and organized criminal gangs using a systematic strategy to try to steal company secrets, which we call *crown jewels*. Such distinctions are extremely important because not all organizations are equally attractive to the different types of cybercriminals.

Partly due to the fact that concepts are often interwoven, cybersecurity remains a troublesome theme to many organization leaders. Nevertheless, this cannot be an excuse to devolve the issue to specialist professionals. It is truly essential that heads of organizations themselves actively lead the crusade for cybersecurity. Within the complexity of cybersecurity, leaders need to consider the relevant issues soundly and, at the very least, pose the right questions. But how should this be done?

TREATING CYBERSECURITY RISK WITH THE PROPER NUANCE IN LINE WITH AN ORGANIZATION'S RISK PROFILE

The seriousness of the cybersecurity risks means that cybersecurity does require boardroom attention—but in the appropriate context. Organizations need to avoid panicked responses that have not been thought through. The media regularly paint a dramatic picture of cybersecurity as if numerous organizations are helpless victims of cybercriminals. Moreover, all types of crime are lumped together, causing anxiety among organizations that is not based on the facts. Small and medium-sized enterprises (SMEs) have a completely different profile than multinationals, and an SME need have few worries about many of the incidents reported in the media.

The truth is more nuanced than the picture presented by the media. The risks are certainly controllable. Cybercriminals are not invincible geniuses, and the government and enterprises have significant knowledge of how to fight cybercrime. But we need to realize that 100 percent security is an illusion and that the pursuit of total security will lead not only to frustration but also possibly to a false sense of security.

In fact, we ought to start considering cybersecurity as "business as usual," as a theme that deserves attention in much the same way as the risk of fire or fraud. These are themes that are tackled by management in a structural way, from a risk-management perspective, with the defenses and responses therefore not founded on the idea of building a system that is completely watertight.

Many organizations need to examine cybersecurity differently. They should not take decisions on the basis of fear of what is happening outside, but reason from the standpoint of their own strengths, from an awareness of the risks run by their own organization, in accordance with the risk profile of the organization and its specific nature.

The starting point of the exploration of an organization's cyber risk is the determination of that organization's risk profile and risk appetite.

Questions that are relevant in determining this risk profile include: "How interesting is the organization to potential cyber criminals?"; "How dependent is the organization on the services of other organizations"; and "How much risk is the organization willing to accept?"

DETERMINING THE CYBER RISK PROFILE

In order to determine an organization's cyber risk profile, we need to use a model that covers the following five aspects as shown in Figure 8.1.

1. What is the organization's internal and external context and environment? In which markets is the organization active? To what extent is the organization dependent on the digitization of the organization's service provision? To what extent is the organization linked to another organization that could form an additional risk in this framework?
2. What could be relevant intended targets within the organization, and also within the chain in which the organization is active?

FIGURE 8.1   An organizational cyber risk profile

3. To which group of cybercriminals, and why, is the organization an attractive target (threats)? Which resources could the attacker deploy?
4. Which vulnerabilities in the organization could cybercriminals exploit? This concerns not only technical vulnerabilities but also human actions. More importantly, what is the level of resilience? How fast can an organization be back in business after a cyber attack?
5. What are the regulatory and legislative requirements with regard to cybersecurity that pertain to the organization?

On the basis of an analysis of the five aspects mentioned above, an organization is able to determine its risk profile as well the amount of risk it is willing to accept (its "risk appetite") and to implement the appropriate set of cybersecurity measures. As stated previously, it will never be possible to achieve 100 percent security, so there is no point in pursuing such an aim!

TREATING CYBER RISK

Cyber risk management programs must consider an organization's risk appetite. Specific cyber risks can and must be treated by applying the necessary measures and by reacting effectively when an organization is subjected to cyber attack. Figure 8.2 addresses the question, how does one select the right set of treatment measures?

In this framework, a number of considerations are relevant.

FIGURE 8.2   Selecting the right set of treatment measures

Focus on Your Crown Jewels

In view of the fact that it is impossible to protect everything, cybersecurity requires special attention regarding the protection of the organization's most valued information. It is therefore vital that an organization specify its crown jewels that need to be protected.

Humans Remain the Weakest Link

It is essential to have technical systems to protect, to identify intruders, and to respond to an attack, but human beings are actually the weakest link in many organizations. However, humans may also be the best asset in the organization's defense, if they are properly informed and trained.

Complementing Preventative Measures with Detective Measures

Whereas organizations once primarily relied on preventative measures to avoid cybersecurity incidents, attention is increasingly being paid to the detection of attacks, in order to enable the organization to react immediately and appropriately. We see a growing use of technical monitoring facilities in many organizations to detect and analyze *alien* traffic.

Focus on an Organization's Capability to Respond

As mentioned previously, we believe it is unfortunately only a question of time before an organization becomes a victim of a cyber incident. Instead of being a helpless victim, an organization can prepare for a serious attack. As such, it is vital for organizations to include the processing of cyber incidents in their crisis plans. An important part of this is the formulation of a protocol to be used in communications during a cyber incident.

Cooperation Is Essential

Besides being able to respond to incidents, it is crucial for organizations to remain up to date and informed of emerging threats, and to learn from other organizations how best to react to incidents. To facilitate this, there are organizations at various levels whose aim is to help other organizations in this area: at national level (the National Cyber Security Centre, for example), at sector level in various International Sharing and Analysis Centers (ISACs), and occasionally there are informal cooperative associations, such as a group of chief information security officers (CISOs) who work together to combat cybersecurity incidents within a particular industry. With the objective of generating a proactive approach to cybersecurity, it is vital to promote the active participation of organizations in such networks, which will help the organization to improve its own resilience. We must not forget, after all, that an incident at another organization is also a potential threat to one's own organization.

ALIGNMENT OF CYBER RISK TREATMENT

Technology alone is not the answer to cybersecurity issues. The answer lies in an integrated approach to cyber risk treatment, focusing on both the softer elements such as governance, culture and behavior, and the harder ones such as technology (Figure 8.3).

The kind of integral approach to cyber risk management shown in Figure 8.3 needs to include the following aspects:

- *Leadership and governance.* An organization's leaders need to demonstrate, in word and deed, that they regard themselves as the owners of cybersecurity, and show that they intend to manage the associated risks adequately.
- *Human behavior.* Cybersecurity involves not only the appropriate technical measures but also the creation of a culture in which people are alert to, and aware of, ways in which they can contribute to security.

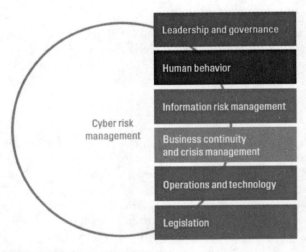

FIGURE 8.3   An integrated approach to cyber risk management

- *Information risk management.* An adequate approach to all-embracing and effective risk management with regard to information provision, also in relation to partner organizations.
- *Business continuity and crisis management.* Good preparation for possible incidents and the ability to minimize the impact of these incidents. This involves crisis and stakeholder management, among other aspects.
- *Operations and technology.* The implementation of checks and control measures in the organization in order to identify the cybersecurity risks and to minimize the impact of incidents.
- *Legislation.* Complying with legislation with regard to information protection.

The application of a holistic model incorporating all the above elements brings the following benefits:

- The minimization of the risk that the organization will be hit by a cyber attack from outside and the minimization of any consequences of a successful attack.
- Better decisions in the field of cybersecurity: the provision of information on measures, patterns of attack and incidents is thus optimized.
- Clear lines of communication on the theme of cybersecurity. Everyone knows his or her responsibilities and what must be done if incidents (or suspected incidents) occur.
- A contribution to a better reputation. An organization that is well prepared and has seriously considered the theme of cybersecurity is able to communicate on this theme in a way that inspires confidence.
- The enhancement of knowledge and competences regarding cybersecurity.
- The benchmarking of the organization in the field of cybersecurity in relation to its peers.

PRACTICING CYBER RISK TREATMENT

In order to continuously manage and mitigate the cyber risks, the organization needs to be able to address these risks in a flexible and ongoing manner. This requires a central and overarching perspective on those risks that require treatment and management attention as in Figure 8.4. An emerging threat landscape, a change in organization activities, and a shift to using new technologies: these are all indicators that the cyber risk landscape is changing. So far, current cybersecurity methodologies and cybersecurity models have not been able to capture this, in practice, in a dynamic way. For an organization to be able to provide a real-time and accurate view of the

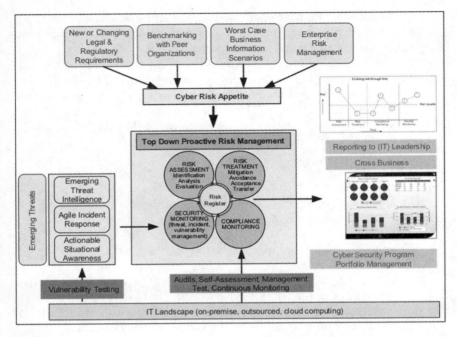

FIGURE 8.4 An overarching perspective over cyber risks requiring treatment

current risk environment would be the next step in the maturity of cyber risk management.

Business as Usual—to Be Integrated into Enterprise Risk Management

Cyber risk management should be to be linked to/integrated in the enterprise risk management (ERM) of an organization. Despite the topic and specific expertise, the approach must be fully aligned to existing risk management processes, and fits the recent developments to rationalize and unify risk frameworks, policies, standards, and processes. The rationalization and unification supports the required consistent risk language and classification schemes within an organization and will therefore be better and more quickly understood by all stakeholders and decision makers.

Cyber risk management must be part of the organization context and must be fully aligned with organization goals and needs. Only then will cyber risk management be able to show its added value by providing insight into organization opportunities and risks that should be avoided. This enables a top-down approach where information risk management (IRM) and ERM are aligned instead of existing in two separate worlds.

Business as Usual—to Be Integrated with the Regular Three Lines of Defense Applies for Model

Cybersecurity risk should be a primary business (first line of defense) responsibility and not be considered solely as an IT responsibility. Preferably, this responsibility should become part of the annual performance objectives of senior management demonstrating the importance and the tone at the top. The main focus for management is and should be addressing the customer needs and satisfaction and ensuring the continued availability of those primary business processes that customers rely on. Accountability and responsibility can be easily provided by utilizing the existing governance structures; hence, the composition and level of seniority is deemed adequate. Senior management should be supported by a multidisciplinary functional team of risk managers, security officers, compliance offices, legal and HR representatives (second line of defense), and included audit as the independent observer (third line of defense) in order to create full transparent and balanced views and supporting the appropriate steering and the right decisions with regard to cyber resilience.

Business as Usual—Managing Your Cyber Risks with a Predefined Risk Appetite

In many organizations it is a common "Pavlovian response" to immediately start drafting and implementing controls when a risk is identified, without asking what level of risk is acceptable. These decisions are often made, although with all good intentions, by cyber risk professionals without consultation with the appropriate business representatives.

The starting point of managing cyber risks is the same starting point of managing enterprise, defining the organization's risk appetite, an exercise to be performed by business representatives instead of cybersecurity specialists. See ISO 31000:2009, *Risk Management—Principles and Guidelines*, which is the overarching risk management standard for most risk management processes. Why can this not be applied for cyber risk management? By selecting cyber as one of the scenarios, senior business management will be able, in conjunction with cyber specialists, to address the relevance of the threat.

More and more organizations formalize risk appetite statements to enable management to maneuver within the agreed and acceptable risk boundaries without constantly being blocked or hindered by risk management processes that are too rigid. Key with determining risk appetite statements is that such statement should contain both quantitative and qualitative components and follows the agreed approval process. The qualitative components are most applicable for cyber risk because the "crystal ball" for quantifying the impact of cyber risk is still based on empiric and rough estimations and is not yet founded on a proven quantitative methodology. Quantifying cyber risk is, unfortunately, still perceived as too complex, academic or mathematical.

We simply miss at this moment in time historical, actuarial data on cyber risks to underpin a quantitative cyber risk model, despite the good efforts of organizations like the World Economic Forum.

Defining the risk appetite for cyber requires a sound and structured process to define the risk appetite of the business, by using the technique of worst-case business information scenario planning. This process must translate the risk appetite into discrete levels of acceptable risk, taking into account factors like changing business models, new and/or changing legal and regulatory requirements, and emerging cybersecurity industry standards. A mechanism that can assist in defining the cyber risk appetite is the use of the annualized loss expectancy (ALE) methodology; expressing all losses to the expected annual loss provides a more consistent approach and evaluation of risks. ALE is defined as expected monetary loss that can be expected for an asset due to a risk over a one-year period; another motivation to relate nonfinancial risks to the financial impact.

A question that is often heard is: does the setting of risk appetite of cyber risks within smaller independent organizations differ from large organizations? No, basically not, most likely the thresholds for analyzing and evaluating risks differ, as larger organizations potentially have larger financial buffers and a higher appetite for risk.

Business as Usual—Using Your Embedded Risk Management Processes

When cyber is assessed as relevant for the organization, they can be assessed and treated by senior management and experienced specialists. The cyber risk assessment process (to identify, analyze, then evaluate risks) should be identical to that used for ERM and is used to arrive at how to priorities risks for treatment. The traditional risk treatment techniques "to avoid, accept, transfer, or mitigate" are on one set of options but they only treat risk as "threats" (risks with negative consequences). Modern-day treatment options also address opportunities (risks with negative consequences). Appropriate combined treatment options are not mutually exclusive, are appropriate to the case in hand, and should be aligned with the international standard ISO 31000:2009, *Risk Management—Principles and Guidelines*' by:

1. Avoiding the activity that gives rise to the risk;
2. Taking or increasing the risk in order to pursue an opportunity;
3. Removing the risk source;

4. Changing the likelihood;
5. Changing the consequences;
6. Sharing the risk with other parties (e.g., risk financing, contracts); and,
7. Retaining the risk by informed decision.

A key element in supporting this unification is to ensure that next to the financial impact criteria, the nonfinancial impact criteria for regulatory, customer, legal, compliance, operational, staff, and reputational occurrences are also being formalized and preferably linked to the financial criteria, meaning that a severe nonfinancial cyber occurrence is considered a high risk and treated equally as risk with a high financial impact.

Business as Usual—Treatment of Cyber Risks

Cyber risk treatment is prioritized, reiterative, and cyclical, with risk owners completing risk and control action plans that balance threat with opportunity to organization objectives and cost-benefit. Appropriate combined treatment options are not mutually exclusive, are appropriate to the case in hand, and should be aligned with the current ISO 31000:2009, *Risk Management— Principles and Guidelines*' standard, as described in the previous section.

Prioritized risk treatment options should be aligned with existing organization objectives and strategies so that there is only a need to spend the money once. If this means that certain investments or improvements in the cyber resilience approach should be postponed, the organization should support and ensure a formal temporary risk assessment process is followed and a well-balanced acceptance and decision process is being followed.

The treatment of cyber risks should not differ from overarching ERM approaches. However, from a cybersecurity and cyber resilience perspective, it could imply that the defined and agreed security baselines and mandatory cyber controls or processes within an organization are being upgraded or enhanced and are subject to a more rigid form of periodic compliance and effectiveness measurement. For example, the organization could decide to monitor not only their crown jewels but all assets, as these are often targeted as stepping stones by the threat actors. By doing so the organization will potentially identify anomalies in their IT environment in an earlier stage, which implies that the response processes can be triggered much earlier as well.

CONCLUSION

The following cyber risk management statement represents those organization capabilities CEO and board expect to be demonstrated in terms of *treating cyber risks.*

TREATING CYBER RISKS

The organization's risk treatment capabilities align with its risk profile, risk appetite and context. Risk treatment methodology is not reinvented for cyber risks but is a subset of the ERM system. Risk treatment covers all cyber risk sources, likelihoods, and impacts. Risk sources include supply chain, cloud, mobile devices, and social media. Impacts are either noninsurable in nature, or insurable in part or whole, and may take various forms (such as fines, reputational damage, loss of customers, loss of employees, and stock devaluation). Impact management preparations are required for insurable risks, crisis management, forensics investigation, customer notification, and business interruption. Cyber risk treatment is prioritized, reiterative, and cyclical. Risk owners complete risk and control action plans that balance threat with opportunity to organization objectives and consider cost-benefit. Appropriate combined treatment options are not mutually exclusive, are appropriate to the case in hand, and are aligned with ISO 31000:2009, *Risk Management—Principles and Guidelines'* by: (1) avoiding the activity that gives rise to the risk; (2) taking or increasing the risk in order to pursue an opportunity; (3) removing the risk source; (4) changing the likelihood; (5) changing the consequences; (6) sharing the risk with other parties (e.g., risk financing, contracts); and (7) retaining the risk by informed decision.

ABOUT KPMG

KPMG operates as a global network of independent member firms offering audit, tax and advisory services; working closely with clients, helping them to mitigate risks and grasp opportunities. Member firms' clients include business corporations, governments, and public-sector agencies and not-for-profit organizations. They look to KPMG for a consistent standard of service based on high-order professional capabilities, industry insight, and local knowledge.

KPMG member firms can be found in 155 countries. Collectively, they employ more than 162,000 people across a range of disciplines. Sustaining and enhancing the quality of this professional workforce is KPMG's primary objective. Wherever we operate, we want our firms to be no less than the professional employers of choice.

We contribute to the effective functioning of international capital markets. We support reforms that strengthen the markets' credibility and their social responsibility. We believe that similar reform must extend to the professional realm.

ABOUT JOHN HERMANS

John is a partner at KPMG Advisory NV–Cyber Lead Partner Europe, Middle East, and Africa. He is responsible for KPMG's cybersecurity services in the Netherlands as well within the EMA region. John is a recognized, frequent speaker on cyber strategies and cyber risk management at national and international conferences. In his daily professional life, John assisted many organizations across the globe in strategizing, planning, and executing their cyber journey. John has trained many supervisory and management board members in how to deal with cyber risk management.

ABOUT TON DIEMONT

Ton is a senior manager at KPMG Advisory NV and a former head of IT risk within the operational risk management office as the chief information security officer (CISO) of an international bank. He has more than 21 years of information and operational risk management experience within the financial industry and has been responsible for developing and implementing IT risk, information security, and cybersecurity strategies; risk dashboards for executive boards and risk committees; aligning IT risk management processes to the operational risk management and nonfinancial risk methodologies and processes, and has been supporting ORM and IRM migrations toward ERM.

CHAPTER 9

Treating Cyber Risks Using Process Capabilities

ISACA
Todd Fitzgerald, CISO and ISACA, USA

Tom stared at the center of the diagram he had penciled (see Figure 1.1). His chief risk officer, Nathan, looked across to their chief of information security, Maria, and invited her to explain the word *process* at the center. Maria obliged, "Process is located at the center of our business model for information security. We understand that cyber risk is an enterprise-wide risk requiring organization-wide solutions. I'll define these processes for you to clarify how they collectively add clear value to our organization. Interrelationships between process and the people, technology, and other enterprise functions determine the effectiveness and efficiency of our cyber risk management system."

CYBERSECURITY PROCESSES ARE THE GLUE THAT BINDS

Maintaining effective cybersecurity processes is too critical to an organization to leave to chance, yet many organizations continue to rely on undocumented processes, tribal knowledge, and paying security professionals to manage routine operational security controls. Cybersecurity processes form the critical piece between those performing the security function and the technology.

Undocumented Processes Result in Tribal Knowledge Dependency

Processes are developed within an organization to include practices and activities to meet objectives through the creation of multiple outputs. Some organizations operate with processes that are either ill defined or undocumented, resulting in inconsistent activities performed and different outputs of differing quality, depending on the individual performing the process. For example, if cyber vulnerabilities are scanned monthly using tool A by employee A and the highly critical vulnerabilities are patched, or fixed, within 7 days, this will provide different results than the employee B using tool B and fixing all vulnerabilities found within 60 days. It would be difficult to be able to articulate the risk posture of the organization if multiple approaches are implemented, as it would be dependent on the individual performing the work. The act of documenting the processes would uncover the use of Tools A and B in use as well and raise the question, "Why are we using two tools, training, and the need for integration to perform the same function?" The different results that come from multiple processes create different outcomes and increase risk.

Undocumented cybersecurity processes create an efficiency and effectiveness issue, as (1) it is assumed that everyone is doing the same thing each time, (2) the processes cannot be universally improved upon, (3) time is wasted communicating processes, (4) junior team members do not have the ability to learn from more senior knowledge of "best practices," and (5) the wheel is reinvented again and again. The lack of documented cybersecurity processes and charts depicting who is responsible, accountable, consulted, and informed (RACI charts) lead to processes being missed, assumptions that processes are being executed when they are not, and uncertainty as to who owns the process and is accountable when the process fails.

Having well-defined processes is important for any business process, so why the particular attention on processes with respect to cybersecurity? The answer is simple: even the slightest failure in one of these processes can cause issues with confidential disclosure, availability, or data integrity of the systems in place to support the mission. In the above example (of not having a consistent vulnerability and patch management process), this could result in critical security vulnerabilities existing on the system that could be exploited by external hackers or insiders, or through carelessness. Executive leadership may assume that the processes are in place and they are being executed on a consistent basis, only to find out that the process was never implemented, the tool was removed, or the individual performing that task was pulled onto another project and no one was informed that the process was no longer being executed. Unnecessary duplication of software application tools and training costs also results.

NO INTRINSIC MOTIVATION TO DOCUMENT

Information technology professionals generally dislike creating documentation of processes since this takes time away from exploring the new technology, creating new applications and databases, or resolving a system or end-user issue. Without clear direction and governance in place to ensure that process development is an organizational priority to support effective and efficient execution to meet the organizational mission, these processes are unlikely to be created, and it should not be assumed that they are. Various standards and frameworks such as ISO 9000 and the International Standards for Assurance Engagements (ISAE) 402 impose documented processes. Specifically, for security, ISO 27001 processes and their artifacts are reviewed by the ISO 27001 registrar to ensure compliance.

Move Routine Actions to Operations

Information security personnel are more expensive resources relative to the computer operations areas that have been optimized for efficiency. Thus, these resources should be leveraged to design the most appropriate processes, with the view of moving these processes to a production operation as soon as possible, executed by less expensive resources. In the preceding vulnerability management example, most of the running of the vulnerability reports could be run by an external security operations center (SOC), or a managed security services provider (MSSP) that operates the process and patches the vulnerabilities according to the risk acceptance level and the priority established by the cybersecurity team designing the process.

This frees up the cybersecurity professional to focus on other high-value efforts versus spending time managing the "routine" operational work. The cybersecurity team could be focused on the exception reports or those cybersecurity items that need further analysis and other potential technology tools to mitigate effectively.

LEVERAGING ISACA COBIT 5 PROCESSES

COBIT 5 processes describe an organized set of practices and activities to achieve certain objectives and produce a set of outputs in support of achieving cybersecurity objectives aligned to enterprise objectives. The processes shown as an appendix to this chapter in Table 9.1, "Cybersecurity Risk and Process Capabilities," are adapted from two professional guides designed to assist in the understanding and implementation of the COBIT 5 Framework, specifically the ISACA COBIT 5 Implementation (COBIT 5, 2012) and COBIT 5 for Information Security (COBIT, 2012) Professional Guides. It clearly presents common business scenarios alongside their corresponding risks and capabilities.

TABLE 9.1 Cybersecurity Risk and Process Capabilities

Risk Sources and COBIT 5 Process Capabilities

Risk Sources		COBIT 5 Process Capabilities
If the scenario is relevant and inherently likely …	*… given these threats*	*… then consider whether these COBIT 5 processes need improvement. Note: In this column, next to each process number is an example from the process to consider. These are not the process names.*
Benefit/Value Enablement Risk		
IT program selection	Incorrect programs selected for implementation and misaligned with corporate strategy and priorities	Alignment of cybersecurity with IT and business frameworks (APO02)
	Duplication among different initiatives	Cybersecurity is integrated with architecture (APO03)
	New and important program creates long-term incompatibility with the enterprise architecture	Innovation promoted in cybersecurity (APO04)
		Establish cybersecurity target investments (APO05)
		Cybersecurity requirements in feasibility study (BAI01)
New technologies	Failure to adopt and exploit new technologies (i.e., functionality, optimization) in a timely manner	Measure effectiveness, efficiency and capacity of cybersecurity resources against business need (EDM04)
	New and important technology trends not identified	Define target state for cybersecurity (APO02)
	Inability to use technology to realize desired outcomes (e.g., failure to make required business model or organizational changes)	IT and cybersecurity architecture aligned with current technology trends (APO03)
		Scan external environment and identify emerging cybersecurity trends (APO04)
		Create feasible new technology solutions while minimizing risk (BAI02)
		Integrate cybersecurity in new technology design (BAI03)
Technology selection	Incorrect technologies (i.e., cost, performance, features, compatibility) selected for implementation	Develop clear information security criteria (APO02)
		Cybersecurity architecture is aligned and evolves with changes (APO03)
		Cybersecurity specifications in line with design (BAI03)
		Security impacts of technology selection (APO13)

IT investment decision making	Business managers or representatives not involved in important IT investment decision making regarding new applications, prioritization, or new technology opportunities	Value management direction and/or oversight for cybersecurity (EDM02) Business and cybersecurity involvement in IT strategic planning (APO02) Cybersecurity Investment fit with target enterprise architecture (APO03) Cybersecurity investments allocated by risk appetite (APO05) Develop cybersecurity budget (APO06) Understanding of business how cybersecurity enables/affects it (APO08) Program management stage-gating (BAI01)
Accountability over IT	Business not assuming accountability over those IT areas it should such as functional requirements, development priorities, and assessing opportunities through new technologies	Executive management accountability for cybersecurity related decisions (EDM01-05) Business, IT-related, and cybersecurity roles and responsibilities (APO01) Clear and approved service agreements including cybersecurity (APO09) Supplier relationship and requirements based on risk profile (APO10) Visible leadership through executive commitment to cybersecurity (BAI05)
IT project termination	Projects that are failing due to cost, delays, scope creep, or changed business priorities not terminated in a timely manner	Cybersecurity roles, reporting and monitoring established (EDM05) Value governance monitoring (EDM02) Resource governance monitoring (EDM04) Program/project management stage-gating (BAI01) Effective portfolio management decision making (APO05) Investment monitoring (APO06) Cybersecurity monitoring process and procedure (MEA01)

(continued)

TABLE 9.1 (*Continued*)

Benefit/Value Enablement Risk

IT project economics	Isolated IT project budget overrun	GEIT policies, organization structures and roles (EDM01)
	Consistent and important IT projects budget overruns	Value governance monitoring (EDM02)
	Absence of view on portfolio and project economics	Resource governance monitoring (EDM04)
		Cybersecurity Investment monitoring (APO06)
		Independent project assessment to ensure cybersecurity requirements included (BAI01)

Program/Project Delivery Risk

Architectural agility and flexibility	Complex and inflexible IT architecture obstructing further evolution and expansion	Define information security expectations (APO01)
		Governance over resource optimization (EDM04)
		Responsive cybersecurity planning (APO02)
		Maintenance of enterprise architecture aligned with cybersecurity (APO03)
		Cybersecurity innovation is promoted (APO04)
		Portfolio management decision making (APO05)
		Agile development life cycle methods include cybersecurity (BAI02,03)
		Maintaining security in an agile and flexible environment (APO13)
Integration of IT within business processes	Extensive dependency and use of end-user computing and ad hoc solutions for important information needs	GEIT policies, organization structures and roles (EDM01)
		Business and IT-related roles and responsibilities (APO01)
	Separate and nonintegrated IT solutions to support business processes	Define cybersecurity strategy and align with IT and business strategies (APO02)
		Align cybersecurity and enterprise architecture (APO03)

		Stakeholders recognize cybersecurity as enabler (APO08) Definition and understanding of business requirements and cybersecurity aspects (BAI02) Define cybersecurity specifications with high-level design (BAI03) Managing organizational changes with regard to cybersecurity (BAI05)
Software implementation	Operational glitches when new software is made operational Users not prepared to use and exploit new application software	Monitor security quality metrics (APO11) Project management (BAI01) Requirements definitions (BAI02) Solution development (BAI03) Managing organizational changes with regards to software implementation (BAI05) Cybersecurity requirements incorporated into infrastructure, process, and application changes (BAI06) Ensure cybersecurity acceptance in test plan (BAI07) Cybersecurity knowledge support through awareness training (BAI08)
Project delivery	Occasional late IT project delivery by internal development department Routinely important delays in IT project delivery Excessive delays in outsourced IT development project	GEIT policies, organization structures and roles (EDM01) Value governance monitoring (EDM02) Investment monitoring (APO06) Program/project management planning and monitoring (BAI01)
Project quality	Insufficient quality of project deliverables due to software, documentation, or compliance with functional requirements	Architecture standards and reuse of cybersecurity components (APO03) Consistent and effective quality management activities (APO11) Program/project quality management planning and monitoring (BAI01)

(*continued*)

TABLE 9.1   (*Continued*)

Service Delivery/IT Operations Risk

State of infrastructure technology	Obsolete IT technology cannot satisfy new business requirements such as networking, security, and storage	Resource management direction and/or oversight (EDM04) Identify potential cybersecurity gaps (APO02) Align cybersecurity and enterprise architecture (APO03) Identifying important cybersecurity trends (APO04) Maintaining security infrastructure (BAI03) Planning for and addressing capacity and performance issues (BAI04) Identify cybersecurity requirements for assets (BAI09)
Ageing of application software	Application software that is old, poorly documented, expensive to maintain, difficult to extend or not integrated in current architecture	Resource management direction and/or oversight (EDM04) Define target state for cybersecurity (APO02) Maintaining enterprise architecture (APO03) Identifying new and important cybersecurity trends (APO04) Maintaining applications with cybersecurity (BAI03) Identify cybersecurity requirements for assets (BAI09) Business process controls (DSS06)
Regulatory compliance	Noncompliance with regulations of accounting or manufacturing	GEIT compliance policies and roles (EDM01) Policies and guidance on regulatory compliance (APO01) Planning for regulatory requirements (APO02) Identifying and defining regulatory requirements (BAI02) Monitoring compliance requirements and current status (MEA03)
Selection/ performance of third-party suppliers	Inadequate support and services delivered by vendors, not in line with SLAs	Effective supplier selection, management, and relationships based on cybersecurity risk (APO10)

	Inadequate performance of outsourcer in large-scale, long-term outsourcing arrangement	Ensure cybersecurity part of procurement planning (BAI03)
Infrastructure theft	Theft of laptop with sensitive data Theft of a substantial number of development servers	Policies and guidance on protection of assets (APO01) References and background checks on new hires and contractors (APO07) Protection of critical assets during maintenance activities (BAI03) Physical security measures (DSS05)
Destruction of infrastructure	Destruction of data center due to sabotage or other causes Accidental destruction of individual laptops	Environmental protection and facilities management (DSS01) Physical security measures (DSS05)
IT staff	Departure or extended unavailability of key IT staff Key development team leaving the enterprise Inability to recruit IT staff	Use certification to develop cybersecurity skill set and enable retention (APO07) Managing tacit knowledge (BAI08)
IT expertise and skills	Lack or mismatch of IT-related skills within IT due to new technologies or other causes Lack of business understanding by IT staff	Definition and development of business and cybersecurity staff competency requirements (APO07) Cybersecurity knowledge support through awareness training (BAI08)
Software integrity	Intentional modification of software leading to wrong data or fraudulent actions Unintentional modification of software leading to unexpected results Unintentional configuration and change management errors	Definition of cybersecurity control requirements (BAI02) Cybersecurity requirements incorporated into infrastructure, process and application changes (BAI06) Ensure cybersecurity part of acceptance testing (BAI07) Establish cybersecurity configuration baselines (BAI10) Access controls (DSS05) Business process controls (DSS06)

(continued)

TABLE 9.1 (*Continued*)

Service Delivery/IT Operations Risk

Infrastructure (hardware)	Misconfiguration of hardware components Damage of critical servers in the computer room due to accident or other causes Intentional tampering with hardware such as security devices	Protection of critical assets during maintenance activities (BAI03) Physical security measures (DSS05) Establish cybersecurity configuration baselines (BAI10)
Software performance	Regular software malfunctioning of critical application software Intermittent performance problems with important system software	Software development quality assurance (BAI03) Planning for and addressing capacity and performance issues (BAI04) Root cause analysis and problem resolution (DSS03)
System capacity	Inability of systems to handle transaction volumes when user volumes increase Inability of systems to handle system load when new applications or initiatives are deployed	Architecture principles for scalability and agility (APO03) Maintaining infrastructure (BAI03) Planning for and addressing capacity and performance issues (BAI04)
Ageing of infrastructural software	Use of unsupported versions of operating system software Use of old database system	Resource management direction and/or oversight (EDM04) Recognizing and strategically addressing current IT capability issues (APO02) Maintaining enterprise architecture (APO03) Identifying new and important technology trends (APO04) Maintaining infrastructure (BAI03) Problems relating to business process controls (DSS03)
Malware	Intrusion of malware on critical operational servers Regular infection of laptops with malware	Policies and guidance on use of software (APO01) Malicious software detection (DSS05)

Logical attacks	Virus attack Unauthorized users trying to break into systems Denial-of-service attack Web site defacing Industrial espionage	Policies and guidance on protection and use of IT assets (APO01) Security requirements in solutions (BAI03) Access controls and security monitoring (DSS05)
Information media	Loss/disclosure of portable media (e.g., CD, universal serial bus [USB] drives, portable disks) containing sensitive data Loss of backup media Accidental disclosure of sensitive information due to failure to follow information handling guidelines	Policies and guidance on protection and use of IT assets (APO01) Protection of mobile and/or removable storage and media devices (DSS05-06)
Utilities performance	Intermittent utilities (e.g., telecom, electricity) failure Regular, extended utilities failures	Relationships/management of key utility suppliers (APO08) Environmental protection and facilities management (DSS01)
Industrial action	Inaccessible facilities and building due to labor union strike Unavailable key staff due to industrial action	Staff relationships and key individuals (APO07) Managing staff knowledge (BAI08)
Data(base) integrity	Intentional modification of data (e.g., accounting, security-related data, sales figures) Database (e.g., client or transactions database) corruption	Information architecture and data classification (APO03) Development standards (BAI03) Change management (BAI06) Managing data storage (DSS01) Access controls (DSS05)
Logical trespassing	Users circumventing logical access rights Users obtaining access to unauthorized information Users stealing sensitive data	Policies and guidance on protection and use of IT assets (APO01) Access controls and security monitoring (DSS05) Contract staff policies (APO07)
Operational IT errors	Operator errors during backup, upgrades of systems, or maintenance of systems Incorrect information input	Staff training (APO07) Operations procedures (DSS01) Business process controls (DSS06)

(continued)

TABLE 9.1 (*Continued*)

Service Delivery/IT Operations Risk

Contractual compliance	Noncompliance with software license agreements (e.g., use and/or distribution of unlicensed software) Contractual obligations as service provider with customers/clients not met	Monitoring service agreements (APO09) Supplier agreements and relationship monitoring (APO10) Software license management (DSS02) Contractual compliance requirements and current status monitoring (MEA03)
Environmental	Use of equipment that is not environmentally friendly (e.g., high level of power consumption packaging)	Incorporation of environmentally friendly principles in enterprise architecture (APO03) Selection of solutions and procurement policies (BAI03) Environmental and facilities management (DSS01)
Acts of nature	Earthquake Tsunami Major storm/hurricane Major wildfire	Environmental and facilities management (DSS01) Physical security (DSS05) Manage continuity (DSS04)

Adapted with the kind permission of ISACA 2016.

The risks related to information technology implementations are noted as "risk sources" in the matrix, and a sampling of the COBIT 5 processes that could be used to mitigate the risk are shown in the far right column as COBIT 5 Process Capabilities. The COBIT 5 Framework contains processes for the enablement of information technology, much of which can apply to cybersecurity practices. The COBIT 5 for Information Security Professional Guide extends the definition of these processes by adding processes specific to cybersecurity.

Components of the Cybersecurity Processes

Each of the cybersecurity processes has a life cycle by which the process is defined, created, monitored, updated, and subsequently retired. New technologies are introduced that may negate the need for a process or significantly alter the process. For example, a cybersecurity policy in the past may have required that sensitive files be placed on a network server and not on the laptop or desktop. A change to the process, by moving to a cloud storage provider with contractual backups or implementing laptops with encryption and backup software, may remove the need to store information on a central network server to ensure the contents are appropriately backed up on a regular schedule.

The cybersecurity process components would include the process description; identification of stakeholders (internal and external), goals, life cycle, and good practices (i.e., process practices, activities, work product inputs and outputs); as well as including metrics for achieving and monitoring the goals and ensuring the stakeholder needs are met.

Cybersecurity Practices and Activities

Enabling processes are developed from practices, activities, and creating detailed activities through increasing levels of detail. Practices are statements of action that develop benefits, provide the appropriate level of risk, and manage the appropriate level of resources to meet the business objectives.

An example of a security-specific practice to support the *Manage Security Services* process would be *Manage Endpoint Security*. This practice would ensure that endpoints (laptop, desktop, server, and other mobile and network devices or software) are secured at a level that is equal to or greater than the defined security requirements of the information processed, stored, or transmitted. Inputs to the process could include the information security architecture, service-level agreements, physical inventory audits, or reports of violations of security of these devices. These practices are somewhat generic and may be adapted for the needs of each enterprise. The organization also decides, through the governing bodies, which practices would apply, the frequency of the practice execution, how the practice is applied (manual or through automated means), and the acceptance of the risk if the practice is not implemented.

Cybersecurity-specific activities provide guidance to achieve the practices. Activities are, in short, the primary actions taken to operate the process. Each of the practices will have a set of either COBIT 5 activities or cybersecurity-specific activities to achieve the operation of the practice. Continuing the *Manage Endpoint Security* practice example, some of the cybersecurity activities may be to configure the endpoints in a secure manner, categorize the types of endpoints and the control needs, identify potential entry point targets of the endpoints, analyze the target attractiveness for each endpoint, implement network monitoring on devices, dispose of endpoints securely, and examine the history of attacks and compare against the current endpoint population.

These activities would be based on generally accepted and good practices. These provide a sufficient level of detail to achieve the cybersecurity-specific practice, would support definition of clear organizational responsibilities (i.e., RACI charts, governance structures), and support the development of more detailed procedures. Some processes may need to be more detailed than others depending on the criticality of the activity and the experience level of the group performing the task.

Different Types of Cybersecurity Processes Work Together

The processes need the input from other enablers to be effective. For example, processes need information as input and also provide information as output to other processes and enablers. The five domains of processes are (1) evaluate, direct, and monitor (EDM); (2) align, plan, and organize (APO); (3) build, acquire, and implement (BAI); (4) deliver, service, and support (DSS); and (5) monitor, evaluate, and assess (MEA).

Evaluate, Direct, and Monitor (EDM) Domain   The EDM domain of processes is geared at providing governance for cybersecurity and is focused on ensuring that the appropriate direction is provided and monitoring mechanisms are in place. Processes to ensure a governance framework and maintenance, benefits delivery, risk optimization, resource optimization, and stakeholder transparency are specified. For example, from Table 9.1, the risk "Obsolete IT technology cannot satisfy new business requirements such as networking, security, and storage" would be addressed through process capability EDM04—Resource Management Direction and/or Oversight. Judgment would be made on whether or not the current cybersecurity resources (people, process, or technology) are sufficient to satisfy the needs of the business. A laptop may have had sufficient processing power, memory, and storage in the past when encryption was not required; however, now that encryption is loaded on the device along with other security controls, the device may no longer be adequate.

Align, Plan, and Organize (APO) Domain   The APO domain of processes contains cybersecurity management processes that are helpful to embed cybersecurity within the IT management framework. They also align the cybersecurity strategy, define the architectural components necessary to support the enterprise architecture, manage the cybersecurity portfolio, set a budget and provision expenses for breaches, manage the training process for cybersecurity professionals, obtain vendor service-level agreements for outsourced services, identify risk and treatment plans, manage cybersecurity innovation with new technologies, and other management practices. Essentially, the APO cybersecurity process capabilities ensure that cybersecurity is appropriately inserted into the processes to support the development of existing and new technology to meet the business objectives.

Build, Acquire, and Implement (BAI) Domain The BAI domain defines process capabilities to assist in the execution of the cybersecurity program. Such capabilities include processes for defining cybersecurity requirements, selecting cybersecurity solutions, embedding cybersecurity in change management processes, managing normal and emergency changes, managing the collective knowledge of cybersecurity practices across the organization, and managing requirements risk. Project management practices are crucial to ensuring that the solutions selected meet the business requirements in a timely and budget-sensitive manner.

Deliver, Service, and Support (DSS) Domain The DSS domain defines those process capabilities that provide operational support and "keep the cybersecurity lights on." These apply to outsourced services as well as internally run services. The cybersecurity operations management is developed with input from the security architecture, information security policies, and facilities information. A process capability exists for identifying, classifying, escalating, and managing security incidents; managing the ticketing system for cybersecurity items; managing problems through root cause analysis and reducing the likelihood of reoccurrence; managing crises, and ensuring that an appropriate business continuity plan and disaster recovery of IT-related equipment and data are in place. Incident response and recovery operations should be integrated with the overall business continuity management program. A key control today for recovering from ransomware attacks is the restoration of the data files using the backups obtained through the documented disaster recovery process. If these controls are not in place and integrated with business continuity, data may be unrecoverable, and if effective processes are not defined, the delay in processing may be unacceptable.

Monitor, Evaluate, and Assess (MEA) Domain This set of management process capabilities in the MEA domain provides the cybersecurity monitoring, self-assessments, and ensuring that reporting requirements satisfying compliance with various laws and regulations are being executed properly. Periodic reviews of cybersecurity through a formal approach are defined. Corrective cybersecurity actions are also tracked and performance is reported. These processes ensure that the appropriate internal control mechanisms for cybersecurity are developed and operating effectively.

COBIT 5 DOMAINS SUPPORT COMPLETE CYBERSECURITY LIFE CYCLE

Each of the COBIT 5 domains contributes to the maturing of the cybersecurity program processes by contributing either governance or management practices and related activities to address the planning, building, or ongoing operation of the cybersecurity environment. The processes are the enablers to provide the who, what, when, and where actions that need to be taken. Holistically, this reduces the risk that actions necessary to protect the confidentiality, integrity, and availability of the information critical to the business are missed.

Why Use a COBIT 5 Process Enabler Approach?

There are other approaches available for specifying cybersecurity control environments, such as NIST Special Publication 800-53, Revision 4, Security and Privacy Controls for Federal Information Systems and Organizations. The purpose of Special Publication 800-53 is to provide guidelines for selecting and specifying security controls for information systems supporting executive agencies of the federal government. The NIST model, in contrast to the COBIT 5 model, is very prescriptive in nature and may be overwhelming to many organizations. These are very detailed definitions and may be best used to compliment and help develop the organization-specific detailed activities to perform the COBIT 5 practices, which in turn, as indicated in the previous section, support the overarching cybersecurity process.

The Center for Internet Security (CIS) and the Centre for the Protection of National Infrastructure (CPNI) promote the *Top 20 Critical Controls* to provide a prioritized set of cybersecurity practices to reduce the risk of cyber attack. These are technical-based controls such as ensuring that accurate inventories of authorized and unauthorized devices are available, secure configurations are created, vulnerabilities are assessed and remediated, administrative privileges are controlled, and so forth, prioritized with increased level-of-control importance. The idea is that by mitigating these cybersecurity gaps the bar is raised for the external hacker to gain access. The controls are important, and this process differs from the COBIT 5 approach as there is less focus on development of processes to support the business objectives and the primary focus is on the technical controls that need to be implemented. These controls, as with the NIST 800-53 controls, are useful in building the detailed activities to support the processes and practices needed; however, the COBIT 5 process enablers are necessary to ensure the right cybersecurity activities are performed efficiently and effectively. These constructs are not readily apparent by using solely the Top 20 critical controls.

The ISO/IEC 27001 security techniques for Information Security Management Systems (ISMS) and the Information Security Forum Standard of Good Practice for Information Security can be used to supplement the processes of the five domains of the COBIT 5 for Information Security framework. The relevant guidance in these standards, along with the NIST 800-53 controls, has been mapped to the COBIT 5 Framework in the COBIT 5 for Information Security Appendices. Using the COBIT 5 framework and the associated processes provides the overarching governance and management assurance that adequate cybersecurity coverage exists from the governance and planning of cybersecurity activities through to the ongoing operation and measurement of the program.

So What Does CEO Tom Get Out of the Process Enablers?

Using the COBIT 5 process enablers provides a very holistic set of cybersecurity processes to manage the cyber risk management system. Once Tom has implemented these processes, it will be clear who in the organization is accountable and responsible for each of the governance and management practices supporting cybersecurity treatment processes, and who else needs to be involved to change or implement the process by being informed or consulted. Tom will have a clear definition of the cybersecurity governance and management practices necessary to achieve each of the cybersecurity processes that make up the cybersecurity program. Tom will also have assurance that the detailed activities are defined and based on good practices, leveraging those technical definitions defined by other standards built on good practices at that level. He will also have the comfort that processes are in place to ensure that the risks inherent in implementing technology have associated processes to mitigate the risk.

Moreover, Tom will have assurance that resources spent on executing processes will add value to the organization by creating cybersecurity-specific outputs used as inputs to follow-on processes, which, taken together, holistically support the business objectives of Tom's organization. Continual review of the processes aids in making clear decisions on the cybersecurity priorities and those processes that need additional investment, or those that can be discontinued or moved to a lower cost of support. Tom will have an integrated program covering multiple processes to support the organization, people, and technology with metrics to measure the effectiveness and efficiency of the cybersecurity program.

CONCLUSION

The following cyber risk management statement represents those organization capabilities CEO and board expect to be demonstrated in terms of *treating cyber risk using process capabilities.*

TREATING CYBER RISKS USING PROCESS CAPABILITIES

Cybersecurity process capabilities provide the governance and management practices necessary to effectively and efficiently align the cybersecurity program with the business enterprise objectives. Detailed activities are developed to support the cybersecurity practices to provide governance (evaluate, direct, and monitor), manage (align, plan, and organize the work), create solutions (build acquire and implement), sustain (deliver, service, and support), and improve (monitor, evaluate, and assess). These processes form a cybersecurity life cycle with defined inputs and outputs based on generally accepted good practices that, taken together holistically, can serve to reduce the organizational cybersecurity risk.

ABOUT ISACA

As an independent, nonprofit, global association, ISACA engages in the development, adoption and use of globally accepted, industry-leading knowledge and practices for information systems. Previously known as the Information Systems Audit and Control Association, ISACA now goes by its acronym only, to reflect the broad range of IT governance professionals it serves. Incorporated in 1969, ISACA today serves 140,000 professionals in 180 countries. ISACA provides practical guidance, benchmarks, and other effective tools for all enterprises that use information systems. Through its comprehensive guidance and services, ISACA defines the roles of information systems governance, security, audit, and assurance professionals worldwide. The COBIT framework and the CISA, CISM, CGEIT, and CRISC certifications are ISACA brands respected and used by these professionals for the benefit of their enterprises.

ABOUT TODD FITZGERALD

Todd is the global director of information security for Grant Thornton International, Ltd., providing strategic information security leadership for Grant Thornton member firms, supporting 42,000 employees in 140 countries. Todd is an ISACA member, prior Information Security Risk Management conference chair, thought leader, and frequent international speaker. Leading large company information security programs for 19 years, Todd is the 2016 Chicago CISO of the Year awarded by ISACA, ISSA, AITP, Infragard, and SIM. Todd is also a 2013 Top 50 Information Security Executive, 2013–2016 Ponemon Institute Distinguished Fellow, and top-rated RSA conference speaker. He is the author of three books (*Information Security Governance Simplified: From the Boardroom to the Keyboard; CISO Leadership: Essential Principles for Success* [ISC2 Press]; and *2014 Certified Chief Information Security Officer (C-CISO) Body of Knowledge*) and a contributor to a dozen others.

CHAPTER 10

Treating Cyber Risks—Using Insurance and Finance

Aon Global Cyber Solutions
Kevin Kalinich, Esq., Aon Risk Solutions Global Cyber Insurance Practice Leader, USA

CEO Tom's objectives include growing sales and reducing costs by efficiently increasing reliance on technology and data analytics. While Tara, his chairperson, and her board of directors are happy with the optimistic financial projections based in part on Tom's embracing technology, the board has also inquired as to whether technology and information asset reliance increases risk to the financial statements from cyber exposures. Can Tom's organization build a quantitative model that addresses cyber exposures in order to maximize efficient allocation of resources, budget, and reporting? If so, can cyber exposures be quantified and cyber risk transferred to insurers in an effective manner? Tom rose to the challenge. He saw to it that his chief financial officer, Gloria, and chief risk officer, Nathan, were collaborating with key internal stakeholders (such as the general counsel, human resources, sales and marketing, product development, treasury, chief information officer [CIO], chief information security officer [CISO], and chief security officer [CSO]) and that they were developing a cyber risk transfer solution aligned with their organization's enterprise risk management system in order to address the total cost of risk (TCOR).[1]

TAILORING A QUANTIFIED COST-BENEFIT MODEL

The reason for the board's ask is simple. A cyber breach, no matter what kind or if it makes the front page of the paper, could have an impact on the organization's balance sheet.[2] The global cost of cybercrime is predicted to hit $6 trillion annually by 2021.[3] This is mapped in Figure 10.1. (D&O Policy is a directors and officers policy.)

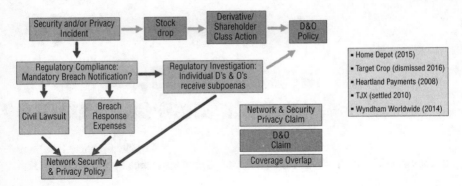

FIGURE 10.1 Financial statement impact

Constraints on Financial Impact Modeling

While we hear about the big cyber hacks, like Sony, TJ Maxx, and the massive October 21, 2016, Internet of Things (IoT)-facilitated attack on Dyn, there are many types of cyber risks that could have a materially negative impact on an organization. System failures, employee mistakes, and simple negligence, such as leaving a laptop or thumb drive in a taxi, are some of the noncriminal cyber perils that can lead to material financial economic losses. In fact, the average cost of a cyber breach ranges from $2 million to nearly $8 million, with eight incidents over $75 million and the largest losses over $300 million, according to publicly disclosed documents.[4] (*Note:* All dollar values in this chapter are U.S. dollars).

However, large portions of the cyber incident studies include damage estimates of subjective intangible assets that are difficult to quantify and almost impossible to insure. For instance, brand and reputation are often cited as the largest portion of a breach loss, which are speculative and largely uninsurable. Similarly, how can one calculate the value of the trade secrets disclosed as part of the 2016 Mossack Fonseca law firm Panama Papers breach? The same issues arise for loss of confidential information regarding mergers and acquisitions from investment banks or new formulas and technology innovations such as algorithms, design plans, and secret proprietary products. The value of trade secrets, proprietary information, and patent infringement is almost impossible to quantify and is virtually uninsurable.

Modeling the Cost-Benefits of Investments in Insurance versus Cybersecurity

Until we develop quantitative models that equate the actual dollar cost of an incident with the return on investment for total mitigation on a *macro*-enterprise level, organizations are simply spending money on information technology security to address *micro*-level issues. Is antivirus software important? Yes, but it is one of literally hundreds of measures and only a small part of cyber exposure issues. Does deployment of enterprise security governance practices moderate the cost of cyber perils? Yes, but what is the marginal incremental benefit of each dollar deployed for cyber risk prevention? Can we measure the total cost of risk value to an organization buying cyber insurance compared to the total cost of risk value of information technology (IT) security in the network layer, versus detection, versus remediation, versus incident response, versus employee training and awareness? Any cyber intelligence system is only as secure as the weakest link in the system, including the people who use it. Cyber insurance underwriters expect such controls to be deployed (along with many others) and that will influence the insurance premium to be paid and scope of coverage obtained.

The CFO should consider modeling their organization's cyber exposure frequency and severity. Figure 10.2 shows one way to frame example cyber exposures to start the quantification process.

Once completed, the CFO can compare the costs involved and perform a cost-benefit analysis of investing another dollar in IT security versus insurance. According to Aon's actual cyber loss claims data, measurable and insurable cyber damage losses are approximately as follows[5]:

- 80 percent = Total damages < $1 million
- 15 percent = Total damages between $1 million and $20 million

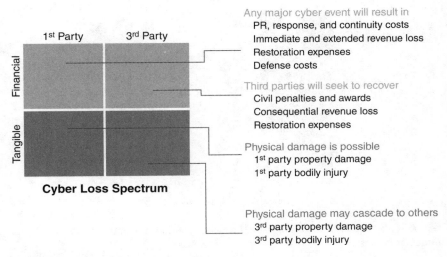

FIGURE 10.2 Cyber risk impacts all quadrants

- 5 percent = Total damages > $20 million (with certain events exceeding $100 million)
- Average = $3.8 million; range between $0 and $300+ million.[6]

Cyber Losses Underinsured Compared to Property Losses

How does this compare to potential losses from other organization perils, such as fires? The probability of any particular building burning down is much less than 1 percent. Yet most organizations spend multiples more in premiums for fire insurance than cyber insurance even though they state in their publicly disclosed documents that a majority of the organization's value is attributed to intangible assets.

The Ponemon Institute conducted the first global research report[7] to examine how entities understand and compare tangible property versus intangible information risks. Figures 10.3 through 10.6 are drawn from this report.

Figure 10.3 represents for organizations the relative value of certain tangible assets (property, plant and equipment) versus certain intangible assets (primarily information assets), with the implication that tangible assets are barely more valuable than intangible assets.

Figure 10.4 compares the total value of the loss that could result from damage to tangible assets versus the loss that could result from damage

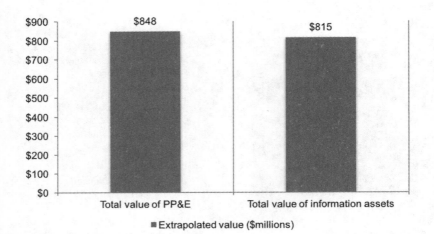

FIGURE 10.3   Asset value comparison: Property, plant and equipment (PP&E) versus information assets

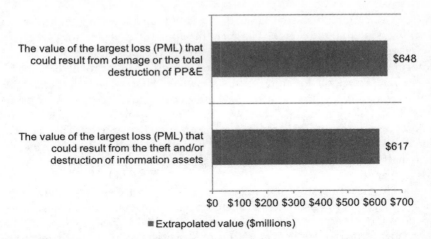

FIGURE 10.4 Probable maximum loss (PML) value for PP&E versus information assets

to intangible assets. Again, the predicted losses to tangible and intangible assets are relatively close.

Cyber-related threats are considered "intangible perils" to organizations and insurers. Figure 10.5 represents for organizations the relative potential financial statement impact of business interruption caused by tangible perils

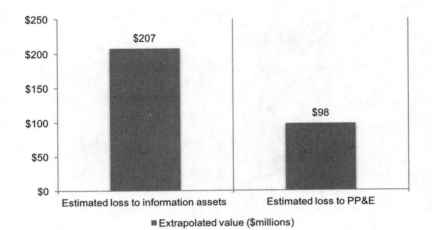

FIGURE 10.5 Impact of business interruption

(i.e., weather, tangible asset damage) versus intangible perils (i.e., malware, hacking, system failure, etc.). These are in estimated dollar terms.

Figure 10.6 represents for organizations the percentage of losses to information assets covered by insurance compared to that for PP&E.

These Ponemon Institute results shown in Figures 10.3 through 10.6 collectively indicate that cyber losses are underinsured compared to property losses. They indicate over four times more insurance cover levels for PP&E over information assets (51 percent over 12 percent). This, despite the value of the assets and largest losses being equal and PPE accounting for only half the comparable business interruption impact ($98 PP&E vs. $207 for information assets).

Such research results also suggest a road map for CFO's to advise their risk managers. CFO's should advise how to appropriately allocate insurance spend on an enterprise-wide risk management (ERM) basis by considering a broader approach to their organization's overall risk profile.[8] Below are a few tips to consider:

- Information technology assets are 39 percent more exposed than property assets on a relative value to insurance protection basis.
- Proliferation of mobile devices, ransomware, social media, third-party vendors/cloud computing, Big Data analytics, and IoT to send cyber risk

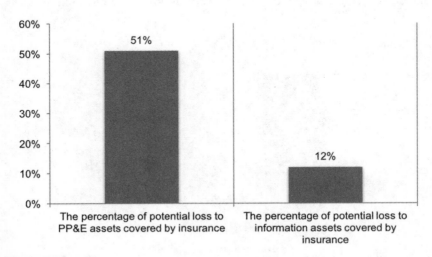

FIGURE 10.6 Information assets covered by insurance compared to PP&E

skyrocketing over next five years (e.g., projected growth in the use of Internet-connected devices will grow from 10 to 50 billion).[9]

- Thirty-seven percent of companies surveyed experienced a "material or significantly disruptive security exploit or data breach one or more times during the past two years, and the average economic impact of the event was $2.1 million."[10]

- The most frequent type of incident was a cyber attack that caused disruption to business and IT operations (48 percent of respondents) followed by 35 percent of respondents who say it was a system or business process failure that caused disruption to business operations.

- Catastrophic cyber losses can result in potential D&O allegations.
    - Process and documentation of determining cyber exposures and considering alternative solutions (such as cyber insurance) could assist in satisfying D&O fiduciary duties with respect to cyber assets.

- Underwriting and purchasing of cyber insurance process can assist to:
    - Satisfy customer and partner cyber insurance contract requirements (i.e., *increase sales*).
    - Stabilize balance sheet, including reduce earnings volatility.
    - Address regulatory guidelines.
    - Reduce TCOR.
    - Enable organization-wide cyber risk management culture.
    - Align cyber insurance solution with enterprise-wide risk management.
    - Avoid D&O allegations.

PLANNING FOR CYBER RISK INSURANCE

Organizations should regularly look at their evolving cyber exposures and solutions to help weather a storm if an incident occurs. Risk and/or insurance managers should collaborate with business units when coordinating and agreeing to prevention, mitigation, and response plans and ensure the pitch is in the board's own language. A cyber risk insurance plan should take into account an organization's planning and desired response. There are four key steps involved.

1. Conduct Pre-Breach Education and Planning

It is important to look at pre-breach planning. Proper planning decreases the frequency likelihood and positively impacts an organization's ability to respond to an incident. A key component of planning is organization-wide education. It is not just about the IT personnel. Education should occur from the board to the basement.

2. Develop an Incident Response Plan and Crisis Management Plan[11]

An incident response plan escalating to a crisis management plan outlines responsibilities, procedures, and decision trees at a high level if an incident occurs that is then not contained within standard IT incident protocols. It is important to keep such plans fresh, as technology and the cybercrime landscape continue to evolve. The plans should consider issues at an enterprise-wide level, not just IT security.

3. Create a Breach Business Continuity Plan[12]

An organization is advised to take a hard look at its capability to recover from a breach. Organizations have business continuity plans in place to weather physical perils that shut down operations. The same should be in place for cyber incidents that bring operations to a halt. This means augmenting an organization's business continuity plan to address technology breaches and the responses required to maintain operations.

4. Review or Implement Cyber Insurance

Conduct an assessment of current insurance policies, such as property and general liability, to determine the potential need for additional coverage and an insurance action plan to address same. The assessment of coverage and gaps can encourage an open dialogue about opportunities to shore up systems and procedures. It can also help identify holes in processes and protocols as well as gaps in insurance coverage that potentially could be filled with cyber insurance.

THE RISK MANAGER'S PERSPECTIVE ON PLANNING FOR CYBER INSURANCE

The risk and/or insurance managers have an important coordination role and should follow a sequence of steps.

First, they should coordinate all *four plans* summarized above.

Second, they should position *cyber insurance* treatment solutions as a subset of ERM system capabilities for the organization. Once the organization's unique cyber risks have been identified, quantified, and collaboratively prioritized, tailored ERM stakeholder protocols should include:

- Ensuring that organization leadership has an appropriate governance structure, particularly reporting on noninsurable cyber risk magnitude.
- Ensuring that the organization has appropriate training through human resources to mitigate breaches via stolen credentials or social engineering.
- Understanding specific cyber vulnerabilities associated with operations.
- Understanding the legal liabilities and financial exposure from IT systems and related customer and vendor contracts.

Third, they should review *vendors and the supply chain* to evaluate potential insurance coverage and contractual indemnities from the organization's vendors. Vendors are often the cause of the cyber peril.[13]

Fourth, they should look for *insurance gaps* by reviewing existing insurance coverages (such as property, general liability, crime, D&O, kidnap and ransom, and professional liability insurance).[14] When identifying cyber coverage gaps, it is useful to leverage external expertise. For instance, it is critical to partner with an insurance broker who has cyber policy wording customization and claims-handling expertise and to consider outside legal counsel to evaluate coverage options. The most popular current combination of cyber-related covers includes third-party defense and liability, business interruption, cyber extortion, and regulatory proceedings. It is also possible to include bodily injury, supply chain, and tangible property damage coverage from IoT exposures.

Fifth, they should prepare the mechanisms of *filing a cyber claim* well in advance of any such event, although one hopes to never file a cyber claim. Such claim mechanisms should be agreed upon in advance with the insurance carrier and set forth in the cyber insurance policy. They include:

- Retention figure your organization is comfortable with paying prior to the insurance kicking in.
- Selection of legal counsel, forensics experts, cyber assessment firms, breach notification firms and credit monitoring firms (if necessary).
- Business interruption "proof of loss" form and calculation.

Sixth, they may also want to consider the use of a *captive insurer* to address cyber exposures, which could provide policy wording flexibility, claims administration, tax advantages, and access to additional program limits.

Seventh, they must stay abreast of cyber insurance *market trends*. This market is still emerging, fast moving, and in a state of flux.

CYBER INSURANCE MARKET CONSTRAINTS

Like any market, cyber insurance is influenced by trends. Some of the trends that have the biggest impact on an organization's cyber insurance decision deal with constraints.

Regulatory Constraints

Organizations should continually review their cyber insurance in light of the growing number of country regulations. For example, the European Union's General Data Protection Regulation new rules become effective May 25, 2018. Among other provisions, these require a 72-hour notification and contemplate fines for the most serious incidents of up to 4 percent of total worldwide annual turnover. Privacy and security laws are on the horizon in other jurisdictions as well.

Capacity Constraints

Several cyber insurers announced new cyber facilities in 2016 with up to $100 million limits per placement and other new cyber capacity. This has increased the generally available stand-alone cyber limits from traditional insurance carriers from approximately $200 million (pre-2015) to approximately $400 million for most organizations in most industries. Add in the potential reinsurance capacity for some large organizations seeking catastrophic coverage and the total global capacity approaches $500 million to $1 billion in select cyber insurance programs with retentions of $10 million to $200 million-plus.

However, there are cyber capacity gaps and/or lack of insurance carrier competition in a number of areas that are in the process of being considered by the insurance market players. Aon Cyber Enterprise Solution™ policy, launched in the fourth quarter of 2016, is intended to address some of the following challenges:

- Large data aggregators with massive amounts of personally identifiable information, including personal health records, such as retail, health care, financial institutions, and hospitality (e.g., hotels and restaurants).
- Organizations with the potential for bodily injury and/or tangible property damage from purely cyber perils (e.g., manufacturing, power/energy, utilities, transportation, agribusiness, driverless cars, and the IoT-connected devices);

- Unauthorized transfer of funds via some combination of hacks (e.g., malware on a system) and social engineering (e.g., employee is tricked into sending a wire transfer at the request of a fake/imposter CFO or CEO such as the $81 million heist from the Bank of Bangladesh via the Federal Reserve Bank of New York).
- Industries where business interruption is of greater concern than breach of personal information, such as transportation, agribusiness, energy, utilities/power, and manufacturing.[15]
- Industries where the *value* of the lost information is most critical, which is generally *excluded* from today's cyber insurance policies, such as investment banks involved in mergers and acquisitions, defense contractors, research labs, and law firms (think Mossack Fonseca breach).

Insurance Placement Constraints

There are over 67 different cyber insurers with over 67 different applications, submission processes, underwriting, policy forms, and claims handling. The key to a successful go-to-market strategy is to tailor what best fits your organization context and to allow time before any potential incident. Figure 10.7 summarizes typical components that make up an optimal cyber insurance program.

Figure 10.8 summarizes minimum timings and insurer steps to place a cyber program. Organizations need to plan around these in order to place an optimal program and tap the global insurance market.

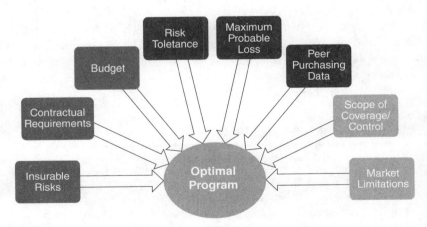

FIGURE 10.7   Optimal cyber insurance components

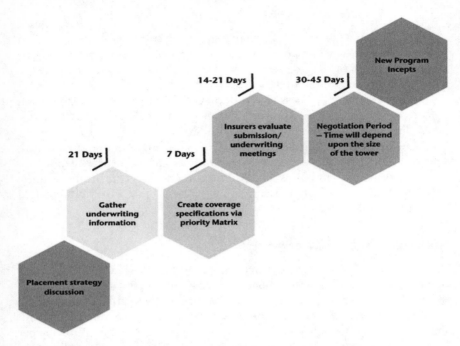

14-21 Days

30-45 Days

New Program
Incepts

21 Days

7 Days

Insurers evaluate
submission/
underwriting
meetings

Negotiation Period
– Time will depend
upon the size
of the tower

Gather
underwriting
information

Create coverage
specifications via
priority Matrix

Placement strategy
discussion

FIGURE 10.8 Cyber insurance placement minimum timings and steps

CONCLUSION

The relationship between cyber risk management and profit margin growth is stronger than correlation; it is cause and effect. The following cyber risk management statement represents those organization capabilities the CEO and board expect to be demonstrated in terms of *cyber risk insurance and risk finance.*

CYBER INSURANCE AND RISK FINANCE

Cyber incident risks are understood in terms of their potential impact on the organization balance sheet and quantified to the extent possible. The cost-benefits of investments in insurance treatment versus cybersecurity treatment are modeled and they are considered for budgeting purposes as complimentary rather than competing investments. A quantitative cost-benefit model to address cyber exposures optimizes the efficient allocation of resources, financial planning, analysis and reporting. Modeling constraints are understood, yet the process is valuable for multiple purposes. Cyber risk is effectively transferred to insurers where appropriate to organization context and where it augments existing insurance covers in accordance with the organizations overall risk management philosophy and appetite. Cyber insurance reduces the TCOR over the long term. Risk and/or insurance managers collaborate with business units when agreeing and implementing plans (i.e., pre-incident education and planning, an incident response and crisis management plan, an incident business continuity plan and, review and/or placement of cyber insurance). Risk and/or insurance managers have an important coordination role. They take appropriate steps to (1) coordinate all the above plans to properly inform management and the board of directors; (2) position cyber insurance treatment solutions as a subset of ERM system capabilities for the organization; (3) review vendors and the supply chain; (4) treat any insurance gaps in existing insurance; (5) prepare mechanisms for filing a cyber claim well in advance of the event; (6) consider the use of alternative options, such as a captive insurer; and (7) stay abreast of cyber insurance market trends, particularly for coverage, capacity, and regulatory constraints.

NOTES

1. "What to Do before, during, and after a Cyberbreach, The CEO's Guide to Cyberbreach Response, https://www.business.att.com/cybersecurity/
2. David Weldon, "A Deeper Look at Business Impact of a Cyberattack," NetworkWorld, August 24, 2016, http://www.networkworld.com/article/3111925/malware-cybercrime/a-deeper-look-at-business-impact-of-a-cyberattack.html?token=%2523tk.NWWNLE_nlt_networkworld_security_alert_2016-08-25&idg_eid=d0c19c2d69484a04b6e58c74d3dfc1b7&utm_source=Sailthru&utm_medium=email&utm_campaign=NWW%20Security%20Alert%20 2016-08-25&utm_term=networkworld_security_alert%23tk.NWW_nlt_networkworld_security_alert_2016-08-25

Above the surface, or well-known cyber incident costs:

Customer breach notifications

Post-breach customer protection

Regulatory compliance (fines)

Public relations/crises communications

Attorney fees and litigation
Cybersecurity improvements
Technical investigations
Below the surface, or hidden or less visible costs:
Insurance premium increases
Increased cost to raise debt
Operational disruption
Lost value of customer relationships
Value of lost contract revenue
Devaluation of trade name
Loss of intellectual property (IP)

3. http://cybersecurityventures.com/cybercrime-infographic/
4. IBM–Ponemon, Global Cost of Data Breach study, June 15, 2016, https://secu-rityintelligence.com/cost-of-a-data-breach-2016/. The 2016 Deloitte study cited above estimates the average costs at twice as much. Deloitte finds "hidden" costs can amount to 90 percent of the total business impact on an organization, and will most likely be experienced two years or more after the event.
5. Aon Global Risk Insight Platform 2016.
6. Deloitte, The 2016 Deloitte study: A deeper look at business impact of a cyber-attack Weldon, August 24, 2016.
7. 2015 Global Cyber Impact Study and Report, sponsored by Aon Risk Services and independently conducted by The Ponemon Institute LLC, surveyed 2,243 companies in 37 countries. http://www.aon.com/risk-services/cyber.jsp
8. Ibid.
9. Cisco, "The Internet of Everything Is the New Economy," September 29, 2015. Online at: http://www.cisco.com/c/en/us/solutions/collateral/enterprise/cisco-on-cisco/Cisco_IT_Trends_IoE_Is_the_New_Economy.html
10. Fred Kaplan, *Dark Territory: The Secret History of Cyber War,* June 2016. "The only completely secure computer is a computer that no one can use. They have given up on the idea that they can somehow make a black box that nobody can get into." http://knowledge.wharton.upenn.edu/article/the-secret-history-of-cyber-war
11. IBM–Ponemon June 15, 2016. Having an incident response team can reduce the cost of a data breach by nearly $400,000 on average, the study's authors said. Moreover, speed makes a difference. The study found that the average time to identify a breach was 201 days; the average time to contain it was 70 days. In general, breaches that were identified in fewer than 100 days cost companies an average of $3.23 million, whereas those found after the 100-day mark cost $4.38 million. Companies with business continuity management (BCM) process-es in place were ahead there, discovering breaches 52 days earlier and containing them 36 days faster than companies without, according to the study's authors.
12. Fred Kaplan, 2016. "The only completely secure computer is a computer that no one can use." Now the Pentagon, for example, is focusing more on what they call detection and resilience. In other words, the trick is to make sure that if somebody gets into your networks, you see this very quickly, and that you can repel them very quickly and repair the damage very quickly. It's come to that.

They have given up on the idea that they can somehow make a black box that nobody can get into.

13. *Affinity Gaming v. Trustwave Holdings Inc.*, 2:15-cv-02464-GMN-PAL, filed December 24, 2015, in Nevada federal court attempts to hold a third-party vendor liable after a breach.

14. Many legacy policies are silent regarding coverage for cyber exposures so courts sometimes grant coverage and sometimes deny coverage under non-cyber-specific policies. For instance, coverage was found in April 2016 under a legacy Travelers general liability policy in *Travelers Indemnity Co. of America v. Portal Healthcare Solutions LLC* (4th Circuit, April 2016). Unauthorized wire transfer for $485,000 found coverage under a crime policy in *State Bank of Bellingham v. BancInsure, Inc.* (8th Circuit, May 20, 2016). However, the trend is for insurance companies to add specific exclusions for cyber exposures to non-stand-alone cyber policies, with some exceptions.

15. In "Lights Out: A Cyberattack, A Nation Unprepared, Surviving the Aftermath," Ted Koppel, *Lights Out: A Cyberattack, A Nation Unprepared, Surviving the Aftermath*, USA, 2016 author Ted Koppel suggests that a catastrophic cyber-attack on America's power grid is likely and that we're unprepared. A 2015 Lloyd's of London/University of Cambridge report, "Business Blackout," sets forth the insurance implications of a cyber attack on the U.S. power grid. The report estimated a hypothetical worst-case scenario of $243 billion to $1,024 trillion in direct and indirect losses, with between $21.398 billion and $71.109 billion in estimated insurance industry losses.

Many property and general liability insurers are inconsistent and/or hesitant to cover cyber exposures likely because there's insufficient actuarial data. Since we don't have sufficient actuarial data for cyber exposures, we should borrow from other complex modeling situations like typhoons, earthquakes, hurricanes, and terrorism—relatively rare events that could have catastrophic impacts.

By combining an objective risk management context based on data analytics, we can learn from natural weather incidents and terrorism threats to develop robust public-private partnerships to help improve our preparedness and reduce losses stemming from a cyber attack.

A number of entities are building actuarial models and cyber resiliency best practices rating assessments, which will facilitate the growth acceleration of the cyber insurance market.

ABOUT AON

Aon plc (NYSE: AON) is a leading global provider of risk management, insurance and reinsurance brokerage, and human resources solutions and outsourcing services. Through its more than 72,000 colleagues worldwide, Aon unites to empower results for clients in over 120 countries via innovative and effective risk and people solutions and through industry-leading global resources and technical expertise. Aon has been named repeatedly as the world's best broker, best insurance intermediary, reinsurance intermediary, captives manager, and best employee benefits consulting firm by multiple industry sources. Visit www.aon.com for more information on Aon.

ABOUT KEVIN KALINICH, ESQ.

Kevin leads Aon's global practice to identify exposures and develop insurance solutions related to Technology Errors and Omissions, Miscellaneous Professional Liability, Media Liability, Network Risk, and Intellectual Property. Kevin is a 2007, 2008, 2009, 2010, 2011, 2012 (Finalist), 2014, and 2016 (Finalist) Risk & Insurance "Power Broker." Kevin has been quoted in numerous publications, including in Ted Koppel's 2015 book, *Lights Out* (along with Berkshire Hathaway's Ajit Jain), the *Wall Street Journal, Time,* and Bloomberg, and a frequent speaker regarding professional liability–related issues in various venues, including CNBC, RIMS, American Bar Association, American Bankers Association, FERMA, World Economic Forum, Stanford Program in Law, Science and Technology, CCH Computer Law Advisory Council, and Association of Financial Professionals. Kevin joined Aon in September 2000, from Altima Technologies, where he served as chief executive officer and led the successful launch of a Web-enabled software product that provides intelligent visualization of network equipment in the areas of telecommunications, data, cables, and computers. Prior to Altima, he was a partner at Chapman and Cutler Law Firm, where he represented domestic and international public and private entities in general corporate matters, intellectual property, M&A, venture capital, institutional investor, and IPO transactions. Kevin holds a JD from the University of Michigan and received his BA degree in economics and mathematics, cum laude, from Yale University.

CHAPTER 11

Monitoring and Review Using Key Risk Indicators (KRIs)

Ann Rodriguez, Managing Partner, Wability, Inc., USA

Tom is in a meeting with his chief risk officer, Nathan, and his chief information security officer (CISO), Maria. Maria is presenting on the progress of the information security program. Tom asks, "How do I know we are doing the right things? That our program is really where it needs to be? That we can really be ahead of this risk?" Nathan hands Tom a graphic one-page report. "Tom, here you can see what we are measuring to indicate risk levels associated with information security risk. These indicators, are already showing improvement given the current state of the program. As you know, 'what gets measured, gets done'; so we are also tracking indicators associated with the program progress. These two sets of data provide a powerful story, which we can use to discuss with the board."

Not many organizations have been known to fail due to a cybersecurity event. This is likely due to strong risk programs to detect and react to threats, and to luck. While no failures have been attributed to cybersecurity events, there are many operational losses that can be attributed to these events. With the velocity and sophistication of these threats constantly accelerating, it is imperative that organizations keep pace with how the risk is considered and the evolution of metrics to indicate potential changes in the risk levels.

The presentation and usage of key risk indicators (KRIs) sit at the pinnacle of strong enterprise-wide risk management (ERM). It routinely appears as an enterprise risk that organizations are concerned with as CEOs consider their strategic objectives and the implications that cyber events (and losses) can have on those objectives. In this chapter, we will discuss some design considerations for effective KRIs and their use—particularly for board and senior management.

DEFINITIONS

Many things are measured within an organization. We will loosely group this entire population of measured things and call them metrics or indicators. These metrics are ultimately clarified by their usage.

Key Risk Indicator

A key risk indicator (KRI) is a metric that permits a business to monitor changes in the level of risk in order to take action. KRIs highlight pressure points and can be effective leading indicators of emerging risks. These are typically forward-looking or leading indicators.[1]

Key Performance Indicator

A key performance indicator (KPI) is a metric that evaluates how a business is performing against objectives. A defined target (typically) provides the benchmark for evaluation of a KPI metric. These metrics are usually backward-looking or lagging indicators.

Key Control Indicator

A key control indicator (KCI) is a metric that evaluates the effectiveness level of a control (or set of controls) that have been implemented to reduce or mitigate a given risk exposure. A calibrated threshold or trigger (typically) brackets a KCI metric. These metrics are usually backward-looking or lagging indicators. Control indicators link with operational or process objectives.

If it is an important indicator, then it is considered *key*. Metrics may have multiple uses. They may inform performance, risk, or control. They are also layered for specific owners and accountable parties—building from control to process to objective, telling a story, and driving action and decisions at each discrete layer.

KRI DESIGN FOR CYBER RISK MANAGEMENT

Every organization has a unique business strategy, risk appetite, and corporate culture. There is also a set of cyber risks that are independent of these factors that come with operating in the digital age. These include risks posed by web sites, e-mail, and digital devices, all of which can be hacked. As such, the specific cyber risks an organization faces will vary as will the program and associated KRIs. As with all KRIs, it is important to design KRIs that provide context to the broader enterprise risk. The layering of KRIs across the range of stakeholders that need information for them to action and govern is an important consideration.

A Risk Taxonomy Provides Clarity

A risk taxonomy is a comprehensive, common, and stable set of risk categories that is used within an organization.

- By providing a *comprehensive* set of risk categories, it encourages those involved in risk identification to consider all types of risks that could affect the organization's objectives.
- By providing a *common* set of risk categories, it facilitates the aggregation of risks from across the organization.

By providing a *stable* set of risk categories, it facilitates comparative analysis of an organization's risks over time.

Having a risk taxonomy is critical when establishing a KRI program, which is critical for anticipating risk. It supports the relationship between metrics measuring control at a granular level with the risk they are mitigating and ultimately the relationship to strategic objectives as seen in Figure 11.1. The taxonomy also provides clarity of accountability and consistency of response and decision making within an organization across the range of stakeholders that use the KRIs.

Organizational Risk

High-level risk statements within the risk taxonomy represent how an organization might view the impact of a control failure within information security. These are essentially the things that could impact the profit and loss (P&L) by disrupting individual business processes and impacting customers. The following three are commonly viewed as risks to most organizations:

- Systems not available as expected.
- Information is exposed inappropriately (to those other than expected).
- Information is inaccurate and cannot be relied upon.

Organization leaders might not immediately care about the details of each control mitigating the various ways in which these risks could be realized; however, they do care about direct negative impact on their P&L and reputation.

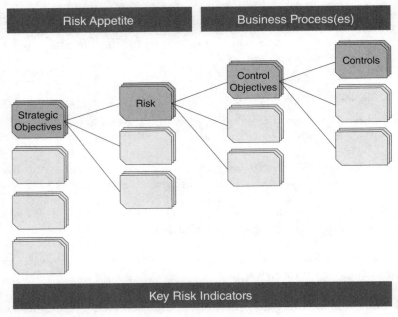

FIGURE 11.1   Risk taxonomy for KRIs

Functional Risk

Cyber risk is a *functional* risk. This means that it is typically managed by the information security organizational function within information technology (IT). It spans the organization and requires clear integration with other functions apart from IT, such as vendor or supplier management, business continuity, and physical security, to name just a few.

Cyber risk as a functional risk type could have an impact on each of our preceding three business risks. Cybersecurity control objectives are aligned to these risks such that, if met, they would substantially reduce the risk. KRIs are designed and implemented to monitor changes in the cybersecurity risk level inherently and residually. These changes would then be reflected in the level of risk to the organization.

KRI Design Links Objectives, Risks, and Controls

KRI design begins with a clear view of the risks that the organization faces and continues with the further synthesis of these risks into control objectives and key controls (as in Figure 11.1). These elements of the risk taxonomy are manifest in the organization's comprehensive cybersecurity program that start with policies and programs guided by industry best practices as well as applicable laws and regulations. The discrete programs form the basis for meeting control objectives which, when met, significantly mitigate the risk.

Organizational threats typically occur in the context of actors, targets, and vectors. We can illustrate how KRIs play a role in telling a story around risk, both inherently and residually, in the following way:

- *Threat actor*—a person or entity who impacts or has the potential to impact the security of an organization. These could be internal, external, or vendors/suppliers.
- *Threat targets*—the things we are trying to protect; things that are valuable to threat actors such as system working correctly, personal information, intellectual property, and so on.
- Threat vectors—paths that threat actors utilize to acquire threat targets; people (our employees, vendors, etc.) or systems or supply chain.

Table 11.1 indicates some examples of KRIs. These are aligned to high-level control objectives that are associated with *threat vectors* (because these are what we can control!) as well as *threat actors*. The KRIs are measured to provide an indication of the risk level and the strength of the program in consideration of our *threat targets*. In Table 11.1, KRIs that may need to be interpreted together are grouped in the column called "Examples of KRIs." The multilayered approach to KRIs is also indicated in differentiating some examples of more detailed *technical KRIs*. Each of these KRI examples may also be separately categorized in one of four categories: incident counts, loss magnitude data, threat data, or control data.

Case Study Where Triggered KRIs Were Apparently Ignored

The Target data breach in 2013 affected over 110 million customers and losses upwards of $250 million.

Hackers accessed the network using an HVAC (heating, ventilating, and air conditioning) supplier's credentials. The HVAC supplier had access to the Target network, and used it to collect temperature and energy usage data from each store. The hackers were able to get the log-on credentials using a phishing e-mail aimed at Target suppliers. They deceived one of the HVAC employees who opened the e-mail, allowing them to infect some of the supplier's computers. The hackers then waited until the malware captured the log-on credentials for Target. The HVAC vendor did not have adequate system protection, so the breach went undetected.

TABLE 11.1 KRI Examples Aligned with Control Objectives

Control Objectives	Examples of KRIs
Employees are trained and behaviors monitored. Culture and awareness efforts are distributed across the organization and monitoring is in place. Behavioral analysis is collecting events, looking at peer analysis, high-risk status, and employee activity and determining where risk hot spots are occurring. (Residual Risk)	% Employee population trained % Employee population randomly tested % Successful test results % Employees with high risk score # Investigations that were legitimate % Investigations that were legitimate # Data loss events due to insiders **Technical KRIs:** Average amount of time between notification of job departure and elimination of corporate access Frequency with which employee access is reassessed % of employee access being reviewed when they change function within the enterprise
Know what is happening externally. Have a process to collect information quickly externally. (Inherent Risk)	# Events across industry # New vulnerabilities detected Loss amounts across industry Peer maturity scores # Regulations applicable % Compliance to regulation
Know what is on the network. Have a complete and current inventory of production systems, IP addresses, devices, operating systems, etc.: their versions, physical locations, owners, function, and who has access. (Residual Risk)	% Completeness of inventory (how much of network has been scanned) % Standardization of configurations across network % High-risk assets under regular access review Rate of compliance with the minimum security baseline **Technical KRIs:** % of employees with "super user" access # of properly configured SSL certificates amount of peer-to-peer file-sharing activity on a company's corporate network # of open ports during a period of time % of third-party software that has been scanned for vulnerabilities prior to deployment
Swift risk assessment for vulnerabilities that affect our system. Have a *complete* and *current* inventory of existing security controls and configurations	% of network security controls mapped % Systems with tested security controls % of high risk assets with weak or non–compliant passwords % High-risk data encrypted % Configuration standardization

and a mechanism for collecting vulnerabilities (*real-time*); *speedy* comparison of vulnerability with existing security controls to flag a vulnerability that could affect our system and a risk assessment process. (Residual Risk)

Vulnerability scan score (considers frequency and automation percentage)
Average incident detection time
Trend of risk assessment timing (from when vulnerability collected)
Technical KRIs:
Botnet infections per device over a period of time

Respond to vulnerabilities based on risk level such that business operations are not impacted.
Have a response time that is based on the risk level and considers business operations. (Residual Risk)

% Patch management program that is automated
Trend of % patches causing business disruption
Average incident response time
Trend of speed of vulnerability response (from when vulnerability collected)
# of unpatched known vulnerabilities

Ensure vendors are risk assessed and access is appropriate.
All vendors are risk assessed based on their access to critical assets (i.e., threat targets) and their approach to fourth parties. (Residual Risk)

% of vendors that are high risk (access to critical assets)
% High-risk vendors with acceptable cybersecurity risk programs
Frequency with which a company reviews its entire list of suppliers and vendors and designates those that are critical
Frequency with which a company verifies its vendor's controls
% of critical vendors whose cybersecurity effectiveness is continuously monitored

---

The Target event illustrates the need for cybersecurity integration in programs such as vendor or supplier management and to have a KRI program that governs response to KRIs.[2]

Using KRIs for Improved Decision Making

The objective of a strong KRI program is to improve decision making within the organization. Ideally, this should be forward looking. Reporting and presentation of the KRIs is both art and science. Much of the art in depicting the view of information security risk is in decoupling the detailed technical metrics and tech-speak, when presenting to senior leadership and board members. Another important consideration if presenting an abundance of

KRIs is to avoid this leading to a false sense of security. Context and messaging are critical.

Stakeholders Want to Be Informed

There are a range of stakeholders in an organization that interact with the metrics measured to indicate changes in risk and control levels. The key stakeholders are typically the board of directors, senior management, chief risk officer, and chief information security officer (CISO) or head of cybersecurity. Differences as to how to present KRIs are directly related to the purview of the stakeholder group. The CISO or head of cybersecurity needs to have the most complete and granular set of KRIs to effectively manage progress and continuous improvement of information security.

Board members and senior management need to understand the inherent and residual risk associated with cybersecurity, as well as the cost of control. In order to understand these metrics, there needs to be a clear relationship of the cybersecurity risk to the organization strategy and to the organization risk appetite, as this is how the inherent risk would be viewed.

Here are the key things the CEO and the board of directors want to know about:

- Cyber risk culture and awareness.
- Inherent cyber risk (i.e., *before* controls are taken into account). Inherent risk level is usually influenced by changes in the threat level; new threat actors, uptick in attacks and sophistication, higher value of threat targets, and so on.
- Residual risk (i.e., *after* controls are taken into account). The level of control we have implemented over the various threat vectors that can be indicated by cyber program status, cyber program maturity, compliance, and peer comparison.
- Actual experience and trends: incidents, losses, policy violations.
- Big-picture metrics: the KRIs that illustrate support for the strategic objectives.

Inherent Risk, Residual Risk, and Big-Picture KRIs

There are several metrics that support *inherent* risk evaluation. Inherent risk arises any time a tool or process can result in potential losses. The aim of security controls is to mitigate inherent risks. This category of risk includes trend of exploits and vulnerabilities across the industry, trend of losses across the industry, and trends of losses that have occurred in companies with similar business models.

Residual risk is that which remains after security controls are implemented. Yes, residual risk is evaluated through metrics for a view of the scope, maturity, and integration of the information security program internally. The KRIs that are designed to indicate the strength of the information security program will be aggregate KRIs, such as percentage of employees trained, percentage of internal infrastructure covered, trend in incidents, response time to mitigate incidents, and trends in losses.

This view of inherent risk and residual risk that is overlaid onto strategic objectives and risk appetite helps an organization understand the cost of mitigation. Table 11.1 represents a useful way to overlay and link these components.

Aligning KRIs to the big picture—that is, the strategic objectives and risk appetite—is imperative for ensuring senior management understanding and support. The way to do this effectively is to align KRIs and design reporting so that the KRIs tell the story that relates to these business objectives.

For example, consider if one of your organization's strategic objectives is to double revenue by expanding the customer base via an online channel. Each of the risks that could impact achievement of that objective must be evaluated and mitigated appropriately. It is quite easy to see that a risk scenario of an external direct denial of service (DDoS) attack would have an impact on customer experience by impacting system availability for customer's transactions. This impact could result in lost revenue and customer retention. From this description, a few KRIs should be apparent, including customer satisfaction and customer retention. These can further be correlated with core system uptime, and the range of control metrics associated with protecting the network perimeter.

Dashboard Samples Tailored to Stakeholders

The cybersecurity and information security disciplines measure many things. They often deploy a robust set of dashboards and reports that are targeted and focused by each stakeholder.

Figure 11.2 represents a sample high-level dashboard with some of the components listed above. These are all aggregated KRIs to provide some information about where the program is and how that relates to the actual experience. Remember that the objective of this reporting is to aid decision making, so these metrics may need to be adjusted to provide more tailored information. For example, the KRIs may be broken by business unit or geography.

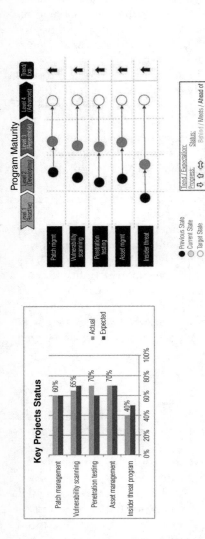

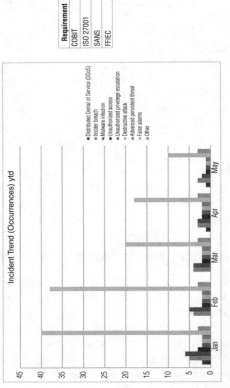

FIGURE 11.2 KRI sample of dashboards and reports

CONCLUSION

There are many metrics associated with the control and outcomes associated with cyber risk management. The usage of these KRIs occurs at numerous levels in a company, from process and program owners, to the CISO and chief risk officer, and to the board and senior management. Effective design of KRIs and their alignment to the big picture will provide stronger engagement with the board and senior management in the company by providing them a not-too-technical look into the risk to achievement of objectives and the program that provides the control. The objective of effective KRI design is to try to be forward looking about the levels of risk and the related readiness to prevent or mitigate an event.

KEY RISK INDICATORS

Specific and tailored cybersecurity key risk indicators (KRIs) are developed to monitor inherent and residual risk levels. These metrics provide leading indication of increasing risk exposure and potential impacts to achievement of strategic objectives and provide a full view across the range of threats. Context is critical in effective KRI design as are ratios, percentages, and always asking the next question to refine the KRI. Response metrics (speed and trend) are important indications of a program's success, which is a key piece of information for senior management and board members.

NOTES

1. Ann Rodriguez and Viney Chadha, *Key Risk Indicators* London, Risk Books, 2016.
2. Ibid.

ABOUT WABILITY

Wability is a management and technical consulting firm that develops more efficient business strategies for Fortune 500 clients by creating and incorporating customized business and technological solutions. Wability focuses on providing the precise talents and skills and strategic advice needed to accomplish client objectives.

ABOUT ANN RODRIGUEZ

Ann has significant experience across financial services in risk management including corporate governance and board reporting, enterprise and operational risk, with focus on technology, information security and third party risks. At GE Capital, Rodriguez established and provided leadership for both the Enterprise and Operational Risk programs. Leading a team of approximately 300 people across a $500 billion global company, she successfully integrated risk management with strategic planning, stress testing, capital planning, and comprehensive capital adequacy review. She established governance structures and provided leadership as chair of the New Products & Initiatives and Operational Risk Management Committees and as a member of the Enterprise Risk Management, Asset Quality, and Model Risk Committees. Rodriguez has held various leadership roles at Wells Fargo, Wachovia, and Goldman Sachs focused on risk governance and regulatory interface, operational risk management, and business management. Ann has an extensive background in consulting, as president of Wability, as lead partner over the Financial Services Consulting at BDO Seidman, and at Price Waterhouse, developing and leading practices in strategy, risk management, operational process excellence, and technology implementations. She has frequently shared her risk management experience, speaking at numerous industry conferences as well as lecturing at the NYU Stern School of Business. She is also author of the book *Key Risk Indicators*, a primer on the metrics required to provide proactive risk management.

CHAPTER 12

Cybersecurity Incident and Crisis Management

CLUSIF Club de la Sécurité de l'Information Français
Gérôme Billois, CLUSIF Administrator and Board Member Cybersecurity at
Wavestone Consultancy, France

The antivirus console administrator is phoning Maria, the chief information security officer (CISO) reporting to Tom the CEO: "… another virus has been detected. I know we struggle with many incidents like this every day, but this one seems very strange. I've never seen it before. It has infected the workstation of a researcher in the R&D lab and it is trying to send loads of data to Internet … the help desk manager just wants the workstation to be reinstalled as soon as possible, saying it's a common incident and nothing to worry about. …"

Maria interjects: "No. This is now an incident needing our incident management process to kick in. Start sending the virus to our forensics experts, then …"

CYBERSECURITY INCIDENT MANAGEMENT

One hundred percent protection capability does not exist in cybersecurity. A cybersecurity incident may always occur—whatever the level of investment. However, it is mandatory that the CEO ensure tailored-to-organization capabilities to differentiate low-impact routine cyber *incidents* from major *crises* that require prompt escalation to effective cyber crisis management in order to avoid high-impact interruption. This chapter shows the CEO how.

When a Cybersecurity *Event* Becomes an *Incident*

There are many definitions for a cybersecurity *incident*. Nearly every standard and framework (such as ISO 27001 and guidelines by the Institute of Risk Management [IRM] UK, the National Institute of Standards and Technology [NIST] and the European Union Agency for Network and Information Security [ENISA]) propose differing approaches. The main question is to define the *specific criteria* to apply to an event that has occurred that may or may not become a cybersecurity incident. These criteria typically represent the impact of the incident on confidentiality, integrity, availability, and traceability for organization assets. However, to stay only with that definition may result in being overwhelmed by a large number of incidents, especially if your organization tries to manage all the incidents related to availability.

A common filter to apply is to ask if the cause of the incident is related to a security breach. For instance, a server whose power supply fails because it is too old will not be classified as a cybersecurity *incident,* but a malicious administrator that accesses information must be. There are many debates as to whether to include in the criteria a suspicion or a vulnerability as an incident (such as those discovered during an audit). These are typically not considered as an incident but are registered as an *anomaly* or *event.* An *incident* is something that has direct and proven impacts.

Qualifying the Two Categories of Incident Sources

Cybersecurity incidents can be classified into two source categories (also known as root causes, risk sources, or inherent causes): internal or external incident sources.

Internal Incident Identification *Internal* incident sources are the primary incident declaration channel by volume. Incidents are usually identified by the information technology (IT) teams such as the network, desktop, or IT surveillance teams, the users through the help desk, or even IT partners. After being analyzed by the IT teams, certain events may be flagged as cybersecurity incidents if the cause of the incident is related to information security (e.g., a breach of confidentiality or system unavailability due to malicious actions or data theft). To make this process operational, communicate a list of the different types of incident you want to track with examples. Start small and increase the list over the years. These technical incidents must be dealt within an appropriate incident management tool of the IT department in order to be efficient and to manage the large "industrial" scale of occurrences.

External Incident Identification *External* incident sources are the secondary incident sources declaration channel by volume. They usually originate from coworkers, external partners, or law enforcement, which may contact the information security team to declare an incident. This is where you will probably encounter the most critical incident and probably need to internally store them in a separate tool to ensure confidentiality as the usual internal IT incident management tools are accessible by hundreds of people.

Qualifying Incidents A structured and formal qualification process must be put in place to ensure that an identified incident will be managed with the appropriate level of attention. Several criteria need to be agreed and used to evaluate incidents. These should include:

- Sensitivity of the data or processes concerned (e.g., research and development [R&D] and data dealt with by VIP's, the Very Important People in the company such as Senior Management).
- The functional perimeter (e.g., number of users or entities impacted).
- The technical perimeter (e.g., number of workstations/servers impacted, partner's systems).
- The probable cause of the cybersecurity incident (e.g., malevolence, human error).

Following this qualification, the incident may be managed normally with predefined processes or it may trigger escalation to the crisis management process.

Follow the Incident Management Policy and Process Steps

The incident management process starts once an incident is discovered and qualified. It follows several steps: identification, containment, remediation, and recovery. All information must be recorded according to a cybersecurity incident management policy, approved at the required level (must be at least CISO and CIO; should be CEO and/or board) and communicated to all concerned parties. Other "must-have" requirements are listed in Table 12.1.

Integrating Incident Reporting with Enterprise-wide Risk Management (ERM)

To report properly on cybersecurity incidents, you need to create a global repository of such information that will be fed by both IT internal and external sources. Data fed from IT internal sources is often automated due to the number of events and the number of people reporting the data. The information security correspondent network is often in charge of declaring the incidents in a centralized tool within large organizations.

TABLE 12.1   Cybersecurity Incident Must-Have Checklist

Requirements	Suggested Content
Cybersecurity incident management policy—includes event and incident definition	Adapted to organization context and explaining the difference between an event, an alert, an anomaly and an incident
Event and incident impact qualification matrix	A matrix with the different criteria to assess the event, decide if it is an incident and evaluate its criticality
Detailed processes	Roles and responsibilities on identification, containment, remediation, recovery and reporting (e.g., using a responsible, accountable, consulted, and informed [RACI] matrix); covering sources whether internal or external (with partners/law enforcement)
Incident response methodologies	"How to" on the most common security incidents (such as viruses, phishing, denial of service)
Incident management reporting	At entity and global level, linked with the ERM tool/applications
Incident repository and follow-up tools	Either through a specific tool/file or within the IT and/or ERM tool/applications

Be warned that it is often difficult to automatically consolidate incidents between organization entities because a single incident may have impacted several entities or be declared/recorded separately with different names and dates. Once consolidated, these incidents may be summarized and imported in the incident repository coordinated by IT collaborating with the ERM function and their ERM umbrella processes. The reporting has to be ultimately presented to the top management of the organization to report threats and the effectiveness and efficiency of the cybersecurity measures in place.

CYBERSECURITY CRISIS MANAGEMENT

A few days later, CEO Tom briefed his board, having received a combined briefing from CISO Maria and chief risk officer (CRO), Nathan, saying, "I'm here to update you on a cyber incident that, unfortunately, escalated into a crisis we had to manage. A cyber attack on our R&D function was detected that infected 30 percent of the R&D lab computers. The attackers were trying to steal our new product intellectual property. We successfully triggered the crisis management process and were able to cut off the attackers before too much was stolen. Due to that swift and efficient response, no communication was required to our stakeholders and regulators, and the financial impacts are limited."

Going from Incident to Crisis Management

We have described so far how to manage standard security incidents. However, the *crisis* management process needs to be triggered by specific circumstances where the usual processes are unable to cope (such as large or multiple incidents occurring simultaneously).

Crisis Management Operating Principles

Cyber crisis management (CCM) is aligned with, and a subpart of, enterprise business continuity management. (For more on business continuity, see Chapter 13.) CCM aims to implement a set of specific organizational and technical measures to allow specially mobilized staff to deploy quickly, effectively, and efficiently during the crisis and respond to potentially unknown situations. CCM ultimately aims to contain impacts and resolve the crisis as quickly as possible.

CCM typically depends on a crisis decision-making unit (CDU) made up of representatives of the organization's top management (e.g., executive committee, board of directors, CRO). This steering role by top management is necessary in order to:

- Mobilize adequate resources urgently and set priorities.
- Allow operations outside of usual processes.
- Quickly validate measures that could impact business processes.
- Manage external communications and crisis disclosure (if required by regulators/laws, if the crisis is directly visible by the general public or if it has been leaked to the press).
- Maintain business continuity to the fullest extent possible in the face of a cyber incident. (See Chapter 13 for a complete discussion of business continuity management.)

The CDU is supported by one or more operational crisis team units who are preincident trained to carry out the CDU's orders and keep the CDU informed of developments. These units typically include:

- A human resources unit covering internal communication and contact with staff.
- A corporate communications/public relations unit that prepares the various communications and manages interaction with the media and external stakeholders.

- A legal unit or representative to log and process filed complaints and notify various external parties.
- A risk function member to coordinate all functions.

Crisis management mechanisms must be documented and tested regularly prior to any crisis. Several aspects need to be covered. These include:

- Human resource aspects such as identification of key people, decision-making mechanisms, and team rotation.
- Logistics such as dedicated workspaces, crisis directory, standby telephones, catering.
- Technical aspects such as defense and investigation capabilities, tools, and so on.

Such mechanisms do not exist today in full in most organizations (except some of the larger ones and in some sectors). These mechanisms are, however, a prerequisite to correctly manage a cybersecurity crisis and are increasingly asked after by boards and external stakeholders such as regulators, credit rating agencies, and insurers.

Structuring and Mobilizing an Operational Cybersecurity Crisis Unit

In the event of a crisis stemming from a cyber attack on the information system, an operational unit needs to be deployed, either as part of a usual information system operational unit or separately. Practical experience over recent years has shown that three teams need to be trained within this unit.

The Investigation Team The investigation team's objective is to identify when the attack started, the vulnerabilities exploited, and consequences of the attack (such as stolen documents or corrupted systems). It analyzes all available internal and external technical elements. It tries to identify the attack's source and the extent of the information system's compromise. The team is made up of digital investigation and forensics specialists focused on reacting quickly to information system crises. Its specialists are often externally sourced and embedded from companies that have a computer security incident response team (CSIRT) or a computer emergency response team (CERT). The targeted organization's technical experts are also integrated into the team to provide an understanding of the context.

The Defense Team The defense team prepares all the technical actions for repelling the attacker and correcting the vulnerabilities exploited during the attack. Its work often goes beyond the acute phase of the crisis in order to consolidate and correct the attacked system in depth and over time. It includes internal specialists with knowledge of the organization's tools and systems combined with external experts with knowledge of the attacker's methods to prevent against any rebound attacks or secondary infections.

The Steering Team   The steering team creates the link between the investigation and defense teams. It also liaises with internal parties (particularly the CDU for decisions and the CRO/ERM function for enterprise support) and with external operational parties (such as law enforcement or government services, depending on context). The steering team gives a business sense to the technical information and provides key elements to prepare a response to the attack across all its dimensions. It passes on relevant information to internal and external communication teams and can also validate communications to ensure that information's technical accuracy and that such information is safe to disclose.

These teams work hand in hand. Investigation provides elements to defense that then put forward plans for steering to approve. Steering follows the various action plans, communicates with all the other concerned parties, and drives the work forward. It must also try to anticipate as far as possible the crisis's next steps by identifying the most likely scenarios that could develop in relation to known attack cases.

The size of these teams may vary widely. A simple attack such as the defacing of Web pages with rhetoric, can mobilize from two to three people sharing the different roles. A more complex attack, bringing about, for example, loss of control of several systems and in particular the information system management infrastructure (such as the active directory), can mobilize tens of people internally and externally for several weeks. The resolution of a complex attack can take over three months and the costs can reach tens of millions of euros.

Tools and Techniques for Managing a Cyber Crisis

The crisis management teams need to have a number of tools and techniques at its disposal to efficiently manage the crisis. A first priority is a *secure crisis management system* (including mail, file exchange, workstations) independent from the attacked information system and administered differently to be able to carry on in the event of a major compromise or destruction of the usual system.

- *Investigation accounts* within technical systems need to be created in advance and deactivated until needed. These avoid having to wait to identify system owners to start off the technical investigations.

- *Forensic software tools* to analyze suspect software are required for launching the software in a risk-free and highly monitored environment (such as confinement through sandboxing).
- *Digital forensic hardware* (such as certified "bit-for-bit" hard disk copying solutions) suitable for legal analysis collection requirements is required.
- *Aggregator tool(s)* that collect and centralize data logs and allow interrogation of records from different systems is required.
- *Threat intelligence tool(s) and techniques* are needed to undertake a far-reaching indicator of compromise (IOC) search with sharing and acquisition capabilities (for technical traces of an attack, such as the IP addresses used or malware signatures). These enable rapid assessment the scale of an attack and rapid exchange of information with peers.
- Specialized tool constraints.

As at time of printing, most organizations do not possess these tools, particularly in the case of IOC search. As there are only some "turnkey" solutions on the commercial market, interested cybersecurity teams are forced to build ad-hoc solutions to respond to such needs. Some of the more advanced incident response service providers have made part of their toolkit available as open source solutions (for instance CERTitude from Wavestone, FIR from Societe Generale or FastIT from Sekoia).

There are several research projects underway at present to define incident response and investigation methods. Understanding of the attacker's actions over time is an essential part of large-scale cyber crisis management where multiple people are working simultaneously on the investigations. The *Diamond Model* by the U.S. Department of Defense and the *Kill Chain* method developed by Lockheed Martin researchers are also of interest.

Cyber Crisis Management Steps

Similar to general crisis management, a full-scale cyber attack management follows four steps, being:

1. Alert and qualification
2. Crisis handling (by carrying out an investigation and a defense plan)
3. Execution and surveillance
4. Crisis closure

The key difference for cyber over general crisis management lies in the cyber specificities, especially regarding how to stop the attack. This section details these specificities within the context of cyber crisis management steps and timings as visualized in Figure 12.1.

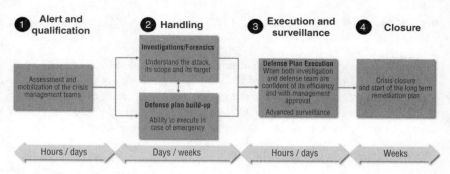

FIGURE 12.1   Cyber crisis management steps

Alert and Qualification   A first incident, whether internal or reported from outside, is enough to trigger the alert. It has to be qualified by the security teams in order to identify its severity and to dispel any doubts. Qualification is based both on system or data sensitivity, on the threat's technical level (e.g., using standard or homemade malware) and on the risk of the incident's spread beyond the initial scope of discovery. If the first analyses show early signs of a well-prepared attack and the target's sensitivity level is high, it is mandatory to trigger the crisis management mechanism using the predefined process.

Crisis Handling: Carrying Out the Investigation and Building a Defense Plan   Once the incident has been qualified, the teams in the cybersecurity crisis unit (i.e., investigation, defense, steering) will begin to investigate and prepare a defense plan.

Starting Investigations   The first team to mobilize is the investigation team. This team deploys the necessary technical means for the investigations. It must respect the principle of absolute discretion in its investigative actions to avoid revealing to the attacker that it has been discovered. The action generally takes several days to bear fruit, sometimes even several weeks in the case of large systems. Gray areas can last for a long time depending on the attacker's ability to cover its tracks. In fact, it is often necessary to leave the attacker to develop freely for a few days in order to understand its *modus operandi* and be able to correctly comprehend its objectives, its level of technical skill, and its tools. The services of bailiffs can often be required to assess the collection of technical traces and track actions in order to remain capable of going through with any legal proceedings. The investigation team progressively prepares an investigation report that sets out its understanding of the attack and its purpose. This report summarizes information about the attacker, the attack's compromise and spread vectors, and the impacted perimeter. It can be used as a basis for legal action such as filing a complaint or notifying the authorities.

Building the Defense Plan   The defense team is mobilized next. Its first actions are to identify the scope of the *emergency zone* by listing the critical assets that must not be compromised under any circumstances, and launching immediate and unconditional actions to repel the attacker—even if their effect is partial and imperfect. This represents an emergency-button type of procedure.

The team's next responsibility is to prepare the defense plan. This contains all the countermeasures needed to eradicate the attack on the impacted perimeters. An appropriate set of countermeasures is deployed all at once in order to prevent the attacker from returning quickly through a nonsecured route. Another set of organizational or technical measures may be positioned over time. These measures may include severing network links or Internet access, isolation of certain business entities, deployment of security patches or new software, changing passwords, and installation of new protective equipment.

The defense plan is dynamic and evolves depending on information from the investigation. At a minimum, it needs to specify the actions to be carried out in the short term and medium term, and ideally in the long term. It also has to identify the actors responsible for these actions, the impacts of their implementation, and finally to follow the execution timeline and progress of these actions once the escalation to crisis management is triggered.

Preparing a defense plan can take from a few hours to several days, although draft defense plans can be elaborated during rehearsal and war games. This depends on the complexity of affected systems, the number of business areas concerned and the reliability of the information coming out of the investigations. The defense team communicates the most critical elements to the steering team, who arbitrate over the impacts and costs with the CDU.

Executing the Plan and Surveillance   The management decision by the CDU to execute the defense plan is certainly the most complex and critical one to make during an information system attack crisis. Executing it may signify a slowdown or even a halt to some organization services, complicating investigation and also revealing to the attacker that its attack has been discovered.

Except in case of emergencies (i.e., the emergency-button procedure), the plan is launched when the investigation team considers they have near-full or full visibility on the attack, and the defense plan is rated as feasible and optimally effective and efficient. The deployment of the plan needs to ensure smooth functioning and solid efficiency by the investigation team using heightened monitoring. Launching the plan can also lead to the deployment of internal or external communication plans based on the visibility or reach of the actions.

Three scenarios are foreseeable from experience with past crises. These depend on the feedback from heightened monitoring. They are:

1. *The threat has been eradicated.* The attacker no longer has access to the information system. The situation is back under control.
2. *The threat has returned.* The attacker accesses the information system via a different *modus operandi* that was not previously observed or discovered during the investigations. It is therefore necessary to restart the investigation and defense processes, being aware that the attacker knows it has been discovered.
3. *The threat evolves.* The attacker launches new actions, which could go as far as attempted mass destruction of the information system (e.g., the wiping of servers and all data) in vengeance or to hide the tracks of its actions.

These scenarios—regardless of their likelihood ratings—need to be anticipated in the defense plan. If "mass destruction" begins, the drastic but considered response of an entire shutdown of the organization information system must be considered by management.

If the defense plan has been carried out successfully, it is necessary to start a return to normal. The reopening of services interrupted or impaired during crisis is organized in coordination with the business lines. This reopening can begin only if the services have been restored to a secure state to prevent the attack recurring.

Crisis Closure   The crisis unit may be stood down on three conditions: once the defense plan has been executed, the systems are back up and running, and if there is no indication of an upsurge or recurrence of the attack. This action must balance speed of normalization with alertness to the return of the attack and threat. Monitoring actions need to carry on long term to be capable of identifying any comeback.

One lesson from past attacks is that certain investigative actions bear results only after several days or even weeks. So what is discovered then can lead to remobilizing the recently dismantled crisis units. In addition, once the attacker has been discovered or driven away, it could deliberately hide him/her to come back stronger later on.

A special remediation project integrating security from the outset is required to drive remediation. This depends on the degree of reconstruction required on the affected information systems. An enterprise debriefing phase, often led by the ERM function or CRO, is also necessary in order to identify all the lessons learned from the crisis.

CONCLUSION

The following cyber risk management statement represents those organization capabilities CEO and board expect to be demonstrated in terms of *incident and crisis management*.

INCIDENT AND CRISIS MANAGEMENT

Low-impact routine cyber *incidents* are differentiated from major *crises* that require prompt escalation in order to avoid high-impact consequences. For *incidents*, all incident sources are detected and classified; routine incident management policy and volume-process steps are practiced and continually reviewed; and incident internal reporting aligns with the ERM system. Process steps include identification, containment, remediation, and recovery. A must-have checklist for incidents is followed. When incidents become unmanageable and/or require escalation, it is escalated by preset criteria to a set of cyber crisis management (CCM) principles. CCM follows these trained-for steps:

1. Alert and qualification.
2. Crisis handling (by carrying out an investigation and a defense plan).
3. Execution and surveillance.
4. Crisis closure.

CCM is steered by a crisis decision-making unit (CDU) (or its equivalent) made up of representatives of the organization's top management. CCM is implemented by an operational cybersecurity crisis unit that is prestructured, tailored to the organization context, and trained to mobilize quickly. It is made up of three teams that work jointly: the investigation team provides digital forensics to the defense team, which build upon plans to be approved by the CDU and applied when appropriate regarding the attack life cycle. These teams are adequately resourced with the technical tools and techniques for managing a modern cyber crisis. Adequate preparation for a crisis event is crucial to the organization and both incident management and crisis management processes are tested regularly with tabletop or in-situation exercises. These are improved over time as new threats arise and the organization evolves.

ABOUT CLUSIF

CLUSIF is the largest association of professionals in France dedicated to information security. It brings together users and providers from all industry branches. Its main goal is to facilitate the exchange of know-how and competences towards an efficient information security management.

ABOUT GÉRÔME BILLOIS, CISA, CISSP AND ISO27001 CERTIFIED

Gérôme is a board member of the cybersecurity practice of the consultancy Wavestone and an administrator of CLUSIF. Since 2001, he has lead projects within multinational companies to tackle cybersecurity challenges, including cybercrime fighting, strategy, and governance definition. He created CERT-Wavestone in 2013 and took part in several large cybersecurity crises driving the investigation and defense teams and dealing with issues at board level. He is currently focused on defining a new security model to embrace digital transformation while protecting valuable assets. He graduated from the engineering school at INSA de Lyon France. He is a regular international conference presenter and media spokesperson and a co-author of "Cyber Security of Industrial Control Systems: How to get started?" © CEPADUES 2014 and "Security and Personal Data Breach" © LARCIER 2016.

ABOUT WAVESTONE

Wavestone is a consulting firm, created from the merger of Solucom and Kurt Salmon's European Business (excluding retails and consumer goods outside of France). Wavestone's mission is to enlighten and guide their clients in their most critical decisions, drawing on functional, sectoral, and technological expertise.

With 2,500 employees across four continents, the firm is counted among the lead players in European independent consulting, and number one in France. Wavestone holds one of the largest cybersecurity and digital trust practice in EMEA (Europe, Middle East, and Africa) with more than 400 consultants.

CHAPTER 13

Business Continuity Management and Cybersecurity

Marsh
Sek Seong Lim, Marsh Risk Consulting Business Continuity Leader
for Asia, Singapore

The business continuity manager, Loretta, spoke solemnly to CEO Tom. "All our information and communications systems and services are under cyber attack. All our data and information files are locked by ransomware."

Tom replied curtly, "But how can this cyber disaster occur? I was given assurances by the internal and external IT experts that our setup is extremely resilient, with the latest state-of-the-art cybersecurity protection and detection systems and services?"

Nathan, the chief risk officer interjected, "The organization took a prudent approach to implement an IT disaster recovery center (DRC), housing all critical servers and databases; including two or more data feeds to ensure critical data are regularly replicated to the DRC."

Loretta chimed in, "Unfortunately, this allowed the attack and ransomware to infect the DRC systems and databases. We do not have an independent IT disaster recovery set up and no secondary back up storage media. The decision was made on the advice that the risk of such a scenario is very low. Our business continuity, crisis management, and communications plans—developed to enable us to recover at an alternate site when the primary site and data center activities are disrupted for a significant period—do not provide the processes and procedures to deal with this cyber disaster."

GOOD INTERNATIONAL PRACTICES FOR CYBER RISK MANAGEMENT AND BUSINESS CONTINUITY

Regardless as to the size or type of your enterprise, is your organization prepared for a cyber scenario like the one Tom is facing? As you read the following sections, refer to the chapter appendix as needed. It contains a glossary of some of the key terms used in this section.

Cyber and the Business Continuity Management System (BCMS)

A business continuity management system (BCMS) can be considered a specialized child and subset of its parent enterprise-level risk management system (ERM). The BCMS uses a business impact analysis (BIA) approach to focus on the critical single points of organization operational failure and crisis and the impact time intervals, processes, and mechanisms to recover the critical organization operations and functions from any disruption. A demonstrable business continuity management capability includes: risk assessment, business impact analysis, implemented recovery strategies, business continuity plan, establishing business continuity/crisis management teams, and review and testing.

A point of failure or crisis may be caused by a cyber breach. When that breach is not managed within the escalation procedures of its sibling cybersecurity incident management system, or it escalates further to a cyber crisis management state, then BCMS and all enterprise functions associated with the BCMS should be engaged.

There may be several approaches that can be adopted to identify and assess key cyber risk scenarios but the focus for business continuity management (BCM) should be on the potential impact from single points of failure over a period of time, and the potential costs and expenses to rectify the problem. The ISO 27000 Information Security family of standards offers a useful information security-based risk assessment approach that focused on the assessing risks to data assets. A standardized risk framework aligned to the ISO 27001 should be tailored to each organization and define the ratings for likelihood of occurrence and the impact criteria based on the confidentiality, integrity, and accessibility (or availability) of sensitive information.

Organizations should identify their risks and measure the effectiveness of their risk treatment and controls. These risks are likely to include:

- Data loss and theft of confidential data.
- Unauthorized access—both intentional and unintentional—by internal and external parties.
- Data loss or corruption when transferring and transmitting data using different communications media and devices.

A key aspect should be to determine the impact to the organization, business, key stakeholders, organization partners, and customers. Sources for impact assessment may come from an organization or sector historical losses or values from past internal incidents, industry surveys, or information from reports provided by relevant experts such as the major international insurers and research agencies like the World Economic Forum.

BCMS Components and ISO 22301

The international BCM standard called "ISO 22301: Societal security–Business continuity management systems–Requirements" provides a framework consisting of international best practices. This framework enables cyber incident and crisis management (ICM) and BCM to be integrated into an organization-wide risk management and response for potential major cyber incidents. Figure 13.1 offers a high level overview of the main cyber response components.

Major cyber incidents can potentially have a significant impact over time, disrupting business and operation activities. Many organizations currently do not have adequate plans established based on maximum probable loss and most credible worst case cyber scenarios, such as a large scale distributed denial of service (DDoS) attacks. Many organizations currently design and implement IT and IT disaster recovery (DR) architectures that have a common physical network infrastructure. Unfortunately, the impact of a corporate or organization-wide cyber incident scenario has not been thoroughly analyzed. Cyber incident responses may be incorporated into existing plans, processes, and procedures—including information and

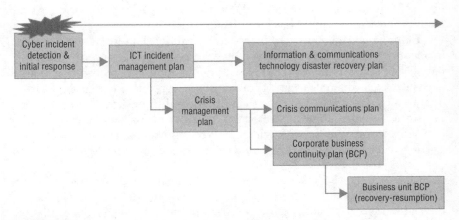

FIGURE 13.1   Conceptual overview of main cyber response components

communications technology (ICT) incident management plan (IMP), IT disaster recovery plan (DRP), crisis management plan (CMP), crisis communications plan (CCP), and business continuity plan (BCP). The ISO 27001 and 22301, international standards for information security and business continuity management systems, respectively, are international best practices and standards that may be used by organizations to implement policies and a framework to address cyber incidents.

The cyber response should include escalation and notification processes to alert the crisis management team (CMT) for incidents that will potentially have a significant impact on the IT services and data, as well as business operations. The cyber response typically has an impact severity matrix as a key component of the IT IMP; which enables an organization to gauge the severity of impact of a cyber attack or incident. The cyber impact severity matrix should constitute or be integrated with the impact matrices and criteria used in risk assessments, business impact analysis, and damage assessments. This facilitates the development and implementation of strategies, plans, processes, and procedures that will provide an integrated and seamless set of response plans (BCP, CMP, CCP, IT IMP, and IT DRP) to address major cyber incidents.

EMBEDDING CYBERSECURITY REQUIREMENTS IN BCMS

BCM and IT DRP traditionally focus on the computer rooms or data center operations becoming inoperable, with significant damages to critical server and network equipment, typically caused by major incidents like power failure or fire. Business continuity and IT disaster recovery plans typically do *not* factor in major disruptions to IT services and business activities arising from cybersecurity issues, risks and attacks.

Enterprise leaders need to be concerned about data loss due to a cyber incident or attack. The impact from the start of an incident needs to be evaluated. The point in time where the last known good data record is available needs to be considered. Today, data protection typically involves replicating data to a remote site; where it is then transferred or backed up to a secondary storage media. Data replicated is typically transported via a wide area network. A potential key risk with significant impact is that the same transporting mechanism allows the same cyber attack to also target the offsite data, and possibly the backed-up data.

Organization users therefore need to evaluate the possibility of relying on earlier versions of data records to support the BCP and IT DRP. The earlier the last known good data record is retrieved from, the bigger the challenge; this implies recreating a larger column of data from alternative records.

BCP and IT DRP recovery prioritization and support resource requirements need to be ascertained in advance. Key areas to reevaluate are IT
resources, IT DR provisions, PC, and other critical infrastructure equipment. Third party and outsourced services should be included in the study.

The impact severity criteria for risk assessment, BIA, damage assessment, and crisis management could be specified based on the number of
critical organization operations and functions, and IT application services
and databases that are affected by a major cyber incident. This should also
take into consideration the time sensitive periods for these functions. Regulatory, statutory, and contractual requirements relevant to the organization
activities also need to be included in the impact severity criteria.

The potential impact of major cybersecurity incidents relating to internal and third-party breaches and private data loss, and the associated consequences on the reputation and image of the organization, the branding of
key products and services, as well as compliance and contractual obligations
also need to be assessed.

Cyber incidents can also result in the disruption of telecommunications
services and infrastructure for a significant period. Today, organizations are
very dependent on the network infrastructure to support internal business
and operation processes, and electronic (including mobile) commerce, so
the unavailability of the telecommunication infrastructure and services will
have grave implications to the organizations—even for crisis management
and communications.

DEVELOPING AND IMPLEMENTING BCM RESPONSES FOR CYBER INCIDENTS

BCP, CMP, and IT DRP typically assume telecommunications infrastructure
(including third-party service providers) is recovered. Besides the telecommunications infrastructure, IT systems, services, and databases at both the
IT production and DR centers may be unavailable for a significant period
of time during a major cyber incident. Therefore, the recovery period of
the IT systems, infrastructure, services, and databases within the prioritized
(planned) time frames need to be validated.

Enhancements to the BCM, CM, IT IMP, and IT DRP responses will
likely be required to ensure the integrated responses adequately address
cyber incident consequences. The minimum operating levels, and corresponding resource and service requirements to support the BCP, CMP, and
IT DRP should be revised to cater for a major cyber incident.

Specialized resources to support the responses will be required—including
consultants and service providers specializing in cybersecurity, cyber forensics,

accounting forensics, crisis management, crisis communications, legal advisors, social media, and news monitoring etc.

The adequacy of the arrangements to support BCM, CMP, IT IMP, and IT DRP need to be validated. Therefore, organizations need to develop and conduct separate and integrated exercises to ascertain that the BCP, CMP, CCP, IT IMP, and IT DRP are effective against a major cyber incident. Independent exercises will validate the adequacy of the BCP, CMP, IT IMP, and IT DRP as individual plans. Exercising the plans in an integrated exercise will validate that the plans, processes, and procedures work seamlessly to mitigate an organization-wide cyber incident.

Organizations need to factor higher expenses and costs associated with the external services and subject matter experts into the BCM and IT DRP budgets. Transferring some of these increased costs through cyber insurance should be included as one of the key risk mitigation measures.

CONCLUSION

The following cyber risk management statement represents those organization capabilities CEO and board expect to be demonstrated in terms of *cyber risk alignment with business continuity management for the enterprise.*

BUSINESS CONTINUITY MANAGEMENT SYSTEM (BCMS)

IT processes are deeply embedded into business and operational processes. A business continuity management system (BCMS) is robust enough to overcome a major cyber incident with an organization-wide impact for a significant period of time (or even threatening the long term survivability of an organization). The BCMS is aligned with the ISO 22301:2012 Societal security–BCMS–Requirements and with the organizational culture, thus making it a strategic management process. The BCMS provides a framework for the organization to implement an integrated response to counter major cyber incidents. Impact severity levels are defined in a standardized impact severity matrix, which should be used or associated with IT incident management plan (IMP), IT disaster recovery plan (DRP), crisis management plan (CMP), crisis communications plan (CCP) and damage assessment. It is also essential to ensure response procedures in these plans are aligned. These are validated by conducting integrated exercises.

APPENDIX: GLOSSARY OF KEY TERMS

Business continuity plan (BCP): Typically made up of the corporate wide or level BCP and the business unit BCPs. The BCPs focus on the continuity, recovery, and resumption of the critical business unit functions (that is, non-technology-based recovery). The corporate BCP contains the corporate level processes and procedures for business continuity, recovery, resumption, restoration, and return to normal operations. The business unit BCPs contain the recovery and resumption processes and procedures for the critical business functions; which were identified and prioritized during the business impact analysis. The prioritization for the recovery of critical business functions is established based on the impact over time when the function is disrupted for a significant period, and the recovery time objectives, which are determined based on internal and external dependencies and time-sensitive and peak processing periods. The recovery point objective of vital data and records will also influence the business continuity priorities.

Crisis management plan (CMP): Contains the processes and procedures for the senior management team to control and ensure coordination of major crisis incidents. The crisis communications plan complements the CMP. It contains the processes, procedures, and templates to manage internal and external communications during a crisis. Together, the CMP and CCP enable organizations to command, control and coordinate information, decisions, and communications during a crisis.

Cyber incident and crisis management plan (ICMP): Documents the processes and procedures for IT teams and management—a framework to respond to and manage cyber incidents. IT may incorporate cyber response incidents into the corporate IT response plan. Crisis management response actions for cyber incident may be embedded in the corporate crisis management plan. IT can incorporate response to cyber incidents in its incident response plan, however, from that point onwards the cyber incident can be treated as any other incident per organization's incident management and crisis management plans.

Disaster recovery plan (DRP): Documents the processes and procedures for the recovery of IT servers, networks, applications, and databases; usually at an alternate site called the IT disaster recovery center. The IT DRP focuses on the technical recovery of IT systems and infrastructure.

ABOUT MARSH

Marsh is a global leader in insurance broking and risk management. In more than 130 countries, our experts in every facet of risk and across industries help clients to anticipate, quantify, and more fully understand the range of risks they face. We assist clients to define, design, and deliver innovative solutions to better quantify and manage risk. We offer risk management, risk consulting, insurance broking, alternative risk financing, and insurance program management services to businesses, government entities, organizations, and individuals around the world. Marsh is a wholly owned subsidiary of Marsh & McLennan Companies (NYSE: MMC), a global professional services firm offering clients advice and solutions in the areas of risk, strategy, and people. With 60,000 colleagues worldwide and annual revenue exceeding $13 billion, Marsh & McLennan Companies include global leaders Guy Carpenter, Mercer, and Oliver Wyman.

ABOUT MARSH RISK CONSULTING

Marsh Risk Consulting (MRC) is a strategic business unit within Marsh. MRC provides innovative risk management and organizational resilience solutions. Working collaboratively with clients, we identify key risks and develop the foundations for effective and sustainable risk management.

ABOUT SEK SEONG LIM, CBCP, PMC

Sek Seong is the vice president and leader BCM & Resilience Service for Asia, Marsh Risk Consulting Singapore. He has been in professional and consulting services for almost 30 years. He specializes in BCM, CM, IT DRP, ISMS, and RM. He develops and implements strategies and plans for clients. Sek Seong has implemented BCMS (with CMP) for many clients, of which at least 25 have subsequently been certified compliant to the ISO 22301:2012 International BCM Standard. He regularly conducts training, speaks at public events, and conducts readiness assessments for clients. He was also on the original core development team that wrote the TR19 Technical Reference for BCM (then relaunched as SS540 Singapore Standard for BCM, which has since been withdrawn as the requirements in this standard are incorporated in the ISO 22301) and the SS507 Singapore Standard for BC-DR for Service Providers.

CHAPTER 14

External Context and Supply Chain

Supply Chain Risk Leadership Council (SCRLC)
Nick Wildgoose, Board Member and ex-Chairperson of SCRLC, and Zurich Insurance Group, UK

CEO Tom looked at his head of procurement/supply chain and operations, Ronald, and asked, "I hadn't thought to take the external context—the supply chain—into account when looking at cyber risk management. Why should we?"

The reply was quick. "The first point is that in an increasingly specialized world where globalized outsourcing has been growing for a number of years, the percentage of an operation's costs that sits in their supply chain is typically between 60 and 80 percent of the total costs." Ronald explained that means that when things go wrong in the supply chain, they can have a dramatic impact on the overall organizational performance. Their globalized nature also means that there are many more opportunities for cyber risk to impact results.

He cited a few statistics from World Economic Forum's "Global Risks Report 2016," which finds risks on the rise in 2016. This, in turn, will be exacerbated by the coming fourth Industrial Revolution. A few facts struck Tom as particularly noteworthy: Evidence is mounting that interconnections between risks are becoming stronger and that these often have major and unpredictable impacts. Cyber attacks are now considered the greatest risk of doing business in North America. They also feature as a top business risk in no fewer than seven other countries, including Japan, Germany, Switzerland, and Singapore. This means that for an organization to be successful, it is imperative to ensure that critical supply chains are adequately protected against cyber threats.

EXTERNAL CONTEXT

Enterprise-wide risk management (ERM) requires that the external context unique to the organization is understood and established. According to ISO 31000:2009, *Risk management—Principles and guidelines*, the process outlines how those ERM parameters and variables, which externally control and influence how the organization achieves its objectives and manages its own set of unique risks. These include specifics for the scope of risk (what risks are inclusions/exclusions/relevant for an organization), risk criteria, and risk policy. External factors include PESTLE (political, economic, societal, technological, legal, and environmental) external factors, and others cited by ISO 31000:

- External stakeholder identification and analysis
- Operating environment
- Competitors
- Government policy
- Community expectations
- Commercial and legal relationships
- Public/professional/product liability
- Economic circumstances
- Natural and unnatural events

External Context Specific to Cyber Risks

The cyber and privacy risks associated with your customers, employees, partners, third-party service providers, and other outside forces must be carefully considered as external factors for the internal organization to manage. The era of hyper-Internet connectivity, the reliance on third-party vendors, and mobility creates a complicated matrix of cyber and privacy exposures and threats. Evaluating all these threats on an enterprise-wide basis effectively requires looking way beyond your network perimeter.

Cyber threats are now regarded as the second of the top three causes of supply chain disruption as in Figure 14.1 according to 74 percent of companies researched by Zurich in 2016. Of the sources for these disruptions, nearly one-third (29 percent) are not even sourced from first-tier suppliers but are "hidden" in third-tier suppliers, as seen in Figure 14.2. Disturbingly, 30 percent of responders report not analyzing their supply chain.

Major enterprises have experienced cyber breaches or business interruptions that have cost hundreds of millions and damage to the brand. While high-profile data breaches during 2014 and 2015 reflected the expanding spectrum of cyber threats, information security experts all agree that

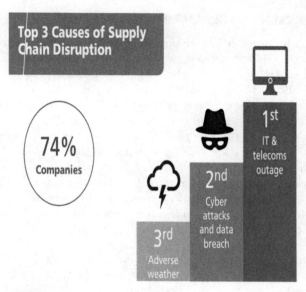

FIGURE 14.1 Top three causes of supply chain disruption

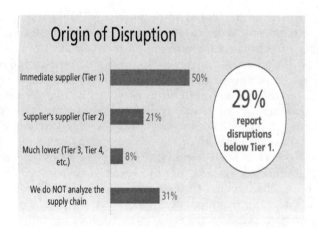

FIGURE 14.2 Origins of supply chain disruption

humans are the root causes of a majority of security incidents and data breaches. The interdependency in your critical global supply chains can have a multiplier effect. For example, a number of your critical suppliers all being affected by the same cyber incident.

External Context and the Supply Chain and Third Parties

As we already know, it is a challenge to be able to operate in your own organization on the matrix or cross-functional basis that is required in order to be able to optimize your cyber risk management practices. There is a further significant level of complexity when you look to interface with a third-party organization. This is because you have to ensure that each third party has the right approach in place to protect your data and to ensure they protect against disruptions to your own critical business processes. As with any interface, there are always opportunities for things to go wrong from a people, process, or systems perspective.

An initial assessment of the third party that you are dealing with can be gained by appropriate use of a *cyber risk management maturity model* within your third party *due diligence*. The extent that you need to validate this can in part be prioritized based on the following:

- Type and extent of access that the third party has to your data.
- Likelihood and impact of a potential third party failure due to a cyber attack on your operational performance.
- Potential reputational impact of the third-party cyber exposure.

An appropriate level of collaboration with the third party is essential to enable this to happen. It is important to realize that this type of relationship has a number of other benefits in terms of innovation or corporate social responsibility initiatives. All of these initiatives share the common requirement of a level of visibility into the processes and systems that are operating.

You also need to be aware in terms of your external context for your cyber risks that the legislative and regulatory requirements faced by your suppliers in the various parts of the world may be very different. These need to be factored into your overall cyber resilience plans.

However, the perceptions and cultures related to individuals operating in key decision-making areas of your external environment are equally important in a global context to the overall resilience that you are able to achieve. If key decision-making individuals in say, a critical supplier, do not have the same perception of the risks faced to your overall supply chain, then you will need to think about the appropriate alternative resilience and data security plans.

There are many examples of potential cyber exposures. Those that are illustrative from a supply chain perspective include:

- Smart cities with traffic control devices on the Internet of Things (IoT) that can be manipulated resulting in accidents, injury, and death or simply gridlock.

- Status of freight movement in trucks, ships, and aircraft is disrupted or manipulated resulting in damage to goods or early, late, or erroneous shipments or general supply chain turmoil impacting suppliers and purchases alike.
- Manipulation of signaling and the controlling the movement of trains.
- Manipulation of air traffic control or control of shipping port activity.
- Disruption of power delivery to critical transport infrastructure.

ZOMBIE ZERO

Example of a Transportation Cyber Attack

Malware doesn't discriminate, but there are certain strains that have been created for particular industries. For example, the logistics malware dubbed "Zombie Zero" by TrapX, underscores the growing security risks faced by shippers and their logistics and transportation partners in a wireless, mobile world where technology changes rapidly.

Logistics firms use scanners to track shipments as they are loaded and unloaded from ships, trucks, and airplanes. Zombie Zero targeted the scanners at shipping and logistics firms for over a year. Once an infected scanner was connected to the victim's wireless network, it attacked the corporate network and the scanned information was compromised (including origin, destination, contents, value, and shipper and recipient information).

There are a number of recommendations that come out of this incident as recommended by TrapX and others:

- Do a design review on all of your original equipment manufacturer (OEM) components, especially those manufactured overseas. This will take a lot of work, but we view it as essential for anyone in the defense industry and highly desirable for most manufacturers that integrate electronic components and chips.
- Consider your strategy to rapidly integrate and deploy software fixes and/or hardware fixes to your end-user customer base, especially if you have a two- or three-tier supply chain.
- Avoid allowing any of these devices to be bootable from a USB port in the production versions.
- Sign the software. This is a mathematical technique used to validate the authenticity of the software.

(continued)

(Continued)

- Run security tests to discover vulnerabilities and help with the design review of OEM components. We recommend using an outside security penetration firm.
- Implement firewalls to resist hacker attacks and only allow specified IP addresses in or out; every device needs one.
- Protect the project management interface from attackers and only allow limited access to the management server.

Transportation Sector Key Role for Supply Chain

The transportation sector plays a key role in the operation of supply chains. These include those in the pharmaceutical sector where lives are literally dependent on them. For many decades, logistics companies have invested most of their time and money into ensuring the integrity of their physical infrastructure and assets. Airlines and express operators have, for instance, been very mindful of the risks to their business of a terrorist infiltration of a bomb on board an aircraft or into a shipping container. However, less attention has been paid to the possibility of an attack on their information technology (IT) systems, which, depending on the source of the threat, could have consequences ranging from inconvenient to catastrophic.

Supply chains dependent on sea freight are perhaps uniquely exposed to cyber attacks. This is due to the way in which shipping has become increasingly channeled through the ever-decreasing number of ports capable of loading and off-loading the largest container ships. For example, a successful cyber attack on a port community system (a system responsible for the coordination of all port activities) of one the big "gateway" hubs, such as Rotterdam or Los Angeles, would have a substantial region-wide economic impact due to the lack of options available for rerouting of ships.

The logistics industry also faces threats, not so much to the control of transport assets, but to the goods themselves, which are being moved or stored. In terms of data, supply chain networks could be described as being inherently insecure, with parties encouraged to share information with their suppliers and their customers. The availability of data heightens the risk that the integrity or confidentiality of that shared information could be compromised. Supply chain management systems facilitate the dissemination of shipment-level information that, while enabling the efficient movement of goods, is also invaluable to criminals. The widespread use of handheld devices and Global Positioning System (GPS) technology in the field is only increasing the risks. Companies understand and manage this risk internally but have difficulty identifying and managing it across a large supplier base and this even includes just their critical suppliers.

The External Context to the Growing Importance of Cyber Risk and IT Failure

The Business Continuity Institute (BCI) has worked with the Chartered Institute of Procurement and Supply (CIPS) and Zurich Insurance over a number of years to understand and survey the status of supply chain resilience. In the six years that the survey has been running, cyber as a cause of disruption has steadily increased reinforcing the importance of cyber resilience in an external context. The key findings from their 2015 report sourced from 537 respondents working in 14 Standard Industrial Classification (SIC) industry sectors (with the majority of these working for companies in excess of 250 employees based mainly in Europe or the United States) are set out below.

2015 REPORT KEY FINDINGS ON THE DRIVERS OF SUPPLY CHAIN DISRUPTION

Business Continuity Institute/Zurich Insurance
SUPPLY CHAIN RESILIENCE REPORT 2015

- Seventy-two percent do not have full visibility of supply chains.
- Seventy-four percent experienced at least one instance of supply chain disruption.
- Fifty percent of disruptions originate from Tier 1, which in turn means there are further exposures lower down the supply chain (Tier 1 means simply those suppliers that supply the organization directly, rather than through another third party).
- In terms of the causes of disruption, the top three causes of supply chain disruption are:
  1. Unplanned IT and telecommunications outage (64 percent).
  2. Cyber attack and data breach (54 percent).
  3. Adverse weather (50 percent).
- The top three drivers of supply chain disruption above are also seen by respondents as being the same top risks in the next 12 months.

BUILDING CYBERSECURITY MANAGEMENT CAPABILITIES FROM AN EXTERNAL PERSPECTIVE

Seven Key Roles to Drive Capability from an External Perspective

The first key aspect of any cyber resilience and protection program in the context of the supply chain is to have the right organizational structure in place. There are a number of stakeholders to consider as you look at your cyber risk management strategy from an external perspective, the most important of which is that you have CEO/board-level sponsorship and support. There are seven key roles as summarized below.

1. *CEO/Board of directors*. Accountable for overall business and organization performance, they have a fiduciary duty to assess and manage cyber risk. Regulators, including the Securities and Exchange Commission (SEC), have made clear they expect organization top leadership to be engaged on the issue. In order for your resilience imperative program to progress you need their support. They can also play a key role in coordinating with critical third parties at an executive-to-executive level.

2. *Chief financial officer (CFO)*. Concerns may range from the potential costs of a cyber event and what the impact could be on the bottom line as well as the reputational impact that such an event might have. They can also play a key role in coordination, building the business case and leading a cyber task force.

3. *Chief risk officer (CRO)/risk manager*. Risk managers can ensure various stakeholders are connected in terms of assessing, managing, and responding to cyber threats. They can also provide access for key decision makers to leading practice methodologies, tools, and understanding.

4. *Legal/Compliance*. As regulations around cyber develop, legal and compliance roles become increasingly important in keeping other stakeholders informed and engaged. And if a cyber incident occurs, lawsuits often follow.

5. *Procurement/Supply chain and operations*. It is absolutely critical that cyber resilience is considered within the context overall supplier due diligence and management. This is often not adequately addressed and becomes even more important where critical data are being exchanged. It is also important that these functions maintain daily operations and workplace stability during a cyber event.

6. *Human resources/employees*. Employees are often the weakest link in supply chain cybersecurity. Simple errors and accidents—or deliberate actions—by employees can lead to costly cyber incidents. Training on

best practices is critical, especially with the rise in sophisticated "spear phishing" attacks targeting specific employees. Employees must be helped to understand the consequences of failure within a supply chain context.

7. *Customers/Suppliers/Logistic providers.* Interactions with customers and suppliers can open you up to an attack. You need to understand the protections they have in place so they do not become the weak point in your cyber defenses.

Cybersecurity Task Force to Focus on Maturity Targets

Establishing a cybersecurity task force must be considered by every organization. Its charter is to take both an internal and external perspective when progressing the organization from the current state of its cybersecurity management system—and its supply chain subcomponents—to that targeted for the future.

The chief financial officer (CFO), with the coordination-support of the chief risk officer (CRO), should establish and lead this formal cross-functional task force. The task force aims to achieve the organization's cybersecurity strategic objectives by reaching out to third parties and identifying the vulnerabilities in the supply chain within their organizations. Who is involved depends on the size and vulnerability of the organization, but appropriate representation from the seven functions mentioned above is required. It may also be appropriate to include key third parties such as outsourcing partners.

Avoiding Silos to Focus on External and Internal Alignment

Silo-biased organization functions create additional challenges for organizations trying to protect themselves from cyber attacks. Systematic preparedness is key; questions like *what*, *when*, *how*, and *if* need to be discussed and analyzed in a holistic manner rather than in silos.

You should have in place an organization that aligns the people, processes, and technology that encompass your cybersecurity response structure. You then need to make clear roles and responsibilities, including, for example, incident response and cyber crisis management plans with critical supply chain partners.

Integrating Supply Chain Capability from an External Perspective

Organizations will have maturity capabilities for cyber risk management to a greater or lesser degree. These will lie in identification, protection, detection, response, and recovery processes that operate in synchronization.

The board will agree on risk acceptance/risk tolerance thresholds. Organizational readiness assessments can be used as a further method of understanding the cyber resilience status of the organization. Recovery scenarios will inform comprehensive recovery planning. Identifying and prioritizing organization resources helps to guide effective plans and realistic test scenarios. This preparation enables rapid recovery from incidents when they occur and helps to minimize the impact on the organization and its constituents (for example, National Institute of Standards and Technology [NIST] Special Publication 800-184). However, organizations need to bolster their maturity capabilities for their cyber risk management system with components that more specifically address the supply chain and external factors perspective. These typically involve the following six factors:

1. *Understanding the risk.* When looking at the business interruption exposure that might be caused by a critical supplier from a cyber disruption, it is key to understand the value at risk as well as the likelihood of disruption. You also need to understand cyber risk in the context of the data that your supplier is holding and the potential they might have to cause you reputational damage.

2. *Information sharing.* It is key that information relevant to cybersecurity is shared appropriately across the internal silos. It is also important that relevant information is shared with critical third parties.

3. *Crisis communications.* A documented, agreed, and tested communication plan needs be prepared based on a tailored set of cyber risk scenarios.

4. *Training/exercising.* As employees can be your weakest links, it is key that your own employees and those from key third parties adequately understand cyber risk processes. War gaming as well as intrusion/penetration testing performed by hired profession hackers can be useful ways to test the robustness of these plans.

5. *Risk transfer tools such as insurance.* These should be considered specifically in terms of third-party and supply chain exposure, where appropriate, in order to provide the relevant balance sheet protection. Insurance providers can also be a useful source of insights into cyber incidents based on their claims data.

6. *Leading practices and open standards.* The use of the leading practices and standards covered in the other chapters of this book should be considered when assessing items from a third-party perspective and how much they have been embedded by critical third parties. It is also important that there is a level of interaction with relevant public bodies, as cyber risk needs to be tackled by a combination of both private and public action.

a. An example of how this might take place is set out based on work carried out by Zurich Insurance and ESADE. (See Table 14.1.)
b. One recommendation arising from this work is for organizations to take targeted actions to mitigate cyber risk such as the mechanism of adopting the SANS 20 Critical Security Controls.

TABLE 14.1 Summary of Private-Sector and Policymaker Recommendations to Improve Global Cyber Governance

Recommendation	Proposed Mechanism
Business	
Greater information sharing to mitigate cyber risk.	Insurance industry via the CRO forum. Anonymized business loss reporting via private-sector–led incentives (e.g., Financial Services Information Sharing and Analysis Center [FS-ISAC]) and public-private bodies (e.g., European Union Agency for Network and Information Security [ENISA]).
Champion common values for global cyber governance in absence of governments' consensus.	Lobby through institutions, particularly privately led initiatives (e.g., CRO forum and multi-stakeholder dialogue forums, such as the World Economic Forum).
Take targeted actions to manage cyber risk.	Adopt SANS 20 Critical Security Controls. Further actions needed for larger organizations.
Enhance general resilience to cyber risk.	Built-in redundancy, incident response, and business continuity planning, scenario planning, and exercises.
Policymaker	
Strengthen those aspects of global governance that have worked properly and isolate them from geopolitical tensions.	Develop informal global cyber networks. Adopt an if-you-build-it-they-will-come approach.
Create a system-wide institution for incident response.	G20+20 Cyber Stability Board.
Enhance crisis management to deal with a potential systemic cyber crisis.	Cyber WHO (World Health Organization).
Seek greater public-private cooperation.	Incentivize alignment of public-private interests on cybersecurity.
Reinforce protection of critical information infrastructures.	Cyber stress tests.

Source: Zurich Insurance and ESADE Business School.

MEASURING CYBERSECURITY MANAGEMENT CAPABILITIES FROM AN EXTERNAL PERSPECTIVE

Supply Chain Risk Maturity Measured by Peer Organizations

The supply chain risk management system can be considered as a specialized *child* and subset of the *parent* overall ERM system. It shares a number of required organization capabilities with its "sibling," that is, the cyber risk management system.

It is particularly important to reach a higher level of supply chain risk management system maturity given the speed and the significant consequences of cybersecurity threats. One way organizations with supply chain exposures can do this is to deploy the supply chain risk management (SCRM) maturity model designed by peer organizations that are members of the not-for-profit the Supply Chain Risk Leadership Council (SCRLC). This model is one methodology and a tool designed to help managers assess and measure their organization's capabilities with respect to managing supply chain risk—which, of course, includes cyber risk. This model is freely available online as a gratis tool for self-assessment of SCRM capabilities.

Given the rising level of global cybersecurity threat, affected organizations should aim to reach a *"proactive" maturity level as a minimum* on the SCRLC maturity model. These are themed across five categories of capabilities (leadership, planning, implementation, evaluation, and improvement). The model produces three output charts that highlight the overall capability of an organization to manage supply chain risks and assessing the organization on a five-stage maturity rating scale (reactive up to aware, proactive, integrated, and resilient).

CONCLUSION

The following cyber risk management statement represents those organization capabilities the CEO and board expect to be demonstrated in terms of *cyber risk external factors, especially the supply chain.*

CYBER RISK EXTERNAL FACTORS AND SUPPLY CHAIN

The external context unique to the organization is established in respect of the cyber risks that are faced, especially in regard to the supply chain. It is a board-level priority to apply this as much to critical third parties as to the internal organization. The focus of organization cyber strategies is equally on developing resilience and protection, not simply on identifying individual cyber risks. External cyber resilience follows five steps to (1) map critical data and value flows for organization, including reputational impact; (2) teach the importance of data security and cyber resilience to employees and to relevant individuals within critical third parties; (3) develop external cyber incident and crisis management response plan(s) appropriate to key scenarios, ensuring regulators are notified where applicable; (4) review and benchmark critical third parties' cybersecurity measures; and (5) track and/or work with policymakers and regulators in the interconnected world of cyber risk public-private partnerships.

ABOUT THE SCRLC

The Supply Chain Risk Leadership Council (SCRLC) is a not-for-profit body made up of global organizations sharing supply chain knowledge. The SCRLC web site offers a supply chain risk management maturity model as an easy-to-use spreadsheet model downloadable for free from http://www .scrlc.com/*. You may then use your own spreadsheet either retained in its original form as a specialized risk maturity model for supply chain, or adapt the maturity level attained on it as the rating to the cyber risk maturity model in the epilogue to *The Cyber Risk Handbook*. We thank the board at the Supply Chain Risk Leadership Council USA, who have kindly granted permission to any reader of this book to download and use their spreadsheet model.

ABOUT NICK WILDGOOSE, BA (HONS), FCA, FCIPS

Nick is a qualified accountant and supply chain professional and has held a variety of senior global financial, supply chain, and commercial positions in a number of industry sectors, working for companies such as Pricewater-houseCoopers, BOC Group, the Virgin Group, and currently Zurich Insurance Group. He has spoken and written on a number of topics related to value chain management. He served on the board of the Chartered Institute of Purchasing and Supply, which is the biggest professional body in the world. He has also served as a specialist advisor to the World Economic

Forum on the topic of systemic supply chain risk and as chairman of the Supply Chain Risk Leadership Council, a select group of multinational companies looking to improve supply chain risk and still serves on the board. He is currently leading the rollout of innovative and award winning supply chain risk products for Zurich Insurance Group, which has given him the opportunity to interact with a large number of multinational companies and understand how they are addressing the real issues they are facing in terms of the globalization of their value chains and the threats they face from a cyber perspective.

CHAPTER 15

Internal Organization Context

Domenic Antonucci, Editor and Chief Risk Officer, Australia
Bassam Alwarith, Head of the National Digitization Program, Ministry of Economy and Planning, Saudi Arabia

"**C**yber risk is an enterprise-wide risk, not just an IT risk. The cyber risk management system comes under the umbrella enterprise risk management system," declared Nathan, the chief risk officer. Tom the CEO looked at Nathan and Grace, his head of human resources, both sitting in his office, and replied, "OK, but what does that mean? Our techies aren't famous for dealing with the rest of the business. In your roles, both of you engage in stewardship and coordination, so tell me how we internally organize. I want to know which functions are accountable and responsible for what, as well as how they are to internally support, consult, and inform each other."

THE INTERNAL ORGANIZATION CONTEXT FOR CYBERSECURITY

There are several international standards and voluntary guidance code approaches to understanding internal organization context. They are voluntary, as they are not mandated by laws.

Standards and Guidance Approaches

One set of standards that can be adapted to cybersecurity is from ISO/IEC 27001:2013 Information Technology–Security Techniques–Information Security Management Systems–Requirements. It covers the essential components for the cybersecurity internal organization context from the perspective of its parent, the information security function. These cover management commitment, information security coordination, allocation of information security roles and responsibilities, authorization process for information processing facilities, confidentiality agreements, contact with authorities, contact with special interest groups, independent review of information security, information security in project management, and segregation of duties.

Another voluntary guidance code approach is ISACA's COBIT 5: Enabling Processes. Its Appendix G is a useful reference and has partly informed the RASCI charts below.

Yet another guidance approach is to adapt the ISO 31000:2009, *Risk management—Principles and guidelines* standard descriptions of internal context for the purposes of cybersecurity and other risks. (For more detail on ISO 31000, see our Chapter 3, Principles Behind Cyber Risk Management). This serves to aid better understanding between the information security, information technology (IT), and other enterprise functions. ISO 31000 brings internal factors for cybersecurity to the fore, such as objectives-led consideration of the organization's internal stakeholders, governance and organization structures, standards, contracts, roles and capabilities, culture, information systems, information flows and decision-making processes. (These other factors are also covered in our other chapters.)

Cybersecurity within the Enterprise

To align the cybersecurity function to other enterprise functions is the clarion call required of modern organizations and their leadership. There is no other way an organization can build the speedy, adaptive, resilient, and responsive capabilities required to face the fast-paced evolving universe of cyber threats (and opportunities).

Effective cybersecurity within the modern organization requires a cyber risk management system. This involves the ongoing, effective and fast deployment of organization *capabilities* to mitigate cyber risk. Waiting to react is *game over*. The system is not only a framework or set of processes, but the ongoing interplay of many capability elements such as people, technology, policies, procedures, practices, third-party relationships, and culture—that is, all those elements or components that make cybersecurity repeatable, consistent, measureable, demonstrable, and responsive, rather than being overly dependent on the ad-hoc vagaries of individuals, silos, and committees.

The cyber risk management system is a subset and child of the parent enterprise-wide risk management (ERM) system and its governance architecture. It is as simple and complicated as that. There is no need to reinvent the wheel in this regard.

The cyber risk management system has a sibling link to the physical security function and to the business continuity management system (BCMS), which also falls under the same parent enterprise risk management system. Leaving aside for the moment where a cybersecurity function may report to, from a risk governance perspective, it is a part of the normal governance and reporting of the ERM system. If not, serious internal gaps may occur at all levels but especially at the strategic, operational, and interdependency levels. A cyber risk advisory committee (or steering committee or equivalents) may form a working party or task force and will naturally report the outputs from the cyber risk management system in the same way the BCM, security, or ERM systems would to, say, a risk and audit committee up to the board.

TAILORING CYBERSECURITY TO ENTERPRISE EXPOSURES

One of the most important roles for the CEO (with board oversight) is to tailor the capabilities of the cybersecurity function to enterprise-wide threats (and opportunities). This means aligning the design of the cybersecurity operating model to the enterprise (and vice versa). It also means making each enterprise function clear on and, accountable for, the set of capabilities the board and CEO expect them to bring to bear to prevent and respond to cyber threat (and opportunity).

Designing Your Own Cyber Risk Function Operating Model

The design of the cybersecurity operating model should be aligned with the ERM function operating model adopted by the enterprise that is already tailored to the organization's objectives, context, and risk profile. As a guide, the template in Table 15.1 is one way to design and assure that these two operating models could achieve the desired levels of alignment. Its content is illustrative, not prescriptive. Until an ERM function is in place, organizations may make alternative arrangements with other heads of functions, typically security or operations/supply chain.

The modern at-risk organization demands that the CEO (with board oversight) directs the alignment of the key functional roles. This means aligning the cybersecurity function and joint activities across the enterprise with other enterprise functions (and vice versa). Not all functions are equally important to cybersecurity and some may have a critical function at certain times (e.g., corporate communications dealing with external media and social media during a cyber crisis). This involves an understanding of

TABLE 15.1 Template for Designing a Cyber Risk Function Operating Model

	Information Security Model	Hybrid Model	Centralized RM Model
Governance and oversight	Always insourced	Cyber and BU risk committees report separately to board/CEO.	*Cyber and business unit risk committees report together under ERM/CRO structure to board/CEO.*
Reporting lines	CISO to head of IT	*CISO to head of IT and dotted line to CRO or head of security but conflict of interest minimized with by reporting to centralized committees.*	CISO reports directly to CRO or head of security and reports to central/board committees.
RM plans and policies	Developed mainly by the CISO, with/without external expert advice, approved by CEO.	*Corporate cyber and risk policy set by the central unit with supporting policies and procedures set by BUs.*	Set at corporate level in consultation with CISO and cascaded down. Includes RM plan and tracked capability maturity improvements.
RM language and methodology	Risk language, processes, and methods left to CISO/BU.	CISO/BU adopts risk language, processes and methods in accordance with central risk policy and risk management plan.	*Central function sets risk language, processes, and methods. Mandates across BUs. Monitors compliance.*
Accountabilities	Set by CISO/BU	*Shared with agreed control ranges and demarcation.*	Primarily rests with a centralized risk function headed by a CRO.
Responsibilities	Set by CISO/BU	*Shared. Defined control parameters.*	Primarily with CRO or centralized risk function.
Risk limits and compliance	CISO/IT managers set risk limits and monitor compliance independently.	*Group-level committee sets risk limits, which the business units operate. BUs may define tolerances, etc., but within group limits.*	Central function sets risk policy, appetite, tolerances. Monitors compliance.
RM info systems	No portfolio reporting capability. Systems differ between InfoSec and across BUs.	*Centralized risk-reporting system in place but CISO/IT manage and own their systems at the specialist technical level.*	Centralized RM information system centralized and deployed across all BUs including InfoSec.

Examples only appear above. Tailor to your organization. Italics represent typical large organization. RM, risk management; BU, business unit; CISO, chief information security officer; CRO, chief risk officer; ERM, enterprise risk management.

the interfaces between the cybersecurity function and the other functions that need to work together and at times team up, before, during, and after a cyber breach or crisis.

Typical Enterprise Functional Roles Most Involved in Cybersecurity *across* the Enterprise

Typical enterprise functional roles most involved in the building and measuring of cybersecurity capability across the enterprise are tabled in Table 15.2. The table depicts the broad relationship and hierarchy of the typical cyber-to-enterprise functional roles. These are the key players who need to work together in building and measuring cyber risk management system maturity.

TABLE 15.2 Typical Enterprise Functional Roles Most Involved in Cybersecurity

Governance		Audit Committee	Internal Audit	Board	
Management					
	Risk committee		CEO		
CISO	CRO	CIO CFO	Legal CSO	COO	HR
InfoSec risk champ	*Digital risk officer*			Supply chain manager	Corporate comms manager
	Insurance manager				
	Security manager				
	Business continuity manager				
Risk management systems for . . .					
	Enterprise				
Cyber	Business continuity				
	Security				

The governance roles are taken up by boards, risk committee(s), and internal audit, and shared by the CEO. The CEO executes strategy and directs executive managers from the CISO across to human resources (HR) with advice from risk committee(s) and/or risk/audit committee who also report to the board and other governance functions.

Aligning these key functions *across* the enterprise   A proven method to analyze, implement, and ensure alignment across functions as charted in Table 15.2 is to use a RASCI matrix. The RASCI matrix is a guidance tool to assist in the identification of roles and assigning of cross-functional responsibilities to a project deliverable or activity. RASCI represents: responsibility, accountable, support, consulted, and informed. RASCI definitions follow:

■ Responsibility: person or role responsible for carrying out or doing the task.
■ Accountable: person or role responsible for ensuring that the whole task is completed, approved, and/or successful.
■ Support: person or role providing support to the task during the implementing of the task/activity/process or service. Typically, a peer or less senior function or advisor.
■ Consulted: person or role whose advice or subject matter expertise is required before and/or during the task in order to complete it.
■ Informed: person or role that needs to be kept informed during and/or after the task, including who should be informed about the task or the decisions to complete task.

Table 15.3 uses the RASCI approach and may be used as a template for tailoring alignment to the needs of any organization. It focuses on the high-level interface between each of the key enterprise functions and their most senior accountable heads, including cybersecurity under the CISO, or the emerging digital risk officer (DRO). It provides a summarized guidance as to how all functions should work together to optimize cyber risk management system maturity. Its content is illustrative, not prescriptive (except that the CISO/DRO should not report to the CIO). This template will require some tailoring to fit the specific structure and needs of each organization.

Aligning Cybersecurity *within* Enterprise Functions

The CEO (with board oversight) should also direct the alignment of cybersecurity *within* each key enterprise function. These functions need to

TABLE 15.3 Aligning Cybersecurity *Across* the Enterprise by RASCI Matrix

Most Senior Functional Heads For ...	Board*	Risk Committee*	Internal Audit*	CEO	CIO	CISO	IS Risk Champ	CRO	DRO (emerging)	Insurance	Physical Security	Business Continuity	CFO	Legal/Compliance	CSO–Strategy	COO	Supply Chain	HR	Corp Comms
Governance, oversight, mandate, tone	A	S	S	R	I	I	I	C	*I*	I	I	I	I	C	I	I	I	I	I
Principles behind cyber RM system	C	C	S	A	C	R	I	C	*R*	I	C	C	C	C	C	C	I	I	C
Cybersecurity policies and procedures	I	I	I	A	C	R	I	C	*R*	C	I	I	I	C		I	I	C	I
Cyber strategy and strategic performance management	I	I	I	A	C	R	I	C	*R*			I	I		R			I	
Cyber standards and frameworks	I	I	I	I	C	R	I	A	*R*		C	C					I		I
Digital risk management enterprise-wide						I	C	C	*A*	R	C	C	C						
Identifying, analyzing, and evaluating cyber risks				I	I	C	R	C	*A*	R	C	C	C	C	C	C	C	C	C
Treating cyber risks			I	I	I	C	R	C	*A*	R	C	R	C	C	C	C	C	C	C
Treating cyber risks using process capabilities			I	I	I	C	R	C	*A*	R	C	R	R	C	C	C	C	C	C
Treating cyber risks using insurance and finance	I	I	I			S		A	*S*	R			R						
Monitoring and review: Key risk indicators	I	I	I			R	C	A	*R*					I					
Cybersecurity incident and crisis management	I	I	I	C	I	R		A	*R*	I		R	C	C		C			C
Business continuity management	I	I	I	C	C	R		A	*R*	I		R	C	I		R	C	C	C
External context and supply chain				I		R		C	*R*							R	A		
Internal organization context			I	A	C	R		R	*R*									I	I
Culture and human factors			I	A	C	R	C	C	*R*					C				R	S
Legal and compliance	I	I		A		S		S	*S*	C			C	R		I	I	S	S

(*continued*)

TABLE 15.3 (*Continued*)

Most Senior Functional Heads For ...	Board*	Risk Committee*	Internal Audit*	CEO	CIO	CISO	IS Risk Champ	CRO	DRO (emerging)	Insurance	Physical Security	Business Continuity	CFO	Legal/Compliance	CSO–Strategy	COO	Supply Chain	HR	Corp Comms
Assurance of cyber RM by all managers	I	I	I	A	R	R	R	R	*R*	R	R	R	R	R	R	R	R	R	R
Independent assurance of effectiveness of cyber RM, governance, and compliance	A		R	I	I	I	I	I	*I*	I	I	I	I	I	I	I	I	I	I
Information asset management				A	R	C		I	*C*			I	C						
Physical security aligned to cybersecurity				A	R			A	*R*		R	C							
Communications and operations management				A	R			I	*R*			I	C						I
Access controls				A	R			I	*R*			I	C						
Cybersecurity systems acquisition, development, and maintenance				A	R			I	*R*			I	C						
People RM				A	C	R	I	R	*R*	I	I	I	I	I	I	I	I	R	I
Cyber competencies/CISO				A	C	R	C	R									R		
Human resources security						I	A	S	*C*	A		R						R	C
Cyber RM system maturity effectiveness	I	A	C	R	R	R		R	*R*				C		I		C		
Corporate communications re cybersecurity	I			A		C	C	C									C		R

*Asteriks indicates governance function rather than executive management function. RM, risk management. Italics indicate an emerging role.

interrelate and team up with the cybersecurity function in order to deliver effective cyber risk management.

Tables 15.4 through 15.21 represent each of the above players. They may be used as guideline templates for any organization to tailor per their needs and objectives. They focus on what *each* of the key enterprise functions and their heads need to do, including cybersecurity under the CISO. As cybersecurity is such a dynamic space, the tables are not meant to be prescriptive and will need revision and tailoring over time. They serve as a useful starting point for debate and framing within any organization as well as a starting point for position description and reward program updates. The only prescription on good governance grounds is that the CISO/DRO should not report to the CIO.

Governance and Risk Oversight Functions for Cybersecurity

Corporate governance and risk oversight roles are taken up by board, risk committee(s), and internal audit reporting to them. The CEO directs management and executes the security strategy encompassing the cybersecurity strategy with advice from risk committee(s) who also report to board and other governance functions. The board of directors and CEO are accountable for overall business and organization performance and they have a fiduciary duty to assess and manage cyber risk. Regulators, including the Securities and Exchange Commission (SEC), have made clear they expect organization top leadership to be engaged on the issue. They can also play a key role in coordinating with critical third parties at an executive-to-executive level.

Leading international practice is to have a risk committee that reports to the full board and report up any cybersecurity matters. Suggested participants are the chairpersons for the board and its subcommittees (such as the audit and finance committee, the operations committee, and the HR committee) and from executive management, the: CEO, CISO/DRO, CIO, CRO, and CFO.

The independent assurance role for cybersecurity is uniquely played by internal audit.

The CEO integrates everything from the boardroom to the server room. The CEO role overlaps the areas of corporate governance and senior executive management. The CEO directs the executive management team from CISO and IT-related management functions right across to people-related functions such as human resources in Table 15.3.

Other key reporting lines to the CEO follow below under both IT-related and enterprise risk-related management functions dealing with cybersecurity.

Executive Management Functions for Cybersecurity

There are several executive management functions interrelated to IT that have a bearing on cybersecurity. But these functions do not all need to report to the CIO, particularly the CISO.

CISO Should Report to CEO The CISO should typically report directly to the CEO in these modern times of high cyber threat with a dotted line to both the CRO and the CIO. A current Internet search shows a strong trend toward CISO reporting to the CEO and it is already legislated this way in certain countries (e.g., Israel).

Variations to Reporting and Titles/Roles Debates over reporting lines are common in modern organizations. Does compliance report to general counsel or CEO? Does risk report to CEO or risk committee or finance or general counsel?

One thing that is clear, however, from a modern-day corporate governance perspective, is that the CISO should be independent of the CIO. Such a reporting line principle avoids potential conflict of interest over cybersecurity strategy execution, time-responsiveness during a crisis and resource allocation. While a CISO reporting to a CIO may have an option to escalate concerns this may not always work well in practice and the CIO may be driven by other imperatives other than those in the best interests of a cyber risk management system. Of course, a reporting line from CISO to CEO does not prevent that CISO from escalating matters over the CEO to the board in the name of good governance if that CEO is not responsive.

The challenge of course, is that modern CEOs are time pressured and some prefer to delegate certain areas to people who have a more detailed understanding for that area. If the CEO needs to delegate direct line reporting by the CISO for practical reasons (e.g., too many reports, low digitization risk exposure by the organization) and is legally free to do so, they can continue to avoid a conflict of interest (if the CISO reports to CIO) by delegating CISO reporting to the CRO. This will reinforce to all enterprise functions that the cyber risk management system is an integrated subset of the ERM system (which the CRO is accountable for).

Alternative options are for the CISO to report to the risk committee or audit and risk committee (but be administered by the CEO's secretariat or the company secretariat). CEOs with immature ERM functions may alternatively look to have the CISO report to the heads of security (physical security) or operations or shared services (if appropriate).

The full-time CISO role is *not* identical to an on-call crisis executive or *crisis action officer* position. (See Chapter 19, "Information Asset Management for Cyber," for a more information on this role.) A crisis action officer is on-call and triggered into action by a standard operating procedure

(SOP) for any type of crisis including—but not exclusive to—a cyber attack. A crisis executive/action officer will not be a CISO who will organize his cybersecurity expert/team separately to deal with incidents leading to crisis situations and will integrate with the wider organization crisis team. (See Chapter 12, "Cybersecurity Incident and Crisis Management," and Chapter 13, "Business Continuity Management and Cybersecurity.") A crisis executive/ action officer typically has the authority, SOP, and resources to do the back-end work for the PR organization, enable business continuity plans, and so on. The plan for a crisis team will clarify who this officer reports to in a crisis, which may include a crisis executive or command center managers. While the crisis executive action officer does not create plans (normally done in quiet times) they are involved in the execution of the plan and will interface with the board and major stakeholders. Once a crisis hits, the plans are executed by the people who are on duty and/or brought in for the occasion.

Larger or more mature organizations have a dedicated security operations center (SOC), command center structure, or sometimes even a cyber-security operations center. (For more on this, see Chapter 19, "Information Asset Management for Cyber," and Chapter 21, "Cybersecurity for Operations and Communications," which stresses the importance of an SOC). The SOC may or may not be part of the CISO's remit, but if so, the CISO will have a dotted line to the CIO. There are managed security service providers (MSSPs) providing SOC as an outsourced service.

The SOC function should be completely integrated with the command center structure. The CISO is typically not part of this command center structure but is brought into the picture if an incident/crisis involves information security. In larger financial institutions, for example, the command center structure is in place but dormant until a need for activation indicated by all the alerts it regularly receives. The head of the command center is on duty (i.e., on duty and on call 24/7 on top of his day-to-day job). There may be a weekly rotation among three or four command center heads, which are senior people but not necessarily the most senior executive managers.

Ownership of information technology falls under chief information officer (CIO).

Ownership of information security falls under the CISO. Some CISOs are already moving toward, or have already transformed, their roles into a DRO role (see Table 15.12).

The CISO should dedicate one of his team members as a part-time risk champion or risk lead. They act as the ambassador to the CRO and other enterprise functions that the CISO's team needs to partner with.

Enterprise Risk-Related Management Functions for Cybersecurity   The CRO is accountable to the CEO and risk/other governance committees for the enterprise risk management system and all its subsystems which include the cyber risk management system for cybersecurity and its sister systems such as the business continuity management (BCM), crisis management and physical security systems. Cybersecurity also involves cyber insurance (products to insure against cyber threat) and finance solutions, which fall under CRO accountability and represent a shared responsibility with the finance function. While in some organizations the insurance function may sit and report to the finance function, the enterprise accountability for the risk of a potential "insurance gap" risk falls to the CRO. Risk officers can ensure various stakeholders are connected in terms of assessing, managing, and responding to cyber risks. They can also provide access for key decision makers to leading practice methodologies, tools, and understanding.

Emergence of the Digital Risk Officer (DRO)   Gartner foresee the emergence of digital risk and the digital risk officer. Their research indicates that more than half of CEOs will have a senior "digital" leader role in their staff by the end of 2015 and by 2017, one-third of large enterprises engaging in digital business models and activities will also have a DRO role or equivalent.[1] The DRO will report to a senior executive outside of IT such as the CRO, a chief digital officer (CDO) or the chief operating officer (COO). Some CISO's are already moving towards, or have transformed, their roles into a DRO role (see below). (Editor note: this extract is taken from our *Chapter 24 People risk management*. At the time of publication, this is still an emerging area and the dividing lines are fuzzy and still not universally agreed or established). Ownership of specialization in enterprise-wide cyber risk management falls under the emerging role of the DRO.

Ownership of insurance and risk finance falls under the head of insurance.

Ownership of physical security, which is in itself increasingly becoming digitized, falls under the head of Physical Security.

Ownership of business continuity management (BCM) falls under the head of BCM. BCM may be agnostic about why assets were lost (i.e., which risk materialized) but their business-impact analysis focuses on "points of failure" including digital data assets.

Ownership of organizational financial matters falls under the CFO. A CFO's concerns may range from the potential costs of a cyber event and what the impact could be on the bottom line as well as the insurance implications an event may have. CFO's can play a key role in coordination, building the business case, and participating on a cyber task force or related committee.

Other Enterprise Management Functions Supporting Cybersecurity

While the above enterprise risk-related management functions are critical partners with the CISO's function and critical to cybersecurity, other enterprise functions have a critical role to play at times such as a cyber crisis and can lend ongoing support to cybersecurity as well. Their contributions and cooperative interaction with the CISO and CRO functions are important. These extend from legal and compliance across to HR and corporate communications.

Ownership of legal matters fall under a legal counsel and compliance officer. Ownership of compliance matters falls under the head of compliance, who may (or may not) report to the legal counsel. As regulations around cyber develop, legal and compliance roles become increasingly important in keeping other stakeholders informed and engaged. Lawsuits often follow if a cyber incident occurs in certain jurisdictions.

Ownership of organizational strategic matters falls under the CSO.

It is critical that cybersecurity is considered within the overall organization context, including the role of procurement/supply chain and operations functions in performing supplier due diligence and management. Interactions with customers and suppliers can create cybersecurity vulnerabilities. The protections these functions have in place need to be understood if they pose a weak point in an organization's cyber defenses. This is often reported as not adequately addressed, particularly where critical data is being exchanged. It is also important that these functions maintain daily operations and workplace stability during a cyber event.

Ownership of organizational operational matters falls under the COO.

Ownership of human resource matters falls under the head of Human Resources. Employees are often the weakest link in the cybersecurity chain. Simple errors and accidents—or deliberate actions—by employees can lead to costly cyber incidents. Training on best practices is critical, especially with the rise in sophisticated "spear-phishing" attacks targeting specific employees. Employees must be helped to understand the consequences of failure within the interconnected organizational context.

Ownership of corporate communications matters falls under the head of Corporate Communications.

TABLE 15.4 RASCI Matrix Cyber Role for Board Members (and Their Delegatory Bodies)

	Is RESPONSIBLE For …	Is ACCOUNTABLE For …	Is SUPPORTED By …	Is CONSULTED By …	Is INFORMED Of/By …
Before cyber crisis (pre-"boom")	* Oversees all organization capabilities to align cyber risks to key organization objectives * Board level advisory cyber committee, chaired by a board member (not IT) * Recordation of all C-suite and boardroom planning, discussion and actions * Culture & reward systems support cybersecurity * Effectiveness of cyber-to-enterprise risk management and internal control systems	* Governance, risk oversight and mandate for the enterprise * Independent assurance by internal audit of cyber risk management * Annual combined cyber risk and assurance report and board-level audit process of regular reviews * Tone at the top * Strategic direction, magnitude of risk it is prepared to take (risk appetite) to achieve objectives (risks of the cyber strategy) * Oversight that risks to delivery of the strategic objectives are managed effectively (Risks to the cyber strategy)	* CEO * Internal Audit independent assurance * Risk committee * Combined assurance by all enterprise units	* CEO * Cyber and risk committees (e.g., tone, strategy, appetite, culture, significance of risks, maturity) * For principles of timeliness, reasonableness, and preparedness	* Cybersecurity policies and procedures * Cyber strategy and strategic performance management * Cyber standards and frameworks * Cybersecurity incident, crisis and business continuity management * Legal and compliance * Significant risks and level of cybersecurity capability maturity
During/after cyber crisis (post-"boom")	* Decision making from crisis response team and business continuity reports sent to C-suite	* Oversight for prosecuting or defending cyber lawsuits * Disclosure of breach to partners, public, and owners of contractually transferred data	* As above * BCM system	* CEO * Cyber and risk committees (e.g., tone, strategy, appetite, culture, significance of risks, maturity)	* Of ITC/InfoSec escalation from incident to crisis * By the internal ITC crisis investigation team report as an input to legal and other action

TABLE 15.5 RASCI Matrix Cyber Role for Risk Committee (RC)

	Is RESPONSIBLE For ...	Is ACCOUNTABLE For ...	Is SUPPORTED By ...	Is CONSULTED By ...	Is INFORMED Of/By ...
Before cyber crisis (pre-"boom")	* Reports to board on monitoring and review of cyber risks, including KRI's input to strategic performance management system * Encouraging a culture that is risk aware and control-minded where risk management is a core competence, entrepreneurial, informed, responsive to constant changes in the risk landscape and is transparent * Steering the alignment between cyber- and enterprise-wide risk management systems * Settles issues aligning management and risk specialty functions to avoid unnecessary escalations to CEO or board	* To the full board * Maturity effectiveness of cyber-to-enterprise risk management system	* Member group of executives by CEO * CISO, CRO, and all enterprise executives * Governance, oversight, mandate, tone	* C-suite boardroom planning, discussion, and actions * All cyber stakeholders for steering * Internal audit * Management and risk functions re: breaches of principles behind cyber risk management system	* Cybersecurity policies and procedures * Cyber strategy and strategic performance management * Cyber standards and frameworks * Risk treatments * Cybersecurity incident and crisis management * Business continuity management * Legal and compliance
During/after cyber crisis (post-"boom")	* Considers crisis response reports and business continuity decision making from top management	* Optimizing risk-informed crisis management decision making	* Board, CEO, CISO, CRO * All enterprise executives	* Risk implications for prosecuting or defending cyber lawsuits (especially for reputation)	* Impending key decision making (e.g., business continuity, insurance, physical security, external notifications, lawsuits)

TABLE 15.6 RASCI Matrix Cyber Role for Internal Audit Function (IA)

	Is RESPONSIBLE For …	Is ACCOUNTABLE For …	Is SUPPORTED By …	Is CONSULTED By …	Is INFORMED Of/By …
Before cyber crisis (pre-"boom")	* Independent assurance to board and management on effectiveness of the cyber risk management system * Evaluate cyber controls and treatment plans for significant risks * Audits and/or reviews of the board-level advisory cyber committee	* High levels of independent and objective assurance via recommendations	* Board and Audit committee governance, oversight, mandate, tone * CEO and executives * Principles behind cyber risk management system	* Board and CEO * Cyber RM system maturity effectiveness	* Combined assurance from other units * Recordation of all C-suite and boardroom planning, discussion, and actions * Board-level audit process of regular reviews * By cyber risk management treatment plans and activities * Cybersecurity policies & procedures * Cyber strategy & strategic performance management * Cyber standards and frameworks * Cybersecurity incident and crisis management * Business continuity management
During/after cyber crisis (post-"boom")	* Fresh postcrisis assurance on changes to the cyber risk management system and board-level advisory cyber committee process	* Revised assurance	* Board and Audit committee * CEO and executives	* Board and CEO	

222

TABLE 15.7 RASCI Matrix Cyber Role for Chief Executive Officer (CEO)

	Is RESPONSIBLE For ...	Is ACCOUNTABLE For ...	Is SUPPORTED By ...	Is CONSULTED By ...	Is INFORMED Of/By ...
Before cyber crisis (pre-"boom")	* Manages all executives and holds them accountable to integrate enterprise-wide cybersecurity * Governance, oversight, mandate, tone * Defines cyber risk appetite aligned with enterprise risk and ensures strategies fall within it * Manages cyber issues by principles of currency, reasonableness, and preparedness * Effectiveness of cyber-to-enterprise risk management and internal control systems * On board-level advisory cyber committee	* CISO/DRO and "connecting the board room with the server room" * Cyber RM system maturity effectiveness * Principles behind cyber risk management system * Cybersecurity policies and procedures * Strategy and strategic performance management * Internal organization context * Culture and human factors * Legal and compliance (e.g., fiduciary duties) * Assurance by all enterprise functions * Information asset management * People risk management * Cyber competencies/CISO hire * Corporate communications	* Board, IA, and Audit committee * CISO/DRO, CRO primarily * Other enterprise executives secondarily	* Board, IA and Audit committee * Cybersecurity incident and crisis management * Business continuity management	* By combined assurance, IA and Board-level audit process of regular reviews * Recordation of all C-suite and boardroom planning, discussion and actions * By ITC/info sec, risk manager * Assessing and treating of cyber risks * Monitoring and review: KRIs Key Risk Indicators * External context and supply chain * HR security
During/after cyber crisis (post-"boom")	* Leading the crisis response team and decision making from crisis response team reports	* Recommendations to Board to prosecute or defend cyber lawsuits * Disclosure of breach to partners, public, and owners of contractually transferred data	* CISO/DRO, CRO, Legal, CorpComms * Crisis response team	* CISO/DRO, CRO * Crisis response team	* Of ITC/ InfoSec escalation from incident to crisis * Crisis response management and recovery * By the internal ITC Crisis Investigation team report as an input to legal and other action

TABLE 15.8 RASCI Matrix Cyber Role for Chief Information Officer (CIO)

	Is <u>R</u>ESPONSIBLE For …	Is <u>A</u>CCOUNTABLE For …	Is <u>S</u>UPPORTED By …	Is <u>C</u>ONSULTED By …	Is <u>I</u>NFORMED Of/By …
Before cyber crisis (pre-"boom")	* Aligning IT and organization strategies * Planning, managing, and resourcing delivery of IT services to support organization objectives * *Avoids* line management of CISO/DRO to avoid conflict of interest (e.g., resourcing, strategy) * Combined assurance	* Physical security aligned to cybersecurity and IT systems * Communications and operations management * Access controls * Cybersecurity systems acquisition, development, and maintenance	* Supports CISO/DRO and vice versa * CRO	* CISO/DRO, CRO, head of BCM * Principles behind cyber risk management system * Cybersecurity policies and procedures * Cyber standards and frameworks * Digital risk management enterprise-wide * Treating cyber risks * Internal organization context * Culture and human factors management * People risk management * Cyber competencies/CISO/DRO	* CISO/DRO and cybersecurity function * Cybersecurity incident and crisis management plans * By board-level audit process of regular reviews * By enterprise managers of alignment requirements (e.g., for business continuity plans, insurance, strategic performance management, legal, HR) * Governance, oversight, mandate, tone * Independent assurance
During/after cyber crisis (post-"boom")			* Support to CISO/DRO and CRO for enterprise-wide management reporting, decision-making and actions (e.g., disclosure of breach to partners, public, and owners of contractually transferred data)	* CISO/DRO, CRO	* Cybersecurity incident and crisis management

TABLE 15.9 RASCI Matrix Cyber Role for Chief Information Security Officer (CISO)

	Is RESPONSIBLE For …	Is ACCOUNTABLE For …	Is SUPPORTED By …	Is CONSULTED By …	Is INFORMED Of/By …
Before cyber crisis (pre-"boom")	* Cybersecurity standards/frameworks, policies, and procedures * Cyber strategy, principles, capability maturity and strategic performance management * Assess, treat, monitor, and report cyber risk and KRIs * Cybersecurity incident and crisis management * Business continuity management alignment * Sharing risk re: external context/supply chain * Internal context for culture, human factors, manages an effective intelligence-based cyber team with specialist competencies (e.g., data scientists, linguists, engineers, analysts, planners, strategists) * Combined assurance * Management of information assets; communications and operations; access control; and systems acquisition, development, and maintenance * Cyber RM system maturity effectiveness * Information security governance (e.g., cyber committee) * Information risk management and compliance * Information security program development and management * Annual combined cyber risk and assurance report and board-level audit process of regular reviews	* To CEO/CRO for security of enterprise information in all of its forms, inclusive of digital assets * People risk management	* Cyber and risk committee and CRO * Legal and compliance * Other enterprise managers * External service providers * Insurance and finance managers	* CEO, CRO re digital risk management enterprise-wide * Manages cyber strategy in co-coalition with CRO and CSO * Inputs for recordation of all C-suite and boardroom planning, discussion, and actions * Contact with authorities and special interest groups	* By external expert providers * By board-level audit process of regular reviews, governance, oversight, mandate, tone * By CEO, CRO, and enterprise managers of alignment requirements * Contact with authorities and special interest groups * Independent assurance
During/after cyber crisis (post-"boom")	* Information security incident management and escalation to crisis management * Inputs via CRO for enterprise-wide management reporting, decision making, and actions (e.g., disclosure of breach to partners, public, and owners of contractually transferred data)		* As above * Corp Comms	* Prosecuting or defending cyber lawsuits * CRO, Legal, Corp Comms * External service providers * Authorities and special interest groups	* Of ITC/InfoSec escalation from incident to crisis management and recovery * By the internal ITC crisis investigation team report as an input to legal and other action

TABLE 15.10 RASCI Matrix Cyber Role for Information Security Risk Champion (ISRC)

	Is RESPONSIBLE For …	Is ACCOUNTABLE For …	Is SUPPORTED By …	Is CONSULTED By …	Is INFORMED Of/By …
Before cyber crisis (pre-"boom")	* Assure/report progress to CISO/DRO, CRO, and Risk committee(s) as required * Risk liaison within and without the InfoSec function for CRO * Coordinates and supports risk owners within function to assess, treat, monitor, and report cyber risks * Enhances risk awareness within function * Update the risk responses on RM information system in a timely manner in coordination with the risk owner(s) * Input to CRO's annual risk management report		* CISO/DRO, CRO * InfoSec team and risk owners * Human resources security	CRO and risk owners to … * Manage the risks assigned to an acceptable level * Articulate and manage the controls on which reliance can be placed * Articulate and manage the action required (with related stakeholders) to achieve target level of risk * Develop and report on Key risk indicators (KRI) * Provide appropriate feedback to the CISO/DRO and CRO on a regular basis regarding progress	* CISO/DRO and cybersecurity functionaries * Governance, oversight, mandate, tone
During/after cyber crisis (post-"boom")	* Inputs via CRO for enterprise-wide management reporting, decision making, and actions (e.g., disclosure of breach to partners, public, and owners of contractually transferred data)	* Risk liaison within and without the InfoSec function	* CISO/DRO, CRO * InfoSec team and risk owners	* CISO/DRO and risk owners to manage the escalated risks	* Of ITC/ InfoSec escalation from incident to crisis management and recovery * By the internal ITC crisis investigation team report as an input to legal and other action

TABLE 15.11 RASCI Matrix Cyber Role for Chief Risk Officer (CRO)

	Is RESPONSIBLE For …	Is ACCOUNTABLE For …	Is SUPPORTED By …	Is CONSULTED By …	Is INFORMED Of/By …
Before cyber crisis (pre-"boom")	* Combined assurance and effectiveness of cyber risk management and maturity improvement * Internal organization context for cyber risk * Annual risk management report, including cyber risk * Member of board-level advisory cyber committee * Intermediary improving communication between C-suite and IT; reconciling opposing drivers (C-suite focus on costs and the bottom line vs. IT focus on the systems and prevention of a cyber event)	* For DRO * For CISO (if delegated by CEO) or dotted line if not * Digital risk management enterprise-wide * Physical security aligned to cybersecurity * Treating cyber risks using insurance and finance * Cyber standards and frameworks * Assess, treat, monitor, assure and report cyber risks and review cyber KRIs * Monitoring and review cyber KRIs * Cybersecurity incident and crisis management * Business continuity management	* Risk and cyber committees * CISO/DRO, IS Risk Champ and competencies * Other risk specialists for BCM, security, insurance, finance, legal/compliance * HR security * Risk support, tools, techniques, and training across functions	* Governance, oversight, mandate, tone * Cyber strategy, principles and strategic performance management * Cybersecurity policies and procedures * External context and supply chain * Culture and human factors * Cyber competencies CISO/DRO * Corporate communications * Appropriate internal control structures with adequate allocation of duties	* Board and CEO mandate, commitment and tone at top * Independent assurance management by Internal Audit * By irregularities, gaps or concerns (and bring to attention of the Board or its committees) * IT Information asset management, asset controls, systems acquisition, etc, * Adequacy and effectiveness of internal control, accuracy and completeness of reporting, compliance with laws and regulations
During/after cyber crisis (post-"boom")	* Lead coordinator of crisis response reports to top management * "Knock-on" risk management (e.g., disclosure of breach to partners, public and owners of contractually transferred data)	* Optimizing risk-informed escalation and crisis management decision making	* As above * Other specialists for Corp Comms, HR, Ops, Supply Chain	* Risk implications for prosecuting or defending cyber lawsuits (especially for reputation)	* Impending key decision making (e.g., business continuity, insurance, physical security, external notifications, lawsuits)

TABLE 15.12 RASCI Matrix Cyber Role for the Digital Risk Officer (DRO)

	Is <u>R</u>ESPONSIBLE For …	Is <u>A</u>CCOUNTABLE For …	Is <u>S</u>UPPORTED By …	Is <u>C</u>ONSULTED By …	Is <u>I</u>NFORMED Of/By …
Before cyber crisis (pre-"boom")	* Digital risk management enterprise-wide * Cybersecurity standards/frameworks, policies, and procedures * Cyber strategy, principles, capability maturity and strategic performance management * Assess, treat, monitor, and report cyber risk and KRIs * Cybersecurity incident and crisis management * Business continuity management alignment * Sharing risk re: external context/supply chain * Internal context for culture, human factors, manages an effective intelligence-based cyber team with specialist competencies (e.g., data scientists, linguists, engineers, analysts, planners, strategists) * Combined assurance * Management of information assets; communications and operations; access control; and systems acquisition, development and maintenance * Cyber RM system maturity effectiveness * Information security governance (e.g., cyber committee) * Information risk management and compliance * Information security program development and management * Annual combined cyber risk and assurance report and board-level audit process of regular reviews	* To CRO for security of enterprise digital-based information and assets * People risk management	* Cyber and risk committee and CRO * Legal and compliance * Other enterprise managers * External service providers * Insurance and finance managers	* Manages cyber strategy in co-coalition with CRO and CSO * Inputs for recordation of all C-suite and boardroom planning, discussion, and actions * Contact with authorities and special interest groups	* By external expert providers * By board-level audit process of regular reviews, governance, oversight, mandate, tone * By CEO, CRO, and enterprise managers of alignment requirements * Contact with authorities and special interest groups * Independent assurance
During/after cyber crisis (post-"boom")	* Information security incident management and escalation to crisis management * Inputs via CRO for enterprise-wide management reporting, decision making, and actions (e.g., disclosure of breach to partners, public, and owners of contractually transferred data)		* As above * Corp Comms	* Prosecuting or defending cyber lawsuits * CRO, Legal, Corp Comms * External service providers * Authorities and special interest groups	* Of ITC/InfoSec escalation from incident to crisis management and recovery * By the internal ITC crisis investigation team report as an input to legal and other action

TABLE 15.13   RASCI Matrix Cyber Role for Head of Insurance (HI)

	Is RESPONSIBLE For …	Is ACCOUNTABLE For …	Is SUPPORTED By …	Is CONSULTED By …	Is INFORMED Of/By …
Before cyber crisis (pre-"boom")	* Treating cyber risks using insurance and finance transfer solutions * Tracking the evolving cyber insurance market and overall risk finance options * Insurance implications from fiduciary duties and "reasonable" action for the "processes" to assess and manage cyber risk * Implications for noncyber and related insurances (e.g., business interruption, directors and officers, public liability insurance, property insurance)	* To CEO for optimizing risk-informed escalation and crisis management decision-making related to insurance and risk transfer	* CISO team, CRO * Security and business continuity managers	* Legal, regulatory and compliance * Cybersecurity policies and procedures * Identifying, analyzing, evaluating, and treating cyber risks	* Governance, oversight, mandate, tone * Cybersecurity policies and procedures * Legal, regulatory, and compliance * Changes to risk management system via CRO
During/after cyber crisis (post-"boom")	* Lead coordinator of information required for cyber insurance claims * "Knock-on" effects for insurance purposes (e.g., disclosure of breach to partners, public, and owners of contractually transferred data)		* As above	* Cybersecurity incident, crisis and business continuity management * Risk implications for insurance and what is noninsurable (e.g., reputation)	* Future insurance ramifications via CRO and reinsurers (e.g., increased premiums)

TABLE 15.14 RASCI Matrix Cyber Role for Head of Physical Security (HPS)

	Is RESPONSIBLE For …	Is ACCOUNTABLE For …	Is SUPPORTED By …	Is CONSULTED By …	Is INFORMED Of/By …
Before cyber crisis (pre-"boom")	* Physical security aligned to cybersecurity * Support HR and CISO for human resources security * Inputs to cybersecurity and business continuity plans, insurance placements	* Physical-to-cyber treatment as enterprise risk, not just IT/InfoSec risk * Physical security-to-cyber strategy risk implications	* CRO, CISO, IS risk champ, BCM and HR manager	* CRO for physical-to-cyber aspects of all C-suite and boardroom planning, discussion and actions * Physical-to-cyber risk management system as subset of ERM system and aligned to business continuity management system (BCMS) * Principles behind cyber risk management system * Cyber standards and frameworks * Identifying, analyzing, evaluating and treating cyber risks	* CRO/CISO requirements for physical-to-cyber risk management system related to physical security of locations, servers, etc.
During/after cyber crisis (post-"boom")	* Physical-to-cyber inputs via CRO as lead coordinator of crisis response reports to top management * "Knock-on" effects for physical-to-cyber management (e.g., disclosure of breach to partners, public, and owners of contractually transferred data)	* Optimizing physical-to-cyber-informed escalation and crisis management decision making	* As above	* CCTV/other evidence and information for physical-to-cyber implications for prosecuting or defending cyber lawsuits (especially for reputation)	* CRO/CISO change requirements to physical-to-cyber risk management system related to physical security of locations, servers, etc. * Relocation to other premises and locations requiring security

TABLE 15.15   RASCI Matrix Cyber Role for Head of Business Continuity (HBC)

	Is RESPONSIBLE For …	Is ACCOUNTABLE For …	Is SUPPORTED By …	Is CONSULTED By …	Is INFORMED Of/By …
Before cyber crisis (pre-"boom")	* Business continuity management aligned to cyber risk management * Coordinates and integrates business continuity and cyber risk escalation management for cyber threats * Aligns cybersecurity to enterprise business continuity plans and considers insurance placements	* To CRO for business continuity of operations, ensuring organization critical functions recover from disruptive events such as a cyber breach or crisis	* CISO, COO, Supply Chain, HC, HSC	* CRO for BCM-to-cyber aspects of all C-suite and boardroom planning, discussion, actions, principles, standards, and frameworks * Cyber incident and crisis management system aligned to business continuity management plan and system (BCMS) * "Points of failure" for cyber information asset management, physical security aligned to cybersecurity, communications and operations management, access control, and cybersecurity systems acquisition, development and maintenance * Identifying, analyzing, evaluating and treating cyber risks	* CRO / CISO requirements of changes to BCM-to-cyber risk management system related to single points of failure to data assets such as servers * Governance, oversight, mandate, tone * Cybersecurity policies and procedures
During/after cyber crisis (post-"boom")	* BCM-to-cyber inputs via CRO as lead coordinator of crisis response reports to top management * "Knock-on" effects for BCM-to-cyber management (e.g., disclosure of breach to partners, public, and owners of contractually transferred data)	* Optimizing BCM-to-cyber-informed escalation and crisis management decision making	* As above	* CISO in order to activate the BC plan	* Changes to risk management system related to physical security of locations, servers, etc. * Possible relocation to other premises and locations * Possible emergency shutdown of systems by CISO

TABLE 15.16 RASCI Matrix Cyber Role for CFO

	Is RESPONSIBLE For …	Is ACCOUNTABLE For …	Is SUPPORTED By …	Is CONSULTED By …	Is INFORMED Of/By …
Before cyber crisis (pre-"boom")	* Treating cyber risks using insurance and finance * Takes cyber risk ownership within their enterprise function to assess, treat, monitor, and report * On board-level advisory cyber committee * Manages financial issues by cyber principles of currency, reasonableness, and preparedness	* All aspects of financial management, inclusive of financial risk and resources needed for cybersecurity * Financial aspects for fiduciary duties and "reasonable" action for the "processes" to assess and manage cyber risk * Financing of cyber strategy and resourcing	* Board-level advisory cyber committee * CEO, CRO, insurance manager	* Financial aspects of all C-suite and boardroom planning, discussion and actions * Identifying, analyzing, evaluating and treating cyber risks * Cyber insurance * Principles behind cyber risk management system * Cybersecurity incident, crisis and business continuity management * Culture and human factors * Legal and compliance * Cyber RM system maturity effectiveness	* By IT/info sec, risk manager and business continuity plans for cybersecurity
During/after cyber crisis (post-"boom")	* Management of a cyber breach costs and bottom-line impacts * Lead on financial decision making based on crisis response team reports * Financial aspects of any disclosure of breach to partners, public, and owners of contractually transferred data		* Board-level advisory cyber committee * CEO, CRO, insurance manager	* Financial aspects for prosecuting or defending cyber lawsuits	* Of IT/InfoSec escalation from incident to crisis management and recovery * By the internal ITC crisis investigation team report as an input to financial decision making

TABLE 15.17 Rasci Matrix Role for Legal Counsel and Compliance (LCC)

	Is RESPONSIBLE For …	Is ACCOUNTABLE For …	Is SUPPORTED By …	Is CONSULTED By …	Is INFORMED Of/By …
Before cyber crisis (pre-"boom")	* Takes ownership within their enterprise function to assess, treat, monitor, and report cyber legal risk and regulatory * Engages stakeholders as regulations change and plans to accommodate regulatory expansion towards widely accepted standards * Pre-defines issues by principles of currency, reasonableness, and preparedness (e.g., cross-border alternate IT processing arrangements during a crisis) * Directs documentation of the cyber risk management "process" * Reviews past contracts, manages future contracts and contractual compliance * Determines if information-sharing partnerships with government or other parties may benefit	* Legal counsel member of board-level advisory cyber committee	* CRO, CISO * Privacy officer monitoring of risk and organization impacts from privacy laws and compliance, or data protection officer under 2018 EU regulations	* Board and CEO governance, principles, and risk oversight for fiduciary duties and "reasonable" action for the "processes" to assess and manage cyber risk * Cyber strategy and implementation of entire "process-oriented" cycle of cyber defense planning, including committee creation, application, simulation, auditing, and recordation * Cybersecurity policies and procedures * Cyber standards and frameworks * Cybersecurity incident and crisis management * Recordation of all C-suite and boardroom planning, discussion, and actions * Insurance terms and conditions * Identifying, analyzing, evaluating, and treating cyber risks	* By board-level audit process of regular reviews * Business continuity management * By ITC/InfoSec, risk manager, and business continuity plans for cybersecurity

(continued)

TABLE 15.17 (*Continued*)

	Is RESPONSIBLE For …	Is ACCOUNTABLE For …	Is SUPPORTED By …	Is CONSULTED By …	Is INFORMED Of/By …
During/after cyber crisis (post-"boom")	* Member of crisis response teams set in action with constant documentation of steps taken and reports sent to C-suite * Internal investigation to record events and actions in preparation for legal action(s) for or against * Manages any bailiffs to assess collection of technical traces for future litigation * Manages any "active defense" and authorization from the foreign network owner before operations are commenced to help limit liability for actions taken * Prosecuting or defending cyber lawsuits * Disclosure of breach to partners in the private and public sector * Notifications to the public and owners of contractually transferred data		* CRO, CISO, HR, CorpComms * Bailiffs	* For advice—either as in-house or outside counsel depending on the potential need to preserve privilege—established immediately and sustained throughout the response	* Of ITC/InfoSec escalation from incident to crisis management and recovery * By digital forensic software managed by ITC/InfoSec * By the internal ITC crisis investigation team report as an input to legal action * By CFO on financial estimations of impacts and prosecution financial support

TABLE 15.18 RASCI Matrix Cyber Role for Chief Strategy Officer (CSO)

	Is RESPONSIBLE For …	Is ACCOUNTABLE For …	Is SUPPORTED By …	Is CONSULTED By …	Is INFORMED Of/By …
Before cyber crisis (pre-"boom")	* Aligns cyber strategy with strategic performance management system * Accepts capability targets as CISO's KPIs and CRO's KRIs input to strategic performance management system * Advisor to board-level advisory cyber committee		* CISO, CRO	* Implementation of cyber strategy and principles * CISO's cyber strategy aligned to organization strategy and objectives * CISO's cyber strategy covers key components that keep up with fast pace of evolving cyber threat universe * Identifying, analyzing, evaluating, and treating cyber risks	* Monitor and review cyber strategy * Cyber KPIs (from CISO) * Cyber KRIs (from CRO) * Cyber RM system maturity effectiveness
During/after cyber crisis (post-"boom")	* Strategic advice to C-suite (e.g., implications for external context, stakeholders, organization objectives)	* Review of cyber strategy	* CISO, CRO	* Disclosure of breach to partners, public, and owners of contractually transferred data if change to external strategic context for organization	* Crisis management and recovery reports

TABLE 15.19 RASCI Matrix Cyber Role for Chief Operations Officer (COO)

	Is RESPONSIBLE For …	Is ACCOUNTABLE For …	Is SUPPORTED By …	Is CONSULTED By …	Is INFORMED Of/By …
Before cyber crisis (pre-"boom")	* Takes cyber risk ownership within their enterprise function to assess, treat, monitor, and report * Sustaining daily operations and business processes * Supply Chain management function and overseeing protections that customers and vendors maintain to guard against attack	* Operation of the enterprise, inclusive of cybersecurity * Overseeing reduction in supply chain and operational vulnerabilities to cyber attack	* CRO, BCM Manager	* Head of supply chain, business continuity plan, and testing execution * Identifying, analyzing, evaluating, and treating cyber risks	* Legal and compliance * By head of supply chain (e.g., of ITC/InfoSec, risk manager, and business continuity plans for cybersecurity)
During/after cyber crisis (post-"boom")	* Lead on coordinating of operational business continuity during crisis	* Managing operations, including customers and vendors	* CRO, BCM Manager * Head of Supply Chain	* By head of supply chain re: executed business continuity plan * Disclosure to customers and vendors	* By head of supply chain (e.g., of ITC/InfoSec escalations, ITC crisis investigation team report, and any customer and vendor intelligence)

TABLE 15.20 RASCI Matrix Cyber Role for Head of Supply Chain (HSC)

	Is RESPONSIBLE For …	Is ACCOUNTABLE For …	Is SUPPORTED By …	Is CONSULTED By …	Is INFORMED Of/By …
Before cyber crisis (pre-"boom")	* Takes ownership within their enterprise function to assess, treat, monitor, and report cyber risk * Sustaining supply chain daily operations and business processes * Managing external dependency risks, especially relationships involving information and communications technology (ICT) with supply chain or third-party risks	* Reducing supply chain and external context vulnerabilities to cyber attack	* COO, CRO, BCM manager	* By COO, business continuity plan and testing execution * Identifying, analyzing, evaluating, and treating cyber risks	* Cybersecurity governance, cyber risk management system, cyber policies and procedures * By ITC/InfoSec, risk manager, and business continuity plans for cybersecurity * Legal and compliance
During/after cyber crisis (post-"boom")	* Lead coordinator business continuity with the supply chain during crisis	* Managing customers, vendors, and other supply chain or third parties	* COO, CRO, BCM manager	* By business continuity plan execution * By any disclosure to customers, vendors, and supply chain	* Of ITC/InfoSec escalation from incident to crisis management and recovery * By the internal ITC crisis investigation team report as an input to risk-informed decision making * By any customer, vendor, and supply chain intelligence

TABLE 15.21 RASCI Matrix Cyber Role for Head of Human Resources (HR)

	Is RESPONSIBLE For …	Is ACCOUNTABLE For …	Is SUPPORTED By …	Is CONSULTED By …	Is INFORMED Of/By …
Before cyber crisis (pre-"boom")	* Cyber competencies/ CISO * Culture and human factors * Manages people issues by cyber principles of currency, reasonableness, and preparedness * On board-level advisory cyber committee * Training on best practices (e.g., countering "phishing" attacks targeting specific employees)	* Cyber competencies/ CISO * Human resources security * Planning and policies for enterprise human resources	* CEO, CISO, CRO * Legal and compliance	* Prioritizing cybersecurity practices and resourcing, including CISO recruitment and retention * Reducing errors or deliberate actions by employees that may lead to costly cyber incidents * People aspects for fiduciary duties and "reasonable" action for the "processes" to assess and manage cyber risk * Cybersecurity policies and procedures * Cyber RM system maturity effectiveness * Cybersecurity incident, crisis and business continuity management * Identifying, analyzing, evaluating, and treating cyber risks	* Governance, oversight, mandate, tone * Principles behind cyber risk management systems * Cyber strategy and strategic performance management * Cyber standards and framework * Internal organization context * By ITC/InfoSec, risk manager, and business continuity plans for cybersecurity
During/after cyber crisis (post-"boom")	* Management of a cyber breach people impacts * Lead on people decision making based on crisis response team reports * People and reputation aspects of any disclosure of breach to partners, public, and owners of contractually transferred data	* Reducing negative cyber breach people impacts * Lead on people decision making based on crisis response team reports * People and reputation aspects of any disclosure of breach to partners, public, and owners of contractually transferred data	* CEO, CISO, CRO, Corp Comms	* People aspects for prosecuting or defending cyber lawsuits	* Of ITC/InfoSec escalation from incident to crisis management and recovery * By the internal ITC crisis investigation team report as an input to people management

TABLE 15.22 RASCI Matrix Cyber Role for Head of Corporate Communications (HCC)

	Is RESPONSIBLE For …	Is ACCOUNTABLE For …	Is SUPPORTED By …	Is CONSULTED By …	Is INFORMED Of/By …
Before cyber crisis (pre-"boom")	* Takes ownership within their enterprise function to assess, treat, monitor, and report cyber risk * Selects and prepares external public relations (PR) experts in case of crisis * At-call advisor to board-level advisory cyber committee * Supports HR training and awareness with broader internal communications on best practices (e.g., countering "phishing" attacks, awareness campaigns to broader employees)		* HR * CRO, CISO	* Alignment of cyber crisis corporate communications as a subset of corporate crisis management/business continuity plan * Proactive internal communications to reduce errors or deliberate actions by employees that may lead to costly cyber incidents * Timely remediation activity to negative social media (both internal or external) * Support HR for people aspects for fiduciary duties * Principles behind cyber risk management system * Identifying, analyzing, evaluating, and treating cyber risks	* By ITC/InfoSec and enterprise manager plans for cybersecurity crisis response and events * Human resources security
During/after cyber crisis (post-"boom")	* Management of internal corporate communication impacts with staff * Management of external public relations (PR) impacts * Outsourced specialist PR or insourced advice for management decision making and crisis team response * Advice on disclosure of breach to partners, public, and owners of contractually transferred data	* Reducing negative cyber breach people impacts * Support to HR for people decision making based on crisis response team reports * Support to HR for people and reputation aspects of any disclosure of breach to partners, public, and owners of contractually transferred data	* HR, legal, and compliance * CRO, CISO	* Outsourced specialist PR * ITC/InfoSec and enterprise manager crisis planning and reactions requiring people communications	* Outsourced specialist PR * By ITC/InfoSec and enterprise manager plans for cybersecurity crisis response and events

CONCLUSION

The following cyber risk management statement represents those organization capabilities CEO and board should be looking to have their organization demonstrate in terms of *cyber risk internal organization context.*

INTERNAL ORGANIZATION CONTEXT

The organization understands its internal context and builds and measures its capability to align all enterprise functions to mutually support the cyber risk management system. The organization operates to the overall principle that cyber risk is an enterprise-wide risk, not just an IT risk. It considers voluntary guidance code approaches that are tailored to the organization. A "cyber risk management system" involves the ongoing, effective, and *fast* deployment of 24/7/365 organization capabilities to mitigate cyber threats. The cybersecurity function and its risk management system is aligned to other enterprise functions and management systems in such a way that the organization has the speedy, adaptive, resilient and responsive capabilities required to face the fast-paced evolving universe of cyber threats (and opportunities). The cyber risk function operating model is appropriately tailored. Cybersecurity is aligned not only *across* the enterprise but *within* each key enterprise function that needs to team up with the CISO/DRO's cyber function. The CEO directs the executive management team from the CISO/DRO and IT-related management functions right across to people-related functions such as human resources. The CRO is accountable for the enterprise risk management system and all its subsystems, which includes the cyber risk management system.

NOTE

1. Gartner, "Gartner Says 2015 Will See the Emergence of Digital Risk and the Digital Risk Officer," 2014, http://www.gartner.com/newsroom/id/2794417, and referred to in our Handbook, Chapter 25, "People Risk Management in the Digital Age."

ABOUT DOMENIC ANTONUCCI

Domenic is a practicing international chief risk officer overseeing cyber-security and a former counterterrorist intelligence officer. An Australian expatriate based in Dubai UAE, Domenic specializes in bringing capabilities within organization risk management systems "up the maturity curve" for enterprise, program, and specialized risks such as cybersecurity. Formerly with Marsh, Shell and Red Cross, he enjoys over 35 years' experience in risk, strategic planning, and business management consulting across many sectors in Europe, Africa, Middle East, Asia, and Australia-Pacific. A specialist with IRM (SIRM), he is a certified ISO 31000 ERM lead trainer and BCMS business continuity lead implementer as well as a former RMP-PMI risk management professional and PMP project management professional. A regular international conference presenter and author, he is the content author for risk maturity model software called *Benchmarker*™ and the author of the book *Risk Maturity Models: Assessing Risk Management Effectiveness*.

ABOUT BASSAM ALWARITH

Bassam is heading the National Digitization Acceleration Program in the Kingdom of Saudi Arabia. He reports to a Ministerial Council headed by the Minister of Economy and Planning. Bassam has led digitization transformation programs in the private and public sector. He is experienced in governance, business continuity, and organizational capability development. Bassam has held various executive positions including chief information officer, chief financial officer, chief operating officer, and chief investment officer. He has worked in the United States with technology companies such as Oracle, and in the Kingdom of Saudi Arabia, where he has held various technology leadership roles.

CHAPTER 16

Culture and Human Factors

Avinash Totade, ISACA Past President UAE
Chapter and Management Consultant, UAE
Sandeep Godbole, ISACA Past President Pune Chapter, India

The head of human resources, Grace, said to Tom, "Just as safety and environment, cybersecurity is the responsibility of each and every employee of the organization." Maria, the chief information security officer (CISO), backed this up: "Of course, Tom, we can't do without the technical side of cybersecurity, but the cultural and human factors are also important. Did you know that the Great Wall of China was first breached by an invader that did not use force but simply bribed guards at the gate?"

A robust cybersecurity "Great Wall of China" should be installed, but the best of the security devices and systems can be compromised, especially due to vulnerabilities arising from human factors. The breach could be motivated by personal benefit or simply a product of ignorance. Since information systems are used by everybody in the organization, the onus of complying with the information security hygiene comes with it. Well-designed security systems, appropriate organizational culture, training, awareness, compliance, and audit play a very significant part in users exhibiting secure behavior. Security protects the confidentiality, integrity, and availability of information assets. It is likely that the need for security is generally accepted within the organization. The trade-off between security, usability, and cost is what makes the choices and decisions quite difficult.

ORGANIZATIONS AS SOCIAL SYSTEMS

Organizations are social systems that are influenced by human factors. Social systems are influenced by drivers such as individual values, thoughts, beliefs, biases, actions, and interactions. Within organizations, most processes and controls even those driven by technology are also influenced by human factors. Let us consider a simple technology control that is omnipresent: *anti-malware solutions*. Organizations where the users are not conditioned to use it effectively but are likely to circumvent it will not derive the value. Successful implementation of security systems is also dependent upon the human factors.

Organizations have multiple stakeholders including employees, customers, vendors, and business partners. The stakeholders influence the organization in multiple ways. The stakeholders participate in various organizational activities and processes. The interactions provide value and also introduce risks. It is important that organizations develop their own risk management culture to address risks comprehensively. Contractors and employees who work alongside them are likely to expose the organization risks. It is therefore important that contractors be included in the cybersecurity risk management as well as the mitigating training and awareness initiatives.

In addition to the contractors, vendor staff and partners bring in an additional risk. In an information technology (IT)-enabled organization, some of the services and components of the IT infrastructure are provided and maintained by vendors. For example, *server virtualization* hardware implemented in the *data center* may be provided and maintained by vendors. Some of the vendors are thus likely to have elevated physical and logical access to the information systems. Vendor staff should be sensitized and trained on the security processes and controls. Mitigation controls need to be implemented to address the risk. These include controls such as activity log monitoring, nondisclosure agreements, security training, and security service-level agreement (SLA). Security expectations and benchmarks help to build an effective security culture.

Cybersecurity Not Merely a Technology Issue

Cybersecurity is not merely a technology issue. Cybersecurity is also a social, cultural, emotional, and behavioral issue. Technology does provide security solutions. These solutions are impacted, however, by the interdependencies and interactions within an organization. For example, inadequate enforcement of the *password syntax* is a technology issue; however, inappropriate usage of passwords by a user is not a technology issue. Inappropriate usage can weaken technology controls. The interplay of the human factors and technology introduces challenges to the technology solutions.

Organizations are not homogenous monoliths but are characterized by diversity. Individual behavior and roles, however, may conflict at times with organizational priorities. For example, the sales team may have prioritized subscribing to a *cloud service* for a quick deployment of an IT solution.

The cybersecurity team is a bit cautious and may recommend additional controls that could delay this transition or impose additional costs. Thus, the aspirations, decisions and actions for different groups of employees may work at cross purposes. The ability to manage this conflict and confrontation therefore plays an important role in managing cybersecurity.

Organizational Culture

Organizational culture is a result of multiple factors, such as regional factors, values, style, decision styles, and ethical standards of leaders. For example, if leaders in an organization do not view *intellectual property* violations of software usage as serious, the organization is likely to have a more permissive culture that condones violations and noncompliance.

Security is not an absolute state but is relative and should be viewed in the context of perceived risk and possible impact. Since risk is probabilistic and futuristic, the perception plays an important role in determining and prioritizing risk. Perception is individualistic and is conditioned by culture.

Culture involves complex variables. Employees are conditioned by their own upbringing, organizational factors and the environment. Since people are unique, it is a challenge for people from diverse backgrounds to converge to form a uniform organizational culture. The environment in which the organization operates also influences culture to a large degree. Organizations that operate under strict regulatory environments are likely to develop and implement a stringent security and compliance culture. The mandatory nature of the requirements is essential to continue business; hence, they tend to become culturally ingrained.

Security policies are essential but not sufficient to promote security. Contradictions between policies and behavior are more likely than consistency guided by policies. For example, an organizational policy may mandate that doors be kept shut and protected using *access control* mechanisms. However, if employees observe that some senior leaders generally violate the policy by tailgating or keeping the doors open, the employees may not view the policy seriously. "Tone at the top" and the related behavior influences the culture and hence behavior of individuals.

Groupthink as a Bias Social psychologist Irving Janis explained the concept of groupthink as a phenomenon seen in certain organizations, teams, and groups. It is a basic component of being part of a group that must be considered by those leading the group. It can be a benefit when groupthink promotes effective security. At the same time, it can also be a detriment. When a group makes faulty or irrational decisions driven by a quest for harmony and conformity within a group, it is an indicator of a dysfunctional or faulty culture. Decisions under such settings are likely to be poor and detrimental to organizational objectives.

Consider a group that is debating *infrastructure architecture*. The group may be composed of network specialists; application and database specialists; security specialists; and finance and the procurement teams. This multifaceted expert group will be effective if the members play their own part well. An enabling culture that nurtures an open, frank, and focused discussion would result in an optimal design and solution. If the phenomenon of groupthink is experienced in the group—with, say, the finance team dominating the "consensus," then security or performance considerations are less likely to be addressed by the group. The outcomes may not be rational or optimal. While the participation of multiple stakeholders is important, participation without an empowering culture can lead to a false sense of rationality.

HUMAN FACTORS AND CYBERSECURITY

People are a very important enabler and determinant of the level of cybersecurity. Security initiatives need to be supported by active, able, aware, and motivated people. For example, a majority of e-mail traffic in the world is spam. Most progressive organizations implement *spam filters* to address this risk. It is possible that some *spam* or *phishing* e-mail could escape the filter and reach users. It is important that users be aware and vigilant to understand the limitations of technology and preserve the security environment through their behavior.

Certain controls are effective only if supported by human diligence and cannot work in isolation. Displaying *photo badges* when on the organization's premises is an example. The control enables employees to challenge those who do not display the photo badge. A combination of technology, process, and people is essential for a security control to be effective and successful.

Douglas McGregor at the MIT Sloan School of Management has defined "Theory X and Theory Y" related to two different perspectives on human behavior, their motivation, ambition, and work ethic. Theory X perceives humans as lazy, lacking ambition, not responsible, and requiring control and supervision. Theory Y, on the other hand, perceives human behavior positively—as rational, motivated, and capable of making correct decisions. A pragmatic and effective approach may recognize that an individual may exhibit both Theory X and Theory Y characteristics in varying degrees at different points in time. A combination of technology, policy, process, disincentives, training, rewards, feedback, and relearning is necessary for effectively guiding and influencing people.

Many of the resources and methods used for implementing technical solutions for security are deterministic. A *firewall* with a defined rule will behave in a predictable manner under defined conditions. This can be determined with reasonable certainty and hence is considered as deterministic. The same cannot be said about people and their actions. This uncertainty about human behavior poses challenges for effective security implementation. Employees may have undergone *anti-phishing* training. The awareness and training is expected to equip employees in responding to phishing attacks. Whether all the trained employees will exhibit desired behavior cannot be determined with certainty. Moreover, behavior of the same individual can vary at different times. The unpredictable and probabilistic nature of human behavior renders it as the weak link in the security chain.

Insider Threats

Insider threats result from the actions or omission of employees, former staff and others who are internal to the organization. They have access to systems and are privy to information that is not generally known to outsiders. Insiders with malicious intent can perform actions that are detrimental to the organization. At other times, the insiders may unknowingly and involuntarily be exploited and used as a conduit for such activities by others.

> PricewaterhouseCooper's Global State of Information Security Survey 2016 respondents reported that incidents attributed to current and former employees remain the two highest sources of security incidents, at 34 percent and 29 percent, respectively, over 2015.[1]

Organizations with dysfunctional cultures, disgruntled employees, and weak work ethic are likely to be at greater risks related to insider threats. Building baseline behaviors for specific roles is a way to detect actions that may seem suspicious. Traditional controls such as segregation of duties, log reviews, and delegation of authority matrix can be used to reduce the risk of malicious insider activity. Modern technology solutions such as security information and event management (SIEM) and data loss prevention (DLP) can build technology defense against this risk.

Social Engineering Threats

Social engineering is an approach employed by attackers to manipulate human behavior in order to breach organization security. Human traits such as bias, human error, blind faith, gullibility, limited awareness, and inconsistent behavior may be exploited. These include actions such as revealing passwords, downloading malware, or disclosing confidential information. Unfortunately, no technology can guarantee a fail-proof solution against social engineering. Engaging people and training them to identify social engineering attacks and defeating them by diligent behavior is the most effective way to address this threat.

TRAINING

Many organizations have training programs for employees across different phases of the employee life cycle. In addition, new initiatives and technology implementations are supported by effective training. Training is used to create awareness, build knowledge, transform behavior, and align employees to a consistent organizational culture. Security and the associated behavior need to be learned. Security training is dynamic, situational, and tailored to specific roles. When social media became omnipresent, organizations experienced the need to train employees about the security risks and responsible behavior in usage of social media. The threat of *ransomware* prompted many organizations to counsel individuals so that the individuals and organization are protected against the risk of ransomware.

Security training can be role specific. New employees may be provided training on acceptable use of technology. Members from the security team may be provided training on certain advanced areas related to vulnerability assessment, security audits and other topics. A *Unix* administrator would be provided training on security features of the operating system.

Gamification, contests, training videos, self-learning computer-based training (CBT), workshops, and awareness-based floor sessions are different ways to administer security training. Each method is suited to different messages and situations. Workshops may be more suited to expert-level detailed training, while floor-level awareness sessions may be quite effective in popularizing new policies or for brushing up on basic security concepts.

While training does build up maturity, awareness, and knowledge, it is not a guarantee that the message is understood uniformly and that it has altered attitudes, behavior, and culture. Evaluation therefore forms an essential part of most training activities. These also serve as effective records and evidence of the training administered to the staff. Sound training prepares individuals to make correct choices even when faced with unique or new situations. For example, a person may have undergone training to help prevent *phishing* attacks. The training may not have covered all the tricks of a fraudster. However, the training may help and prepare the individual to respond even in a different scenario.

FRAMEWORKS AND STANDARDS

The significance of human factors is not a matter of subjective interpretation but has found its place in the standards that are globally accepted by professionals and organizations. A useful way to address human factors is considered in the three leading cybersecurity frameworks and standards—ISO 27001:2013, business model for information security (BMIS) and National Institute of Standards and Technology (NIST)—which are addressed below.

ISO 27001:2013

ISO 27001:2013 is a globally accepted standard for Information Security Management Systems (ISMS). Some of the controls included in the standard are related to the human factors are Organization of Information Security, Human Resource Security, Asset Management, and Access Control. These controls are either associated with the human factors or simply influenced by it.

Business Model for Information Security (BMIS)

The business model for information security (BMIS) represented in Figure 16.1 was developed by University of Southern California and adapted by ISACA. The model defines four elements and six dynamic interconnections between the four elements. The elements defined by BMIS are people, process, technology, and organization.

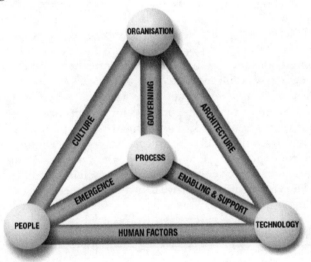

FIGURE 16.1 The ISACA business model for information security (BMIS)
Source: COBIT 5 Implementation ©2012 ISACA. All rights reserved. Used by permission.

Organizations generally define processes to enable performing repetitive tasks. Over time, the human factor influences the processes to bring in some variance, adaption and adoption. Human factors can influence the implementation and outcome of technology that is implemented. Acceptance and support of the human element is vital to the success of technology.

BMIS defines culture as a pattern of behaviors, beliefs, assumptions, attitudes, and ways of doing things. The organizational culture is formed over time by strategy, organizational design, and behaviors. Individuals bring their own cultures and form subcultures in the workplace. The interplay of both of these influences the organization.

To improve the information security program, managers need to examine and understand culture. They must extend the culture's strengths and recognize or improve its weaknesses to be effective in its approach to security. BMIS has identified certain actions and initiatives that can help the culture to become more favorable toward security.

Recognizing the influence of culture may mean that you try to align culture to the intended security outcome or that you recognize how culture impede or promote security and leverage it. Models such as BMIS help organizations to focus on the elements and interactions to develop security within the organization.

NIST Framework

The President of the United States issued an executive order on "Improving Critical Infrastructure Cybersecurity" in 2013. In response to the executive order, NIST developed a "Framework for Improving Critical Infrastructure Cybersecurity." The core framework defines five functions: identify, protect, detect, respond, and recover. Each function is further supported by categories, subcategories, and informative references. Many of the categories have an implicit or explicit people component that is addressed or that influences the outcome. Some of these categories include asset management, business environment, governance, risk management and strategy, access control, awareness and training, detection process, response planning, communication, and recovery planning. Considering that these have an inherent human element the significance of organizational and individual culture is apparent as part of the cybersecurity initiative.

TECHNOLOGY TRENDS AND HUMAN FACTORS

The ever evolving nature of technology and its applications results in a dynamic environment. *Digital technologies* including the four *SMAC applications (social, mobile, analytics, and cloud)* are currently driving organization innovation. The urge to share information instantly enabled by these technologies is a great benefit but at the same time it is also a cybersecurity risk. Trends such as *teleworking* and *bring your own device (BYOD)* require appropriate risk management and cultural sensitization. It is important that the employees and vendors understand not only the benefits but also the associated cybersecurity risks in the usage of technology. The cultural shift necessary to securely deploy the new technology is therefore very important.

Measuring Human Behaviors for Security

Measurement is essential for any factor to be quantified, evaluated, and improved. This can be more challenging for intangible factors. People behavior and culture lend themselves to evaluation using qualitative approaches:

1. *Simulation.* Observing the behavior of people by simulating real life scenarios. For example, a simulated *phishing* exercise to evaluate security culture.
2. *Classroom evaluation.* People can be administered tests in a classroom to gauge knowledge and awareness about cybersecurity practices.
3. *Audits.* Audits related to cybersecurity readiness and compliance serve as an effective and possibly an independent oversight mechanism for evaluation.
4. *Data analytics.* Data analytics provides an opportunity to measure compliance and provide quantification.

Reducing Cyber Risks That Occur Due to Human Mistakes

One interesting methodology for managing the human risks to information security is through awareness and behavior management called Human Impact Management for Information Security (HIMIS). The objective is to reduce information security risks that occur due to human mistakes as represented in Figure 16.2. HIMIS views the human factor as two distinct but interdependent components: "awareness" and "behavior." Awareness is "to know" and behavior is "to do or to react." High awareness does not mean that information security risks due to human mistakes are less. Positive change in behavior is the key.

To achieve confidence that information security risks due to human risks have reduced, it is necessary to have more security awareness and responsible behavior from the workforce while handling information. A survey is conducted to measure 14 security practices (referred to as ESP, short for expected security practices) that must be followed by the surveyed organization's workforce. HIMIS helps you to (1) define the information security awareness and behavior requirements, (2) build a strategy for awareness

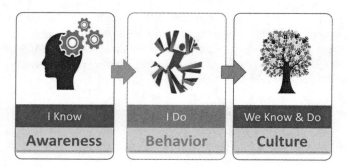

FIGURE 16.2   HIMIS methodology to reduce cyber risks that occur due to human mistakes. Reprinted with the kind permission of Anup Narayan, founder and CEO of Information Security Quotient, www.isqworld.com.

and behavior management, (3) deliver the program, and (4) verify whether the awareness has increased and whether behavior of the workforce has improved while handling information. The HIMIS methodology is built on the belief that the true reward of a good information security awareness program is positive change in behavior.

CONCLUSION

The following cyber risk management statement represents those organization capabilities CEO and board expect to be demonstrated in terms of *cyber risk culture and human factors*.

CULTURE AND HUMAN FACTORS

Management treats the organization as a social system influenced by human factors. While culture involves complex variables and multiple stakeholders (including employees, customers, vendors, and business partners); a tailored risk management culture addresses cyber risks comprehensively. Cybersecurity is treated not merely as a technology issue but as a mix of social, cultural, emotional, and behavioral issues where potential conflicts and contradictions are managed. Cyber risk treatments (including controls) combine technology with nontechnology treatments and are fast paced to match the threat. Organization decision making avoids biases such as groupthink. The culture is resistant to human factors such as insider threats and social engineering threats. Active, able, aware, motivated, and trained people, vendors, and other stakeholders support cybersecurity. Employee training programs cover different phases of the employee life cycle and are role specific where appropriate. An appropriate set of standards and qualitative approaches are used for measuring and evaluating people behavior and culture.

NOTE

1. PwC Global State of Information Security Survey 2016, http://www.pwc.com/gx/en/issues/cyber-security/information-security-survey/data-explorer.html

ABOUT ISACA

As an independent, not for profit, global association, ISACA engages in the development, adoption and use of globally accepted, industry-leading knowledge and practices for information systems. Previously known as the Information Systems Audit and Control Association, ISACA now goes by its acronym only, to reflect the broad range of IT governance professionals it serves. Incorporated in 1969, ISACA today serves 140,000 professionals in 180 countries. ISACA provides practical guidance, benchmarks and other effective tools for all enterprises that use information systems. Through its comprehensive guidance and services, ISACA defines the roles of information systems governance, security, audit, and assurance professionals worldwide. The COBIT framework and the CISA, CISM, CGEIT, and CRISC certifications are ISACA brands respected and used by these professionals for the benefit of their enterprises.

ABOUT AVINASH TOTADE

Avinash is an ISACA past president (UAE Chapter), Institute for Internal Audit (IIA) member and an experienced information security and information assurance professional. A management consultant, he currently is the MD of Avcon Consulting Services. He has experience with multinational workforce cultures and assurance of cybersecurity, SCADA security, business continuity, and IT governance. A former senior vice president for internal audit for Emirates Global Aluminium (EGA) in the UAE, he is a Certified Management Accountant (United States) and Chartered Electrical Engineer (United Kingdom) with certifications in CISA, CGEIT, CISSP, Java, and ISO 27000, 9000, 14000 and 20000. He frequently speaks at international professional seminars and conferences about cybersecurity, corporate governance, continuous auditing, ERP controls, and the like.

ABOUT SANDEEP GODBOLE

Sandeep Godbole is an ISACA-CISM Excellence Award winner for Asia, an ISACA past president (Pune Chapter India), and an experienced information security and information assurance professional. He currently works for a U.S.-based IT service company as General Manager for Information Security. He has experience with multinational workforce cultures and cybersecurity with organizations such as Deloitte, Tata Motors, and Emirates Airlines. Certified in CISM, CISSP, CGEIT, CISA, and CEH, his experience spans domains including security governance, security implementation, and cybersecurity, as well as security standards and frameworks. He holds a graduate degree in computer science and postgraduate degree in business administration. He is a sought-after speaker at international conferences that include EuroCACS conferences (Manchester, Barcelona, London, Copenhagen,) as well as c0c0n, TieCon, iSafe, and others. Sandeep has contributed articles related to security in industry publications and also in social media.

CHAPTER 17

Legal and Compliance

American Bar Association Cybersecurity Legal Task Force
Harvey Rishikof, Chair, Advisory Committee to the Standing Committee on Law
and National Security, USA
Conor Sullivan, Law Clerk for the Standing Committee on National Security, USA

Lawyers. Tom reluctantly swiveled away from his workstation to face the creatures before him. There sat two of the breed, ties drawn tight around their necks and dark suits set in stark contrast to the beige office. His general counsel Alain, spoke first: "Tom, I know you asked our office to advise you today about what legal and compliance capability we can bring to bear for cybersecurity, so I brought with me one of our staff attorneys who's had prior experience with cyber. As you know, lawyers are like wolves; we never travel alone. We actually have several worrisome conclusions which we think you really should consider."

It is beneficial to spend some time understanding the legal paradigms that drive cyber law today. For our purposes, it is worth examining the legal frameworks in the two places modern organizations are perhaps the most likely to do business subject to cyber regulations: the European Union and the United States. Before doing so, let us overview how the regulatory dots are connected as in Table 17.1.

EUROPEAN UNION AND INTERNATIONAL REGULATORY SCHEMES

The European Union has recently established a unified cyber law system beyond the 1995 EU Data Protection Directive.[1] The current EU Data Protection Directive was enacted in 1995, and was the original effort at determining data regulations within the European Union.[2] In this directive, the processing of personal data—data which could be used to identify an individual—must be transparent, have a legitimate purpose, used in a means

TABLE 17.1 Connecting the Regulatory Dots

WHAT to Protect	WHY Protect It	Protect from WHOM	Protected by WHOM	Typical Methods
Personal data of employees and customers	Human rights/ regulatory imposts versus Big Data, identity stealers, etc.	Hackers/criminals for profit/gain Hackers for ideological reasons States/governments for access/gain (e.g., FBI/Apple 2016)	Organizations Regulators	Regulations Enforcement Compliance
Intangible organization assets (e.g., trade secrets, other intellectual property)	For business sustainability (optional to organizations)	Hackers/criminals for profit/gain Hackers for ideological reasons States/governments for access/gain (e.g., FBI/Apple 2016)	Organizations	Regulations Enforcement Compliance
Market infrastructure (e.g., finance, telecom and energy markets)	For national security (sometimes regulatory imposts)	Terrorists Other states/ governments for gain Own states/ governments for access/gain (e.g., FBI/Apple 2016)	Organization security Government security agencies	Regulations Enforcement Compliance

proportional to the reason the data was initially collected, and provide some information to the subject about their retained rights to the data.[3]

The upcoming application of the General Data Protection Regulation (GDPR) builds on these protections for personal data, placing further obligations on data processors—notably to create a data protection officer (DPO), creating a lead supervisory authority for EU cyber regulations, creating a "right to erasure," and increasing the requirements for consumer consent to data collection.[4] These imposts are placed on the organization processing or controlling the data to the extent it happens within the European Union, or regardless of where the processing takes place—as long as the data processed is related to goods or services offered within the European Union.[5] The GDPR also known as EU Regulations (EU) 2016/679 has been passed by the European Parliament, but will not be phased in until May 25, 2018.[6]

Transfer of Data Out of the EU, Including the United States

The GDPR also updates the 1995 Data Protection Directive's limitations on the transfer of personal data to countries outside of the European Union, further defining what determines that a country provides "adequate protection" of the data to avoid ancillary agreements.[7] The United States has negotiated an exception to this rule in the "E.U.–U.S. Privacy Shield," which went into effect in August 2016.[8] The Privacy Shield provides companies that transfer data across the Atlantic with a clear set of legal standards and protections surrounding consumer data that must be followed to participate in commerce with the European Union. U.S. corporations will be subject to compliance review with the U.S. Department of Commerce, as well as redress mechanisms set up to ensure that access to the data by government agencies will be as limited as possible.[9]

An auxiliary bill working its way through the EU government is the Network and Information Security Directive (NISD). It has similarities to the GDPR by way of its broad footing but mainly concerns nations and critical infrastructure (CI).[10] Under NISD, countries are to designate cyber response contact points in their governments and specific companies as "operators of essential services," while the selected companies have expanded cybersecurity expectations and an incident notification requirements.[11]

Post-Brexit United Kingdom

In regards to the United Kingdom's planned withdrawal from the European Union, in all likelihood the United Kingdom will continue to abide by EU privacy laws until the exact moment the union is broken, but there is little beyond conjecture to determine what would happen post-"Brexit."[12] Assuming that there is no "adequacy decision" immediately available from the European Commission when the United Kingdom exits—determining that the United Kingdom's cyber laws are strong enough to be compliant with the EU policies—companies would have to implement "standard contractual clauses" or "binding corporate rules" to transfer data from the European Union to the United Kingdom immediately after the exit.[13] These clauses are approved by the EU government as sufficient to provide adequate safeguards to the privacy and data rights of EU citizens.[14]

International Organization for Standardization (ISO)

The ISO is an international nongovernmental organization dedicated to setting international standards for organization activity. ISO 27001 and 27002 encompass the ISO's take on managing information security risks, providing a method to identify risks, plan to address them, and implement controls. ISO 27001 is organized in a "plan-do-check-act" manner similar to other ISO programs, making interaction with other ISO programs, such as ISO 22301 for business continuity management systems, possible if not encouraged. While compliance with ISO standards are not outright required by regulations, the close relationship between cybersecurity methods, risk management, and organization planning makes ISO's organizational offerings across multiple perspectives potentially advantageous.

U.S. REGULATIONS

The U.S. national security paradigm has changed massively since the "age of innocence" pre-September 11. If that time of innocence is termed as "Security 1.0," the world now anxiously sits in "Security 3.0" awaiting the emergence of "Security 4.0."

The events of 9/11 led to the quick enactment of "Security 2.0" where regulations prioritized physical security and critical infrastructure security, but cybersecurity was still largely focused on preventing mischievous hackers more than malicious disruption of critical infrastructure.

"Security 3.0" defines the modern world as we know it where there is recognition of the importance data plays to the world and there are some regulations to protect personal information, but what overall role the government should play in ensuring cybersecurity is still in flux. Threats from criminals, hackers, espionage, and potentially the military in a time of war has created a volatile space. Creating a single common cybersecurity framework has been challenging when faced with questions of federalism, agency politicking, and technological advancement.

Finally, "Security 4.0" seems to be emerging from an increasingly interconnected world, driven by a Big Data economy and the increasing Internet of Things. In this era, regulators and organizations will have to focus more on proactive prevention of cyber events rather than reactions, and not just for organizations within their nation—but for organizations that span the world. Security 4.0 presents new, monumental challenges to the existing national security paradigms which will only be addressed with time.

Cybersecurity Negligence Remains Undefined

One method to avoid traditional negligence liability in a U.S. court is by proving that the standard of care, set by the legislature or judicial precedent, has been met. But as yet there has been no clear, defined standard of care set in the question of cybersecurity negligence.[15] Instead, a patchwork of state, federal, and international laws and regulations have combined to form a rough guideline: steps to secure data must be "reasonable" or "appropriate"—taking the relevant circumstances into account—in order to avoid liability.[16] To satisfy this requirement of reasonableness, a company should use a risk assessment process and craft a cybersecurity plan based off the findings.[17]

Until recently, there was little guidance beyond industry report recommendations on what sort of process or measures were enough to be "reasonable" for companies in industries without specific cyber regulations.[18] Currently, the U.S. private sector has been gravitating toward the U.S. National Institute of Standards and Technology's (NIST) published cyber framework. NIST was originally given the responsibility to create the framework by Executive Order 13636, but the responsibility was then codified by the Cybersecurity Enhancement Act of 2014. Adapting to the NIST framework is currently voluntary for non–critical infrastructure (CI) companies, but company partnerships between non-NIST-compliant companies and CI are restricted, driving further adoption of the NIST standards throughout the economy. A similar scheme is rapidly being implemented within the federal contracting industry, requiring contractors to adopt specific data security standards to remain competitive for government contracts. As a result, more public-private business transactions are voluntarily becoming dependent on both parties having a NIST satisfactory level of cybersecurity. (Chapter 6 surveys standards and frameworks and contains a detailed section on NIST).

Specific U.S. Industry/Sector Regulations

While general laws on cybersecurity are sparse in the United States, some specific industries are highly regulated. As mentioned previously, *critical infrastructure (CI)* organizations must abide by the NIST framework as well as cooperate with the Department of Homeland Security, the Cyber Threat Intelligence Integration Center, and law enforcement with regard to cyber incident reporting and response.

The *telecommunications* sector is voluntarily covered by the NIST framework and is encouraged to hold regular meetings between the FCC and individual companies to discuss cyber programs for risk management.

Energy producers have similarly been put on the NIST framework from the Department of Energy's Cybersecurity Framework Implementation Guidance and our regulated by specific regulatory bodies, such as the Federal Energy Regulatory Commission.

For *government contractors*, there has been a similar strengthening of cyber rules. In August 2015, the *Department of Defense (DOD)* released for the Defense Industrial Base (DIB) a revised version of the "Safeguarding Rule," which requires companies contracting with DOD to implement a more expansive set of security controls.

Many other *federal agencies* are considering similar rules, with the Office of Management and Budget considering a comparable rule to apply to all contractors.

Financial services have had significant past regulation in regards to cyber, requiring compliance with rules set down by the Federal Financial Institution Examination Council on behalf of a slew of federal regulatory agencies. Companies that deal in *securities and futures* have been similarly regulated to necessitate the adoption of an information system security program (ISSP). The ISSP must meet certain generally accepted standards or risk censure by regulating organizations, pushing more industries into adopting the NIST framework. The Securities and Exchange Commission (SEC) has signaled an increased emphasis on *advisors* having adequate cyber policy, rather than on responses to a breach and the harm suffered by the client. The Financial Industry Regulatory Authority (FINRA) has also created a report on cybersecurity best practices, pertaining to cybersecurity planning for *broker-dealers*.

The *health care* industry must abide by a series of regulations under the Health Insurance Portability and Accountability Act (HIPAA), which were split into a "Privacy Rule" and "Security Rule." The Privacy Rule establishes standards for the protection of certain personal health information.[19] The Security Rule acts on the protections laid out by the Privacy Rule by addressing "technical and nontechnical safeguards that organizations called 'covered entities' must put in place to secure individuals' 'electronic protected health information' (e-PHI)."[20] The Security Rule seeks to ensure the protection of personal health information while allowing new technologies to improve patient care.[21]

The previous examples are just a selection of some industries with specific regulatory schemes already being developed. Tom would be well served by asking his legal counsel to compile a more comprehensive list of regulations that pertain to his specific industry, simply to ensure that if regulations or guidelines exist, they are either being met or are being addressed in upcoming plans.

General Fiduciary Duty in the United States

The FTC has brought several regulatory actions against companies for failing to prevent unauthorized access to consumer information as "unfair or deceptive acts."[22] The settlements from these cases can involve increased information security requirements or long running independent audit schemes.[23] There are also state and federal laws that support private actions against companies for unfair and deceptive trade practices, data breach notification, and failure to timely notify—in addition to negligence or breach of contract claims.[24] There is no single federal notification rule, so depending on which state the corporation has interests, differing state regimes apply.

Corporate boards have a general duty to protect corporate assets, reputation, and goodwill.[25] This typically includes overseeing systems to manage risk to the organization's operations—including cyber risks.[26] While the technical nature of cyber-based threats may be foreign to the typical corporate board, the same common-sense, due-diligence approach that the board applies to other duties should be applied to cyber as well. The directors should have an understanding of the cyber risks that face the company and create an appropriate advisory team to determine what the "best practices" are to mitigate those risks. Boards should also engage in oversight of the programs in place, procedures, trainings, and any disclosures.[27]

The general trend of U.S. cyber regulations seems to point toward increased adoption of a "best practices" regime. While noncritical industries may not be directly regulated into following the NIST framework, the costs of not adopting such practices may outweigh the benefits, considering the potential legal penalties, regulatory fees, and loss of organization opportunities with more regulated industry.

Forecasting the Future U.S. Cyber Regulatory Environment

The general trend of U.S. cyber regulations seems to point toward increased adoption of a NIST-driven "best practices" regime. While noncritical industries may not be directly regulated into following the NIST framework, the costs of not adopting some clear cybersecurity practices may outweigh the benefits—considering the continuing growth in cyber attacks against organizations in conjunction with potential legal penalties, regulatory fees, and loss of organization opportunities for those who lack "adequate" or "reasonable" protection schemes.

However, it should be noted that NIST is not the end-all-be-all of cyber resources. Standards from the SANS Institute, Open Web Application Security Project, and the Control Objectives for Information and Related Technology have also been referenced in recent regulatory expansions, offering readily available ancillary standards by which a company could use to design a legally "reasonable" cyber program.

COUNSEL'S ADVICE AND "BOOM" PLANNING

In the cybersecurity world, a cyber-event is typically referred to as a *boom*, with all pre-event planning actions taking place *left of boom* and all reactionary measures happening *right of boom*. In the context of this boom centric framework, a typical CEO should seek to foster a multidisciplinary team to deal with cyber concerns. In planning or in response to a cyber incident, coordinated action will be needed across multiple disciplines to help mitigate damage and recover functionality.[28] A CEO will also seek close cooperation with legal counsel both left of boom and right of boom. Cybersecurity lawyers can help protect networks, systems, and data before they are compromised, as well as help mitigate the consequences of any cyber incident that does occur.[29]

Table 17.2 represents a RASCI-style summary of the role of legal counsel and compliance both before and during/after a boom.

Left of Boom

According to *A Playbook for Cyber Events*, "The most important period of time in a company's response to a cyber incident likely occurs before the incident occurs."[30] Cyber breaches can happen quickly, not be detected for months, and then erupt into a volcano of trouble when discovered. Because of this volatility, the best way for a CEO to prepare the company for the legal requirements and ramifications of a breach is in substantial planning left of boom.

Without a specifically articulated regulatory standards for liability in a cyber incident scenario, the CEO and board should take steps to combat allegations of negligence or a violation of their fiduciary duty by showing that a *reasonable* degree of security has been put in place to guard against a cyber incident. While the definition of what qualifies as a reasonable degree of security is still up for debate, a *process-oriented* form of *reasonableness* is now widely adopted.[31] To satisfy a process-oriented standard, the CEO should develop a process to identify risks, delineate plans to deal with those risks, then implement the plans with requisite oversight.[32] Actions taken toward fulfilling a process may have to be proven to regulators, shareholders, and judges in the event of a data incident, which makes the recordation of all C-suite and boardroom planning, discussion, and actions imminently important.

The basic process could be designed and executed by a board level advisory committee, comprised of multidisciplinary professionals with some cyber familiarity. This *cyber committee* would be responsible for identifying cyber risk points and sensitive data, leading the creation and practicing of incident response plans, and ensuring that new security measures are constantly being incorporated into company's cyber security apparatus—such as widespread data encryption practices depending on the data system.[33] A system for reporting cyber intrusions internally, with external partners

TABLE 17.2 RASCI Matrix Role for Legal Counsel and Compliance

	Is RESPONSIBLE For …	Is ACCOUNTABLE For …	Is SUPPORTED By …	Is CONSULTED By …	Is INFORMED Of/By …
Before cyber crisis (pre-"boom")	* Takes ownership within their enterprise function to assess, treat, monitor, and report cyber legal risk and regulatory * Engages stakeholders as regulations change and plans to accommodate regulatory expansion towards widely accepted standards * Pre-defines issues by principles of currency, reasonableness, and preparedness (e.g., cross-border alternate IT processing arrangements during a crisis) * Directs documentation of the cyber risk management "process" * Reviews past contracts, manages future contracts and contractual compliance * Determines if information-sharing partnerships with government or other parties may benefit	* Legal counsel member of board-level advisory cyber committee	* CRO, CISO * Privacy officer monitoring of risk and organization impacts from privacy laws and compliance, or data protection officer under 2018 EU regulations	* Board and CEO governance, principles, and risk oversight for fiduciary duties and "reasonable" action for the "processes" to assess and manage cyber risk * Cyber strategy and implementation of entire "process-oriented" cycle of cyber defense planning, including committee creation, application, simulation, auditing, and recordation * Cybersecurity policies and procedures * Cyber standards and frameworks * Cybersecurity incident and crisis management * Recordation of all C-suite and boardroom planning, discussion, and actions * Insurance terms and conditions * Identifying, analyzing, evaluating, and treating cyber risks	* By board-level audit process of regular reviews * Business continuity management * By ITC/InfoSec, risk manager, and business continuity plans for cybersecurity

(continued)

TABLE 17.2 (Continued)

	Is RESPONSIBLE For …	Is ACCOUNTABLE For …	Is SUPPORTED By …	Is CONSULTED By …	Is INFORMED Of/By …
During/after cyber crisis (post-"boom")	* Member of crisis response teams set in action with constant documentation of steps taken and reports sent to C-suite * Internal investigation to record events and actions in preparation for legal action(s) for or against * Manages any bailiffs to assess collection of technical traces for future litigation * Manages any "active defense" and authorization from the foreign network owner before operations are commenced to help limit liability for actions taken * Prosecuting or defending cyber lawsuits * Disclosure of breach to partners in the private and public sector * Notifications to the public and owners of contractually transferred data		* CRO, CISO, HR, CorpComms * Bailiffs	* For advice—either as in-house or outside counsel depending on the potential need to preserve privilege—established immediately and sustained throughout the response	* Of ITC/InfoSec escalation from incident to crisis management and recovery * By digital forensic software managed by ITC/InfoSec * By the internal ITC crisis investigation team report as an input to legal action * By CFO on financial estimations of impacts and prosecution financial support

in government or industry, and with regulatory or contractually required contacts should be developed and tested.

A *board-level audit process* should also be created to regularly review the advisory committee's actions, plans, and recommendations. As previously mentioned, the audit's methodology and findings should be written and preserved, as well as boardroom discussion over the audit's results. In addition to audits, cyber incident simulations can help identify holes in a potential cyber response plan, as well as demonstrate dedication to a reasonable degree of "process" protection.

Legal should be deeply involved in the left of boom timeframe beyond articulating any applicable state or industry data regulations and directing documentation of the process. Past *contracts* should be revisited to ensure that included standards for the protection of proprietary information are being met, while future contracts should be written and examined with cybersecurity risks in mind.

Legal can help determine whether *information sharing* partnerships with government or with similar companies might be beneficial to a company's cybersecurity prospects.

There should also be a discussion over the purchase of specific cyber *insurance* for organizations, which manage considerable cyber risks.

Boom and Right of Boom

After a boom occurs and the organization is notified of the breach, a quick reaction holds the key to mitigating damage from the breach—thus mitigating the potential expansion of liability from the breach.

The first response to a boom should come from the *implementation of the prepared plan.* Any response teams should be set in action with constant documentation of steps taken, with reports sent to the C-suite. A conversation with legal counsel—either with in-house or outside counsel depending on the potential need to preserve privilege—should be established immediately and sustained throughout the response to the crisis.

From the input of legal counsel, *compliance* with notification and data protection regulations pertaining to the subject industry should be adhered to. Beyond notification requirements, disclosure of the breach to partners in the private and public sector may create opportunities to gain further resources and information to mitigate damage. There may be some worry that disclosure to the government or public could harm the reputation of the company, this risk should be discussed and a strategy set. Owners of contractually transferred data should be notified as to the status of the breach and the confidentiality of their data. Notifying the public, and specifically those who might have had information disclosed by the breach, also warrants discussion with legal and other relevant parts of the company.

As the response plan is implemented, an *internal investigation* should be created to record events and actions. If possible, observing the movements and tactics of the attackers within information systems can help inform how to scrub their access to the system, as well as providing known failure points to strengthen in future defensive measures.

While an *active defense,* actively hacking back the hacking party, might seem attractive as a means to harry the offenders or to find out what data has been stolen, from a legal perspective it may do more harm than good. Using active defense beyond one's own networks can expose private organizations to expanded liability, including liability for attacking another network.[34] If an active defense is necessary, receiving authorization from the foreign network owner before operations are commenced could help limit liability for actions taken.

CONCLUSION

The following cyber risk management statement represents those organization capabilities CEO and board expect to be demonstrated in terms of *cyber risk legal and compliance.*

LEGAL AND COMPLIANCE

The legal and compliance issues surrounding cybersecurity are predefined by principles of currency, reasonableness, and preparedness such that the organization is prepared for the legal requirements and ramifications of a breach. An organization must work with its legal professionals to ensure any currently applicable data security regulations are met while planning to accommodate regulatory expansion towards widely accepted standards. Legal should be integrally involved in the entire "process-oriented" cycle of cyber defense planning, including: committee creation, application, simulation, auditing, and recordation. The C-suite must stay appraised on the process to ensure compliance with fiduciary duties and "reasonable" action (typically, to identify risks, delineate plans to deal with those risks, then implement the plans with requisite oversight). Actions toward fulfilling a "process" are able to be proven to regulators, shareholders, and judges in the event of a data incident via the recordation of all C-suite and boardroom planning, discussion, and actions. The basic "process" should be designed and executed by a board level advisory *cyber committee*, comprised of multidisciplinary professionals with some cyber familiarity. A *board-level audit process* regularly reviews the advisory committee's actions, plans, and recommendations.

LEFT OF BOOM

Before any cyber event, legal counsel not only articulates any applicable state or industry data regulations but directs documentation of the "process," reviews *past contracts* and manages *future contracts* with cybersecurity risks in mind. Legal can advise on the purchase of specific cyber *insurances* and determine whether *information-sharing* partnerships with government or with similar companies might be beneficial.

RIGHT OF BOOM

During and after any incident, legal counsel is part of the response teams set in action with constant documentation of steps taken and with reports sent to the C-suite. Advice by legal counsel—either with in-house or outside counsel depending on the potential need to preserve privilege—should be established immediately and sustained throughout the response to the crisis. From the input of legal counsel, *compliance* with notification and data protection regulations pertaining to the subject industry is adhered to. Beyond notification requirements, *disclosure* of the breach to partners in the private and public sector may create opportunities to gain further resources and information to mitigate damage (while balancing internal concerns over potential harm the reputation of the company by such disclosure). *Owners* of contractually transferred data should be notified as to the status of the breach and the confidentiality of their data. *Notifying the public*, and specifically those who might have had information disclosed by the breach, also warrants discussion with legal and other relevant parts of the company. An *internal investigation* should be created to record events and actions. If an "active defense" is contemplated, receiving authorization from the appropriate public authorities and foreign network owners before operations are commenced could help limit liability for actions taken.

NOTES

1. http://ec.europa.eu/justice/data-protection/reform/index_en.htm
2. http://eur-lex.europa.eu/legal-content/EN/TXT/PDF/?uri=CELEX:31995L0046 &from=en (Art 1.)
3. Ibid, Art 3.
4. https://www.technologylawdispatch.com/2016/04/privacy-data-protection/the-data-protection-directive-is-dead-long-live-the-general-data-protection-regulation/
5. Ibid.
6. Ibid.
7. http://ec.europa.eu/justice/data-protection/international-transfers/adequacy/index_en.htm;http://eur-lex.europa.eu/legal-content/EN/ALL/?uri=celex%3A52012PC0011 (Art. 41)
8. http://europa.eu/rapid/press-release_IP-16-2461_en.htm
9. Ibid.
10. https://www.crowell.com/files/Regulatory-Forecast-2016-Crowell-Moring.pdf (p. 30)
11. Ibid.
12. https://www.crowelldatalaw.com/2016/06/privacy-cybersecurity-weekly-news-update-11/
13. Ibid.
14. http://ec.europa.eu/justice/data-protection/international-transfers/transfer/index_en.htm; http://ec.europa.eu/justice/data-protection/international-transfers/binding-corporate-rules/index_en.htm
15. http://www.tilj.org/content/journal/50/14%20SHACKELFORD%20PUB%20PROOF.pdf, p. 11
16. Harvey Rishikof and H. George, *A Playbook for Cyber Events* (Washington, DC: ABA Press, 2014), 39–42.
17. Ibid., p. 49.
18. http://www.tilj.org/content/journal/50/14%20SHACKELFORD%20PUB%20PROOF.pdf, p. 13.
19. http://www.hhs.gov/hipaa/for-professionals/security/laws-regulations/
20. Ibid.
21. Ibid.
22. http://www.sidley.com/~/media/files/newsinsights/publications/2014/03/board-oversight-of-cybersecurity-risks/files/view-article/fileattachment/board-oversight-of-cybersecurity-risks–march-2014.pdf
23. Ibid.
24. Ibid.
25. http://www.sidley.com/~/media/files/newsinsights/publications/2014/03/board-oversight-of-cybersecurity-risks/files/view-article/fileattachment/board-oversight-of-cybersecurity-risks–march-2014.pdf
26. Ibid.
27. Ibid.

28. Cyber Playbook 5.
29. Cyber Playbook 5.
30. Cyber Playbook.
31. Handbook 49.
32. Handbook 48.
33. Playbook 5.
34. See Playbook 7.

ABOUT THE CYBERSECURITY LEGAL TASK FORCE

The American Bar Association's Cybersecurity Legal Task Force examines the risks posed by criminals, terrorists, and nations that hope to steal personal and financial information, disrupt critical infrastructure, and wage a new kind of warfare on a battlefield of ones and zeros. The Task Force serves as a facilitator of collaboration, information exchange, and policy identification in the emerging field of cybersecurity law.

ABOUT HARVEY RISHIKOF

Harvey Rishikof is co-chair of the American Bar Association National Cybersecurity Legal Task Force. He formerly served as Chair of the American Bar Association Standing Committee on Law and National Security and currently serves as its Advisory Committee Chair. He is senior counsel at Crowell & Moring, LLP and is the former dean of the National War College in Washington, D.C., where he also chaired the department of national security strategy. Mr. Rishikof is a lifetime member of the American Law Institute and the Council on Foreign Relations. Mr. Rishikof was a senior policy advisor to the Director of National Counterintelligence, ODNI, a federal law clerk in the Third Circuit for the Honorable Leonard I. Garth, a social studies tutor at Harvard University, attorney at Hale and Dorr, AA to the Chief Justice of the United States, legal counsel for the deputy director of the Federal Bureau of Investigation, and dean of Roger Williams School of Law. Currently, he is also an advisor to the *Harvard Law Journal* on national security and serves on the Board of Visitors at the National Intelligence University. He has written numerous articles, law reviews and book chapters. Mr. Rishikof and Roger George recently co-authored *The National Security Enterprise: Navigating the Labyrinth* (Georgetown Press, 2011); *Patriots Debate with Steward Baker and Bernard Horowitz* (ABA Press, 2012); and *A Playbook for Cyber Events*. (ABA Press, 2014).

ABOUT CONOR SULLIVAN

Conor is a joint Law and Masters of Public Administration candidate from Syracuse University's College of Law and Maxwell School of Citizenship slated to graduate in 2018. He is specializing in national security law and is currently working as a Summer Law Clerk for the American Bar Association's Standing Committee on National Security. Conor has had work published by the Syracuse University Honors Program, *The End of the Means: Using the Arab Spring Revolutions as a Case Study for Machiavelli's The Prince*, as well as by the National Defense University Press, *Responding to Russia after the NATO Summit: Unmanned Aerial Systems Overmatch in the Black Sea*.

CHAPTER 18

Assurance and Cyber Risk Management

Stig J. Sunde, Senior Internal Auditor (ICT), Emirates Nuclear Energy Corporation (ENEC), UAE

Mark, the chief audit executive (CAE) looks directly at Tom the CEO, "Are there any intruders inside your organization information systems already? How do you know? How does the board obtain reasonable assurance that you as CEO and the executive team are managing cyber risks effectively? Optimal combined assurance to the board and to you as CEO is obtained by coordinated efforts by different organization functional units."

CYBER RISK IS EVER PRESENT

Cybersecurity is defined by ISACA as protecting information assets by addressing threats (risks) to information processed, stored, and transported by internetworked information systems. Cyber risks are risks that occur due to the interconnectivity of information and communications technology (ICT) systems. For modern organizations, these connections are present within the organization, between it and its suppliers and customers, and with its employees or on employee own devices. In addition, there are operations technology systems in the form of process control systems or industrial control systems. In some cases these are connected to the organization's computer network for remote maintenance and monitoring. These industrial control systems are used in the production of products and services such as electricity, production of food, cars, and present in hospital equipment, nuclear plants, and aviation controls. The Internet of Things (IoT) provides many benefits to organizations at large as well as individuals, but requires adequate controls of the risks that come with it.

The key challenge is ensuring digital service availability while maintaining integrity and confidentiality of your systems. The key characteristic of cyber risks is that they require ongoing and continuously monitoring of the effectiveness of the risk-mitigating controls. Your systems are online and interconnected 24/7. This, combined with increased threats from more organized and highly skilled professional adversaries, makes the efforts required to protect your systems extremely demanding. Thus, protection must be a combined effort by different parties of the organization, or different Lines of Defense, to be further explained in the following.

WHAT THE INTERNAL AUDITOR EXPECTS FROM AN ORGANIZATION MANAGING ITS CYBER RISKS EFFECTIVELY

The protection starts with understanding the organization objectives and strategy, what the organization wants to achieve and what is required to "get you there." To get you there will most likely require interconnected systems to deliver digital services supporting the achievement of your goals through digital services delivered to different organization functions. For each digital service the organization should assess the vulnerabilities and potential threats (and opportunities), at three levels—the *application* level, the *database* level, and the *infrastructure/network* level.

Which organization goals depend on which digital service? Are they agreed? With the understanding of what is important and critical to the organization, it is possible to identify which digital services are critical to achieving its objectives. Unfortunately, this link is not always clear to many organizations. In a changing environment, this link will require systematic efforts to establish, and to maintain in an organized way.

So the full process consists of a set of steps. These can be summarized as follow:

1. Understand the organization objectives.
2. Map the digital services to the organization objectives.
3. Assess cyber risks—these will spotlight the critical digital services and assets.
4. Treat cyber risks.
5. Monitor the risks and effectiveness of implemented cyber risk treatments, including controls.
6. Report by management to CEO and board on the effectiveness of the treatments and cyber breach incidents.
7. Obtain independent assurance and independent reporting to the board.

Risk Assessment Expected by Internal Audit

Risk assessment(s) starts by recording the vulnerabilities and potential threats to each of the components behind each digital service once we know which digital services are important and critical for achieving organization objectives. This work must be done properly and must be comprehensive. Focus on what is critical to the organization and score the inherent risk accordingly. Then develop the risk treatments (including mitigating controls) in line with organization risk appetite and tolerance and to the cost/benefit of the organization. A complete implementation of the treatments must aim to reduce the residual risk to an acceptable level. Of course, the cybersecurity domain has its own technical vocabulary where threats are described in more detail (i.e., threats, threat sources, threat events, threat agents, and attack vectors). This risk assessment is the responsibility of the management.

The Case for Combined Assurance Model

The auditor will also look critically at the governance structure set up to manage the cyber risks, and *who is doing what*. Given the characteristics of cyber risks, there must be evidence of a set of layered management controls in place to ensure that cyber risk treatments are effective *now, now, and now*—continuously 24/7. These require a set of combined efforts by different organization functional units to accomplish the required comfort in order to provide assurance to the CEO and the board that these controls are working.

One popular model of achieving reasonable assurance is the Combined Assurance framework. This was developed initially by the European Confederation of Institute of the Internal Auditors (ECIIA) and Federation of European Risk Management Associations (FERMA) as guidance to the 8th EU Company Law Directive. Figure 18.1 is an adaptation of the combined assurance approach. This approach centers on different functions to provide different *lines of defense* to protect the organization. Figure 18.1 includes three lines of defense where the first two are the responsibility of the CEO to apply and manage, while the third is left to an independent assurance by internal audit.

The number of lines is not so important as long as the full range of protections are in place, are well managed and the appropriate level of overall combined assurance is provided. The combined assurance approach and its lines of defense should be understood as a conceptual view for presentation purposes. In reality, the lines are not clear-cut because there will be

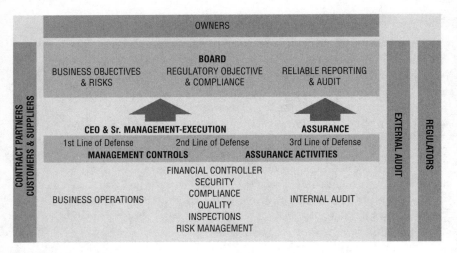

FIGURE 18.1   Combined assurance approach

organization functional units with responsibilities and activities overlapping the lines. Moreover, different organizations will have different ways of structuring this. What is critical is that an orchestrated effort is required between different units (lines of defense) and between assurance activities around cyber risk treatments being systematically executed (while minimizing duplicated work efforts) such that they can be input into one combined assurance report to the CEO and the board. The three-lines-of-defense model is intended to clarify who is doing what, while maintaining the cooperation and coordination of the different functions to ensure the processes work effectively (and to avoid *silos*).

The Role for an Information, Communication, and Technology (ICT) Unit

In terms of "who does what" in managing cyber risk reiterative assessment and treatments, the ICT unit is typically best placed to implement technical cyber risk treatments, including controls. The ICT-managerial controls in organization or business operations should ensure that subordinates complete the work as instructed and adhere to policies and procedures. ICT operations will deploy tools to monitor any security threats and have a process in place to resolve security incidents. Moreover, they will deploy and maintain escalation mechanisms for severe security incidents.

The Role for a Cybersecurity-Specific Line of Defense

A cyber (and information) security unit would be another line of defense responsible for conducting the cyber risk assessments. They must operate in close collaboration with the ICT operations unit, the enterprise-wide risk management (ERM) unit, and organization strategy unit. The organization strategy unit and/or ERM unit would provide the full set of organizational objectives, and ICT would provide the list of digital services and assets to support the organization's functions. ERM, in collaboration with cybersecurity team, will capture the outcome of cyber risk assessments and record them for the tracking of the risks and the implementation of the treatments. In practice, a more detailed and technical tracking of cyber risks may be done by the security unit, while the ERM unit tracks and monitors these risks in more generic terms.

The security team must establish the information security policies in line with the outcome of the cyber risk assessments. The security unit would be responsible for conducting security reviews of cyber risk treatments to obtain assurance that treatment and controls are working. Additional monitoring tools will probably be required to implement this within the ICT environment. This must be done in close collaboration with the ICT operations and follow an agreed change management process before being introduced in a production environment.

The ICT operations unit and the cybersecurity unit represent the front line of cyber defense. Ensuring quality and maturity of the processes to manage cyber threats are the key responsibility of these two units. Assurance is achieved by mature executions in ICT operations; with managerial controls reviewing that the execution is in line with requirements. These must also be supported by further reviews by the security unit, ensuring the cyber treatments are working.

Both ICT operations unit and cybersecurity unit will report on the effectiveness of the controls either directly to CEO or an executive body on a periodic basis, and immediately for any severe cybersecurity incidents. The security unit should be reporting to a different executive officer than the ICT unit. This is important to ensure security objectives are not compromised by other priorities in organization or business operations. But this also requires adequate protocols in place between security unit and the ICT operations on how to cooperate and work together. This working relationship is key to manage cyber risks effectively.

Roles for ERM and Organization Strategy to Work Closely with ICT

The ERM unit is responsible for managing risks together with the risk owners in business operations and across the organization. The ERM team works closely with both the ICT operations unit and security unit in recording and monitoring cyber risks. The ERM unit will be responsible for coordinating the combined assurance reporting to the CEO and the board (or via an audit or a risk committee of the board). Note that the ICT operations unit and Security unit is expected to have a much more detailed register of risks, including all digital assets linked to digital services as well as to organization objectives and to risk treatments.

The organization strategy unit (or its equivalent) is responsible for the business strategy and cascading business objectives down to organization or business operations, and monitoring the performance and reporting back to CEO. This reporting should capture risks related to each organization objectives, providing an improved basis for executive management to make risk-informed decisions. Note that this reporting is different from the combined assurance reporting, the latter providing assurance to the CEO and the board that treatments of, in this case, cyber risks are well implemented and working effectively.

Roles for Compliance and Quality Assurance

Another layer of assurance will be provided by the compliance unit and the quality assurance unit (or their equivalents). This layer is made up of another set of reviews. These are less frequent and focus on ensuring adherence to both regulatory requirements and internal procedural requirements. The quality assurance unit would typically be involved in any information security audits (such as internal audits of ISO 27001 on information security). The Compliance unit capture and monitors all regulatory requirements (as a minimum) and interact with the business operations to verify compliance and report status.

Both the compliance unit and quality assurance unit are managerial tools reporting to different executive officers, thus providing independence from the organization operations being reviewed/audited. This avoids conflict of interest and segregates duties.

The CEO Obtains Combined Assurance

With the application of the combined assurance model the CEO obtains assurance from the first and second line of defense. This is effective when the role of the different lines of defense are clearly defined, the processes are clear, the organization "silos" are broken in terms of a mature processes matrix, working their way across the different functional units and lines of defense.

HOW TO DEAL WITH TWO DIFFERING ASSURANCE MATURITY SCENARIOS

Back to the key question: how do the CEO and the board obtain assurance that the cyber threats are effectively mitigated? Again, the key with cyber risks are their continuous presence, which requires continuous attention and ongoing responses. The two most common scenarios of assurance are presented below.

Scenario 1: Mature Assurance

In Scenario 1, there is well-established and mature governance structure in place with well-established processes in line with the combined assurance model described previously. In this scenario, the third line of defense by way of the internal audit (IA) unit conducts audits of the processes in place and test if the controls/treatments are working effectively. IA reports this to the board, normally via an audit committee. The different lines of defense are mature and working well, both individually and in cooperation among the different units. There will typically be less assurance efforts required from the third line of defense (internal audit) in such a mature cyber risk–focused organization where strong first- and second-line defenses are working effectively. The IA unit will conduct its risk assessment; review the existing processes for managing cyber threats, the treatments/controls in place, and conduct "walk-throughs" to validate the design and the implementation of the treatments/controls. The more management has well-implemented controls working effectively, the less required of IA. In this case, IA will validate the information presented in the combined assurance report prepared by the ERM unit, and add the assurance activities conducted by IA for each of the risks.

Scenario 2: Less Mature Assurance

In Scenario 2, there is low maturity of governance structure and the processes for managing the cyber risks, and/or no concept of combined assurance is in place. Less mature organizations will have to take more conservative security approaches until adequate cyber threat–mitigating capabilities are built up. This will require IA to conduct more comprehensive audit reviews. These are likely to have strong recommendations to significantly reduce the use of internetworked solutions with external parties until better internal capabilities are built up (depending on the organization objectives and business needs). This may effectively reduce the organization's ability to achieve the objectives if more conservative security measures are required. Assurance activities from third line of defense will be more frequent in this scenario and larger effort required.

COMBINED ASSURANCE REPORTING BY ERM HEAD

Cyber risk is an enterprise risk. The ERM unit should be the coordinator of the combined assurance reporting to the CEO. It is *not* the role of internal audit to do this management reporting. An extended or combined assurance report, including the activities of IA as the third line of defense, should be presented to the board (or the audit committee of the board) by the head of ERM. Internal audit conducts audits on the organization and provide independent assurance on the reported information, which then is presented to the board.

The combined assurance report should include the following information:

- The cyber risks from the risk register.
- The related organization objective (the cascaded ones).
- The treatments (controls) in place to mitigate the threats.
- The current/residual risk ratings.
- Assurance/review activities by first line of defense (i.e., the organization front-line units, such as operations).
- Assurance/review activities by the second line of defense (i.e., the organization support units, such as ERM).
- Independent assurance activities by the third line of defense (to be provided by the internal audit unit).

Table 18.1 represents an illustrative sample for such a combined assurance report.

CONCLUSION

The cyber risk management statement over the page, represents those organization capabilities CEO and board expect to be demonstrated in terms of *cyber risk assurance*.

TABLE 18.1 Combined Assurance Report Illustrative Sample

		CYBER RISK & TREATMENT INFORMATION				MANAGEMENT CONTROLS			CEO & BOARD	
					Current/ Residual Risk		ASSURANCE ACTIVITIES			
ID	Cyber Risks	Business Objective	Treatments/ Controls			BUSINESS OPERATIONS FIRST LINE OF DEFENSE	SUPPORT & BACKOFFICE SECOND LINE OF DEFENSE	INTERNAL AUDIT THIRD LINE OF DEFENSE	CEO Comments	Board Comments
1	Loss of confidentiality in digital services	Exceed regulatory requirements and ensure protection of business sensitive information								
1A	Access to sensitive information by unauthorized individuals	Restrict access to sensitive information	ICT Operations: Access Management Controls Procedure Established		MEDIUM	Business Units: 1. Approves the access to digital services for each individual. 2. Confirms periodically the validity of approved accesses for each individual. No deviations observed in the last three reviews.	ICT Operations: 1. Conducted self-assessments of the procedure and its implementation. No deviations observed in last two self-assessments. 2. Conducted logical access reviews with confirmations from business units on validity of granted access to individuals. No deviations observed in the last three reviews. Quality Assurance: QA conducted an internal audit of the ISO 27001 Information Security controls and observed three deviations pertaining to the access management	Audit of the Logical Access Process conducted in Q1. Five observations where made during the audit, of which four resolved before the final report was issued. The last observation was lack of timely disabling read access to one services (low risk). Internal Audit has reviewed the provided information for this line item and does not have any further concerns to be raised. Residual risk rating is reasonable justified.		
1B	Loss of integrity of information within digital services	Reliable Business Performance Information provided to decision makers								
2										
2A										
2B										
3	Loss of availability of digital services	Ensure Effective Business Operations								
3A	Risk of Denial-of-Service attach	Ensure availability of critical business services	ICT Operations: Intrusion Detection Systems are implemented and monitoring controls established		MEDIUM	ICT Operations: The IDS status is monitored 24/7. No deviations oberved since last reporting.	Security: Security conducted review of the treatment/controls mitigating the DoS threats. No significant deviations were observed, while some process improvements where recommended (low risk).	Internal Audit conducted and audit last year on cyber security, which included reviewing the mitigations implemented for the DoS treats. No significant observations were made. Residual risk rating is reasonable justified.		
3B										
4	Risk of theft of digital assets	Ensure Safeguarding of Assets								
4A										
4B										

279

CYBER RISK ASSURANCE

The board and CEO must ensure the necessary organization capabilities to align cybersecurity with key organization objectives. Cybersecurity should include a cyber risk assurance framework/methodology as a structured approach to conducting assurance activities in a coordinated manner across an organization. This for the purpose of gaining confidence that cyber threat mitigations are working effectively, and to convey this conclusion to stakeholders such as the CEO and the board, supported by independent assurance provided by internal audit. It ensures that different assurance activities by different business units are coordinated and complementary to each other. It recognizes the special characteristics of cyber threats, and the requirement to have strong cybersecurity governance in place to validate cyber threat treatments (controls/mitigations) continuously, for the benefit of protecting the organization in a balanced manner in its pursuit of achieving the business objectives. Balanced manner means assessing the cyber risks with the right skill sets and providing a balanced and informed basis for decisions on how and what treatments are right for the organization, without hindering the performance of the business. It adds value by reducing duplication of work activities and thus costs, and makes the protection stronger (maintaining confidentiality and integrity of information) while ensuring availability of digital services to support and enable the business achieving the business objectives.

ABOUT STIG SUNDE, CISA, CIA, CGAP, CRISC, IRM CERT.

Stig J. Sunde, CISA, CIA, CGAP, CRISC, IRM Cert., has over 20 years' experience in governance, risk management, and compliance with strong focus on information security and IT governance. Following years of experience with PwC, KPMG, the Office of the Auditor General of Norway, and the European Court of Auditors (the EU audit body), Stig J. Sunde now works as senior internal auditor (ICT) with Emirates Nuclear Energy Corporation on one of the largest nuclear energy programs, where four nuclear plants are soon to deliver power. Stig is also trained in information security of Industrial Control Systems by U.S. Homeland Security (Idaho ICS program for utilities sector). Stig J. Sunde is a former board director of ISACA Norway and a former member of The IIA's Advanced Technology Committee, responsible for the GTAG-series. Stig can be reached on LinkedIn at http://ae.linkedin.com/in/sjsunde.

CHAPTER 19

Information Asset Management for Cyber

Booz Allen Hamilton
Christopher Ling, Executive Vice President, Booz Allen Hamilton, USA

As Tom begins to piece together his company's cyber risk management plan with Nathan, his chief risk officer (CRO), and Nasir, his crisis action officer, Tom recalls a recent news story of a major company crippled by a cyber attack. "That sounds bad," Tom says, "but it would never happen to us. We perform regular security updates and are fully compliant with security requirements." Nathan cautions, "Tom, compliance is only a small piece of an incredibly lethal and complex cybersecurity puzzle. What was good enough years ago leaves companies open for a crippling attack today." Nasir chimes in, "Information is power. The more effectively our organization protects our own information assets and detect and respond to threats in a broad, holistic manner, the more likely we will be to keep sensitive information out of hackers' hands."

THE INVISIBLE ATTACKER

Holiday season is usually a time of plenty for North American retailers. But in December 2013, a giant retail company got a surprise worse than a stocking full of coal: the credit card information of 40 million customers had been stolen via point-of-sale (POS) systems in the company's stores. An additional 70 million customer records containing names, addresses, phone numbers and e-mail addresses were also exposed.

This was no ordinary breach. Hackers began their assault by infiltrating the network of one of the company's heating, ventilating, and air conditioning (HVAC) vendors. Like many large operations, this giant retail company used an outside vendor to monitor temperatures and energy consumption inside its stores. Whenever outages occurred, the HVAC vendor conducted troubleshooting and addressed issues remotely. This helped the giant retail company save money and increase energy efficiency—but it also created the perfect backdoor for hackers to begin their attack on the company's network.

Once inside, hackers moved laterally through the company's systems, seeking out vulnerabilities to gain access to ever-more-sensitive data. They eventually reached the POS system, where they installed malware—invisible to virus scanners—that gathered information with every swipe of a card in one of the company's stores. The stolen data was stored on hacked servers throughout the world, and then sold on the Dark Web.

Attackers had access to the company's network for more than two weeks. When customer data was exfiltrated across the Web, a computer security firm hired by the company alerted the security team at the company's headquarters in Minneapolis.

Yet even after the alarm had been sounded, the company did not act soon enough. It believed itself to be compliant with latest security protocols, and thus had no reason to act. Only when the Department of Justice notified the company about the breach did it begin to investigate what had gone wrong. By then, it was too late: 70 million pieces of personal information had been exposed. And 46 percent of the company's typical holiday profits were lost.

A TROUBLING TREND

While this company's breach is one of the largest and most well known in recent years, it is far from the only company to be hit. Other large, multinational organizations have been the victims of cyber attacks, leading to millions in lost revenues and erosion of customer trust.

Frequent attacks across industries demonstrate that the cyber threat is real, and the impact to organizations substantial. Why, then, are so many companies behaving as though checking the basic requirement box is enough? The time for organizations to develop mature, detailed, and highly integrated plans to manage risk is now. These plans should be based on new frameworks and tools that can evolve as threats change and allow senior executives to conduct cost and risk trade-offs for their investments.

Organizations cannot control how or when a cyber attack will occur. They can, however, control the speed and effectiveness of their response.

THINKING LIKE A GENERAL

Cyber attacks may be new to major news headlines, but in reality, tactics like malware—and attacks like the one that took down the company in the example above—have existed for decades. The difference: these attacks once took place only between nations and militaries, the only entities with the funds and expertise to conduct cyber espionage.

Now, the problem has trickled down to organization-to-consumer organizations, and companies are ill-prepared to defend themselves. As in the example above, corporations often take a compliance-based approach to cybersecurity. They bring in accounting firms to conduct audits, and once they have satisfied all requirements, they consider their work complete. But every major company that has been hit has been technically compliant.

Similarly, when a breach occurs, most companies focus on fixing technical problems. They concentrate on finding and removing intruders, while ensuring that the lights remain on and causing minimal disruption. While these activities are important, the impact of a cyber breach can reverberate far beyond a company's systems and organization operations. Depending on the intrusion, it also may create a customer problem, a legal problem, an operations problem, a policy problem, a lost-revenue problem, and a communications, public relations, regulatory, and brand reputation problem.

Traditional organization problem solving and planning approaches are no match for this new reality. A rapidly unfolding cyber crisis demands confident decision making and execution. To best defend themselves against attacks, organizations should think more like militaries. They must take a proactive approach to defense, continuously strengthening their safeguards while preparing themselves for the worst.

THE IMMEDIATE NEED—BEST PRACTICES

Military planners prepare for specific mission scenarios that require clear communications and precise coordination among numerous actors. In developing effective, integrated response plans that lead to successful crisis management, companies should follow three main principles:

1. **Create a contingency plan and document it in a handbook.**
   Organizations should identify in advance what kind of cyber crises could occur. They should examine high-probability and/or high-impact scenarios and identify possible stakeholders who would be affected. This means analyzing how these potential scenarios could impact finances, operations, legal, and other activities, as well as investor relations,

customer relations, regulatory affairs, and other external-facing entities. Once a company has mapped out possible scenarios and plans, they should create handbooks (or *playbooks*) that ensure a coherent, coordinated response.

2. **Conduct war games to improve the plan and train staff.**

War gaming can provide insights into anticipated cyber incidents and planned responses, helping organizations refine their plans and identify all the capabilities required for an effective response. Games should also include scenarios assuming a cyber incident is successful, which will orient the company into a physical response. Not all organizations will have the resources to create plans for every possible scenario. To make best use of resources, teams should conduct games based on situations that are most likely to occur or will inflict the most damage.

Response plans and playbooks should be exercised regularly, perhaps once per quarter, to ensure that responders understand their roles and have practice carrying them out. This is essential to a unified response when an incident occurs. Having a plan is not the same as being prepared. Training is essential.

3. **Appoint a crisis action officer to create and execute plans.**

Every company should have a single person or function responsible for preparing for and responding to cyber crises. This role can be called the *crisis action officer* or *crisis executive*. Too often, these functions are dispersed among different players. This leads to a lack of coordination in planning and preparation, and a lack of effective execution during a cyber crisis. A crisis action officer should understand how the technical aspects of a breach could impact the entire enterprise, including the risks it would pose. He or she should be specifically trained for the position and should have the ability to lead joint decision making by calling together various corporate functions.

A crisis action officer should not, however, share blame for contributing to a cyber crisis. This will allow him or her to focus efforts on guiding the company in the event of an attack. This individual would report directly to the CEO during a crisis and would be accountable for managing crises effectively.

CYBERSECURITY FOR THE FUTURE

Many companies have already implemented these steps. For those who have not, such actions should be considered an immediate priority.

But while these precautions may protect companies today, they are far from future-proof. As the technologies used to carry out cyber attacks increase in sophistication, the strategies organizations use to defend themselves must evolve as well. There are a number of cutting-edge approaches that organizations should begin to consider as they move toward true military-grade cybersecurity.

From Exploitation to Attack

Computer network operations is another concept that originated with the military and now has applications for organization. It refers broadly to actions that an entity takes to increase their own information security, while denying security to their enemies. It has three components: computer network defense (CND), computer network exploitation (CNE), and computer network attack (CNA).

CND is self-explanatory. CNE and CNA are more complicated. CNE refers to cyber espionage and is passive, while CNA refers to infiltrations that destroy or disrupt data or systems and is destructive. Until now, companies have prepared themselves primarily for exploitation: gathering of secure customer data, for example. Moving forward, they must begin to protect themselves against attack as well, putting contingencies into place for possible deletion or corruption of data.

Reimagining the Attack Surface

How exactly does CNA occur? That depends on an organization's attack surface. An attack surface is the sum of all possible entry points to an environment. It can include software, hardware, firmware, networks, and people. Organizations can minimize their risk of attack by reducing the size of their attack surface, or the number of points of entry into their systems.

They can also reduce the connectedness of various parts of their networks using firewalls and encryption, reevaluating which employees have access to what data, and using real-time monitoring for anomalies. These changes will help organizations not only stop hackers in their tracks but reduce the mean time between threat detection and remediation. In the case of recent attacks, weeks passed before the attack surface was modified. Today, updates should occur in minutes or seconds.

OODA: Observe, Orient, Decide, and Act

Another way organizations can begin to protect themselves from CNA is by taking a lesson from Air Force pilots. During the Korean War, pilot John Boyd observed that U.S. F-16s lagged behind Russian MIG-15s in speed and maneuverability. Yet the American planes consistently bested their opponents in dogfights, in part because of their use of what Boyd called the

OODA loop. The OODA loop is a decision making cycle that consists of four parts: observe, orient, decide, and act. If an individual or organization can continually evolve and move through this cycle faster than a competitor can, they can disrupt the enemy's own OODA loop, and can often win despite other disadvantages.

The concept of the OODA loop has frequently been applied to organization decision making, and will be especially useful for minimizing threats in the emerging cybersecurity landscape. Instead of waiting for attacks to occur, companies can attempt to thwart would-be hackers by staying one step ahead, constantly adapting and refining their networks and security protocols.

New Opportunities for Network Agility

Companies will be able to close their OODA loops by making changes to the attack surface of their software environments in real time. The advent of software-defined networks (SDNs) will make this easier than ever. A step away from reliance on hardware-based routers and switches, SDNs will allow network administrators to constantly monitor and change attack surfaces as necessary based on identified threats.

In this way, today's security operations centers (SOC) will evolve into true command-and-control centers for operations. While the command-and-control model gives ultimate decision-making authority to the commander, this approach relies heavily on joint decision making among all the relevant functions to ensure realistic evaluation of options, collaborative action planning, and a high probability of success.

TIME TO ACT

The cyber reality companies now face is daunting to say the least. But organizations cannot allow themselves to be paralyzed by fear. Nor can they continue to tell themselves "it will never happen to us." Cyber attackers are becoming more sophisticated—and more destructive—every day. The time is now for all organizations to modernize their information security operations and prepare themselves for a future filled with even more advanced threats.

CONCLUSION

The following cyber risk management statement represents those organization capabilities CEO and board expect to be demonstrated in terms of *information asset management* for the future.

INFORMATION ASSET MANAGEMENT

The organization takes a proactive approach to address threats by controlling the speed and effectiveness of its response to cyber attacks. It adopts true military-grade cybersecurity approaches by being proactive in defense, continuously strengthening safeguards while preparing for the worst. A contingency plan handbook documents how to respond in the event of an attack. Plans are rehearsed through regular wargames, staff training, and responses adapted over time. Plans and training include changes to threats, in order to reduce mean time between detection and remediation. A dedicated crisis action officer (reporting to the CEO) creates and oversees response planning. The security operations center (SOC) is evolving into a true command-and-control center for operations. Computer network operations are considered as actions that an organization takes to increase their own information security, while denying security to its enemies.

ABOUT BOOZ ALLEN HAMILTON

Booz Allen Hamilton has been at the forefront of strategy and technology for more than 100 years. Today, the firm provides management and technology consulting and engineering services to leading Fortune 500 corporations, governments, and not-for-profits across the globe. Booz Allen partners with public- and private-sector clients to solve their most difficult challenges through a combination of consulting, analytics, mission operations, technology, systems delivery, cybersecurity, engineering, and innovation expertise.

With international headquarters in McLean, Virginia, the firm employs more than 22,500 people globally and had revenue of $5.41 billion for the 12 months ended March 31, 2016. To learn more, visit www.boozallen.com/international (NYSE: BAH).

ABOUT CHRISTOPHER LING

An executive vice president at Booz Allen Hamilton, Christopher Ling leads the firm's international organization providing a range of services to the public and commercial/private sectors of several countries (services include: strategy and policy, digital, strategic innovation and software development, technology and analytics, operations, human capital and learning, and engineering services).

Prior to leading the international organization, Mr. Ling led the cyber organization across the full spectrum of capabilities, including computer network exploit, computer network attack, and computer network defense. He has developed new and innovative cyber capabilities, which leverage lessons learned from the national intelligence community for application to commercial organizations, focusing on cyber maturity models, predictive intelligence, and network emulations.

Mr. Ling specializes in developing high-level strategies to innovate and improve intelligence support to operations, focusing on quantifying investments to create new value and improve capabilities. He has 25 years of experience managing intelligence and information technology system concept definition, trade analyses, requirements, modeling, and simulations at both the programmatic and the detailed technical levels.

CHAPTER 20

Physical Security

Radar Risk Group
Inge Vandijck, CEO, Radar Risk Group, Belgium
Paul Van Lerberghe, CTO, Radar Risk Group, Belgium

The head of security, Flory, is impressing on CEO Tom that ". . . physical asset security—not just digital asset security by the IT department—is also important. One without the other does not work."

"OK," Tom replied, "but I need to understand exactly how."

Flory lists several physical risk scenarios in her mind such as:

- A break-in and theft at the data center.
- An imposter physically penetrating their facility pretending to be a visitor or supplier and stealing laptops or leaving lots of USBs on desks hoping someone will eventually plug it in or using latest desktop internal phones to gain digital access, or other means of gaining access to data assets (e.g., network).
- Social engineering by the adversary becoming friendly with guards and physically penetrating the location to gain access to data assets (e.g., network).
- Blackmail and other pressures on guards.
- An employee insider and collusion or sabotage.

In the end, Flory decides to explain a plan to build a state-of-the-art physical security risk management system in order to assist the IT information security function by considering various physical security threat scenarios such as theft, sabotage, and break and entry to the data center.

TOM COMMITS TO A PLAN

Tom commits to what he calls *Tom's plan* on the advice of Flory, his head of security. It sets out how to plan, implement, monitor and review a physical security management system. Figure 20.1 represents how Tom plans to report to the board by working through the following steps:

1. Get a clear view on the physical security threat landscape as it relates to cybersecurity.
2. Understand how the physical security system's organization specifically relates to cybersecurity: Who does what? What are the resources and competences available?

FIGURE 20.1   Tom's plan to build a state-of-the-art physical security risk management system

3. Identify the security controls that are in place as they relate to cybersecurity.
4. Evaluate the effectiveness of controls by calculating the probability of interrupting an adversary.
5. Map and evaluate the cost-efficiency of the controls in place based on their total cost of security.
6. Get a clear view on how mature the physical security risk management system is, how it supports and augments cybersecurity, and on its compliance with applicable laws and regulations (e.g., Tier requirements for data rooms).

GET A CLEAR VIEW ON THE PHYSICAL SECURITY RISK LANDSCAPE AND THE IMPACT ON CYBERSECURITY

Tom needs to get a clear view on the physical security risk landscape as it may impact cybersecurity. So he considers:

- Why may adversaries be motived to target the digital assets of the organization?
- What are digital information asset targets?
- Where are these digital information asset targets located?
- How will adversaries potentially operate?
- With what means will adversaries potentially operate?
- When will adversaries most likely attack?
- Who are our adversaries?

If cyber risks that may affect the objectives of the organization are not clearly assessed, there is an exposure that some cyber risks are not secured, undersecured or oversecured. In terms of capabilities, the organization might have invested in the wrong security controls.

Effective identification and profiling of physical security risk scenarios rests on seven elements. Figure 20.2 depicts these. A good understanding of physical security risks will enable the design of the right security measures in a step-by-step approach.

Step 1 is to establish the internal and external context in which his organization seeks achievement of the objectives. The ISO 31000:2009, *Risk management—Principles and guidelines* standard provides excellent guidelines. Elements in the *external* context that can play a role in Tom's cyber risk assessment include the legal, regulatory, technological, and competitive environment. Other elements to consider are relationships with and perceptions and values of external shareholders. The organization's *internal* context may

FIGURE 20.2   How to identify physical security risk scenarios using seven key elements

include governance, organizational structure, roles and accountabilities, the information systems, information flows, and decision-making processes.

Finally, set the context of the risks that require assessment: Does the organization need to focus on cyber risks with a criminal intent, or does it also include cyber risks that can have nonintentional causes? Figure 20.3 represents a stepped approach to such risk assessment.

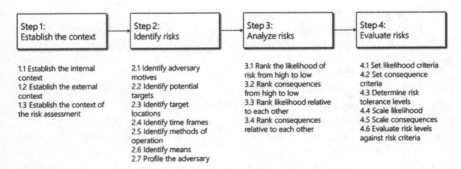

FIGURE 20.3   Risk assessment stepped approach

Step 2 documents criminal cyber risks. This involves:

- What are adversaries' potential motives to commit cybercrime? For example, espionage, sabotage, fraud based on money gain, frustration, revenge.
- Why may our organization be a target? Which information assets does our organization possess that are attractive for adversaries? For example, R&D, client information, trade secrets.
- Where are these target information assets located? For example, in the cloud, network, data rooms, printed, tablets.
- When do adversaries attack, are their vulnerabilities in timing? For example, during maintenance, e-mail exchanges.
- How do adversaries operate? For example, hacking, direct denial of service (DDoS) attack, social engineering, infiltration, breaking and entry.
- With what means do adversaries attack? For example, exploits, social engineering skills, breaking and entry material.
- Who may be adversaries executing a cyber attack? For example, staff, competitors, activists, terrorists.

A list of identified cyber-crime risk scenarios delivers a clearer view on the risk landscape since not all these scenarios have the same likelihood or consequences.

Step 3 ranks the likelihood of the identified risk scenarios from high to low and does the same for the consequences. This can be refined by taking into account the current security controls in place to arrive at residual risk.

Assuming that the two highest-ranked cyber risk scenarios based on likelihood of occurrence are *theft* and *sabotage,* then the risk identification statements may read as follows:

1. *Theft* (with motive money gain) of information on new product release (target), stored on servers in the data room (target location) during server maintenance (time frame) through unauthorized server access (MO) using a stolen access token (means) by a criminal pretending to be maintenance staff organized by a competitor (profile).
2. *Sabotage* (with motive bringing reputation damage to the organization out of frustration) of the organization's web site (target) which is managed in the cloud (target location), anytime (time frame) through hacking the web site (MO) by exploits (means) by an internal IT staff member (profile).

The board will likely want to know how much more likely is scenario 1 (theft) is relative to scenario 2 (sabotage) and equally in terms of

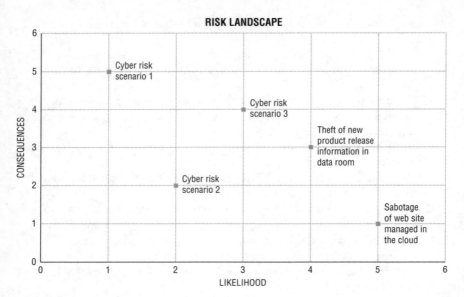

FIGURE 20.4   Risk landscape heat map example

consequences. The risk landscape analysis of risk scenarios in Figure 20.4 is helpful to a board as a heat-map format. The board will have an immediate clear view on the various cyber risk scenarios and the organization's risk criteria should indicate whether or not the various cyber risk scenarios fall within acceptable tolerance levels.

MANAGE OR REVIEW THE CYBERSECURITY ORGANIZATION

Once there is an understanding of the probability of interrupting the identified cyber risk scenarios, the organization can move to analyze organization roles and responsibilities, resources and competence management. To complete Tom's plan for physical security to augment and support cybersecurity, use a RASCI methodology to detail who does what by following the eight steps shown in Figure 20.5.

The RASCI matrix is a powerful tool to assist in the identification of roles and assigning of cross-functional responsibilities to a project deliverable or activity. RASCI represents: responsibility, accountable, support, consulted, and—informed.

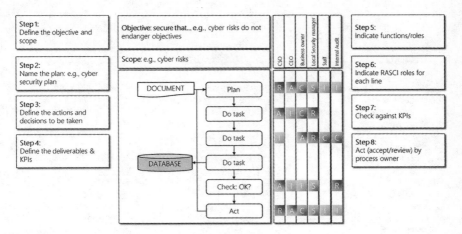

FIGURE 20.5   Tom's RASCI plan for the physical security organization

RASCI definitions follow:

- Responsibility: Person or role responsible for actually doing or completing the task.
- Accountable: Person or role who ensures that the whole task is completed, approved and/or successful (often called the "approver" or "owner" of the task).
- Support: Person or role responsible for providing support to the task.
- Consulted: Person or role whose subject matter expertise is required *before* and/or during the task in order to complete it.
- Informed: Person or role that needs to be kept informed during and/or informed *after* the task (including the status of task completion).

DESIGN OR REVIEW INTEGRATED SECURITY MEASURES

Now that Tom has a clear view on the cyber-related physical security risk landscape of his organization, he is ready to design and/or review organizational and technical security measures to deter, delay, detect, alarm, and respond to adversary attacks.

This starts with evaluating if the security measures in place do effectively deter, detect, alarm, delay or respond to the identified cybersecurity risks. If not, scarce resources may have been allocated on the wrong security controls.

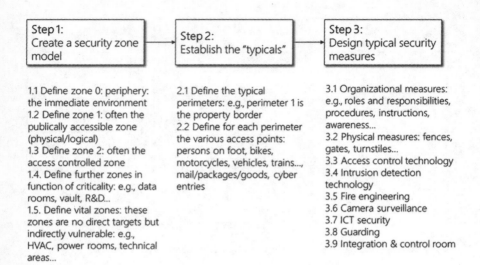

FIGURE 20.6   "Typical" physical security design in three steps

One leading method uses a three-step approach to designs and/or reviews typical physical security measures as shown in Figure 20.6. This is based on organizational measures, physical security, access control, intrusion detection, camera surveillance, information and communications technology (ICT) security alarm handling and response.

Step 1 is to consider the various security zones that are in place both physically and virtually and create a model. If a security zone model does not exist, one should be developed to organize a layered defense-in-depth. In the conceptual zone model in Figure 20.7, the largest-area shaded zones indicate the least critical areas, the medium-area shaded zones indicate zones with higher criticality and the darkest-shaded smallest zones are locations with high criticality that an adversary may be more likely to target.

Step 2 is to consider and evaluate the various typical perimeters. These include the various perimeter and perimeter accesses—both physical and logical. This should take the Tier certification requirements into account for the server- or data room. The Telecommunications Industry Association, a trade association accredited by ANSI (American National Standards Institute) defined four levels (called tiers) of data centers in a thorough, quantifiable manner. TIA-942 was amended in 2008 and again in 2010. TIA-942: Data Center Standards Overview describes the requirements for the data center infrastructure. The simplest is a Tier 1 data center, which is basically a server room, following basic guidelines for the installation of computer systems. The most stringent level is a Tier 4 data center, which is designed to host mission critical computer systems, with fully redundant

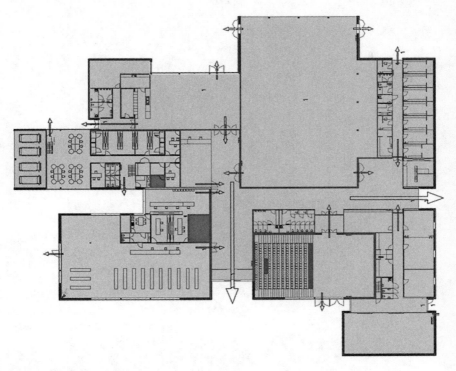

FIGURE 20.7   Security zone model example

subsystems and compartmentalized security zones controlled by biometric access controls methods. Another consideration is the placement of the data center in a subterranean context, for data security as well as environmental considerations such as cooling requirements.

Now, consider a cyber risk scenario that involves *break and entry*. There needs to be a clear view on what measures are in place for the various perimeters and perimeter access points. If the board member asks how the organization has secured the outer perimeter of its sites, the following "typical" security design in Figure 20.8 will give the board a clear insight and can be tailored to the organization.

Step 3 is to become well informed about the various physical security measures that are in place and how they relate to cybersecurity. These measures include:

- Organizational measures: For example, roles and responsibilities, procedures, instructions, awareness, and so on.
- Physical measures: Fences, gates, turnstiles, etc.

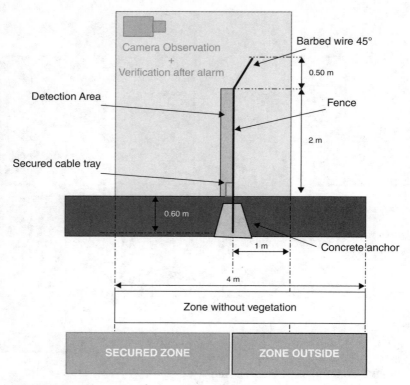

FIGURE 20.8 Typical security design example

- Access control technology.
- Intrusion detection technology.
- Fire engineering.
- Camera surveillance.
- Guarding.
- ICT security: Firewalls, anti-malware.
- Integration and control room.

Figure 20.9 depicts the key objectives and various purposes for security measures. While guarding can also act as a corrective measure, most security measures are preventative and detective in nature. That is, to deter the adversary, to detect the adversary, to raise an alarm, to assess the alarm and to respond to the alarm.

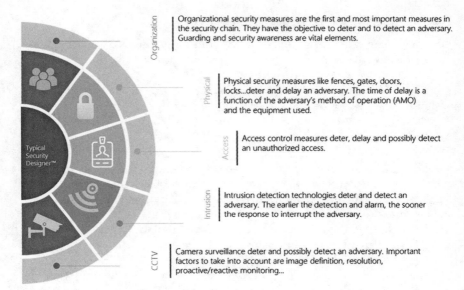

Organization
Organizational security measures are the first and most important measures in the security chain. They have the objective to deter and to detect an adversary. Guarding and security awareness are vital elements.

Physical
Physical security measures like fences, gates, doors, locks...deter and delay an adversary. The time of delay is a function of the adversary's method of operation (AMO) and the equipment used.

Access
Access control measures deter, delay and possibly detect an unauthorized access.

Intrusion
Intrusion detection technologies deter and detect an adversary. The earlier the detection and alarm, the sooner the response to interrupt the adversary.

CCTV
Camera surveillance deter and possibly detect an adversary. Important factors to take into account are image definition, resolution, proactive/reactive monitoring...

FIGURE 20.9 Key objectives for security measures

It takes some effort to plan, implement, monitor, and review security controls. Use the following tips:

- Be clear on the security goals.
- Apply technology by defense-in-depth.
- Integrate technology in a smart way.
- Take into account the impact of the environment on technology.
- Set clear functional requirements.
- Define the optimal locations.
- Choose the right technology.
- Install technology according to good workmanship.
- Organize maintenance.
- Use technology in the way it is intended for.

REWORKING THE DATA CENTER SCENARIO

Let us evaluate the security objectives and controls for the data center scenario we have begun.

Understanding Objectives for Security Measures

Let us evaluate the security objectives by continuing the risk scenario identified earlier, as follows:

Theft of information on a new product release, stored on servers in the data room during server maintenance through unauthorized server access using a stolen access token by a criminal pretending to be maintenance staff.

First, evaluate what security controls are in place to *deter* an adversary trying to gain unauthorized access to the data room in this particular scenario. Are alert people around? Are visible security controls in place? Are strong access rights based on need to have access?

Second, evaluate what security controls are in place to *detect and alarm and to assess* an adversary in this particular scenario:

- Alert people around? Yes, alert people around can identify that the criminal is not part of the maintenance staff.
- Access control system? No, access will be granted through the stolen access card unless a good procedure is in place to immediately block an access card when reported stolen. A higher degree of security would be to have double or even triple access controls in place:
  1. An access card is something you have.
  2. A pin code is something you know.
  3. Biometry like a fingerprint, eyes, or vein patterns is something you are.
- Camera surveillance? Yes, potentially, if designed to detect a person gaining access with a stolen access card. This would require an integration between the access control system and the camera surveillance system and an operator verifying that the picture of the person entering the control room is the rightful owner of the access badge. Face recognition software is also an option.

Third, evaluate what security controls are in place to *delay* the adversary in this scenario. Locks and robust doors and walls will have no effect in this scenario since the adversary has access to the data room through a stolen access card and pretending to be a maintenance technician. Evaluate the measures in place to delay an adversary trying to get digital access to the information on the new product release.

Fourth, evaluate what security controls are in place to *respond to the alarm*. Are guards on site? What is their response force time? Are controls for lockdown in place?

Understanding Controls for the Data Center Scenario

The impact of all of these controls on all barriers on the path to the target (i.e., the data room in this scenario) need to be considered. What controls are in place to gain access to the first perimeter, the controlled zone, and, finally, the data room in this scenario?

Integration of controls is one element to consider. For example, an integration of physical security and intrusion detection in the case of the control room can give an operator information on the status of doors. An integration can also automatically close doors in an alarm situation. Integration of camera surveillance and access control can initiate automatic steering of a preset in camera surveillance triggered by an access control action or provide pop-up camera images.

How the *environment* affects technology is another element to consider. For example, if the data room walls are made of fabric, an enforced door will have no impact.

The *functional requirements* for technology can vary. For example, resistance times vary for the different physical security measures for doors, windows, and roof skylights, or the throughput time of access control systems.

The *location and the use* of security controls when choosing the right new technology (such as physical security measures, access control, camera surveillance, intrusion detection) is another element to consider. Often, many legacy controls have been installed, but they are not in line with current or future organization expectations or needs. Therefore, the right new technology needs to take account of the objectives of each new security control that is newly required. This includes defining the functional needs of each new measure to augment those currently in place. And not only the technical objectives, but also the procedural and operational objectives (e.g., a camera needs "line of sight" to provide to good footage, a right height, and an angle).

The *right security equipment* can now be chosen once each "typical" security design element is defined. The technical specifications for such equipment must match the security goals and must be suitable to operate in the organization's specific Tier environment. The correct equipment to install can be vital, such as choosing a door made from wood or metal for its type of magnetic contact.

The *installation* of this equipment needs to be considered even though the right security equipment can be found most of the time. Clarity is needed as to how security equipment and material will be installed. The installation must be done taking into account at least the basic installation requirements for security controls (e.g., according to the prioritized security zone model) and the possibilities to overrule the detection of the equipment. Certain arrangements must be specified up front. These include, for example, that a magnetic contact must be installed at the most secured zone, that cabling is located at this same zone, that locks are not larger than the door leaf, or that the inclination on the fences are towards the less secured zones.

The technology needs to be *correctly used*. Just wearing a badge does not mean anyone needs to have access to all locations. People make use of wedges to keep doors open. Alarms are not followed up.

Maintenance is another key attention point. If controls are in place and are currently used but are not well maintained, then they may lose their mitigation effectiveness. Examples of poor maintenance include badges of employees who left the company that are still being enabled with all their access rights and cameras not functioning due to broken cabling, condensed dome cameras, or video loss.

CALCULATE OR REVIEW EXPOSURE TO ADVERSARY ATTACKS

Now that there is a clear view on the cyber risk scenarios and the various security controls in place, it is possible to simulate the path of an adversary and the probability of interrupting the adversary.

Simulating the Path of an Adversary

The organization's capabilities in physical security risk management in terms of the probability of interrupting the identified cyber risk scenarios can be done by simulation of the probability of interrupting an adversary along a certain path. A security system accomplishes its objectives by either offering deterrence or a combination of detection, delay, and response—in the physical as well as the digital sense. Timing is everything. A clear understanding is required of the various timing aspects related to the identified cyber risk scenarios and how the timings are related to the controls in place. This can become quite technical and may be better left to security experts.

Figure 20.10 shows the four steps involved in simulating the probability of interrupting an adversary along a certain path of physical attack on a location holding data assets.

Calculating the Probability of Interrupting the Adversary

A variety of considerations are taken into account when calculating the probability of an organization being able to interrupt the path of an adversary for each cyber risk scenario. These include:

- T1: What is the penetration time to target?
- T2: At what time will a cyber attack be detected and alarmed?

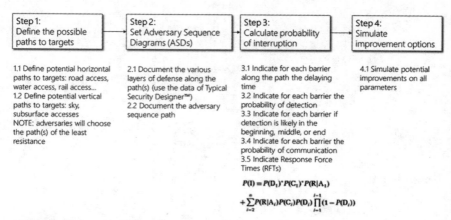

Step 1: Define the possible paths to targets	Step 2: Set Adversary Sequence Diagrams (ASDs)	Step 3: Calculate probability of interruption	Step 4: Simulate improvement options

1.1 Define potential horizontal paths to targets: road access, water access, rail access...
1.2 Define potential vertical paths to targets: sky, subsurface accesses
NOTE: adversaries will choose the path(s) of the least resistance

2.1 Document the various layers of defense along the path(s) (use the data of Typical Security Designer™)
2.2 Document the adversary sequence path

3.1 Indicate for each barrier along the path the delaying time
3.2 Indicate for each barrier the probability of detection
3.3 Indicate for each barrier if detection is likely in the beginning, middle, or end
3.4 Indicate for each barrier the probability of communication
3.5 Indicate Response Force Times (RFTs)

$$P(I) = P(D_1)^* P(C_1)^* P(R|A_1)$$
$$+ \sum_{i=2}^{n} P(R|A_i) P(C_i) P(D_i) \prod_{i=1}^{i-1} (1 - P(D_i))$$

4.1 Simulate potential improvements on all parameters

FIGURE 20.10 Adversary path analyzer in four steps

- T3: What is the intervention time once the attack is detected and alarmed?

The first step to evaluate the probability of interrupting a cyber attack is to define the potential path(s) to target(s). These potential paths are a function of the cyber risk targets, target locations, time frames, method of operation, and access to means. In terms of identified cyber risk scenarios, consideration is to given to either potential horizontal paths (such as road access, water access, rail access) or potential vertical accesses (such as sky access) and to subsurface access in combination with access points to data asset access points for a cyber attack. Figure 20.11 captures the essential three points in time to mitigate an adversary attack.

Once potential paths to targets are assessed in view of (1) the shortest distance to target, (2) the lowest chance to be caught and, (3) the lowest consequences when caught, then the second step is to evaluate the various controls in place along the path. Here, a two-dimensional Adversary Sequence Diagram (ASD) is a valuable tool to evaluate this as in Figure 20.12. The ASD will help to define the paths an adversary will use to reach his target. Once the paths are defined and the control measures in place are inventoried, the time of resistance can be calculated.

The probability of interrupting an adversary's attack is *not* the sum of all resistances divided by the intervention time. Rather, it is based on these probability (*p*) factors:

- The delaying time of each barrier.
- The probability of detection at each barrier.

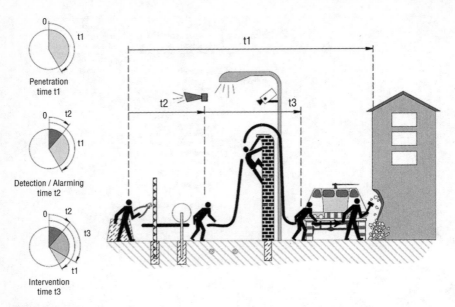

FIGURE 20.11   The three points in time to mitigate an adversary attack

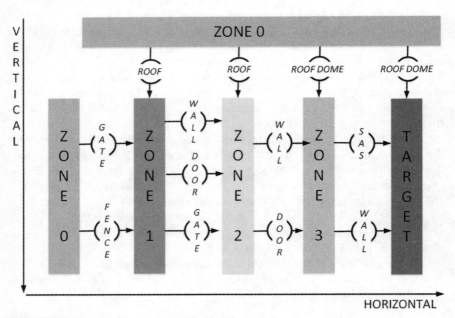

FIGURE 20.12   Adversary Sequence Diagram

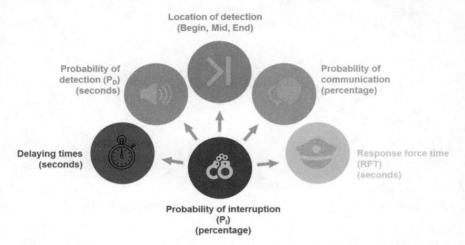

FIGURE 20.13   Probability (*p*) factors for interrupting an adversary's attack

- The location of detection: at beginning, middle, or end of the path.
- The probability of communication with response forces.
- The response force time.

Figure 20.13 looks at these *p* factors for interrupting an adversary's attack.

OPTIMIZE RETURN ON SECURITY INVESTMENT

Tom's next—and perhaps biggest—challenge is to demonstrate how to optimize the costs and benefits of security to protect and create value. Bringing the right arguments to demonstrate return on security investment (ROSI) is not an easy task, but it is certainly not a mission impossible. The challenge is to present a clear link between the investment in security and the value added through securing the achievement of organization and information security objectives.

Costs for security are often regarded as a necessary evil and often driven by a need to meet regulatory obligations. In a mature risk management organization, the link between security and the value added is well understood as the security optimum: the point where the optimal costs for cybersecurity equals the marginal benefits. Figure 20.14 shows this crossover point in a line graph.

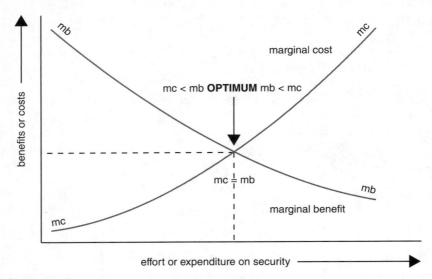

FIGURE 20.14   Optimizing return on investment

CONCLUSION

The following cyber risk management statement represents those organization capabilities CEO and board expect to be demonstrated in terms of *cyber risk physical security* to support and augment cybersecurity.

PHYSICAL SECURITY

Physical security risk scenarios are identified, analyzed and evaluated within the context of a cyber-related physical security risk landscape for the organization. Organizational and technical physical security measures to deter, delay, detect, alarm, and respond to adversary attacks are designed and/or reviewed in order to support and augment cybersecurity. Exposure to adversary attack scenarios are calculated or reviewed by simulating the path of an adversary and calculating the probability of interrupting the adversary. A RASCI-based plan for the physical security organization is implemented. The link between security and the value added is understood as the point where the marginal benefits exceed or equal their optimal costs.

ABOUT RADAR RISK GROUP

Radar Risk has developed a number of trademarked methodologies that have been outlined in this chapter above. Tom's plan for cyber risk management capabilities is based on Securifyer™, a methodology that gives guidance on the planning, implementation, monitoring and review of a physical security management system. Crime Profiler™ is a method to identify physical security risk scenarios based on seven key elements of offender motives, potential targets, vulnerable locations, attack methods and means, vulnerable times, and offender profiling. Typical Security Designer™ is a three-step method that designs the organizational and technological security measures for optimal management of security risk scenarios. Path Analyzer™ is a four-step method to simulate an adversary's path and provide a higher level of security. Path Analyzer™ is a method to calculate the probability (p) factors for interrupting an adversary's attack. Radar Scanner™ measures the maturity of a security management system and compliance with a range of security laws and regulations such as International Ship and Port Facility Security (ISPS) Code, Customs-Trade Partnership Against Terrorism (C-TPAT) and the security-related ISO standard.

ABOUT INGE VANDIJCK

Inge is the CEO of the Radar Risk Group, a cooperative global network of risk management experts headquartered in Antwerp, Belgium, and New York. She is an economist and experienced enterprise risk management professional, specialized in security with a broad perspective on risk causes whatever their nature: criminal, natural, technological, or human error. Inge developed the Radar Risk's Management Thought Process and has applied it in in the public and private sector with European, federal, regional, provincial and local governments, police, airports, seaports, oil and gas companies, energy and nuclear facilities, public transport, financial institutions, pharma and biologicals, the museum sector, the diamond industry, automobile industry, and food industry.

ABOUT PAUL VAN LERBERGHE

Paul is the Radar Risk Group's CTO. He is an engineer and guest lecturer at the University of Antwerp and preparing his PhD at the UGent/UAntwerpen, faculty of Law & Criminology: "The impact of security awareness on security scenarios in organizations." He started his security career as a development engineer where he gained experience in the conception and integration of physical security technologies such as access control systems, intrusion detection, fire engineering, camera surveillance, and control rooms. Paul has in-depth expertise in security technology and strong abilities to apply security technology from a risk and objectives point of view. Moreover, he knows all about the vulnerabilities in physical security technologies that adversaries exploit.

CHAPTER 21

Cybersecurity for Operations and Communications

EY

Chad Holmes, Principal, Cybersecurity, Ernst & Young LLP (EY US)
James Phillippe, Principal, Cybersecurity, Ernst & Young LLP (EY US)

CEO Tom challenged Maria, his chief information security officer (CISO). "I'm told ISO 217001 has at least 10 categories of operations and communications requirements relevant to cyber risk. But I want you to boil it down. Are we confident we understand how the threat landscape in the digital world applies to our organization and strategy and how to mature our prioritized operational cybersecurity capabilities around this?"

DO YOU KNOW WHAT YOU DO NOT KNOW?

Big Data. Smart devices. The Internet of Things. Robotic process automation. Behavioral analytics. 3D printing. The increasing digitization of your organization is yielding rewards in efficiency and cost-effectiveness. What is not as clear are the increasing risks that these advances are bringing to your organization's operations.

You should understand these risks, and how to prevent them from damaging your organization. You need insight into not only the vulnerabilities of your IT systems, but to the data those systems produce, looking deeply into your organization environment. You have to gain fluency in the current portfolio of threats, how they are detected, and what strategies your organization needs to follow in order to treat them.

You may be tempted to assign responsibility for this effort with your information security leaders and team. Is not the solution in firewalls and virus protection software? If it were that simple. Cybersecurity is an organizational problem that requires a comprehensive enterprise-wide organization solution, one that starts with visibility and provides insight. Both come from data and the analytical discipline to discover its secrets.

Uncovering the threats is just part of the solution. Your security team needs to predict how threats will unfold and inform the strategies to treat them.

There are five crucial areas that need your focus:

1. Threat landscape
2. Data and its integrity
3. The digital revolution
4. Your organization and organizational changes
5. Your people

We propose that your organization's security operations are likely obsolete, and not adequately prepared to face the challenges that are literally changing day by day. In this chapter, we examine these critical five carefully, and we illustrate what your organization's response should be.

THREAT LANDSCAPE—WHAT DO YOU KNOW ABOUT YOUR ORGANIZATION RISK AND WHO IS TARGETING YOU?

Some threats are explicit, a deliberate effort to breach your defenses and steal intellectual property. These can be Hollywood-style hackers, bypassing your firewall and exposing vast amounts of critical information, or they can be small, subtle attacks that ship information outside your organization by exploiting side doors and hidden windows. Who are these people? What do they want? What tactics do they use?

Information security is changing at a rapidly accelerating rate. Threat actors are increasingly relentless, making the response to information security incidents an ever more complex challenge.

According to EY's Global Information Security Survey 2015, 36 percent do not have a threat intelligence program, with a further 30 percent only having an informal approach, while 5 percent say that their organization has achieved an advanced threat intelligence function.

DATA AND ITS INTEGRITY—DOES YOUR RISK ANALYSIS PRODUCE INSIGHT?

Think of the amount of data your organization processes each day across multiple departments and disciplines. Now consider the additional data that is created in the background at a systems level as that processing occurs.

Now think about what your organization's strategy is for accessing, analyzing and evaluating data to reveal actionable insight. In particular, understanding the motivations and aims of threat actors to predict issues before they arise is the current cutting edge of information security.

For example, attackers may alter rather than steal your data. Imagine financial results changing to provoke errors, data analysis corrupted, or introduction of additional data to complicate your own. As innovation relies entirely on intellectual property, your risk multiplies as the scope of attacks intending to compromise that property widens. These threats complicate staffing, as the shifting landscape challenges knowledge and processes.

Fifty-seven percent say that lack of skilled resources is challenging information security's contribution and value to the organization (EY, 2015).

DIGITAL REVOLUTION—WHAT THREATS WILL EMERGE AS ORGANIZATIONS CONTINUE TO DIGITIZE?

Attackers have avenues into your organization apart from the usual channels, thanks to several factors:

- Organizations are transforming and moving into the digital era.
- The adoption of the cloud and the Internet of Things are gaining traction.
- The near-continual demand for access to information among people of all levels throughout the organization.

Can we predict the changes in the threat environment that this revolution brings?

Cybersecurity helps make the digital world fully operational and sustainable. Cybersecurity is key to unlocking innovation and expansion, and by adopting a tailored and risk-centric approach to cybersecurity, organizations can refocus on opportunities and exploration. The operational imperatives of safety, quality, and productivity depend on such innovation, and the cybersecurity ramifications of the ongoing digital revolution can reveal much about the eventual success of an organization's efforts.

Vendor consolidation brings unforeseen complications, including increasing gaps in visibility, lack of access to appropriate data, security countermeasure orchestration breaking down, security playbooks falling apart, and data security weakening. In digital, that can mean security response delays, data integrity, and connectivity and process issues, all of which can affect operations and risk to be compromised.

Eighty-eight percent of respondents do not believe their information security fully meets the organization's needs (EY, 2015).

CHANGES—HOW WILL YOUR ORGANIZATION OR OPERATIONAL CHANGES AFFECT RISK?

When the organization contemplates partnerships, marketing initiatives, mergers or acquisitions, how does it lever security intelligence? It's an axiom that balancing risk and reward is the key to sustainable organization success, but you should be aware of *unseen* risk, just as in other areas of the risk environment.

Ownership of data and information can become muddied during periods of change; security processes and procedures are set aside, and lines of responsibility are blurred. Strategic decisions can overbalance an organization in one area, leaving it vulnerable in another. Internal communication of significant organization decisions and strategies frequently omits the security infrastructure—they do not know what they do not know.

Twenty-seven percent say that data protection policies and procedures are informal or that ad hoc policies are in place (EY, 2015).

PEOPLE—HOW DO YOU KNOW WHETHER AN INSIDER OR OUTSIDER PRESENTS A RISK?

Cellular telephones, portable hard drives, USB drives, social media, tablets, laptops—it is common for employees, customers, vendors, and suppliers to have direct access to your networks whether they are inside your facility or not. The security of these channels is only as effective as the countermeasure you have deployed, which is sometimes just a password that they have chosen.

Well-intentioned people can be led astray. Phishing involves posing as a reputable entity in electronic communications with the aim of manipulating the recipient to reveal confidential information. To most eyes, the communication seems authentic, and the request to reply or click a link quite reasonable. The result, however, ranges from exposing passwords to releasing personally identifiable information, to encryption of data, to infecting a device with malware.

How should you evaluate these risks?

Fifty-six percent expect the most likely source of a cyber attack to be an employee. Thirty-six percent expect an external contractor working on-site. Only 31 percent of all third parties are risk-rated and have appropriate due diligence applied (EY, 2015).

WHAT'S HINDERING YOUR CYBERSECURITY OPERATIONS?

- "Smart" devices and services bring a mass of data, increasing vulnerabilities for exploitation; automation removes humans from decision-making processes. What is the appropriate balance between efficiency and security?

- Social media and "bring your own device" (BYOD) with employees, customers, citizens "always on" and sharing information—not fully appreciating the implications for privacy and confidentiality. How can organizations get employee attention that leads to positive behavior?
- Human frailty remains a serious risk, and one that's difficult to manage. How should organizations evaluate people's readiness for operating in a more security-minded way?
- Rafts of new legislation and regulations are forcing changes in processes, which means that other vulnerabilities are created, further changing the threat landscape, and the attack surface of an organization. What roles do governmental factors play in risk assessments?

CHALLENGES FROM WITHIN

Organizations need to know which threats represent the most urgent risk to the operation of your organization. You need a framework that brings together a communication strategy, cyber threat information, and the treatment options so that you can ask better questions, get better answers, and make better decisions. Security teams can have a hard time translating a broad vision or top-line strategy to a direct impact on specific critical assets.

Acting upon cybersecurity intelligence requires organizational discipline and integrated strategy. Figure 21.1 summarizes how a *security operations center (SOC)* acts as the linchpin between cybersecurity threats and effective response and management.

Translating intelligence into action for organizations is hardly simple. Figure 21.2 offers a checklist to get started. It sets up the organization for the more specific steps it can take now that follows in the next section.

WHAT TO DO NOW

Cyber risk prevention relies on the communications and operations teams' support. Your organization should undertake the following tasks immediately.

Drive for Clarity

The lack of linkage down to physical assets, applications and ultimately data is a root cause for many of the communication and prioritization challenges. In the ideal situation, when a security operations team detects a potential compromise of a system, they should be able to communicate its organization impact. To be able to do that, they need to clearly understand what data

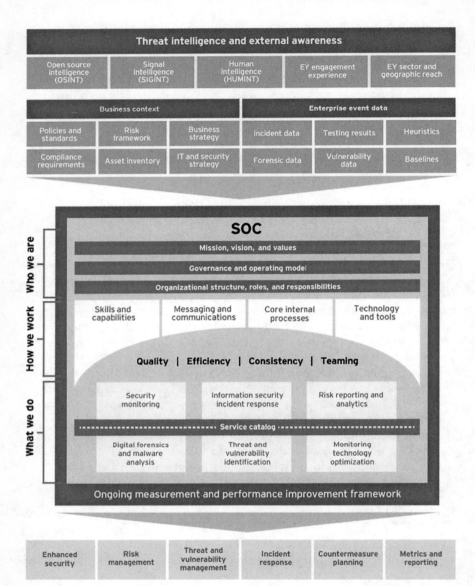

FIGURE 21.1 The big picture: How your organization can integrate and expand your cybersecurity protocol

Do's and don'ts for getting started:		
Do	get your executive leadership team on your side.	✓
Don't	understate the full cost of building a SOC. Avoid surprises and hidden costs and communicate openly to secure the needed funding.	✗
Do	develop strong governance processes for accountability and oversight and define rules of engagement with other areas.	✓
Do	build a capable team.	✓
Don't	start with the technology. Understand your needs first and then find technical solutions (new or existing) that fit.	✗
Do	enable repeatable outcomes through formal processes, procedures and protocols.	✓
Do	understand your most prized assets and tailor SOC operations accordingly.	✓
Do	use available information to enhance decision-making and response efforts.	✓
Don't	underestimate the value of collaboration. Build a work environment that fosters teamwork and enables effective operations.	✗
Do	keep up with the ever-changing threat landscape through continuous improvement practices.	✓

FIGURE 21.2   Checklist of do's and don'ts for getting started

is on what system, the value of that data, and what could go wrong with the organization if the system were to become unavailable, lost, or have an integrity issue or be compromised.

Fill in the Knowledge Gap

Understanding both the strategic and technical elements of the threat environment is challenging, and experience is a great teacher. Operations teams need front-line experience with behavioral analytics, insider threats modeling, advanced persistent threats groups, communication strategies, and state-sponsored actors. Your executive teams may not have this background, and the gap can create a frustrating communication issue, where security feels they must educate executives to enable them to make sound decisions and provide support. Executives accustomed to not knowing the details of such matters can be in denial about their complexity, increasing risk. Who wants to create a tense culture around security within the executive suite?

Understand the Speed of Change

We have designed security infrastructure historically on the premise that steady and continuous investments and an effort to "move the needle" year over year will allow organizations to keep pace and address the evolving threat landscape. Not anymore.

Security challenges are accelerating alongside the digital transformation, including robotics, artificial intelligence, analytics and so on, as mentioned earlier. New technology breeds broader attacks. You and your team do not have time to enact a multiyear investment strategy; your organization needs tools right now to disrupt, safeguard and recover from the next threat.

To push past the comfortable confines of "business as usual," you need to understand how attackers think and how they act; your security team has to think like the attackers, understanding how they manipulate these new attack opportunities.

Know Your Assets

Understanding your critical organization risks and knowing what attackers may want from your organization enables you to establish targeted defense through prioritization (of assets, people, organization areas) and hardening of vulnerabilities. Assessing the threat landscape particular to your organization (based on your operating environment, critical assets, and organization strategy) allows you to understand the most likely threat actors and methods they may use, which can be played out in scenarios to gauge readiness.

This all informs your SOC and should be the basis on which it will support your organization. Putting in place a more advanced SOC and using cyber threat intelligence to effectively align operations helps enable you to conduct "active defense operations," where you send intelligent feelers to look for potential attackers, analyze and assess the threat, and neutralize the threat before it can damage critical assets. Similarly, you can use an advanced SOC to operate in the same way and actively hunt down unwanted anomalies or confirmed attackers in your systems.

Make Cyber Risk More Tangible

You need a comprehensive threat radar that covers a variety of indicators and can raise communication triggers when a certain threshold is crossed. Each time your SOC analysts identify an attack in early stages, they can demonstrate value by extrapolating the damage that otherwise would have been caused had the scenario played out to its worst case. Organizations can continue adding to that value chain by adopting an "active defense" process.

In "active defense," you gain a dynamic and proactive component to security operations, integrating and enhancing existing security capabilities to yield greater effectiveness against attackers. Adopting an iterative cycle with built-in mechanisms for continuous improvement, you can realize gains in efficiency, accountability, and governance capabilities, which translate directly into improved return on investment (ROI).

Adapt to Your Environment—Establish/Improve Your SOC

The most essential action for organizations is to either set up or revisit an SOC that brings together the relevant systems and constituencies required to monitor, analyze, and respond to the threat environment. A mature SOC can prioritize what needs to be protected by defining the communication strategies and leveraging advances in technology to operate more efficiently and effectively. The initiation, integration, and advancement of core SOC capabilities is crucial to the success of security operations.

An effective SOC has these characteristics.

- *Monitoring and response.* The SOC monitors for threat indicators to detect attacks before critical company services are disrupted or high-value assets compromised. SOC personnel also conduct investigations to determine cause and scope of security incidents, coordinate containment, and recovery and communication activities.
- *Cyber threat intelligence* capabilities are more than simply data. Intelligence is information from sources from technical logs to news reporting that has been analyzed. It should quantify and qualify threats, be timely, accurate, actionable and relevant, and be used to establish a threat level and drive appropriate strategic and tactical countermeasures. A mature cyber threat intelligence program also provides forecasting to inform an organization's decision makers and support operations.
- *Vulnerability management* is the function responsible for proactively identifying, assessing and consistently managing the organization's exposure to cyber attacks, and tracking, validating and providing metrics

on the remediation of vulnerabilities. It must be integrated into other enterprise functions and should encompass all vulnerabilities.

- *Today's SOCs have the task of monitoring enormous volumes of data* to find pieces of information that signify an event worthy of action or further review. The SOC can bring unique value to that effort by using behavior-based analytics on the data providing visibility into trends and patterns that may have been obscured otherwise. Through that analysis we are able to innovate in real time, reducing development life cycles by orders of magnitude. This shifts the traditional security operations paradigm from reactive to proactive and enables agility and innovation at the speed of attackers.

Adapt Your Organization

In the age of digital transformation, the speed of change, combined with ineffective communications, a lack of understanding of what is important and an executive knowledge gap, creates an environment in which security operations teams are not able to be as agile as needed. In response, organizations are recognizing the opportunity to leapfrog their competitors and threats by avoiding attachment to prior investment decisions. That requires a high level of executive sponsorship and awareness of security, as well as confidence that outcomes may be more easily achieved through new technologies and concepts.

CONCLUSION

The following cyber risk management statement represents those organization capabilities the CEO and the board expect to be demonstrated in terms of *cybersecurity for communications and operations.*

OPERATIONS AND COMMUNICATIONS

The organization initiates, integrates and advances core security operations center (SOC) capabilities to detect, prevent and respond to cybersecurity situations. A mature SOC prioritizes what needs to be protected, matures communication strategies and leverages advances in technology to operate more efficiently and effectively. It delivers not only monitoring and response services to detect and remediate cyber threats but—with the combination of cyber threat intelligence, analytics, and orchestration capabilities—it provides ways organizations can detect and respond in minutes. The organization drives for clarity on the linkage between its business objectives down to its physical assets, organizational risks, applications, and ultimately data, in order to avoid communication and risk challenges. It builds in remediation automation to fill in any gaps, is responsive to the speed of change, and knows its assets. It makes cyber risk management more tangible with an "active defense" process. It adapts to cyber environmental changes quickly by analyzing gap improvements and remains adaptive with a mature and integrated set of security operations capabilities, powered by data science, automation, and an analytics platform. This enables the visibility, context, and insight needed to proactively protect its data, intellectual property, and brand.

ABOUT EY

EY is a global leader in assurance, tax, transaction and advisory services. The insights and services we deliver help build trust and confidence in the capital markets and in economies the world over. We play a critical role in building a better working world for our people, for our clients and for our communities.

ABOUT CHAD HOLMES

Chad Holmes is a principal, CTO, and Strategy, Technology and Growth leader for the EY Advisory Cybersecurity practice. Chad has over 18 years of experience in cybersecurity and has held leadership roles in high-tech security companies, health care, architecture, and financial organizations.

ABOUT JAMES PHILLIPPE

James Phillippe is a principal in Advisory at EY. He serves as EY's Global Cyber Threat Management leader, which includes responsibility for the global network of Advanced Security Centers (ASCs). James has over 18 years of experience and has held a leadership role within the ASCs since their creation in 2002.

CHAPTER 22

Access Control

PwC

Sidriaan de Villiers, Partner—Africa Cybersecurity Practice, PwC South Africa

CEO Tom, addressing Maria, his chief information security officer (CISO), demanded, "In five words, tell me what is the most important thing to know about access control that is different when it comes to cybersecurity."

Maria shot back, "Manual controls are simply ineffective."

TAKING A FRESH LOOK AT ACCESS CONTROL

While the cybersecurity risk landscape has dramatically mutated, the approaches that organizations rely on to manage cyber risks have not kept pace. Traditional information security models do not address the realities of today. These models are still largely technology focused, compliance based, and perimeter-orientated, while aiming to secure the back office. IT security hygiene is often lacking, and ineffective access controls contributed directly to the half billion personal records lost or stolen in 2015. (See the foreword for more details.)

It is time to take a fresh look at access controls—to understand how going digital changes the fabric of your organization. This journey starts with the implementation and integration of the latest technologies, trends and platforms, including cloud computing, mobile technologies, and Big Data analytics, allowing stakeholders to interlink their social media environments on shared smart devices for personal and business usage. With the proliferation of Internet of Things (IoT) devices and the expectation of being *always connected, always online*, consider the question: is our access control model still supporting our organization goals and addressing the right risks?

An effective cybersecurity program starts with a strategy and a foundation based on risks. According to PwC's "Global State of Information Security Survey 2016," 91 percent of the participants had adopted a risk-based cybersecurity framework. Although many organizations are using an amalgam of frameworks, the two most frequently implemented guidelines are the ISO 27001 and the cybersecurity framework of the U.S. National Institute of Standards and Technology (NIST). Risk-based frameworks can help organizations design systems, measure effectiveness, and monitor goals and risks for an improved cybersecurity program.[1]

Access control refers to the mechanisms and techniques used to ensure that access to assets is authorized and restricted based on organization and security requirements. The access control sections below, including the definitions given, are largely based on the ISO/IEC 27001:2013 (E) international standard, developed to provide requirements for establishing, implementing, maintaining and continually improving an information security management system (ISMS).[2] Particular attention must be paid to the distinction between "can/may" and "should" and "must". "Can" and "may" mean the following guidance can be considered as an option, whereas "should" is highly recommended, and "must" a necessity or requirement.

ORGANIZATION REQUIREMENTS FOR ACCESS CONTROL

The access control principles and activities covered below should be designed and formulated based on the organization and information security requirements for access control, with an overall aim of limiting access to information and information-processing facilities.

Based on a proper understanding of the organization, including its strategy, goals, and objectives, as well as the outcome of a risk assessment, the organization should formulate its access control policy with due consideration of the principles of *need to know* and *need to use*. The access control policy, including the sections discussed below, should be documented, approved, implemented, and reviewed based on the nature of the organization and its related security requirements. In determining the organization requirements, it is important to have a comprehensive understanding of your cyber threat landscape and your digital assets, including your company's "crown jewels." Many organizations have found that it is overly resource-intensive to implement maximum protection over all of their information components and information-processing facilities. The organization requirements for access controls should thus be crafted and modeled based on the specific nuances within the organization; they should support the overall organization goals, while protecting what matters most.

USER ACCESS MANAGEMENT

A large percentage of cybersecurity incidents stem from compromised login credentials. Attackers often follow the path of least resistance. They might search for the likes of unused user accounts (IDs), accounts with default passwords (the password set at installation and documented in the installation manuals), and accounts with easy-to-guess passwords. Therefore, to achieve the overall access controls objective, specific focus is required on user access management.

User Registration and Deregistration

The first step in providing access to a system is to create a user ID or user account; this process is also referred to as identity management. The process should apply to all types of users for all systems and services. User IDs should be unique to ensure accountability when access activities are logged and monitored. Therefore, sharing of user IDs should be prohibited, except where a process or device requires a user ID, for example, where an ID is required for a program that manages the backup function. This type of user ID is often a cyber attack entry target, so it is recommended that it be restricted to a physical device or that it is classified as a nondialogue user that cannot be used other than for the role for it was created.

Any request to register a new user should be approved by an organization or application owner or the reporting line manager. This applies to single sign-on integration, automation, workflow, or self-service solutions. At user ID creation, the user must acknowledge the conditions for access and adherence to relevant policies. The user ID or account should be created according to the documented naming convention. When a user resigns from the organization or when access is no longer required, the user ID should immediately be deregistered, removed, or locked on all systems. This will require effective integration with the organization's human resource (HR) processes.

Manual user registration and deregistration has been replaced with workflow-based processes or advanced identity and access management (IAM) solutions. These IAM solutions have become a requirement in large multisystem environments, where thousands of identities and access rights are managed across geographical systems and organizational boundaries, including employees, contractors, customers, partners and vendors.[3] For today's complex requirements, organizations need intelligent IAM solutions.

User Access Provisioning

After the registration of a new user ID, a process called user provisioning— commonly referred to as entitlement management—is followed to allocate user rights and privileges to the user so they can access information or resources. The objective should be to design and allocate rights and privileges in such a way that user access is restricted according to "need to know" and "need to use" principles and the user's role and purpose, meanwhile ensuring the segregation of duties (SOD). Role-based access control (RBAC) can be used to achieve this.

RBAC is an approach used to manage user rights and privileges (roles). It is intended to reduce the cost of security administration and ensure consistency of access principles. Permissions to perform certain system-based operations are assigned to specific roles, and roles are then allocated to users based on their function within the organization. As permissions are not assigned directly to users but only acquired through the assumption of roles, managing user rights is a matter of assigning predefined roles. Other access control approaches include mandatory access control (MAC), discretionary access control (DAC), rule-based access control (RAC), attribute-based access control (ABAC), history-based access control (HBAC), and identity-based and organization-based access control.[4]

A request for the allocation of rights and privileges to a user should be based on formal approval from the relevant organization or resource manager, in line with the agreed organization rules. An end-to-end trail of evidence should be retained of the user provisioning process followed for each request.

Management of Privileged Access Rights

The allocation of privileged (superuser) access to a user generally goes against the above overall access objective of ensuring restricted user access and the segregation of duties. User accounts with these roles are prime cyber attack targets and should be restricted, protected and controlled.

- It is sometimes necessary to give a superuser temporary access to fix errors, perform upgrades or deal with incidents—functions that cannot be carried out using normal support roles. In these exceptional instances, there are a number of controls that should be considered: Design and approve a superuser role to be used when required.

- Assign the superuser role or open the superuser ID based on special approval or a formal break-glass procedure requiring an incident to be reported in the incident management system.
- Send an automated alert to the security manager and organization manager when the role is activated or opened.
- Ensure that the activities performed by the superuser are logged (protected from manipulation) and promptly reviewed by the security manager and organization manager.
- Remove the role or lock the user ID as soon as the incident has been closed.
- It is strongly recommended that this procedure be automated or that tools are used in support thereof.

When an application user requires privileged access on an ongoing basis because of special circumstances, again the question must be asked: How is the risk managed? Special approval should be required, and the organization should design and implement adequate internal controls to mitigate the risk. A combination of the controls listed above should be considered.

New technologies are becoming available to assist with managing superuser access, from application-level to database-level access. Manual controls are simply ineffective.

Management of Secret Authentication Information of Users

The allocation and management of secret authentication information should be controlled through a formal process. The authentication information must remain secret at all times. This may be challenging if passwords or PINs are still being used as an authentication method, especially if supported by manual processes. Hackers may target stages of the authentication cycle through intensive organizational reconnaissance, social engineering, or other techniques.

When using a manual process to create user IDs or accounts, the user must be informed what the initial sign-on process is. Either the initial log-in will not require a password, or the initial password must be communicated to the user. The user is required to change the password within a specified time, and upon first log-in. Furthermore, when a user requires a password reset, it is critical that the identity of the user be validated before the password is reset. Communication is required between the function that will perform the reset and the user, including the new password. The user needs to log in with the reset password and then change the password within a period of time or upon next log-in so as to ensure secrecy.

It is clear from the preceding explanation that a manual process is open to attack. Hackers can intercept the passwords or use standard passwords applied by the organization during user creation and password reset. Technology should be considered to ensure the secrecy of authentication information, including one-time PINs (passwords) that are system generated and distributed via mobile phone, self-service password resets, integrated IAM solutions, and the like. Are passwords still an effective authentication method? Clearly not.

Review of User Access

Over time, a person's role within the organization may change. For instance, user rights and privileges (allocated roles) might evolve as a result of promotions, transfers, terminations, or changes in responsibilities.

To ensure that access rights are still appropriate, access is restricted and the segregation of duties is in place, allocated user access should be formally reviewed at regular intervals. The frequency of reviews should be based on the risk classification of the systems or data involved. The application, resource, or system owner; line manager; or head of department concerned needs to review the list of users with their allocated access rights, following the documented process. The user access reviews can be integrated with modern governance risk and compliance (GRC) solutions, although it will still require manual activities.

For the review to be effective, the review group must be small enough and known to the reviewer, and the access information should be nontechnical to ensure that the reviewer can interpret the access he or she is responsible for. The reviewer should return the review results to the access maintenance group. Where it has not been confirmed that a user's access has been reviewed, that user's access should be suspended. This may seem drastic, but access control discipline is of crucial importance in the cyber world in which we operate.

As regards intelligent access management, this is an area where Big Data analytics on IAM data and log files in combination with access management intelligence could play a major role in the defense against cyber attacks. This will move us closer to "ongoing user certification," reduce ineffective manual activities, and identify unusual behavior, while requiring human intervention only when exceptions have been flagged.[5,6]

Removal and Adjustment of User Rights

The human resources function should notify the access maintenance group of terminations to ensure that user IDs are immediately locked or deleted. This should preferably be automated so as to ensure the timely and effective termination of the user ID from all systems. The same controls described earlier should apply in the case of changes to access rights and privileges (user roles).

USER RESPONSIBILITY

The people component is often seen as the weakest link in the cyber chain. People are not equally diligent or knowledgeable when following processes or making decisions. As a result of leave arrangements, use of temporary staff, handover of responsibilities, and human emotional and physical well-being, manual controls are not consistently effective. Attackers will use social engineering, spoofing, phishing, brute-force attacks, and many other methods to obtain confidential information or to get a user to perform an activity that will compromise the organization.

Users must be trained in information security, and continuous awareness campaigns should remind them of cyber risks and the techniques used by hackers. Users must understand the importance of keeping their authentication information secret and their authentication devices secured at all times. Organizations should provide advice to users on how to select complex passwords and how to remember them, as writing them down will compromise the organization. Users must be aware of the access control policy, and they must understand the importance of full compliance and what their roles and responsibilities are in relation to information security.

SYSTEM AND APPLICATION ACCESS CONTROL

There are a number of fundamental requirements that need to be in place in order for an access control system to function at a basic level.

Information Access Restriction

Access to information and application systems must be restricted in accordance with the access control policy, on a need-to-know and need-to-use basis.

Secure Log-in Procedures

Access to systems and applications must be controlled by a secure log-in procedure that provides valid user identification, confirmed via effective authentication that is based on the risk profile of the information. Passwords are the most common way to authenticate as it is the simplest and most cost-effective authentication technique. But due to advanced hacking techniques and the exploitation of human behavior (ignorance and intentional or unintentional activities), we need more robust ways to protect valuable assets. As mentioned earlier, 91 percent of respondents to PwC's latest Global State of Information Security Survey reported that they are already using advanced authentication for some forms of access.[7]

Organizations that use a risk-based approach should be able to classify data and users, and should implement higher levels of authentication or multilevel authentication for high-risk areas.

Advanced authentication can replace passwords or be used as part of multifactor authentication. This includes fingerprint identification, retina scanning, speech and type pattern recognition, confirmation via mobile devices, and security tokens. "In the near future, data analytics or adaptive authentication could make authentication easier and safer for consumers. The next big challenge for authentication will be the expansion of the 'Internet of Things.' Should this device be allowed to unlock my car or unlock my home?"[8] Prepare for it.

Password Management System

Where passwords are used for authentication, the system must be interactive and ensure quality passwords. This includes enforcing the following conventions:

- Minimum length
- Prevention of historical passwords
- Regular changes
- Using special characters
- Using numeric values
- Mixed cases for alpha characters
- Avoidance of standard dictionary words, common passwords, or coherent phrases

Use of Privileged Utility Programs

Utility programs are often used to support the organization. However, any utility programs that are capable of overriding systems or bypassing controls should be restricted and tightly controlled. Due to the less restrictive access rights of utility programs, they are often targeted by hackers.

Access Control to Program Source Code

Access control to program source code should be restricted, as unauthorized access could result in exposure via backdoors, Trojan horse activities, and so on.

To protect the source code, consider deploying a combination of the following techniques to prevent malicious intent:

- Ring fence the source code storage area via segmentation or build an air-gap between the storage area and the Internet, as well as employees.
- Encrypt the source code.
- Implement very strict access controls to the source code areas.
- Perform peer code review to detect backdoors or other malicious code.
- Run software scans to find vulnerabilities.
- Electronically compare code.
- Automated system integrity checks to ensure the right code is in production.
- Strong automated version control.
- Automated code migration.

MOBILE DEVICES

As mobile devices increasingly become part of our lives, and as businesses start to harden their on-site security, cybercriminals will focus more on mobile devices. Most organizations now allow corporate-issued or employee-owned mobile devices to connect to their networks and business applications. This is where the corporate/business and private worlds become interweaved. A user may now use the same device to read mails (business and private), open confidential attachments, make appointments, surf the Internet, make mobile payments, and use several social media applications, all while connected to an unsecured Wi-Fi network in a public location. Does this sound familiar?

Risks associated with the use of mobile devices can include unauthorized access via unsecure Wi-Fi connections; loss or theft of data; mobile malware; phishing and spyware; the creation, use, or distribution of inappropriate content; organizational reputation; or simply having a confidential conversation over a cellular phone in a public place. Often, users store various log-in credentials on their mobile devices and if the device is compromised, then access to multiple business or private systems and applications is compromised. In this way, mobile devices can become an easy entry point for cybercriminals. Figure 22.1 shows how attacks on IoT devices

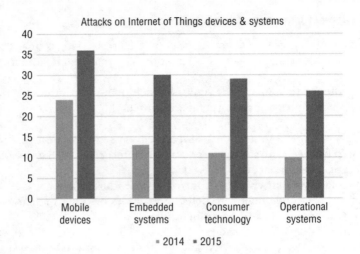

FIGURE 22.1   "The Global State of Information Security Survey 2016"
Source: PwC, "The Global State of Information Security Survey 2016." Content is
reprinted with the kind permission of PwC.

have increased in percentage terms for 2015 over 2014, according to PwC's
"Global State of Information Security Survey 2016."[9]

The modest mobile phone that was launched in the early 1990s has
now become a sophisticated and powerful mobile computing device that
is adding new levels of complexity to cybersecurity as it evolves ever further. Organizations can deal with mobile cyber threats by setting up mobile
device management policies. This is no simple task. You have to navigate
your way through a complex debate involving user expectations, productivity, and mobile freedom, and compare that to the mobile device risk to
the organization. Ultimately, the benefits of mobility are in danger of being
outweighed by the increase in your cyber risk.

Not all mobile devices offer the same security features. You therefore
have to decide if you will allow all mobile brands and ranges of devices
to connect to the organization's network and applications. You can reduce
your mobile cyber risk by using virtual private networks (VPNs), encrypting
data (static and in motion), and having passwords on all devices. Through
the central management of remote devices you can also locate a device, perform a remote lock or a data wipe, and enforce authentication—preferably
multifactor authentication. You can also monitor device usage, and continuous feedback to the user community can change user behavior. Making users
aware of mobility risk is therefore extremely important. Users should turn

off all features and functions that they do not use, and all business systems and applications that are accessed by mobile devices should be secured via identity and device management, authentication, encryption, and privilege management. It is also a good idea to consider third-party solutions for anti-virus, antispam, and intrusion detection. It is anticipated that native device software and third-party solutions will develop rapidly in this regard. (See Chapter 4 for more sample policy content for mobile devices and BYOD).

TELEWORKING

Teleworking or telecommuting is an arrangement where an employee uses computers and other telecommunication devices to work from a location other than the normal workplace, for instance, from home. This is often a temporary arrangement to assist an employee with their work–personal life balance or a particular set of circumstances, or where contractors or temporary staff are employed. While the human resource and potential cost benefits of allowing telecommuting are obvious, it does increase the cyber risk to an organization. The physical security within the telecommuter's environment may not be as strong as at the workplace; people may share equipment or use unsecure communication and personal applications on it; and the hardware, software, and security arrangements in respect of the equipment and its configuration may not comply with corporate standards. It is also very difficult to detect noncompliance. The organization could consider a number of practices to reduce the related risk:

- *Policy development.* A clear policy is required to ensure that user behaviors, actions, and practices are acceptable. The roles, responsibilities, benefits, and conditions must be clear, and physical, logical, and paper-based security requirements must be well known.
- *Use of equipment.* If the organization provides the equipment, it has more control—it is easier to ensure that the equipment is configured and loaded with the same software and that the same protection is used as in the workplace. If staff are allowed to use their own computers, it is very difficult to achieve the same level of protection as in the workplace. The organization will have to be prescriptive about, for instance, the use of the equipment and licensed software, firewalls, and antivirus and spyware software.
- *Encryption.* Due to the physical access risk, all PCs and storage devices, including removable media, have to be encrypted to protect all stored data.
- *Secure communication.* All electronic communication with the workplace should be via a VPN, connected only to secure networks.

- *Log-in.* Adequate log-ins using proper identification and strong authentication controls are required.
- *Support.* Telecommuters should be provided with the necessary technical support.
- *Training.* Ongoing technical and cyber awareness training should be provided.
- *Audits.* Compliance audits should be performed as required.
- *Access management.* Those business systems and applications that are accessed by telecommuters should be secured using identity and device management, authentication, encryption, and privilege management.

Telecommuters should be treated the same as third parties that require access to your environment—provide them with a strong set of baseline standards, audit them, and treat all interactions with them cautiously.

OTHER CONSIDERATIONS

Cybercriminals are always on the lookout for crown jewels, those core digital assets that, if compromised, may seriously damage or even ruin your business. Valuable and confidential information, including your crown jewels, need protection.

Cryptography could be an effective way to protect your information. Consider the end-to-end process and ensure that information is always encrypted, whether stored (static) or in transit. Encryption can be used for a variety of applications, including hard drives, flash drives and other removable media, e-mails, critical Web transactions, and external communications.

Another aspect to consider is network security. General network controls include the implementation of procedures for network equipment identification and management; defining roles and responsibilities; strong authentication control (device and user authentication); the segregation of duties; firewalls and routers that are correctly configured; and, of course, encryption. It is also essential to focus on the logging and monitoring of network activity, including the use of advanced intrusion detection systems (IDSs). Despite these controls, however, there are no guarantees than attackers will not (eventually) gain access to your network. This is where network segmentation or zoning can protect your crown jewels. By zoning the network, you can limit the number of devices, users, and applications that operate in highly protected areas, thereby making it more difficult for attackers to access your more sensitive digital assets.

CONCLUSION

The following cyber risk management statement expresses those organizational capabilities that the CEO and board expect to be demonstrated in terms of *access controls and cyber risk.*

ACCESS CONTROLS

The organization understands that the overall objectives and general principles of ITC access control remain largely the same as for traditional information security. But cyber risk requires that smart processes and next-generation technology be added to achieve current access control objectives. The organization avoids manual controls, embraces automation, and deploys access control intelligence to stay ahead of attackers. Its access control structure is effective. Cyber savvy and informed people, including third parties, leverage technology and are capable of identifying and reporting potential suspicious behavior and activities. Competent people use smart processes to bind these elements together to achieve enterprise-level goals.

NOTES

1. PwC. "The Global State of Information Security Survey 2016," 2015, www .pwc.com/gsiss
2. British Standards Institute, "Information Security Management Systems (ISMS): Requirements of ISO 27001:2013 Training Course, Implementing ISO/IEC 27001:2013, Information Technology-Security Techniques and Information Security Management Systems—Requirements," BSI Standards Limited, 2013.
3. Hitachi ID Systems, Inc., *User Provisioning Best Practices,* 204, 8–12. Available online: https://www.scribd.com/document/76682662/User-Provisioning-Best-Practices
4. PwC. *Information Security—A Strategic Guide for Business,* Pricewaterhouse Cooopers LLP, November 2003.
5. C. Sullivan, "Accelerating Access Management to the Speed of Hacks," *ISACA Journal,* 2015, 43–46.
6. PwC. "Building Digital Trust—The Confidence to Take Risk," 2014. Available online: http://www.pwc.co.uk/cyber-security/insights/building-digital-trust-to-take-risks.html
7. PwC. "The Global State of Information Security Survey 2016," 2015, www.pwc .com/gsiss

8. Wall Street Journal, Custom Studios, and PwC. "Broader Perspectives—A Cybersecurity and Privacy Hub," July 2016. Available online at http://www .sponsoredcontent.wsj.com/pwc/broader-perspectives/beyond-passwords/
9. PwC. "The Global State of Information Security Survey 2016," 2015, www.pwc .com/gsiss

ABOUT PWC

With offices in 157 countries and more than 208,000 employees, we are among the leading professional services networks in the world. We help organizations and individuals create the value they're looking for, by delivering quality in assurance, tax, and advisory services.

At PwC, we see cybersecurity and privacy differently. We don't just protect organizational value; we create it—using cybersecurity and privacy as tools to transform organizations. By bringing together capabilities from across PwC, we seek to understand senior leaders' perspectives on cybersecurity and privacy in the context of strategic priorities so they can play a central role in organizational strategy. By incorporating tactical knowledge gathered from decades of projects across industries, geographies, programs, and technologies, PwC can create and execute holistic start-to-finish plans.

ABOUT SIDRIAAN DE VILLIERS, PWC PARTNER SOUTH AFRICA

Sidriaan started his career in IT, where he gained experience as a programmer, systems analyst, and project manager for retail applications and networking environments. He then joined PwC as an IT auditor in 1990 and started to specialize in ERP controls and security. Due to his ERP experience, he has been involved in a number of international engagements in countries that included Namibia, Botswana, Zimbabwe, the Middle East, the United Kingdom, the United States, Switzerland, and Greece. With 30 years of experience in IT, computer auditing, risk management, data analytics, and system development life-cycle assessment, he is now responsible for the PwC Africa cybersecurity practice. He often lectures on controls- and security-related topics at colleges and universities in South Africa and is a regular cybersecurity presenter. More recently, he delivered a paper on controls and security in an ERP environment at the ORACLE Africa user group conference in Swaziland and was the keynote speaker at an ERP conference in Tel Aviv (Israel). Sidriaan holds BCom (Information Systems) and BSc (Hons Computer Science) degrees. As a member of ISACA, he completed the CISA certification in 1998, CISM in 2007, and CRISC in 2011.

CHAPTER 23

Cybersecurity Systems: Acquisition, Development, and Maintenance

Deloitte
Michael Wyatt, Managing Director, Cyber Risk Services, Deloitte Advisory, USA

"It looks like we have some real exposure." The words so softly addressed to Tom by his general counsel, Alain, slowly sank in. So what happened? A small marketing department in a third-tier market decided that the customer relationship management (CRM) solution offered by headquarter does not meet their needs. So they went ahead, found this very affordable cloud-based solution, and were up and running in no time. And now the cloud provider had a data breach. IT was never involved in managing this application. Nobody seems to know what data was stored there. There is a chance that data from all customers globally was loaded into the cloud. And the contract with the cloud provider does not give us any leverage to do our own investigation.

There is an increased push on business functions to drive value for the company in a short time frame. Thus, business functions are likely to look into technology solutions, including disruptive technologies, to increase automation, optimize processes, reduce costs, and achieve competitive advantage. Too often, cybersecurity is treated as something to be added or "bolted on" to existing applications and systems. This chapter is intended to help executives understand the foundational elements needed to establish a solid risk-aware process to acquire, develop, and maintain information systems.

BUILD, BUY, OR UPDATE: INCORPORATING CYBERSECURITY REQUIREMENTS AND ESTABLISHING SOUND PRACTICES

Today's information technology is characterized by fast changing, increased connectivity (e.g., Internet-of-Things [IOT], cloud computing, mobile networking), and ever increasing data volume. A more interconnected and interdependent information technology (IT) environment results in increased business impact from cybersecurity incidents. To reduce risk in such a dynamic environment, cybersecurity through a strong posture has become a must-have aspect in the information systems development life cycle. As with mechanical engineering, it is far better to design safety and security into the solution rather than attempting to augment a completed product. Cybersecurity needs to be interwoven into the information system development life cycle instead of waiting to add compensating controls until right before putting the system into production.

This section provides an overview of the application life cycle as shown in Figure 23.1 and provides guidance on the typical controls that can be considered by an organization in each phase of the life cycle.[1]

Governance and Planning

Implementing a strong cybersecurity program is more than deploying the latest cybersecurity tools. Even leading security tools have limitations and integration with legacy systems may be difficult. The onus of cybersecurity lies with the people bringing it to life, which includes end users as well as IT

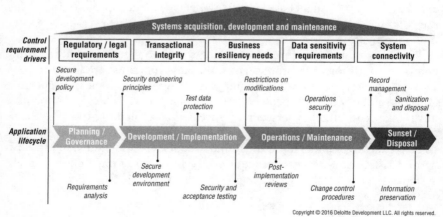

FIGURE 23.1   Application life cycle and typical controls

professionals. In addition, strong cybersecurity organizational culture starts at the top of the organization, requiring involvement from the CEO as well as the chief risk officer, chief operating officer, chief information officer, and other senior leaders. Without strong executive support, cybersecurity is a compliance exercise or, worse yet, simply an IT problem rather than an enterprise risk management issue. Establishing clear guiding principles and policies outlining security processes sets clear expectations with relevant stakeholders (e.g., information security, IT development, business procurement).

Define Security Requirements   To define security requirements, first an organization must define its risk appetite. At what level does the risk introduced by a business decision outweigh its benefits? At what point is a control introduced too expensive or could hinder business growth? And if risk management requirements slow down business growth, is it still justified as it enables sustainability of the business? Security requirements do differ from organization to organization and from industry to industry. While a bank may choose to encrypt all customer-related data, it may be not cost effective for a wholesaler. While the investment in applying the control may be the same, the potential impact of a breach differs significantly. As you define security requirements, identify the "crown jewels" of your organization and how to protect them.

Applicability of controls are typically determined through an application risk assessment driven by the information processed, business criticality, and type of application (e.g., customer facing versus internal). This application risk assessment follows an established methodology (based on the security requirements) and should be completed at the beginning of each project, ensuring alignment of the requirements with business needs and application characteristics. Incorporating this application risk assessment early in the project planning phase is more effective and economical than adding security to already developed or acquired technologies.[2]

Establish Policies and Procedures: The Guiding Principles for Effective Cybersecurity Programs   The application security policies and procedures establish when and how the application risk assessment should be applied. They also specify the controls being applicable based on the security requirements identified during the risk assessment. Without appropriate policies in place, the adoption of leading cybersecurity practices is left to the good intentions of the individual team members. The application security policies and procedures typically also cover controls such as and limited to secure coding methodologies, cybersecurity reviews, quality gates, and impact analysis of application changes.

Rules typically have exceptions. There will be applications for which it is not feasible to implement all controls required by policy. The exception approval and risk acceptance process should enable transparency into the risk exposure, as well as the business case. Depending on the risk exposure sign-off should involve the right level of leadership and obtaining the appropriate sign-offs.[3]

Development and Implementation

Based on the outcome of the application risk assessment and policy prescriptions, the organization can define or design the appropriate security features and controls. Strong cybersecurity relies on the *defense-in-depth* principle; it is by adding relevant layer of controls (e.g., access control, encryption, and monitoring) that the expected level of protection is achieved. Thus, security design is done in consideration of the broader security architecture and systems connectivity. Additional technically focused risk assessments (e.g., technical architecture, systems interfaces, and programming language) may supplement the initial application risk assessment.

Safety First: the Importance of Secure Engineering and Development Practices As described previously, cybersecurity considerations should be incorporated tightly within the application life cycle. Organizations can achieve this by adopting secure engineering practices and enabling a security-focused mindset in the development life cycle.

Secure engineering approaches are focused on *cybersecurity by design,* a concept that applies security to all of the layers of an information system's design, from the business process to the technology platform. By taking an engineering approach to cybersecurity, analysis can be performed both on the system and within program modules to ensure design and implementation of the appropriate security controls.

Some of the leading practices within secure engineering include adding fail safe procedures to handle errors and maintain data integrity for critical failures and validation of the inputs to protect against commonly exploited vulnerabilities, such as cross-site scripting and Structured Query Language (SQL) injections. Secure engineering guidelines should also include effective code design practices, including the use of tools to examine code for security vulnerabilities (system flaw or weakness that can be exploited by an attacker) as well as peer code review.

A security-focused mind-set in the development and test environment is important as well. Historically, developers have enjoyed complete control over the code they write and the data used during development. Depending on the sensitivity and criticality of the information system, additional cybersecurity controls may be warranted. Organizations should consider the use of well-defined code repositories with version control and check-out processes to mitigate code defects. Data sets used in development and testing environment should be sanitized from any confidential data to prevent undue access by developers.[4]

Security and Acceptance Testing: Cybersecurity Leading Practices   Too often, organizations evaluating an application for acceptance, whether externally sourced or internally developed, focus solely on functional requirements. It is important that cybersecurity requirements be included in the process.

As systems are developed, security testing is conducted to verify that systems are complying with security requirements and producing outputs as expected and only as expected. Applications are reviewed (in a pre-production environment that closely replicates the production application environment) from the perspective of a malicious individual. The purpose is to determine whether vulnerabilities exist (that may not by detected through secure code reviews) within the application that a cybercriminal can leverage to gain unauthorized access to sensitive information and cause disruption to services.

Preparations include creation of a detailed schedule of activities and test inputs and expected outputs under a range of conditions, as well as development of documentation to capture test results. The security testing process is incomplete if not followed up by collaboration with development and architecture teams for risk classification and prioritization, remediation strategies, and verification of remediation effectiveness.

Independent cybersecurity testing by external experts may be conducted for critical systems. Testing should not be limited to in-house developed systems; third-party software providers should allow procuring organizations to test software or, at a minimum, provide evidence of independent testing. Note that if not included in the purchase contracts, suppliers will be reticent to agree to vulnerability testing of their proprietary code base by customers or independent third parties. The best time to address the need to test supplier provided software is during the procurement cycle and contract negotiations.

Testing, Testing, One, Two, Three: Protection of Test Data   While testing applications, it is important that the test data used emulates production data as closely as possible. One of the most common practices in testing information systems is to simply extract production data and load it in the test environment. However, organizations could face cybersecurity incidents in these test environments, leading to exposure of sensitive and confidential data. Many organizations have suffered tremendous losses of personally identifiable information (PII) and protected health information (PHI) due to a test environment lacking basic cybersecurity controls.

For critical and sensitive information systems, the same level of cybersecurity controls used in production need to be applied in the test environment. Organizations should also consider practices like obfuscation (masking of identifiable details) for the test data and additional controls like authentication, encryption and audit logging. Organizations should also consider the procedures for disposal and termination of testing environments upon completion of the process.[5]

Maintenance and Operations

Once the system is implemented, appropriate change management processes are necessary to ensure that the migration of the system to production is done with minimal risks of disruption. Postimplementation reviews may be performed to ensure security features operate properly in production.

Risk of Impact: Cybersecurity Change Control Considerations A change to an application or system can negatively affect the availability, confidentiality or integrity of an information system. This is why change control, fundamentally an IT process, has become an important cybersecurity control.

Numerous organizations have faced operational outages, reputational damage, and financial losses due to poor change control procedures, including a lack of communication between stakeholders, lack of conducting business impact analysis, and making changes to production environments instead of to a staging environment and promoting the changes to production. Hence, it is recommended that organizations develop detailed change control policies and procedures beginning with the design phase of a project through maintenance and operations.

Leading change control practices include use of a formal review process that evaluates the change. The review process includes risk assessment and impact analysis of the existing information system's cybersecurity controls. To compensate for changes that have unforeseen impacts, back out procedures to revert to the prechange state are strongly recommended.

Organizations can further reduce the risk of impact by having a staging or test environment that mirrors the production environment but is isolated in case the change has unforeseen outcomes. Finally, it is important that documentation of the information system be updated to reflect the change.

To Change or Not to Change, That Is the Question Vulnerabilities as well as general IT operating risks are often introduced through the modification of packaged software. In this context, modification refers to changes to the software code itself rather than configuration settings made available by the software developer. For example, when a user uses a "rootkit" to modify the operating system on a mobile device, built-in security controls are bypassed, making the device and the information on it vulnerable to hackers.

It is recommended to restrict modifications to packaged software. However, for exceptions, organizations should consider the following aspects and assess the exception based on business needs and risk acceptance criteria. Modifying packaged software often makes the software more difficult to support by the organization and the vendor. It also may lead to instability or performance issues and may make it difficult to upgrade to future versions. Modifications to packaged software also warrant a high level of scrutiny and process adherence from a change control perspective.[6]

Secure Operations   Once a system or an application is up and running in production, a number of ongoing security activities should be done to maintain security features as per the requirements (e.g., certificate/key management, patch management). For more information on security operations, see Chapter 21.

Sunset and Disposal

Decommissioning a system is more than pulling the plug out or discarding the hardware. Appropriate planning and processes are necessary to archive data, sanitize and dispose systems safely, based on information sensitivity.

Decommissioning a System: Nothing Left Behind   With continual technology evolution and breakthrough, information systems often become obsolete or are transferred to a different technology platform. It is imperative to follow an end-to-end disposal process to effectively decommission a system.

The starting point is to design a disposal or transition plan in compliance with legal regulations, government policies, and license agreements. The transition plan outlines the steps to preserve information and manage records. Archived information, whether content based, management, or operational, comes in handy not just for migration to a new system or future reactivation, but also for developing secure future systems. When archiving data, applicable laws and regulations requirements (e.g., retention period) should be addressed; organizations operating across multiple international locations should be particularly careful with various requirements.

Once the data are preserved, all of the old information system digital media can be sanitized and disposed. The system is shut down and discarded followed by security review of the closure. The sanitization and disposal process should consider the information confidentiality level to apply the appropriate sanitization techniques in consideration of the risks.

The index of archived information (location and retention attributes), media sanitization records, hardware and software disposal records, and system closure verification should be documented.[7]

SPECIFIC CONSIDERATIONS

Organizations can build their information systems in many ways, such as the traditional development process, purchase of readily available software, or use cloud/software as a service (SaaS) applications.

- *Commercial off-the-shelf (COTS) applications.* Applications developed by vendors and installed on the organization's information systems. These applications are usually purchased outright by organizations with usage based on licensing agreements.
- *Cloud/SaaS applications.* Applications developed by service providers or vendors and installed on the provider or vendor information system. Organizations typically have an on-demand or pay-per-usage metrics.
- *In-house developed applications.* Applications developed, installed, and maintained by the organization using internal teams and/or contractors.

Commercial Off-the-Shelf Applications

Broader availability of products at lower costs has driven the use of COTS products to fulfill business needs in organizations. Purchasing a software from a vendor, even prominent vendors, does not mean it is free from vulnerabilities or include relevant security features for your organization's needs.

As part of the assessment of applications, organizations should evaluate the following risks:

- Organizational risks may include misalignment between the business needs and the product features, not identifying the right end users, and exposing sensitive data through the product.
- Product risks may include inefficient management of security patches and vulnerabilities, nonfulfillment of business and functional requirements, and gaps between available controls and security needs (e.g., encryption not present).

It is also beneficial to consider the vendor's track record and history of security responses and development quality.

In order to manage these risks, an effective policy needs to establish and validate security requirements during the procurement process. It is crucial to include security requirements during software selection, whether procurement is driven by the technology or business functions.

As with in-house developed software, penetration testing and vulnerability scanning of the COTS applications prior to production rollout is necessary to provide reasonable assurance of the new solution's security posture. Remember the right to evaluate COTS products should be negotiated as part of the procurement and contracting process.

Cloud/SaaS Applications

Cloud/SaaS applications are rapidly becoming the norm today with systems potentially connecting and transferring data over the untrusted public Internet. While many organizations find it beneficial to use such cloud/SaaS applications, additional cybersecurity controls for such systems should be considered, especially for the following risks:

- The vendor IT infrastructure database might have weak cybersecurity, exposing the organization to attacks and breaches even if the application fulfills all security requirements.
- Availability of ready-to-use cloud services (e.g., storage, content management and collaborative tools) and need for flexibility may encourage business functions and project teams to use unapproved services, bypassing the security requirements definition and evaluation process.
- Legal and regulatory risks should also be considered when using cloud services (e.g., privacy requirements, cross-border transfer restrictions if provider is located in a different country).

When considering using cloud/SaaS applications, cybersecurity due diligence on the provider should be performed in addition to the review of application security features. Due diligence activities may include review of provider cybersecurity policies, provider contract reviews, data protection audits, baseline security controls, and incident response process. Particular attention should also be given to contracts with the providers, ensuring cybersecurity requirements are included as well as a clause allowing joint investigations in case of cybersecurity incident at the provider impacting your organization's data or application. Organizations may also consider adding an indemnification clause requiring the provider to indemnify the organization in case of a data loss. Indemnification clause is a good incentive for the provider to tighten up its cybersecurity controls.

In-House Developed Applications   While custom software development is typically under the domain of technology officers and cybersecurity functions, business executives also need to consider the associated security risks and understand the impact to the organization:

- When developing an application, the focus is on achieving the business goals and very often security is overlooked, (e.g., an application handling confidential information with no encryption and inadequate authentication). Misalignment between security needs and actual security features may lead to a breach.
- Developing complex applications with thousands of line of code and interconnected systems is a very error-prone activity; coding errors may result in application vulnerabilities and may not be detected if the testing only focuses on application business functionalities.

Detailed code reviews can be established to identify security weaknesses in the code through automated scanning tools and escalating to manual reviews for detailed inspection of issues.

It is beneficial to consider building secure development enablers, such as acquiring secure coding tools (e.g., static code scanning, vulnerability scanning tools developed by leading security institutes like SysAdmin, Audit, Network and Security [SANS] Institute, Community Emergency Response Team [CERT]).

Do not assume developers are security experts by default; it is important to provide regular training with a focus on secure code development and the security pitfalls of coding. These training sessions should focus on high-risk areas of weakness including, but not limited to, topics such as information leakage, input validation, and error handling.

CONCLUSION

The following cyber risk management statement represents those organization capabilities CEO and board expect to be demonstrated in terms of *cybersecurity systems acquisition, development, and maintenance*.

CYBERSECURITY SYSTEMS ACQUISITION, DEVELOPMENT, AND MAINTENANCE

The organization's effective and reliable information systems are efficient and cost effective and achieve competitive advantages. Building and buying information systems are the result of careful business and risk-based decisions. Appropriate security requirements that are commensurate to the risks, are defined, implemented and tested before moving the application into production. Cybersecurity is "by design" and integrated into the organization applications. Policies and procedures must ensure that cybersecurity are addressed through the development or acquisition life cycle in line with the following guiding principles: (1) security requirements should be identified up front based on the risks; (2) the security requirements should be included in the application development and selection processes; (3) the security requirements should be tested for effectiveness pre- and postimplementation; (4) when using cloud/SaaS providers, cybersecurity due diligence should be conducted; and (5) developers should be trained on secure coding practices, and the developed code should be inspected for security defects.

NOTES

1. National Institute of Standards and Technology. *Security Considerations in the System Development Life Cycle,* Special Publication 800-64, 2008.
2. International Standards Organization 27002, "14.1. Security Requirements of Information Systems." In *Information Technology–Security Techniques–Code of Practice for Information Security Controls.* Switzerland, Edition 2, October 2013.
3. National Institute of Standards and Technology. *Framework for Improving Critical Infrastructure Cybersecurity,* Version 1, 2014.
4. International Standards Organization 27002, "14.2. Security in Development and Support Processes." In *Information Technology–Security Techniques–Code of Practice for Information Security Controls.* Switzerland, Edition 2, October 2013.
5. International Standards Organization 27002, "14.3. Test Data." In *Information Technology–Security Techniques–Code of Practice for Information Security Controls.* Switzerland, Edition 1, February 2010.
6. The Open Web Application Security Project, "The Ten Most Critical Web Application Security Risks," 2013. Available online: https://www.owasp.org/index.php/Top_10_2013-Top_10
7. National Institute of Standards and Technology, "3.5. SDLC Phase: Disposal." In *Security Considerations in the System Development Life Cycle.* Special Publication 800-64, 2008.

ABOUT DELOITTE ADVISORY CYBER RISK SERVICES

Deloitte Advisory's cyber risk services help complex organizations more confidently leverage advanced technologies to achieve their strategic growth, innovation, and performance objectives through proactive management of the associated cyber risks. With deep experience across a broad range of industries, Deloitte Advisory's more than 3,000 cyber risk services practitioners provide advisory and implementation services, spanning executive and technical functions, to help transform legacy IT security programs into proactive, secure, vigilant, and resilient cyber risk programs. Deloitte Advisory cyber risk services works with clients worldwide to better align cybersecurity investments with strategic business priorities, establish improved threat awareness and visibility, and strengthen the ability of organizations to prepare for, defend against, and thrive in the face of cyber incidents.

ABOUT MICHAEL WYATT

Michael Wyatt has a broad background of over 27 years' experience, specializing in cybersecurity program development and identity management. Michael serves as a Managing Director in Deloitte Advisory's Cyber Risk Services practice where he leads the digital identity management solution offering. He is responsible for helping clients address their cybersecurity program development, identity enabled digital transformation, privileged access control and identity access governance needs. Prior to joining Deloitte in 2007, Michael held cybersecurity leadership positions with Sun Microsystems, Waveset Technologies, and IBM/Tivoli.

CHAPTER 24

People Risk Management in the Digital Age

Airmic
Julia Graham, Deputy CEO and Technical Director at Airmic, UK

Tom the CEO was chatting with Grace, his head of human resources (HR): "Do you remember that John Connor, a central character in the science fiction series *The Terminator*, believed that a war between humans and machines would occur?" Tom asked. He summarized the 2003 film, *Rise of the Machines,* the third film in the *Terminator* series: The president faced pressure to activate Skynet to stop a computer virus that was infecting computers all over the world. Grace finished the story for Tom. "Yes, toward the end of the film, John reached Crystal Peak, a nuclear base hardened against nuclear attack. He discovers that the facility is not Skynet's core but a nuclear fallout shelter and that Skynet has no core because it was actually the Internet and the source of the virus spreading the whole time. Judgment Day begins as nuclear missiles are fired at several locations around the world, killing billions of people."

RISE OF THE MACHINES

Fiction perhaps, but a decade on from the making of *Terminator 3,* fiction is becoming fact. Technology is infiltrating the world from every angle—from in-home sensors to telematics, and wearable devices; information is flowing between people, devices, and companies without any human intervention. But human intervention will remain important in the new normal of the digital world. Man will continue to be at the center of organizations, doing what man can do better than machines by adding value through creativity. However, man cannot be programmed like a machine, and it is man's ability in the area of creativity that can at the same time be both an asset and a liability. In the film *Rise of the Machines,* man was the weakest link—his misreading of the scenario resulted in disaster. People make bad decisions for a whole range of reasons: they get tired and lose concentration, become scared and lose the ability to think rationally, or are demotivated and resentful.

ENTERPRISE-WIDE RISK MANAGEMENT

Like risk, there is no commonly accepted definition of *people risk,* but for the purpose of this chapter the following definition taken from Blacker and McConnell will be used: "the risk of loss due to the decisions and non-decisions of people inside and outside of the organization."[1] This definition looks at people through the lens of the individual and the organization, including employees, managers, and directors, from different functional and governance perspectives and external stakeholders including customers, suppliers, competitors, regulators, government bodies, the general public, and local communities. All can touch the organization and all can influence the achievement of the organization's purpose and objectives and the operation of its business model.

The context of people risk is broad ranging from routine decision making to complex analysis—and it is often the routine decision made badly through carelessness or maliciously by intent that can create the greatest severity of risk. Even worse is a poor decision communicated effectively, spreading its success like a financial disease. The careless use of a portable device can expose huge amounts of data, which even in quite recent times required a computer the size of a small car and the release of simple but personal data has the potential to create enormous reputational harm and financial consequences and penalties. Where the context of people risk varies from more conventional approaches is that people are viewed as an aspect of enterprise risk and across the organization, and not through unconnected operational silos. Viewed this way, the potential for aggregation and interdependencies of risk inside and outside the organization can be more readily identified, assessed, and treated. Consequently, people risk is not solely the domain of the human resources department, and people risk in the digital age is not solely the domain of the technology or information security department—it is a cross-functional enterprise-wide activity.

The People Risk Management System

People risk should form part of the risk management system of the organization rather than operate as a separate or silo—in any context including the digital world. The digital environment is, then, part of the overall internal and external context of the organization, which should embrace all of the organization's economic and social activities. This approach will help to ensure that risk management and associated controls are proportionate, reasonable and achievable. This approach also facilitates the assignment of responsibility for risk across the organization. This approach is not rocket science but common sense. However, digital risks are often left to those who "best understand" them—there is an inherent fear of the unknown. Nobody likes to appear ignorant, and when questions about technology are raised, it is too easy to look the other way and expect those on the technology team to field the answers. Everyone today needs some level of digital knowledge. Effective enterprise-wide people risk management demands upskilling of knowledge in the organization, starting at the board and working up from the front line. As the typical key holders to the lock of training budgets, human resources have a key role to play in realizing this objective. The cross-functional management of people risks will help to ensure that training is appropriately targeted and delivered.

The Digital Governance Gap

Most executives take managing risk seriously. Yet crises continue to emerge as organizations continue to neglect basic oversight and processes and to identify training needs and fulfill them.

The perceived value of both tangible and intangible assets is relatively similar, with just 3 percent difference according to Ponemon Institute research. On average, the total value of tangible assets reported was $872 million, compared to $845 million for intangible assets. When asked to estimate an average figure for the loss or destruction of all their intangible assets (or probable maximum loss/PML), again the estimation was similar ($638 million for intangible assets, compared to $615 million for their tangible assets). In contrast, both the impact of business disruption to intangible assets and the likelihood of an intangible asset or data breach occurring is seen as significantly greater than for tangible assets."[2]

According to a report from KPMG the speed of technology change will be exponential with data and data analytics the biggest area of investment. Forty-one percent of the CEOs who responded believing their business will be significantly transformed over the next three years.[3] There are deep implications as the world moves toward a demand for business leaders who are more inventive big-picture thinkers, who can create a vision of change and frame it positively in this context. This does not imply that today's leaders cannot be tomorrow's leaders, but it does point toward the need for a change in the balance of leadership teams to reflect the knowledge, skills and expertise of the digital world. This change demands a confidence in leaders to manage their reshaped teams and in forging new directions. Yet despite a 56 percent rise in boardroom ownership of cyber risk, the majority of firms are still failing to conduct or estimate the financial impact of a cyber attack, according to Marsh.[4] The next step for the majority of respondents companies with a basic understanding is to conduct in-depth analyses into the issues, involving multiple groups within the organization, including information technology, executive management, legal, and risk management.

Cyber risk should be approached as an economic risk integrated with the business model and form part of the organization's risk management and decision-making systems. Forming a cross-disciplinary team to focus on identification of the risks and the impacts they may have on the business was considered an important step organizations should take. However, there was little evidence of the majority making this commitment. The U.K. government used a nontechnical governance questionnaire to assess the extent to which boards and audit committees understand and oversee risk management measures that address cybersecurity threats to their business. The report concluded that U.K. companies have improved their understanding of cyber risks—yet 33 percent of boards have set and understood their appetite for cyber risk, which means 67 percent have not. Sixteen percent of boards have a very clear understanding of where the company's key information and data assets are stored with third parties, which means that 84 percent do not.[5] A report from insurer AIG reported that only half of the boards surveyed were taking external views on emerging risks into account.[6] These reports taken collectively imply that boards are confident in their management of digital governance and cyber risk, while exhibiting a degree of complacency in making this assessment without sufficient command of the subject. Is there a *cyber governance gap*?

TOMORROW'S TALENT

Many of the biggest organizations in the world have been built on foundations of "left-side brain excellence," or logical and sequential management. The left side of the brain is especially good at recognizing events that occur one after the other and in controlling serial behaviors. On the other hand, the right side of the brain has an ability to interpret things simultaneously. It is the equivalent of the enterprise risk management side of the brain! "The left hemisphere of the brain specializes in text, the right hemisphere specializes in context."[7] Pink's work is not new, but it does have the sense of a theory evolving into fact. One of the biggest people risks organizations face is their inability to attract and retain talent at all levels of the organization, including the top. "The Cyber Governance Gap" is perhaps an indication that the top of many organizations in this regard is lagging behind. The two sides of the brain, of course, work together—it the growing respect and recognition of the value of people who exhibit "right-side brain" tendencies that is different. The emphasis of those who are entrepreneurs and start disruptor businesses are unlikely to have a left-side emphasis. The point and the risk is that organizations need both.

The Digital Quotient

An expression used to describe the needs of the digital age is the *digital quotient (DQ)*. According to Prashant Ranade, the vice chairman of Syntel, a leader can increase his or her DQ through the six following strategies:

- *Managing the unknowable.* Recognize the boundaries of his/her own expertise and develop a network of experts to provide a strong foundation of knowledge.
- *Entrepreneurship.* Identify trends so it's possible to scale strong ideas and cut losses to minimize the damage that comes with taking necessary risks.
- *Mind mapping.* See the big picture and establish clear boundaries that keep the primary goals in mind.
- *Discerning at speed.* Understanding quality information and processing it clearly, at the speed of business.
- *Succeeding in the customer age.* Meeting customer expectations and setting the ground rules for interactions.
- *Inspiring with technology.* Using technology to tap each individual's talents, skills, and best work.[8]

For many decades, the notion that the smartest people make the best leaders was a widely held belief. The idea of smartness—as measured by the intelligence quotient (IQ)—was viewed as a primary determinant of success, and it was commonly assumed that people with high IQs were destined for lives of accomplishment and achievement throughout their careers. Traditional leadership qualities like intelligence, toughness, determination, and vision are important, but tomorrow's truly effective leaders will also need to display a high degree of emotional intelligence, which includes qualities like self-awareness, inspiration, empathy, and social and relationship management skills.

"With digital technologies like mobility, social networks, Big Data analytics, and cloud now deeply embedded in every aspect of our personal and professional lives, today's business leaders need to possess a completely new set of capabilities in addition to IQ and EQ to succeed in the digital age."[9]

Digital Leadership and the Emergence of the Digital Risk and Digital Risk Officer

At the end of the 1990s, the role of chief information officer (CIO) was ebbing out of fashion. Technology and information were increasingly viewed as commodities, and if the organization saw the value of a CIO, it was typically a junior managerial position. Everything now looks quite different. Organizations are now hungrier for knowledge about digitization and the ability to mine and manipulate data. Cries for CIOs is not new, but lack of focus on their value has perhaps led to the risk that suitable talent is in short supply. The CIOs that do exist are perhaps not as well equipped today and they need to be for tomorrow. Digital transformation requires expert leadership. According to KPMG, the number of CIOs with more senior reporting lines has doubled in recent years.[10] Recognition of the "Cyber Governance Gap" and the risks associated with this should see the relevance and importance of the CIO to organizations as a trusted expert and advisor.

Commentators on the professional scene foresee the emergence of a new breed of information and technology oriented professional. The digital risk and digital risk officer are likely to emerge in prominence and in number. Research by Gartner indicates that more than half of CEOs will have a senior "digital" leader role in their staff by the end of 2015 and by 2017, one-third of large enterprises engaging in digital business models and activities will also have a digital risk officer (DRO) role or equivalent."[11]

The ability of businesses to keep up with the predicted exponential change in the use of technology and information means it is almost inevitable that technology failures and information breaches will increase and that technology and information teams will struggle to keep pace with disruption and subsequent fixes. Technology, the Internet of Things and more traditional security technologies will have interdependencies demand a risk-based approach to governance and integration as part of the business model and the management of this. "Digital risk management is the next evolution in enterprise risk and security for digital businesses that are expanding the scope of technologies requiring protection. Digital risk officers will require a mix of business acumen and understanding with sufficient technical knowledge to assess and make recommendations for appropriately addressing digital business risk," said Paul Proctor, vice president and distinguished analyst at Gartner. "Many traditional security officers will change their titles to digital risk and security officers, but without material change in their scope, mandate, and skills they will not fulfill this role in its entirety."

The DRO is, however, not "more of the same"—the responsibilities of a DRO are not the same as those of the chief information technology officer (CTO) or chief information security officer (CISO). The DRO and CTO and CISO are complementary, and these roles are likely to continue and to co-exist. Think of a financial function analogy and the responsibilities of the chief financial officer (CFO) and the head of management accounting and the head of financial control. The responsibilities are similar but also differ-ent—the seniority and reporting lines are radically different. The DRO will become the natural "go to" person for the board on technology and infor-mation as regards risk and controls assessment and as regards the executive or C-Suite addressing future business opportunities and strategy. The DRO will work with peers including the CFO, general counsel (GC), Data Protec-tion Office (DPO), compliance, chief risk officer (CRO), and digital market-ing, and sales and operations team leaders.

Where will this new breed of DROs come from? DROs are likely to surface from the community of CTOs and CISOs. What will set the DRO apart is management. This is not only a technically informed role; it is a leadership role. New knowledge and skills will be required and not all cur-rent role holders will be able to rise to the fresh challenges of operating at a higher level.

Technology and information teams have been allowed to "do their own thing." These functions were viewed as operational or "support" and as long as business could be maintained, disruptions avoided and "yes" was uttered when new developments were demanded, the functions were left alone. Now they are in the spotlight. For organizations that have already taken the leap of change, life will evolve albeit change and the pace of change will quicken. Elsewhere there will be a "churning" of talent as organizations seek to increase their digital talent pool.

A new "superset" of technology and information professionals will challenge current organization structures, the definition and division of responsibilities, knowledge, skills, and the tools and language required to systematically, effectively, and efficiently identify, assess, define, and man-age technology and information risks and opportunities. Modifying existing teams to include the spectrum of digital risk is not an option. Future tech-nology demands skills and tools deployed in a different cultural context to current technology, information, and security teams.

Digital enterprise risk management (DERM) will demand the adop-tion of enterprise-wide risk management (ERM) and the collaboration this demands. The potential to deliver the performance benefits recognized by adopting ERM opens up to the digital world as regards cost efficiencies, greater risk assurance for business processes, and quality of business per-formance. Digital risk management capability requires a demolition and reengineering of current organization structures and responsibilities and development of new capabilities in security and risk assessment, monitoring, analysis, and control. Demolition is a powerful word, but the transformational changes predicted in the digital age will not wait for evolutionary change.

"By 2019, the new digital risk concept will become the default approach for technology risk management," said Proctor. "Digital risk officers will influence governance, oversight, and decision making related to digital business. This role will explicitly work with non-IT executives in various capacities to better understand digital business risk and facilitate a balance between the need to protect the organization and the need to run the business. However, the cultural gap between IT and non-IT decision makers presents a significant challenge. Many executives believe technology—and therefore technology-related risk—is a technical problem, handled by technical people, buried in IT. If this gap is not bridged effectively, technology and consequent business risk will hit inappropriate levels and there will be no visibility or governance process to check this risk."[12]

CRISIS MANAGEMENT

In order to be resilient, organizations must have clear processes to in place to respond to threats.

Cyber Crisis Management Can Have a Number of Unique Characteristics

Typically the domain of the information technology function, cyber-related incidents must be managed at an enterprise-wide level. An effective digital business model bridges including technology and information, the business, finance, human resources, legal, and risk management. Accountability and solid decision making are essential to facing cyber threats. Before disaster strikes, it is absolutely necessary to have a clear operating model in place.

The Dynamics of a Successful Crisis Management Team
- Strong but consultative leader.
- A pool of potential team members with competence and skills mix suitable for a portfolio of crises.
- Relevant team members deployed according to the needs of the crisis.
- Optimum size between 6 and 10.
- Trained and rehearsed against multiple scenarios.

Some organizations have found that crises emerge when they neglect to manage "front-line" behavior and culture (which is the first line of defense against risk). Having a strong risk culture does not necessarily equate to taking less risk—risk confident organizations may feel able to take more risk and at times of stress and pressure following an incident are likely to have a higher "chance" of survival. McKinsey has undertaken research which indicates that some people have characteristics which enable them to respond quickly.[13]

A crisis can help an organization to integrate risk management and digital risk management including crisis response, but this is better tested in rehearsal than in real time!

RISK CULTURE

Despite high profile failures of risk management in recent years, the cost and probability of failure is often underestimated internally and externally, including the time required to fix the problem. Risk taking remains a fundamental driving force in business: when managed correctly it drives competitiveness and profitability. However, when managed unsuccessfully, the results can be devastating.

The role of senior management in ensuring companies manage their risk successfully is of critical importance. Encouragingly, this is increasingly recognized in official guidelines. The Financial Reporting Council's risk guidance published in October 2014 stated that the board should take "ultimate responsibility for risk." And the FRC's most recent risk guidance, "Corporate Culture and the Role of Boards," published in July 2016, states that senior executives should "get out of the boardroom" to understand how their firms are behaving.

The importance of this is backed up by research commissioned by Airmic which identified "underlying weaknesses that made them especially prone to both crises and to the escalation of crisis into a disaster." These weaknesses were found to arise from seven key areas, two of which were: board "risk blindness" and a risk "glass ceiling." In other words, risk information did not flow freely up to senior management, usually due to cultural and structural barriers. The result was a failure of the board to properly recognize and engage with risks inherent in the business.[14]

The risk of the "glass ceiling" includes "risks arising from the inability of risk management and internal audit teams to report to and discuss, with both the 'C Suite' (leaders such as the Chief Executive, Chief Operating Officer and Chief Financial Officer) and NEDs."[15]

Recognizing if your company suffers from board risk blindness is not always easy, but there are red flags to look out for. Two of the key indicators for assessing "board risk blindness" are: tracking how and when people speak up and how their words are responded to; and how risk responsibilities are embedded in role responsibilities and reward systems.

Risk culture is not a new concept but it has gained traction and importance since the financial crisis. Risk culture is dynamic; it can be a mixture of formal and informal processes and may exist in more than one form. However, it is important that risk culture is set within the overall framework of the organization's vision, mission, corporate culture, and risk management system. And, most importantly, it comes from the boardroom.

CONCLUSION

There is no blueprint for managing people risk generally, or in the Digital Age. However, instilling a digital regime comprising technology, business, risk and people solutions as part of the building blocks of an enterprise-wide people risk management system as part of the organization's overall risk management system, is a great place to start!

The following cyber risk management statement represents those organization capabilities CEO and board expect to be demonstrated in terms of *people risk in the digital age.*

PEOPLE RISK MANAGEMENT SYSTEM

Management understands that people are not machines and cannot be programmed. An enterprise-wide people risk management system includes technology, business, risk, and people solutions that avoid operational silos. It forms part of the enterprise risk management system where people risk is not solely the domain of the human resources (HR) department or the technology or information security departments. People risk controls are proportionate, reasonable and achievable. Organizational knowledge upskilling starts at the board and works up from the front line. HR uses training budgets to appropriately target and deliver cross-functional training. Any digital governance gap is bridged by in-depth analysis and a cross-disciplinary team including IT, executive management, legal, and risk management. Talent is recruited balancing future needs for both left- and right-brain thinkers and leaders develop or increase their digital quotient.

The organization manages all forms of digital risk and may deploy a specialized digital risk officer if appropriate. Crisis management capabilities, resources, and relationships enable rapid and appropriate response appropriate to not only an emergency, but also to react to small changes that could ultimately develop into a disaster. Senior management nurture a risk-taking culture that drives competitiveness and profitability.

NOTES

1. Keith Blacker and Patrick McConnell, *People Risk Management: A Practical Approach to Managing the Human Factors That Could Damage Your Business* (Section 2.1). London: Kogan Page, 2015. E-ISBN 978 0 7494 7136 1.
2. Ponemon, EMEA Cyber Impact Research, 2015. Retrieved from www.slideshare.net/GraemeCross2/ponemon-2015-emea-cyber-impact-report
3. KPMG, "Now or Never—Global CEO Outlook," 2016, https://home.kpmg.com/xx/en/home/media/press-releases/2016/06/2016-ceo-outlook-next-3-years-more-critical-than-previous-50.html
4. Marsh, "UK Cyber Risk Survey Report 2016," 2016, https://www.marsh.com/uk/insights/research/uk-cyber-risk-survey-report-2016.html
5. U.K. Government, "Cyber Security Breaches Survey," 2016, https://www.gov.uk/government/uploads/system/uploads/attachment_data/file/521465/Cyber_Security_Breaches_Survey_2016_main_report_FINAL.pdf
6. AIG, "Tech Risk: Are Companies Ready?" 2016, https://www.aig.co.uk/content/dam/aig/emea/united-kingdom/documents/Insights/tech-risk-are-companies-ready.pdf
7. Daniel H. Pink, *A Whole New Mind: Why Right-Brainers Will Rule the Future.* NY USA: Riverhead Books, 2005.
8. CEO.com, "Leadership in the Digital Age," 2016, http://www.ceo.com/operations/leadership-in-the-digital-age/
9. Ibid.
10. Mark Samuels, "The Unexpected Return of the CIO," ZDNet, September 20, 2016, http://www.zdnet.com/article/the-unexpected-return-of-the-cio/
11. Gartner, "Gartner Says 2015 Will See the Emergence of Digital Risk and the Digital Risk Officer," 2015, http://www.gartner.com/newsroom/id/2794417
12. Ibid.
13. McKinsey, "Managing the People Side of Risk," 2015, Retrieved from http://www.mckinsey.com/business-functions/risk/our-insights/managing-the-people-side-of-risk
14. Airmic, "Roads to Ruin," 2014. Retrieved from https://www.airmic.com/technical/library/roads-ruin-analysis
15. Ibid.

ABOUT AIRMIC

Airmic is the association for everyone who has a responsibility for risk management and insurance for their organization. Members also include company secretaries, finance directors, and internal auditors as well as risk and insurance managers. We support our members in a range of ways: through training and research, by sharing information, through our diverse special program of events, by encouraging best practice, and by lobbying on subjects that directly affect risk managers and insurance buyers. Above all, we provide a platform for professionals to stay in touch, to communicate with each other and share ideas and information. The more people who take part in our activities, the more valuable we become.

ABOUT JULIA GRAHAM

Julia is the Deputy CEO of Airmic, the U.K. association of risk and insurance professionals. She heads the development of a technical agenda which includes strategic thought leadership on risk and insurance issues and the learning and development needs of Airmic members. Julia has been a risk and insurance professional for over 40 years, most recently before joining Airmic, as director of risk management and insurance at the global law firm DLA Piper. Julia is a Fellow of the Chartered Insurance Institute, Fellow of the Business Continuity Institute, U.K. lead expert for the development of the global risk standard ISO 31000:2009, *Risk management—Principles and guidelines*, immediate past president of the Federation of European Risk Management Associations (FERMA), and a nonexecutive director of several captive insurance companies. In what spare time remains she enjoys spending time being told what to do by her two daughters and sorting out her new home in Wiltshire.

CHAPTER 25

Cyber Competencies and the Cybersecurity Officer

Ron Hale, PhD, CISM, ISACA, USA

Tom and his team have journeyed through the discovery of the benefits and risks of the digital organization and have come to an understanding of how the organization will need to move forward in implementing an innovative and enabling cybersecurity program. This program needs to be organization focused and responsive to the changing threat landscape. To implement such an organization-wide program Tom needs someone with the right skills and attributes. The role of the CISO is not only one that requires a strong command of security technology. It is even more critical that the CISO be an organization contributor and organizational leader as well.

THE EVOLVING INFORMATION SECURITY PROFESSIONAL

As the need to protect information from compromise and misuse, and the capabilities of hackers have changed over the years, so too has the role and responsibility of information security professionals. The role that is perhaps experiencing the greatest change is that of the chief information security officer (CISO). In the early days of what was initially called data security, there was little need for someone to lead protection activities. Security was mainly a matter of maintaining access lists within products such as the RACF, Top Secret, or ACF2. While technical staff responsible for these systems might have been given a security specific title, they were part of the information technology (IT) department, indistinguishable from other technical specialists within that group.

As information systems evolved from megalithic mainframe computing to a distributed model, leveraging the power of networks, personal computers, and client server architectures, the need for dedicated information security specialists became evident. It was no longer sufficient to define user permissions in the access control system software. It was now necessary to specialize in areas such as risk management, protection architectures, application security, and incident response to meet organization needs related to the increased complexity of the information systems environment. It was even more important to have a leader who not only had broad knowledge of the various technical focus areas within an information security program, but who could also drive the security strategy and align it with the goals and priorities of the organization.

Information systems have become more distributed and at the same time increasingly integrated into organization processes. Attacks are common, attackers are more sophisticated, and the damage resulting from incidents is escalating. Attackers have evolved from lone individuals who in the early days were mainly interested in exploring systems, to sophisticated cybercriminals, terrorists, and agents of nation states. Attacks have evolved from Web page defacements to now include cybercrime, where the objective is financial gain or market advantage. Interest in information security has risen to the board where cybersecurity is among their top concerns. With heightened risk and a need for greater visibility into information security, the chief information security officer (CISO) has become a necessary role. The CISO is often not only a technical specialist but is the organization lead managing the complexities of a program that is an essential part of enterprise and operational risk management.

THE DUALITY OF THE CISO

There are two sides to the CISO: the technical specialist and the executive strategist. Both roles are equally important, as the CISO must understand both the necessary cybersecurity products and how to implement them in line with the organization's overall strategy and objectives.

Technical Specialist

Obviously, to lead the information security organization, the CISO needs to be well versed in security concepts and strategies and in the products that are a core part of a protection architecture. The CISO needs to be a technical specialist who knows the nuts and bolts of information and cybersecurity and who can address the broad requirements and technical aspects of the security program. Much of this domain specific craft knowledge is encompassed in the common body of knowledge defined by the International Information System Security Certification Consortium, or (ISC)2. As the information security profession was forming, it became evident that there needed to be some way to distinguish accomplished and capable professionals from those who did not have the knowledge or experience required to be an information security professional. A group of distinguished practitioners came together to form (ISC)2 and to develop the taxonomy of knowledge that was immediately accepted as the knowledge base of the profession. In 1994, the common body of knowledge was created and became the basis for the Certified Information Systems Security Professional (CISSP) certification. This body of knowledge undergoes an annual review to ensure it remains current and that it reflects existing technical knowledge requirements for information security professionals. The common body of knowledge encompasses eight domains[1]:

1. Security and Risk Management
2. Asset Security
3. Security Engineering
4. Communications and Network Security
5. Identity and Access Management
6. Security Assessment and Testing
7. Security Operations
8. Software Development Security

Executive Strategist

While an understanding of the technical specializations necessary of an effective information security program are essential, there is also a critical need for practitioners to understand the organization and how information security supports organization growth and development. The security practitioner needs to be able to work as an essential part of enterprise and operational risk management. This is particularly true for the CISO, who, as the chief executive representative of information and cybersecurity within the organization, needs to be able to support the organization and integrate the security program into the strategic initiatives and operational activities of the organization.

A 2016 study by executive recruiter Korn Ferry identified that 80 percent of CISOs say their jobs have a very high visibility and accountability orientation, which is higher than other managers at the same reporting level.

TABLE 25.1   Key Attributes for Information/Cybersecurity Executives

Competencies	Experience
Strategic, global thinker (sees big picture)	Depth of technical experiences
Thinks outside the box	Understands evolving regulatory and
Analytical (digs deeply into issues)	legal environment
Possesses "business savvy" (understands	Has (successfully) dealt with/handled
how information is used in daily	security incidents in the past
operations)	
Balances competing priorities	
Communicates and influences broadly	
(board, senior management)	
Attracts, builds, and leverages talent	
Traits	**Drivers**
Learning agile (can adapt to the	Seeks high visibility and
new and different)	accountability roles
Flexible	Strives to be agents of change (not
Tolerance for ambiguity	agents of "no")
Intellectually curious	Must "thread the needle" to balance
Bias for action	driving change with managing
	enterprise risk
	Pursues close engagement with
	organization leaders (works to add
	value)

Source: With the kind permission of Korn Ferry USA.

The researchers identified that more CISOs are reporting outside of the traditional IT structure. Instead, there is an increasing trend for the CISO to report with a more strategic orientation; to organization leaders such as the head of risk management, the general counsel, the chief operations officer (COO), or the CEO. This strengthens the position of information security as being an organization critical service rather than a technology specialization within IT.

The evolving orientation of information security has resulted in a change in expectations as to what skills and expertise the security lead in the organization must have. It is no longer as important to only be a strong technologist. It is becoming more critical that the CISO understands how to address technical information protection requirements from the perspective of an organization strategist. Table 25.1 identifies the key attributes required for CISOs as identified in the Korn Ferry research.[2]

JOB RESPONSIBILITIES AND TASKS

To identify the specific accountabilities, responsibilities, knowledge requirements, and skills that are necessary for those who lead information security programs, ISACA conducts periodic job task assessments. These global assessments bring together empirical data gathered from CISOs as well as insights from industry leaders and subject experts to define the CISO position in terms of the tasks they perform and the knowledge required in this role. These are the basis for the Certified Information Security Manager (CISM) certification that has been offered by ISACA since 2003.

According to the most current research conducted by ISACA, the CISO as an organization executive needs to have broad professional capabilities that can be summarized in terms of the following four task and knowledge domains:

1. Information Security Governance
2. Information Risk Management and Compliance
3. Information Security Program Development and Management
4. Information Security Incident Management[3]

Information Security Governance

As the lead for information security governance in the organization, the CISO establishes and maintains a framework and supporting processes that ensure that the information security strategy is aligned with organization goals and objectives. This governance framework supports overall governance activities within the organization and contributes to efforts to ensure that information risk is appropriately managed and that information security program resources are managed responsibly. Within this governance responsibility, the CISO is responsible for defining the goals and objectives of the security program, aligning them with organizational goals and objectives, and developing and implementing the policy, procedures, and guidelines required as part of the program. As the champion for information security within the organization, the CISO seeks to gain organizational support and commitment for the security program at all levels within the organization. As a contributor to the organization's ability to manage information and technology risk, the CISO identifies external influences to the organization (e.g., technology, organization environment, risk tolerance, geographic location, legal and regulatory requirements) to ensure that these factors are addressed by the information security strategy. The CISO will also establish, monitor, evaluate, and report metrics to provide management with accurate information regarding the state of risk, the impact on the organization, and the effectiveness of the information security strategy.

To be the lead for information security governance and to integrate this into the overall governance structure of the organization, the CISO has certain knowledge requirements. These include:

- The fundamental concepts of governance, how they relate to information security, and the relationship between information security and organization goals, objectives and functions.
- Methods to implement the security governance framework.
- Internationally recognized standards, frameworks, and best practices.
- Strategic budgetary planning and reporting methods.
- Methods to obtain commitment from senior management and support from other stakeholders.
- Organizational structures and lines of authority.
- Methods to select, implement, and interpret metrics.

Information Risk Management and Compliance

The second area of CISO professional competence involves information risk management and compliance. This area of expertise is focused on the management of information and technology risk. The CISO is responsible for integrating information risk management into organization and IT process and for promoting consistent and comprehensive information risk management processes across the organization. This can include establishing and maintaining processes for information asset classification to ensure that measures taken to protect assets are proportional to their organization value. The CISO ensures that risk and vulnerability assessments are conducted periodically and develops risk treatment plans and programs to manage risk to acceptable levels. The CISO also evaluates controls to determine if they are appropriate and effective and monitors risk to ensure that changes are identified and managed. When there is a gap between current and desired risk levels the CISO reports these and will develop or assist in developing and implementing needed changes. In their compliance role the CISO identifies legal, regulatory, organizational and other compliance requirements, and builds programs to ensure continued compliance. While the CISO has these responsibilities depending on the organization structure some accountability may be shared with other organization executives including the chief risk officer.

To accomplish their risk management responsibilities, the CISO has certain knowledge requirements. These include:

- Information asset classification and valuation methods.
- Risk and vulnerability assessment and threat analysis methodologies.

- Legal, regulatory, organizational and other requirements for information security.
- Sources of information regarding emerging threats and vulnerabilities.
- Risk assessment and analysis methods.
- Risk treatment strategies and methods and how to apply them.
- Security controls and countermeasures.
- Control baseline modeling and its relationship to risk based assessments.
- Risk reporting, monitoring and review requirements.
- Techniques for integrating risk management into organization and IT processes.
- Maturity-gap and other gap analysis techniques.
- Security controls and countermeasures and the methods to analyze their effectiveness.

Information Security Program Development and Management

A major part of the CISO's responsibility is the development and management of the information security program. As part of this responsibility the CISO needs to align and integrate the security program with other organization functions and ensure that the program advances the information security strategy. The security architecture, which integrates the program elements addressing people, process, and technology forms the basis for the security program. Since security is part of everyone's responsibility, the CISO leads programs to ensure security is part of the organizational culture through awareness programs. As an organization unit leader and representative of the security program across the organization, the CISO needs to implement and communicate information about the effectiveness and efficiency of security program and provide periodic reports to executives and board members.

To accomplish these management responsibilities, the CISO has certain knowledge requirements, including:

- Identify, acquire, manage and define requirements for internal and external resources.
- Establish, communicate and maintain organizational information security standards, procedures, guidelines and other documentation to support and guide compliance with information security policies.
- Establish and maintain a program for information security awareness and training to promote a secure environment and an effective security culture.
- Integrate information security requirements into organizational processes.

- Integrate information security requirements into contracts and activities of third parties.
- Establish, monitor, and periodically report program management and operational metrics to evaluate the effectiveness and efficiency of the information security program.

Information Security Incident Management

The last area of expertise and action required of the CISO is that of the security incident manager. As cyber threats too frequently lead to security incidents, the CISO is responsible for developing and maintaining incident detection capabilities as well as the ability to expeditiously respond to limit damage and to return the organization to normal activities. To accomplish this increasingly critical activity, the CISO has certain knowledge requirements including:

- Establish and maintain an organizational definition of, and severity hierarchy for, information security incidents.
- Establish and maintain an incident response.
- Develop and implement processes to ensure the timely identification of information security incidents.
- Establish and maintain processes to investigate and document information security.
- Establish and maintain incident escalation and notification.
- Organize, train, and equip teams to effectively respond to information security incidents in a timely manner.
- Test and review the incident response plan periodically to ensure an effective response to information security incidents and to improve response capabilities.
- Establish and maintain communication plans and processes to manage communication with internal and external entities.
- Conduct postincident reviews to determine the root cause of information security incidents, develop corrective actions, reassess risk, evaluate response effectiveness, and take appropriate remedial actions.

CONCLUSION

As information and information technology have evolved, and as they have become central to how organizations serve their market, the role of the defenders in information security departments has changed. Information protection professionals have evolved from having a minor technical role in administering access credentials to being at the forefront of defending information assets from misuse and compromise. The leader of information and cybersecurity activities has evolved from a technical specialist to the executive strategist responsible for the protection of organization assets and the domain expert for the board and executive management. While knowledge of information security technologies and techniques is important, it is increasingly critical that the executive CISO brings organization acumen and leadership qualities to this important position.

COMPETENCIES AND THE CISO

Cybersecurity is a top concern for boards and executive management. The cybersecurity leader in an organization needs not only to have broad technical capabilities across information security domains, but leadership expertise and the ability to effectively guide the organization in implementing an effective, holistic and enterprise-wide cyber program. This program needs to address organization structure, people, process, and technology, but also the critical dynamic components of culture, governance, human factors, and the enablement of processes through technology. More critically, in this rapidly changing environment, the CISO needs to recognize emergent conditions and the opportunity and threats that these present. The CISO requires competencies in four areas: (1) Information Security Governance, (2) Information Risk Management and Compliance, (3) Information Security Program Development and Management, and (4) Information Security Incident Management.

NOTES

1. (ISC)2, "CISSP Domains," https://www.isc2.org/cissp-domains/default.aspx, 2016.
2. Aileen Alexander and Jamey Cummings, "The Rise of the Chief Information Security Officer," *People & Strategy* 39 (1), Winter 2016, pp10-13.
3. ISACA, "CISM Job Practice Areas," http://www.isaca.org/Certification/CISM-Certified-Information-Security-Manager/Job-Practice-Areas/Pages/default.aspx, 2016.

ABOUT ISACA

As an independent, nonprofit, global association, ISACA engages in the development, adoption, and use of globally accepted, industry-leading knowledge and practices for information systems. Previously known as the Information Systems Audit and Control Association, ISACA now goes by its acronym only, to reflect the broad range of IT governance professionals it serves. Incorporated in 1969, ISACA today serves 140,000 professionals in 180 countries. ISACA provides practical guidance, benchmarks, and other effective tools for all enterprises that use information systems. Through its comprehensive guidance and services, ISACA defines the roles of information systems governance, security, audit and assurance professionals worldwide. The COBIT framework and the CISA, CISM, CGEIT, and CRISC certifications are ISACA brands respected and used by these professionals for the benefit of their enterprises.

ABOUT RON HALE

Ron is an organization executive, scholar practitioner, mentor, and thought leader with experience in executive management and in leading organizations in the governance and management of information and information technology in particular as it relates to organization innovation and the protection of information. Over 30 years, as a senior practitioner and thought leader, he has helped organizations understand threats and risks related to information and information systems and how to build effective programs to govern and implement effective protection and recovery programs. As the chief knowledge officer for ISACA, he has led and contributed to the development of leading practice aids for practitioners and enterprises.

CHAPTER 26

Human Resources Security

Domenic Antonucci, Editor and Chief Risk Officer, Australia

Grace, the head of human relations, is in CEO Tom's office for the last time before Tom is to present to the board. Tom said, "Well, Grace, I've heard nearly everyone mention something that also seemed to involve your HR function. Can you just spell out the basic capabilities for human resources security that you are responsible for in HR?"

If people are said to be the weakest links in any security system, then the HR function and its processes have a role to play. As the needs of organizations and their HR functions of varying size and maturity may differ, let us summarize in this chapter recommended capabilities expected of lower-, mid-, and higher-maturity HR functions. For more detail on what constitutes the HR function's process maturity, refer to the SEI capability maturity model approach.[1]

NEEDS OF LOWER-MATURITY HR FUNCTIONS

Some HR functions are small or at lower-levels of HR process capability maturity. Here, managers take basic and possibly some managed levels of responsibility for managing and developing their people within the cybersecurity and enterprise functions. No matter how small or immature, there is no excuse for not communicating to staff minimum protocols or a standard for HR cybersecurity.

An Example Human Resource Security Standard

For heads of HR in a hurry, the City University of Hong Kong Human Resource Security Standard is a public domain document that can be tailored quickly and at no cost to suit any size or type of organization.[2] This type of document should not remain a stand-alone document just for cyber-security, and can be integrated on behalf of cybersecurity into any existing organization HR manual or portal.

The document's 10 pages are straightforward. Its contents include a policy statement, objectives, types of users (including contractors and third-party users) and covers all key aspects for the three-stage cycle (akin to ISO 27000): prior to employment/engagement, during employment/engagement, and at termination or change of employment. Responsibilities are covered for the human resources office, central information technology (IT) and departmental IT service owners, information security unit, all other enter-prise units and employees, and third-party users.

NEEDS OF MID-MATURITY HR FUNCTIONS

Some HR functions are mid-size or at mid-levels of HR maturity. Here, man-agers take more managed-level practices (such as managing performance, training, communication, and coordination) within the cybersecurity and enterprise functions. At these HR maturity levels, there is no excuse for not meeting appropriate standards and training for HR cybersecurity even if the standards are not necessarily certifiable.

Capabilities to Meet a Certifiable International Standard

While the National Institute of Standards and Technology (NIST) and other voluntary information security standards are also available, the most popu-lar and international of standards is ISO/IEC 27001:2013,[3] which can be purchased at a small cost. The ISO 27000 family of standards help organi-zations keep information assets secure. ISO 27001 is the international stan-dard against which an Information Security Management System (ISMS) can be certified. This standard outlines the requirements of a certified ISMS that will help you demonstrate regulatory compliance and information secu-rity risk management.

Clause 6.1.3 of this standard describes how an organization can respond to risks with a risk treatment plan. An important part of this is choosing appropriate controls. Annex A is akin to a catalog of security controls that an organization can select from and totals 114 controls. A.7 in Annex A targets six controls that are specific to *Human Resource Security* and covers three key areas: controls that apply *before, during, or after employment*. The overall objective of HR security is to ensure that all employees (including contractors and any users of sensitive data) are qualified for and understand their roles and responsibilities of their job duties and that access is removed once employment is terminated. More specific objectives and details on the six controls can be found under these sections of ISO 270001:2013:

A.7 Human Resource Security

During Employment

1. *Screening.* Includes background verification checks at escalating levels for different staff, contractors and third parties with different screening tests (e.g., background screen, credit check, physical examination, drug testing, sample job tasks).
2. *Terms and conditions of employment.* Contracts clarify mutual responsibilities between the organization and parties.

During Employment

1. *Employee orientation for new employees.* Includes workshops, signed acknowledgments, and manager and supervisor explicit supports to ensure that each person within the organization must be vigilant when it comes to protecting information systems.
2. *Ongoing education, awareness, and training.* Delivered to defined calendars (annually, biannually, etc.) appropriate to the employee's job roles and responsibilities with a minimum requirement for all employees to undergo general training on basic information security practices and/or acknowledge their basic understanding of the organization's security policies and procedures.
3. *Disciplinary process.* For security breaches.

Termination and Change of Employment

1. *Responsibilities.* Where the HR function is generally responsible for the overall termination process and works together with the supervising manager, with controls to protect the organization's interests in a managed way with the appropriate return of all equipment and removal of all access rights using a checklist of actions that must be taken without exception.

A checklist for a secure employee departure is readily available in more detail online.[4] Here is a summary of the content an organization should tailor to its own needs:

Checklist for a Secure Employee Departure

❑ *Conduct an exit interview with the employee*—with their supervisor and the IT team, including how they can be reached if the company needs to get in contact after their last day.

❏ *Retrieve organization mobile devices* and backup discs, USBs, etc.
❏ *Deactivate organization e-mail addresses and remote access accounts*—include a process for former employee e-mails to be forwarded to their supervisor to ensure continued communications with external customers.
❏ *Change passwords*—ensuring that nothing, including the organization Twitter account, is left in their name if they worked in the organization's social media area.
❏ *Collect all company-related keys, pass cards, and ID cards*—include informing the security team.
❏ *Change PINs or passwords to any corporate credit cards or financial accounts*—include any corresponding bank statements and any other material that could contain financial information.
❏ *Prepare for challenges*—be prepared for a potentially negative reaction, so forewarn your IT and security teams, so that they can immediately implement the exit process.

NEEDS OF HIGHER-MATURITY HR FUNCTIONS

Some HR functions operate within large organizations or at higher-levels of HR maturity. Here, managers evidence more predictable- and optimizing-level practices within the cybersecurity and enterprise functions (such as organizational performance alignment and continuous capability improvement). At these HR maturity levels, there is there an increasing array of more sophisticated tools, techniques and solutions for advanced cybersecurity. These include certified professional and academic programs.

Certified Professionals

Organization awareness, education, training and internal communications may all lead up to certification of professionals available in various countries with reputable institutions. In the United Kingdom for example, various certifying bodies offer a Certified Professional (CCP) scheme as an important step in creating a unified standard for those working in the U.K. Cyber Security industry according to Government Communications Headquarters (GCHQ). GCHQ is a British intelligence and security organization responsible for providing signals intelligence and information assurance to the British government and armed forces. The CESG Certified Professional (CCP) scheme is a certification framework for competent information assurance (IA) professionals. Individuals can choose to be certified in one or more specified IA roles, at several levels of competency. The CCP originated with U.K. national security, then was extended to the government sector, then the private sector.

Academia

Certain universities are increasingly becoming Centers of Excellence to enhance the cybersecurity knowledge base. In the United Kingdom, GCHQ and the Engineering and Physical Sciences Research Council (EPSRC) have recognized 11 U.K. universities as having an established cybersecurity research pedigree based on their academic excellence, impact, and scale of activity and research in areas that underpin cybersecurity.

CONCLUSION

The following cyber risk management statement represents those organization capabilities CEO and board should be looking to have their organization demonstrate in terms of *human resources (HR) security.*

HUMAN RESOURCES (HR) SECURITY

As a minimum, staff protocols or a standard for HR cybersecurity are in-effect and updated. For *pre-employment,* protocols include roles and responsibilities, screening for insider and other threats, and terms and conditions of employment. For *during employment,* protocols include management responsibilities, information security awareness, organization awareness, education, training and internal communications and, a disciplinary process. For *termination or change of employment,* protocols include termination responsibilities, return of assets, and removal of access rights. A checklist is always used for secure employee departure. Larger organizations and/or higher HR maturity functions look for continuous capability improvement by exploiting an array of more sophisticated tools, techniques and solutions for advanced cybersecurity.

NOTES

1. CMU/SEI Capability Maturity Model (P-CMM) Technical Report, Version 2.0, 2nd ed., July 2009.
2. City University of Hong Kong Human Resource Security Standard, October 19, 2015, pp. 1–10, http://www6.cityu.edu.hk/infosec/isps/docs/pdf/05.CityU%20 -%20Human%20Resource%20Security%20Standard.1.1.pdf

3. ISO 31000:2009, *Risk management—Principles and guidelines'*, ISO 1st ed. 2009-11-15.
4. Ryan Francis, "Checklist for a Secure Employee Departure," August 3, 2015, http://www.csoonline.com/article/2953594/data-protection/how-companies-should-secure-their-networks-when-an-employee-leaves.html#slide1

ABOUT DOMENIC ANTONUCCI

Domenic is a practicing international chief risk officer overseeing cyber-security and a former counterterrorist intelligence officer. An Australian expatriate based in Dubai UAE, Domenic specializes in bringing capabilities within organization risk management systems "up the maturity curve" for enterprise, program, and specialized risks such as cybersecurity. Formerly with Marsh, Shell and Red Cross, he enjoys over 35 years' experience in risk, strategic planning and business management consulting across many sectors in Europe, Africa, Middle East, Asia, and Australia-Pacific. A specialist with IRM (SIRM), he is a certified ISO 31000 ERM lead trainer and BCMS business continuity lead implementer, as well as a former RMP-PMI risk management professional and PMP project management professional. A regular international conference presenter and author, he is the content author for risk maturity model software called *Benchmarker*™ and the author of the book *Risk Maturity Models: Assessing Risk Management Effectiveness*.

Becoming CyberSmart™: a Risk Maturity Road Map for Measuring Capability Gap-Improvement

Domenic Antonucci, Editor and Chief Risk Officer (CRO), Australia
Didier Verstichel, Chief Information Security Officer (CISO) and Chief Risk Officer (CRO), Belgium

Tom prepared his last slides for presentation to the Board with a quiet sense of satisfaction. His chief risk officer Nathan, had summarized the assessments of the current state of enterprise-wide capabilities to deliver an effective cyber risk management subsystem to the existing enterprise-wide risk management (ERM) system. These assessments were sourced from all functional heads. As CEO, he knew the board expected to see future gap improvements in these capabilities. As he saw his chairperson, Mara, enter his office, he quietly smiled. He held a new confidence that his organization had a way to measure and track capability gaps.

BACKGROUND

Improving risk management maturity improves trust and reliability in the organization's ability to achieve its objectives, to report its risk profile(s), and to add value to the organization. More mature enterprise risk management (ERM) systems deliver researched bottom-line, top-line and other "hard" benefits for an organization such as the tripling of the bottom-line.[1] There is no reason the same does not apply for the ERM subset, a *cyber* risk management system.

Enterprise risk management system capabilities mature over years at staggered rates unique to your organization. The same is true for a *cyber* risk management system except they have a greater "need for speed" to meet the velocity and dynamism of the cyber threat landscape. "Maturity" means a current or future state, fact, or period of evolving development, quality, sophistication and *effectiveness* (it is not necessarily age-dependent). A "maturity model" is a simplified system that "road-maps" improving, desired, anticipated, typical, or logical evolutionary paths of organization actions that are repeatable. The ascending direction implies progression that increases organization effectiveness over time (albeit subject to stasis and regression).

Benchmarking against self (and others) is the most powerful tool for measuring gap improvements in the capabilities that make up the cyber risk management system. It benchmarks your current baseline capabilities against targeted self-improvements over time. This delivers the right set of specific cybersecurity capabilities within an enterprise risk management system best tailored to your organization. This serves to continually assess and assure effectiveness.

BECOMING CYBERSMART™

CyberSmart™ capabilities may be rated by a simple rating approach. This applies an assessor score of between 0 to 4. Assessors are typically the CISO and/or Risk and/or Internal Audit functions, as well as external independent assessors. These ratings scales are based on robust criteria adapted from the HB156 ISO and IIA-backed maturity assessment five-point scale methodology for in-evidence implementation of each capability.[2] Table E.1 explains in detail how to attribute a score of between 0 and 4 on a five-point scale for rating of CyberSmart™ capabilities.

TABLE E.1   CyberSmart™ Five-Point Scales for Rating of Capabilities

Assess This Score for Each Scale …	Description: Ask If the Organization Capability Is …	Example
0 = Nil.	Nonexistent, nothing in place, achieved, in effect (0%), or known. No capability. Unaware or no recognition of need. Not part of culture or mission.	Policy X not in current management mind-set.
1 = Starting.	Starting to be put in-place, achieve or in-effect (say 0–<30%). Insignificant, limited, or starting capability as intent not action. Management mandate or some recognition of intent and need may exist but still lacks engagement or execution. Approach is ad hoc, disorganized, without communication or monitoring. People unaware of responsibilities.	Policy X still being planned or written before approval.

2 = Partly.	Partially in place, achieved, or in effect (say 30–<60%). Capability exercised to some extent so as to create/protect value. Practices/controls are in place but are not documented. Mandate backed by commitment evidenced by reinforcement practices by management. Operation dependent on knowledge and motivation of individuals. Effectiveness not adequately evaluated. Many practice/control weaknesses exist and are not adequately addressed; the impact can be severe. Management actions to resolve practice/control issues are not prioritized or consistent. People aware in part of their responsibilities.	Policy X approved in writing or informally communicated by management. Now in early stages of being introduced as a business process with awareness/training, etc., so people partly have the knowledge and experience to perform the process.
3 = Largely.	Largely in place, achieved, or in effect (say >60–<90%). Capability effectively practiced or with proficiency which creates/protects value. There is a largely effective enterprise-wide risk management practice and internal control environment. People aware and largely discharge their responsibilities.	Now in latter stages of being largely integrated by aware/trained/capable people with evidence of implementation by management for informed decision making (e.g., reports providing management with the right information at the right time and/or methodologies that adequately analyze data and information).
4 = Fully.	Fully in place, achieved, or in effect (say >90%) at all times in all places. Capability practiced towards the optimum or serves as model for others so as to create/protect value. People fully aware, trained where appropriate and discharge their responsibilities as an integrated part of the way they work and make decisions. Some use of technology applied appropriately to automate practices/controls to gain efficiencies or reduce cost or duplication. Management checks and balances in-place so as to continuously improve.	Policy X fully integrated and continuously improved (where appropriate) with systems and information to meet tomorrow's needs such that practices (and internal controls) are monitored, measured, reported and fed back so management is confident that they are effective and efficient.

The maturity model we have dubbed CyberSmart™ appears in Table E.2. It is in matrix form for ease of transfer to a spreadsheet by any organization at no cost. It aggregates the cybersecurity capability building blocks from each chapter in the *Cyber Risk Handbook* based on the capabilities noted by each subject matter expert. As an illustration only, it shows a current or baseline score of 46 percent Index rising over future periods of implementation to targeted Indices of 69 percent, 82 percent, and 92 percent. Of course, these ratings, targets and periods must be tailored to each organization. These scores and targets may be integrated into the enterprise strategic performance management system as a key performance indicator (KPI) and also used as a key risk indicator (KRI) for the assessment of effectiveness of the ERM system by both the independent Internal Audit function as well as ERM and other management functions. "Becoming CyberSmart™" goes to an operating principle that improving how risk-smart your capabilities are for cybersecurity is a journey, not a destination.

TABLE E.2 CyberSmart™ Maturity Model: A Risk Maturity Road-Map for Measuring Capability Gap Improvement

Maturity Capabilities and Chapter Reference for Details	Rating	Gap for Improvement Notes	Target Rating by DD/MM/YY	Target Rating by DD/MM/YY2	Target Rating by DD/MM/YY3
PART ONE: GOVERNANCE AND RISK OVERSIGHT					
Chapter 2 Cyber risk oversight. Boards and senior management around the world have relied on traditional ERM and internal audit paradigms to help them oversee cyber risk. These paradigms need to change if boards and senior management are going to meet the new expectations. More of the same cybersecurity approaches will not do the job. Boards need to insist that all ERM and internal audit work is directly linked to their organization's top value creation and value preservation objectives and require regular reports on the state of residual risk linked to those objectives. Cybersecurity needs to be focused on its potential impact on key business objectives, not as a priority on its own regardless of its impact on the organization's sustained success. To accomplish this shift boards and senior management must call for fundamental change in the way ERM and internal audit services are delivered.	3		4	4	4
Chapter 3 Principles guide actions. Actions are taken by people in order to achieve the goals and objectives of an enterprise. Principles form the foundation of desirable and positive behavior for people in carrying out their respective responsibilities. Risk management principles in a COBIT 5 approach *meet stakeholder needs* by being transparent, inclusive, dynamic, iterative and responsive. Principles *covering the enterprise* guide people to create and protect value, tailor to their own environment, and explicitly address uncertainty. In *applying a single, integrated framework,* being systematic, structured and timely is key. *Enabling a holistic approach* is supported by making risk considerations integral in all processes and decision making, while considering human factors, and using the best available data. Finally, the principle of facilitating continual improvement through a risk maturity strategy aligns naturally with activities and processes found in *separating governance from management.*	3		3	4	4

(continued)

TABLE E.2 (*Continued*)

PART ONE: GOVERNANCE AND RISK OVERSIGHT

Chapter 4 Policies and procedures. Cyber risk policies. An appropriate mix of tailored cyber risk management-specific policies and procedures guide processes, practices, and organization risk management activities. These put cyber risk principles into effect and are systematically applied through the cyber risk management process. The organization can demonstrate to all stakeholders how it manages cyber risk. At a minimum, policies and procedures are fully in effect to cover mobile devices, ransomware, social media, third-party vendors/cloud computing, "Big Data analytics," and Internet of Things. Various approaches are deployed to make such risks the responsibility of all employees, and not just the IT function. A cycle of continuous improvement throughout the organization allows development along the risk maturity curve. The policies provide a platform for companies to maximize digital opportunities while managing the threats associated with advances in technology, data-driven insight, and evolving work practices.	2	3	4	4
Chapter 5 Strategic performance management system. The organization has a strategic performance management system to measure implementation of a tailored cyber strategy delivering digital resilience. The cyber strategy shares the organization's business risks, target state capabilities, target state level of protection and required initiatives. The organization goes beyond cyber risk-mitigating controls and considers cyber a capability-building enabler. A digital resilience assessment frames a baseline maturity to a set of metrics (KPIs/KRIs) of three types: measuring progress against initiatives, measuring overall level of capability, and measuring protection to specification for the most critical information. The metrics align with an appropriate set of principles and are automated, simple, repeatable, and on-demand. There is a forum to cascade for each of the three dimensions the aligned initiatives, markers, activities, actions, and resources (people and funding) necessary to drive each action to successful completion. Tracking the "status" and "progress" of each initiative surfaces the blockers and bottlenecks to the cyber strategy.	1	3	3	3

Chapter 6 Standards and frameworks. The appropriate mix of global key standards and frameworks for cybersecurity are in evidence, monitored, reviewed and tailored to the organization context. These include voluntary codes such as the ISO/IEC 27000 series, COBIT 5, NIST, ISF, SANS Top 20 controls, IT-CMF, WEF, and ENISA. These can be tailored singly, or in combination and with local regulatory codes that may apply to the organization. They provide the organization with effective cyber risk management guidance and benchmarking. Management understands that consistently applied good practice beats sporadic pockets of "best" practice. There is a road map for implementation of the cyber risk management system and to establish the required capabilities to keep it functioning, monitored and up to date. Cyber-related risks are treated and included in enterprise risk management (ERM) like any other risk to an organization and are aligned with the umbrella ISO 31000:2009, *Risk management—Principles and guidelines* standard.

PART TWO: PROCESSES

Chapter 7 Assessing cyber risks (identifying, analyzing, and evaluating). The organization realistically assesses the vulnerabilities of its digital system components not just for technology flaws (such as in design, encryption, event logging, or software malfunction) but for human factors. Trusted insiders present the highest risk (motivated either by malice or more commonly by accident) as well as third-party contractors, vendors, or temporary workers (essentially privileged users). The organization commits to a robust and structured approach to assessing and managing risk and an information risk assessment methodology. This involves a six-part approach to (1) generating an integrated view of information risk; (2) realistically assessing worst case; (3) mapping different types of threats, both malicious and accidental; (4) assessing vulnerabilities to different threat events and the strength of any controls already in place; (5) evaluating risk appetite and likelihood of a successful threat; and (6) developing practical approaches to addressing the information risks which have been identified. Other factors examined include organization capability, security culture, commitment, people competence, user privilege patterns, technology, leadership, policy, and environment. There is a balance between regulatory compliance and doing everything

(*continued*)

TABLE E.2 *(Continued)*

reasonable to protect mission-critical information. Cybersecurity maturity avoids barriers separating data security from the organization's core business functions and does not rely on device-centric safeguards. The focus begins and ends with the organization's data: how it is protected, which data is truly mission-critical, what behaviors need to be protected against, and who really needs to access it and when.

Chapter 8 Treatment. Treating cyber risks. The organization's risk treatment capabilities align with its risk profile, risk appetite, and context. Risk treatment methodology is not reinvented for cyber risks but is a subset of the enterprise risk management (ERM) system. Risk treatment covers all cyber risk sources, likelihoods and impacts. Risk sources include supply chain, cloud, mobile devices, and social media. Impacts are either noninsurable in nature or insurable in part or whole, and may take various forms (such as fines, reputational damage, loss of customers, loss of employees, and stock devaluation). Impact management preparations are required for insurable risks, crisis management, forensics investigation, customer notification, and business interruption. Cyber risk treatment is prioritized, reiterative, and cyclical. Risk owners complete risk and control action plans that balance threat with opportunity to organization objectives and consider cost/benefit. Appropriate combined treatment options are not mutually exclusive, are appropriate to the case in hand, and are aligned with ISO 31000:2009, *Risk management—Principles and guidelines*: (1) avoiding the activity that gives rise to the risk; (2) taking or increasing the risk in order to pursue an opportunity; (3) removing the risk source; (4) changing the likelihood; (5) changing the consequences; (6) sharing the risk with other parties (e.g., risk financing, contracts); and (7) retaining the risk by informed decision.

2	2	3	3

Chapter 9 Treatment using process capabilities. Cybersecurity process capabilities provide the governance and management practices necessary to effectively and efficiently align the cybersecurity program with the business enterprise objectives. Detailed activities are developed to support the cybersecurity practices to provide governance (evaluate, direct, and monitor), manage (align, plan, and organize the work), create solutions (build, acquire,

1	2	3	4

and implement), sustain (deliver, service, and support), and improve (monitor, evaluate, and assess). These processes taken together form a cybersecurity life cycle with defined inputs and outputs based on generally accepted good practices that, taken together holistically, can serve to reduce the organizational cybersecurity risk.

Chapter 10 Treatment using cyber insurance and risk finance. Cyber breach risks are understood in terms of their potential impact on the organization balance sheet and quantified as far as possible. The cost-benefits of investments in insurance treatment versus cybersecurity treatment are modeled and they are considered for budgeting purposes as complimentary rather than competing investments. A quantitative cost-benefit model to address cyber exposures optimizes the efficient allocation of resources, financial planning, analysis, and reporting. Modeling constraints are understood. Cyber risk is effectively transferred to insurers where this is appropriate to organization context and where it augments existing insurance covers. Cyber insurance reduces the total cost of risk (TCOR) over the long term. Risk and/or insurance managers collaborate with business units when agreeing and implementing plans (i.e., pre-breach education and planning, an incident response and crisis management plan, a breach business continuity plan and, review, and/or placement of cyber insurance). Risk and/or insurance managers have an important coordination role. They take appropriate steps to (1) coordinate all the above plans to properly inform management and the board of directors; (2) position cyber insurance treatment solutions as a subset of ERM system capabilities for the organization; (3) review vendors and the supply chain; (4) treat any insurance gaps in existing insurance; (5) prepare mechanisms for filing a cyber claim well in advance of the event; (6) consider the use of a captive insurer; and (7) stay abreast of cyber insurance market trends, particularly for capacity and regulatory constraints.

Chapter 11 Monitoring and review using key risk indicators (KRIs). Specific and tailored cybersecurity KRIs are developed to monitor inherent and residual risk levels. These metrics provide leading indication of increasing risk exposure and potential impacts to achievement of strategic objectives and provide a full view across the range of threats. Context is critical in effective KRI design as are ratios, percentages and always asking the next question to refine the KRI. Response metrics (speed and trend) are important indications of a program's success, which is a key piece of information for senior management and board members.

0 1 2 3

0 1 2 3

(continued)

TABLE E.2 (Continued)

PART TWO: PROCESSES

Chapter 12 Incident and crisis management. Low-impact routine cyber incidents are differentiated from major crises that require prompt escalation in order to avoid high-impact consequences. For incidents, all incident sources are detected and classified; routine incident management policy and volume-process steps are practiced and continually reviewed; and, incident internal reporting aligns with the ERM system. Process steps include identification, containment, remediation, and recovery. An incident "must-have" checklist is followed. When incidents become unmanageable and/or require escalation, it is escalated by preset criteria to a set of cyber crisis management (CCM) principles. CCM follows trained-for steps: (1) alert and qualification; (2) crisis handling (by carrying out an investigation and a defense plan); (3) execution and surveillance; then (4) crisis closure. CCM is steered by a crisis decision-making unit (CDU) (or its equivalent) made up of representatives of the organization's top management. CCM is implemented by an operational cybersecurity crisis unit that is prestructured, tailored to the organization context, and trained to mobilize quickly. It is made up of three teams that work jointly: the Investigation team provides digital forensics to the defense team, that build upon plans to be approved by the CDU and applied when appropriate regarding the attack life cycle. These teams are adequately resourced with the technical tools and techniques for managing a modern cyber crisis. Adequate preparation for a crisis event is crucial to the organization and both incident management and crisis management processes are tested regularly with tabletop or in-situation exercises. These are improved over time as new threats arise and the organization evolves.	1	3	4	4
Chapter 13 Business continuity management system (BCMS). IT processes are deeply embedded into business and operational processes. A business continuity management system (BCMS) is robust enough to overcome a major cyber incident with an organization-wide impact for a significant period of time (or even threatening the long term survivability of an organization). The BCMS is aligned with the ISO 22301:2012 Societal Security–BCMS–Requirements and with the organizational culture, thus making it a strategic management process. The BCMS provides a framework for the organization to implement an integrated response to counter major cyber incidents. Impact severity levels are defined in a standardized impact severity matrix, which should be used or associated with IT incident management plan (IMP), IT disaster recovery plan (DRP), crisis management plan (CMP), crisis	1	3	3	3

384

communications plan (CCP), and damage assessment. It is also essential to ensure response procedures in these plans are aligned. These are validated by conducting integrated exercises.

PART THREE: ORGANIZATIONAL STRUCTURES AND DESIGN

Chapter 14 External context and supply chain. The external context unique to the organization is established in respect of the cyber risks that are faced, especially in regard to the supply chain. It is a board-level priority to apply this as much to critical third parties as to the internal organization. The focus of organization cyber strategies is equally on developing resilience and protection, not simply on identifying individual cyber risks. External cyber resilience follows five steps to (1) map critical data and value flows for organization, including reputational impact; (2) teach the importance of data security and cyber-resilience to employees and to relevant individuals within critical third parties; (3) develop external cyber-incident and crisis management response plan(s) appropriate to key scenarios, ensuring regulators are notified where applicable; (4) review and benchmark critical third-party cyber-security measures; and (5) track and/or work with policymakers and regulators in the interconnected world of cyber risk public-private partnerships.

Chapter 15 Internal Organization Context. The organization understands its internal context and builds and measures its capability to align all enterprise functions to mutually support the cyber risk management system. The organization operates to the overall principle that cyber risk is an enterprise-wide risk, not just an IT risk. It considers voluntary guidance code approaches that are tailored to the organization. A "cyber risk management system" involves the ongoing, effective, and *fast* deployment of 24/7/365 organization capabilities to mitigate cyber threats. The cybersecurity function and its risk management system is aligned to other enterprise functions and management systems in such a way that the organization has the speedy, adaptive, resilient and responsive capabilities required to face the fast-paced evolving universe of cyber threats (and opportunities). The cyber risk function operating model is appropriately tailored. Cybersecurity is aligned not only *across* the enterprise but *within* each key enterprise function that needs to team up with the CISO/DRO's cyber function. The CEO directs the executive management team from the CISO/DRO and IT-related management functions right across to people-related functions such as human resources. The CRO is accountable for the enterprise risk management system and all its subsystems, which includes the cyber risk management system.

0	3	3	3
2	3	3	3

(continued)

385

TABLE E.2 (*Continued*)

PART FOUR: CULTURE, ETHICS, AND BEHAVIOR

Chapter 16 Culture and human factors. Management treats the organization as a social system influenced by human factors. While culture involves complex variables and multiple stakeholders (including employees, customers, vendors, and business partners); a tailored risk management culture addresses cyber risks comprehensively. Cybersecurity is treated not merely as a technology issue but as a mix of social, cultural, emotional, and behavioral issues where potential conflicts and contradictions are managed. Cyber risk treatments (including controls) combine technology with nontechnology treatments and are fast paced to match the threat. Organization decision making avoids biases such as Groupthink. The culture is resistant to human factors such as insider threats and social engineering threats. Active, able, aware, motivated and trained people, vendors and other stakeholders support cybersecurity. Employee training programs cover different phases of the employee life cycle and are role specific where appropriate. An appropriate set of standards and qualitative approaches are used for measuring and evaluating people behavior and culture.	2	2	3	3
Chapter 17 Legal and compliance. The legal and compliance issues surrounding cybersecurity are predefined by principles of currency, reasonableness, and preparedness such that the organization is prepared for the legal requirements and ramifications of a breach. An organization must work with its legal professionals to ensure any currently applicable data security regulations are met while planning to accommodate regulatory expansion towards widely accepted standards. Legal should be integrally involved in the entire "process-oriented" cycle of cyber defense planning, including committee creation, application, simulation, auditing, and recordation. The C-suite must stay appraised on the process to ensure compliance with fiduciary duties and "reasonable" action (typically, to identify risks, delineate plans to deal with those risks, then implement the plans with requisite oversight). Actions towards fulfilling a "process" are able to be proven to regulators, shareholders, and judges in the event of a data incident via the recordation of all C-suite and boardroom planning, discussion, and actions. The basic "process" should be designed and executed by a board level advisory cyber committee, composed of multidisciplinary professionals with some cyber familiarity. A board-level audit process regularly reviews the advisory committee's actions, plans, and recommendations. Before any cyber event, legal counsel not	2	2	3	4

only articulates any applicable state or industry data regulations but directs documentation of the "process," reviews past contracts, and manages future contracts with cybersecurity risks in mind. Legal can advise on the purchase of specific cyber insurances and determine whether information-sharing partnerships with government or with similar companies might be beneficial. During and after any incident, legal counsel is part of the response teams set in action with constant documentation of steps taken and with reports sent to the C-suite. Advice by legal counsel—either with in-house or outside counsel depending on the potential need to preserve privilege—should be established immediately and sustained throughout the response to the crisis. From the input of legal counsel, compliance with notification and data protection regulations pertaining to the subject industry is adhered to. Beyond notification requirements, disclosure of the breach to partners in the private and public sector may create opportunities to gain further resources and information to mitigate damage (while balancing internal concerns over potential harm the reputation of the company by such disclosure). Owners of contractually transferred data should be notified as to the status of the breach and the confidentiality of their data. Notifying the public, and specifically those who might have had information disclosed by the breach, also warrants discussion with legal and other relevant parts of the company. An internal investigation should be created to record events and actions. If an "active defense" is contemplated, receiving authorization from the appropriate public authorities and foreign network owners before operations are commenced could help limit liability for actions taken.

Chapter 18 Assurance. The board and CEO must ensure the necessary organization capabilities to align cybersecurity with key organization objectives. Cybersecurity should include: A cyber risk assurance framework/methodology is a structured approach to conducting assurance activities in a coordinated manner across an organization. This is for the purpose of gaining confidence that cyber threat mitigations are working effectively, and to convey this conclusion to stakeholders such as the CEO and the board, supported by independent assurance provided by internal audit. It ensures that different assurance activities by different business units are coordinated, and complement each other. It recognizes the special characteristics of cyber threats, and the requirement to have strong cybersecurity governance

3

3

3

4

(continued)

387

TABLE E.2 *(Continued)*

PART FOUR: CULTURE, ETHICS, AND BEHAVIOR

in place to validate cyber threat treatments (controls/mitigations) continuously, for the benefit of protecting the organization in a balanced manner in its pursuit of achieving the business objectives. Balanced manner means assessing the cyber risks with the right skill sets and providing a balanced and informed basis for decisions on how and what treatments are right for the organization, without hindering the performance of the business. It adds value by reducing duplication of work activities and thus costs, and makes the protection stronger (maintaining confidentiality and integrity of information), while ensuring availability of digital services to support and enable the business achieving the business objectives.

PART FIVE: RESOURCES IN INFORMATION ASSETS

Chapter 19 Information asset management. The organization takes a proactive approach to address threats by controlling the speed and effectiveness of its response to cyber attacks. It adopts true military-grade cybersecurity approaches by being proactive in defense, continuously strengthening safeguards while preparing for the worst. A contingency plan handbook documents how to respond in the event of an attack. Plans are rehearsed through regular war games, staff training, and responses adapted over time. Plans and training include changes to threats, in order to reduce mean time between detection and remediation. A dedicated crisis action officer (reporting to the CEO) creates and oversees response planning. The security operations center (SOC) is evolving into a true command-and-control center for operations. Computer network operations are considered as actions that an organization takes to increase their own information security, while denying security to its enemies. — 2 — 3 — 3 — 3

PART SIX: RESOURCES IN ARCHITECTURE SERVICES, INFRASTRUCTURE AND APPLICATIONS ASSETS

Chapter 20 Physical security. Physical security risk scenarios are identified, analyzed, and evaluated within the context of a cyber-related physical security risk landscape for the organization. Organizational and technical physical security measures to deter, delay, detect, alarm, — 3 — 3 — 3 — 4

388

and respond to adversary attacks are designed and/or reviewed in order to support and augment cybersecurity. Exposure to adversary attack scenarios are calculated or reviewed by simulating the path of an adversary and calculating the probability of interrupting the adversary. A RASCI-based plan for the physical security organization is implemented. The link between security and the value added is understood as the point where the marginal benefits exceed or equal their optimal costs.

Chapter 21 Operations and communications. The organization initiates, integrates and advances core security operations center (SOC) capabilities to detect, prevent and respond to cybersecurity situations. A mature SOC prioritizes what needs to be protected, matures communication strategies, and leverages advances in technology to operate more efficiently and effectively. It delivers not only monitoring and response services to detect and remediate cyber threats but, with the combination of cyber threat intelligence, analytics, and orchestration capabilities, it provides ways organizations can detect and respond in minutes. The organization drives for clarity on the linkage between its business objectives down to its physical assets, organizational risks, applications, and ultimately data, in order to avoid communication and risk challenges. It builds in remediation automation to fill in any gaps, is responsive to the speed of change and knows its assets. It makes cyber risk management more tangible with an "active defense" process. It adapts to cyber environmental changes quickly, by analyzing gap improvements and remains adaptive with a mature and integrated set of security operations capabilities, powered by data science, automation and an analytics platform. This enables the visibility, context and insight needed to proactively protect its data, intellectual property, and brand.

2   3   3   3

Chapter 22 Access controls. The organization understands that the overall objectives and general principles of ITC access control remain largely the same as for traditional information security. But cyber risk requires that smart processes and next-generation technology be added to achieve current access control objectives. The organization avoids manual controls, embraces automation and deploys access control intelligence to stay ahead of attackers. Its access control structure is effective. Cybersavvy and informed people, including third parties, leverage technology and are capable of identifying and reporting potential suspicious behavior and activities. Competent people use smart processes to bind these elements together to achieve enterprise-level goals.

2   3   3   3

(continued)

TABLE E.2 (Continued)

		3	3

PART SIX: RESOURCES IN ARCHITECTURE SERVICES, INFRASTRUCTURE AND APPLICATIONS ASSETS

Chapter 23 Systems acquisition, development, and maintenance. Cybersecurity systems acquisition, development, and maintenance. The organization's effective and reliable information systems are efficient, cost effective and achieve competitive advantages. Building and buying information systems are the result of careful business and risk-based decisions. Appropriate security requirements that are commensurate to the risks, are defined, implemented and tested before moving the application into production. Cybersecurity is "by design" and integrated into the organization applications. Policies and procedures to ensure cybersecurity are addressed through the development or acquisition life cycle in line with the following guiding principles: (1) security requirements should be identified up front based on the risks; (2) the security requirements should be included in the application development and selection processes; (3) the security requirements should be tested for effectiveness pre- and postimplementation; (4) when using cloud/SaaS providers, cybersecurity due diligence should be conducted; and (5) developers should be trained on secure coding practices and the developed code should be inspected for security defects. — 2, 3, 3, 3

PART SEVEN: RESOURCES IN PEOPLE, SKILLS AND COMPETENCIES AS ASSETS

Chapter 24 People risk management system. Management understand that people are not machines and cannot be programmed. An enterprise-wide people risk management system includes technology, business, risk and people solutions that avoid operational silos. It forms part of the enterprise risk management system where people risk is not solely the domain of the human resources (HR) department or the technology or information security departments. People risk controls are proportionate, reasonable and achievable. Organizational knowledge upskilling starts at the board and works up from the front line. HR uses training budgets to appropriately target and deliver cross-functional training. Any "digital governance gap" is bridged by in-depth analysis and a cross-disciplinary team including IT, executive management, legal, and risk management. Talent is recruited balancing — 3, 3, 4, 4 future needs for both left- and right-brain thinkers and leaders develop or increase their digital quotient (DQ). The organization manages all forms of Digital Risk and may deploy a specialized digital risk officer (DRO) if appropriate. Crisis management capabilities, resources and relationships enable rapid and appropriate response appropriate to not only an emergency, but also to react to small changes that could ultimately develop into a disaster. Senior management nurtures a risk-taking culture that drives competitiveness and profitability.

Chapter 25 Competencies. Competencies and the CISO. Cybersecurity is a top concern for boards and executive management. The cybersecurity leader in an organization needs not only to have broad technical capabilities across information security domains, but leadership expertise and the ability to effectively guide the organization in implementing an effective, holistic and enterprise-wide cyber program. This program needs to address organization structure, people, process and technology but also the critical dynamic components of culture, governance, human factors, and the enablement of processes through technology. More critically, in this rapidly changing environment, the CISO needs to recognize emergent conditions and the opportunity and threats that these present. The CISO requires competencies in four areas: (1) Information Security Governance; (2) Information Risk Management and Compliance; (3) Information Security Program Development and Management, and (4) Information Security Incident Management.

2   3   4

Chapter 26 Human Resources (HR) security. As a minimum, staff protocols or a standard for HR cybersecurity are in effect and updated. For preemployment protocols, include roles and responsibilities, screening for insider and other threats, and terms and conditions of employment. For during employment, protocols include management responsibilities; information security awareness; organization awareness, education, training and internal communications; and a disciplinary process. For termination or change of employment, protocols include: termination responsibilities; return of assets and, removal of access rights. A checklist is always used for secure employee departure. Larger organizations and/or higher HR maturity functions look for continuous capability improvement by exploiting an array of more sophisticated tools, techniques, and solutions for advanced cybersecurity.

2

1   2   3   4

CyberSmart™ TOTAL AS INDEX RATING OUT OF 100%:   47%   69%   82%   92%

NOTES

1. Domenic Antonucci, *Risk Maturity Models: How to Assess Risk Management Effectiveness* (London: Kogan Page, 2016).
2. Ibid.

ABOUT DOMENIC ANTONUCCI

Domenic is a practicing international chief risk officer overseeing cybersecurity and a former counter-terrorist intelligence officer. An Australian expatriate based in Dubai UAE, Domenic specializes in bringing capabilities within organization risk management systems "up the maturity curve" for enterprise, program, and specialized risks such as cybersecurity. Formerly with Marsh, Shell and Red Cross, he enjoys over 35 years' experience in risk, strategic planning and business management consulting across many sectors in Europe, Africa, Middle East, Asia, and Australia-Pacific. A specialist with IRM (SIRM), he is a certified ISO 31000 ERM lead trainer and BCMS business continuity lead implementer as well as a former RMP-PMI risk management professional and PMP project management professional. A regular international conference presenter and author, he is the content author for risk maturity model software called *Benchmarker*™ and the author of the book *Risk Maturity Models: Assessing Risk Management Effectiveness*.

ABOUT DIDIER VERSTICHEL

Didier is an experienced chief information security officer (CISO) as well as a chief risk officer (CRO) with a background in the financial sector. He is currently a freelance consultant in ICT security and enterprise risk management, with a client base that includes BNP Paribas Fortis and ING Belgium. He is also a member of the Strategic Advisory Board of Sonavation Inc, a leader in ultrasonic fingerprint readers. He sat on the Information Security Forum (ISF) advisory board in 2012 and 2013. Didier worked for SWIFT, the Brussels-based global financial messaging system, from 1994 through 2014. He was a program manager and led the Y2K program (among many key initiatives) up to the year 2000. From 2000 to 2005 he was director of the Worldwide Networks department, where his main achievement was the development of a global multivendor secure IP network. He was then appointed director of the Enterprise Security and Architecture department in 2005 and combined the CSO and CISO functions. His responsibilities were IT architecture, security strategy and technology, security risk management, security policies and compliance, as well as corporate security. He was appointed CRO in January 2011. Before joining SWIFT, Didier held various ICT functions at Europay (now Mastercard Europe), where he started his career in 1982.

This glossary defines commonly used terms in cybersecurity in an enterprise-wide risk management (ERM) context. Words in *italics* have their own separate glossary entries, so please see cross listing for a complete understanding of definitions.

Access controls – Mechanisms and techniques used to ensure that access to assets is authorized and restricted based on *organization* and security requirements.

Assessing risk-management effectiveness – To evaluate or diagnose how well an *organization risk management system* is doing the right things (*effectiveness*) to manage *risk*. For internal audit/board: an objective written assessment of the effectiveness of the system of risk management and the internal control framework to the board.

BCP – See *business continuity plan (BCP)*.

Benchmarking – The use of internal or external points of reference or standards against which *risk management system* and *effectiveness* may be compared, checked, or assessed.

Board – The board of directors responsible for *organization* risk oversight and their equivalents in public agencies and not-for-profits.

Boom – A term for a cyber event with all pre-event planning actions taking place left of boom and all reactionary measures happening right of boom.

Business continuity plan (BCP) – Is typically made up of the corporate wide or level BCP and the business unit BCPs. The BCPs focus on the continuity, recovery, and resumption of the critical business unit functions (i.e., from a disruption).

Capabilities – Specific and repeatable abilities, faculties, or powers of an *organization* enabling it to collectively deliver organization objectives in the face of threats and to leverage opportunities.

Capability level – An indicator, position, or stage on a scale of quantity, extent, rank, or quality of organization *capabilities*.

Capability maturity model (CMM) – A model based on the maturation of one specific *organization process capability* such as software development.

Chief information security officer (CISO) – A traditional role for a manager dedicated to information security, including digital and nondigital assets and information.

Cloud computing – A service-provider model for enabling on-demand network access to a shared pool of configurable computing capabilities or resources (e.g., networks, servers, storage, applications and services) that can be outsourced.

CMP – See *crisis management plan (CMP)*.

Combined assurance – The joint and aligned organization assurance processes by the management and internal audit functional lines to maximize *risk management*, governance oversight, and control effectiveness, and optimize overall assurance to the audit and risk committee and *Board*.

Combined assurance report – An extended or combined assurance report—including the activities of internal audit as the third of *three lines of defense*—presented to the *board* (or the audit committee of the board) by the head of ERM.

Competency – An underlying ability of an individual (not an organization) to perform a job or task properly or excel at it by combining a set of observable knowledge, skills, and attitude, which often result in work behaviors.

Corporate governance – A framework of rules and practices by which a *board* of directors ensures accountability, fairness, and transparency in a company's relationship with its all stakeholders.

Crisis management plan (CMP) – Contains the processes and procedures for the senior management team to control and ensure coordination of major crisis incidents. The crisis communications plan (CCP) complements the CMP. It contains the processes, procedures, and templates to manage internal and external communications during a crisis. Together, the CMP and CCP enable organizations to command, control and coordinate information, decisions, and communications during a crisis.

Crown jewels – The most valuable digital assets or information to an *organization*.

Cyber risk management system – A subset of the *risk management system* specific to *cybersecurity capabilities*.

Cyber risk sources – Any root and other causes that give rise to a cyber risk such as supply chain, social media, ransomware, cloud computing/third-party vendors, Big Data analytics, the Internet of Things (IOT), and BYOD/mobile devices.

Cyber space – An interdependent network of information technology infrastructures, that includes the Internet, telecommunications networks, computer systems and embedded processors and controllers.

Cybersecurity – Protecting information assets by addressing threats (risks) to information processed, stored, and transported by internetworked information systems (ISACA) or protecting computers, networks, programs, and other digital data and digital assets from unintended or unauthorized threats while optimizing opportunities.

Cybersecurity negligence – Not legally defined as yet; remains unclear as to the standard of care required or steps to secure data that must be "reasonable" or "appropriate"—taking the relevant circumstances into account—in order to avoid liability.

Effectiveness – To produce a desired or intended result and a focus or mantra on "doing the right things" within *organizations*.

Digital quotient (DQ) – New sets of capabilities in addition to IQ and emotional quotient (EQ) to succeed in the digital age including organization leadership competencies to cope with the digital revolution in technologies such as mobility, social networks, Big Data analytics, and cloud.

Digital risk officer (DRO) – An emerging role for a *risk manager* dedicated to cybersecurity, typically reporting to the chief risk officer or chief executive officer.

Disaster recovery plan (DRP) – Documents the processes and procedures for the recovery of IT servers, networks, applications, and databases; usually at an alternate site called the IT disaster recovery center. The IT DRP focuses on the technical recovery of IT systems and infrastructure.

DQ – See *digital quotient (DQ)*.

DRO – See *digital risk officer (DRO)*.

DRP – See *disaster recovery plan (DRP)*.

Effective decision making – A cognitive and managerial process alongside an integrated *risk management system* for making the right decisions when faced with choice(s) to achieve and optimize organization objectives or outcomes.

Efficiency – Commonly, the ratio of the useful work performed by a machine or in a process to the total energy expended or heat taken in and a focus or mantra on "doing things right" in terms of achieving organization objectives faster, better, or cheaper.

Enterprise – Synonymous with *organization* covering private, public, and nongovernmental organization sectors.

Enterprise-wide risk management (ERM) – Typically synonymous with *risk management* for all sectors; also used to emphasize an integrated and holistic "umbrella" approach delivering objectives by managing *risk* across an *organization*, its silos, its risk specialist, and other subfunctions and processes.

ERM – See *enterprise-wide risk management (ERM)*.

Fiduciary duty – Applies to cyber cases as it does to other cases in the United States and elsewhere, where corporate boards have a general duty to protect corporate assets, reputation, and goodwill; relevance for cyber cases includes failing to prevent unauthorized access to consumer information as "unfair or deceptive acts" or unfair and deceptive trade practices, data breach notification, and failure to timely notify and negligence or breach of contract claims.

Framework – "a basic structure of something (Webster's)" such as ideas, concepts, guidelines, rules, checklists, requirements, facts, or physical parts.

Incident and crisis management plan (ICMP) – Documents the processes and procedures for IT teams and management—a framework to respond to and manage cyber incidents. IT may incorporate cyber response incidents into the corporate IT disaster recovery plan. Crisis management response actions for cyber incident may be embedded in the corporate crisis management plan.

Key control indicator (KCI) – A metric that evaluates the effectiveness level of a control (or set of controls) that have been implemented to reduce or mitigate a given risk exposure. A calibrated threshold or trigger (typically) brackets a KCI metric. These metrics are usually backward-looking or lagging indicators. Control indicators link with operational or process objectives.

Key performance indicator (KPI) – A metric that evaluates how a business is performing against objectives where a defined target (typically) provides the benchmark for evaluation of a KPI metric and the metrics are usually backward-looking or lagging indicators; may include a risk maturity model assessment index rating or measure.

Key risk indicator (KRI) – A metric that permits a business to monitor changes in the level of risk in order to take action and to highlight pressure points that can be effective leading indicators of emerging risks or changes in risk as they are typically forward-looking; may be represented by part of whole of *risk maturity model* assessment index rating(s) or measure(s).

King III Code – 2009 – Leading corporate governance code for universal application in terms of quantity and quality of *risk management* guidance with detailed, specific and clear requirements for risk management by board, internal audit, risk, and other functions.

Levels – The steps, classes, or tiers of overall *risk management* capability or *capabilities,* often themed into modules as a *component* within a *risk maturity model.*

Likert Scale – A statistical method of ascribing quantitative value to qualitative data to make it amenable to statistical analysis. Commonly used in questionnaires as a five- or seven-point scale (scoring step). Sometimes stepped with negative and positive values to a neutral midpoint. Sometimes stepped in ascending sophistication, quality, or other measure.

Maturity – Concept relating to the current or future state, fact, or period of evolving development, quality, sophistication, and *effectiveness* (not necessarily age dependent).

Maturity model – A simplified system that "road-maps" improving, desired, anticipated, typical, or logical evolutionary paths of *organization* actions. The ascending direction implies progression increases organization *effectiveness* over time (albeit subject to stasis and regression).

Measurement – A quantitatively expressed reduction of uncertainty based on one or more observations. For risk maturity models, may be expressed as an overall index score to 100 percent, within which certain percentiles equate to ascending *maturity* levels and/or as *Likert scales* to assess the *capabilities* being assessed to arrive at the overall score.

Organization – Synonymous with enterprise as in ERM; an administrative structure in which people collectively manage one or more services/activities as a whole, share senior management, and operate under a set of policies.

People factors – Influences on *cybersecurity* as opportunities and threats from staff as "insiders," third parties acting as "trusted insiders" and human error, bias, and behaviors; human beings are often described as the "weakest link" in the *cyber risk management system.*

Reasonable assurance – To check for correctness and truthfulness; achieved when the *risk* is at an acceptable level according to common sense and logic; while (1) acknowledging that it is not possible to assert absolutely and certainly that an event will (or will not) occur, and (2) qualifying that while a standard conforms to known limits, it is not excessive in any way (http://www.businessdictionary.com/definition/reasonable-assurance.html)

Risk – The effect of uncertainty on objectives where the effect is a deviation from the expected—positive and/or negative.

Risk assessment – A stepped approach after understanding internal and external context to the organization, in three steps: risk identification, risk analysis, and risk evaluation, enabling prioritization for risk treatment (including controls).

Risk management – Coordinated activities that direct and control an *organization* in pursuit of its objectives and with regard to *risk*.

Risk management plan – A scheme within the *risk management* framework specifying the approach, the management components, accountabilities and resources to be applied to the management of *risk* and how to implement *risk maturity strategy* (ISO 31000:2009, *Risk management—Principles and guidelines*); and, how to implement the improvement outputs "road-mapped" by a *risk maturity model*.

Risk management system – The repeatable and interconnected mechanisms and initiatives organizing the right *organization capabilities* to deliver *risk management effectiveness;* inputs and desired risk management outputs-to-outcomes; may include risk management information systems.

Risk manager – Typically, a risk officer/functionary within a full- or part-time dedicated *risk management* function to technically support line managers who remain the *risk* owners and managers. Sometimes extended to mean all board, executive, and staff members who all share risk management accountability.

Risk maturity model – An abbreviation for a *capability maturity model* specialized to an expanded set of *risk management system capabilities*. It represents a diagnostic tool using levels of *maturity* to track gap improvement of the right organization capabilities designed to deliver risk management effectiveness. More correctly and in full: a *risk management system capability maturity model*.

Risk maturity strategies – To develop and implement schemes to *improve risk management maturity* alongside all other aspects of their organization.

Risk specialty or subdisciplines – A group label for sub-ERM disciplines such as safety and health and related organization functions such as legal.

Risk treatment options – Controls and anything that modifies risk; if aligned with ISO 31000:2009, *Risk management—Principles and guidelines*, they will be tailored to (1) avoiding the activity that gives rise to the risk; (2) taking or increasing the risk in order to pursue an opportunity; (3) removing the risk source; (4) changing the likelihood; (5) changing the consequences; (6) sharing the risk with other parties (e.g., risk financing, contracts); and (7) retaining the risk by informed decision.

Silo factor – A state where department-based management of organization activity and/or compartmentalized risk management activities may result in a narrow, parochial view of risk that prevents management from understanding risks facing the entire enterprise.

Standards – Commonly, a level of quality or attainment or a required or agreed level of quality or attainment; formally, the most commonly agreed standard by accredited technical bodies for risk management representing nations, that is, ISO 31000:2009, *Risk management—Principles and guidelines*. For cybersecurity, standards/frameworks include: ISO/IEC 27000 family; COBIT 5 for Information Security; NIST Special Publication 800-53 Revision 4 Security and Privacy Controls for Federal Information Systems and Organizations; ISF Standard of

Good Practice for Information Security; Center for Internet Security (CIS) Top 20 Critical Controls; IT-CMF:ISM; PCI-DSS; and European Union Agency for Network and Information Security (ENISA).

Tailoring – To align the *risk management* approach to the unique-to-organization objectives, internal and external context and risk profile(s). For *risk maturity models,* tailoring is driven primarily by choice and quality of the *capabilities* content and *scales* and influenced by external and internal *benchmarking*, model design of *components,* and other techniques and methods.

Three lines of defense/offense – An assurance approach relying on *risk management* co-operation between the organization front line managers and operating functions, support functions, and internal audit function. "Defense/Offense" relates to risk management functions combining *capabilities* to create as well as protect organization value and/or to deal with *risk* sources with either/both or alternating negative or positive consequences. *Source:* The IIA which adapted it from ECIIA/FERMA Guidance on the 8th EU Company Law Directive, article 41 https://na.theiia.org/standards guidance/Public%20Documents/PP%20The%20Three%20Lines%20of%20Defense%20in%20Effective%20Risk%20Management%20and%20Control.pdf

Index